W9-CSI-835

"This lady is organized . . . well-researched guide."
San Francisco Chronicle Book Review

". . . almost overwhelmingly full of detailed information. Excellent."
San Diego Tribune

"We had a great time on our California vacation.
Weekend Adventures was essential both during planning and execution.
Thank you for a wonderful guide!"
Joleen Chambers, parent, Annapolis, MD

"Ms. Meyers has left no stone unturned in researching the recreation
opportunities available in the northern half of the state."
Travelin'

"Carole Terwilliger Meyers writes intelligently about family fun.
She finds places kids like that adults can stomach. And vice versa."
Alice Kahn, reporter, San Francisco Chronicle

"The guide is very well organized . . . Highly recommended."
Pacific Sun

". . . a gold mine of travel tips."
The Montclarion

"Carole's weekly family outing suggestions are welcome reminders of
what a wonderful area of the world we live in. Sometimes all we need
is another's enthusiasm to put sparkle in our day!"
C. J. Bronson, Bay Area radio personality

"Whenever we need a break from the city routine,
I reach for my copy of *Weekend Adventures*. It's the greatest guidebook
around for families who want to explore Northern California."
Dixie Jordan, Editor, Parents' Press

"Enjoyable to read . . . and loaded with photos."
Small Press

". . . easy-to-follow format."
Booklist

WEEKEND ADVENTURES

– FOR CITY-WEARY PEOPLE –

Also by Carole Terwilliger Meyers:

Miles of Smiles: 101 Great Car Games & Activities
San Francisco Family Fun
Eating Out With the Kids in San Francisco and the Bay Area
How to Organize a Babysitting Cooperative and Get Some Free Time Away From the Kids
Getting in the Spirit: Annual Bay Area Christmas Events
Eating Out with the Kids in the East Bay

FIFTH EDITION

WEEKEND ADVENTURES

– FOR CITY-WEARY PEOPLE –

OVERNIGHT
TRIPS IN
NORTHERN
CALIFORNIA

CAROLE TERWILLIGER MEYERS

Enlarged and updated edition of *Weekend Adventures for City-Weary Families: A Guide to Overnight Trips in Northern California*, copyright ©1977, 1980.

Published by: CAROUSEL PRESS
                P.O. Box 6061
                Albany, CA 94706-0061
                510/527-5849

Library of Congress Cataloging-in-Publication Data

Meyers, Carole Terwilliger.
    Weekend adventures for city-weary people, overnight trips in
northern California / Carole Terwilliger Meyers. -- Enl. and updated
ed.
        p.   cm. -- (Weekend adventures for city-weary people,
overnight trips in the U.S.A.)
    Includes indexes.
    ISBN 0-917120-12-4
    1. California. Northern--Guidebooks.   2. Family recreation--
California, Northern--Guidebooks.   I. Title.   II. Title: Overnight
trips in northern California.   III. Series: Meyers, Carole
Terwilliger. Weekend adventures for city-weary families. overnight
trips in the U.S.A.
F867.5.M48   1992
917.9404'53--dc20   92-7864
                                                            CIP

Printed in the United States of America

10 9 8 7 6 5 4 3 2 1

for Gene

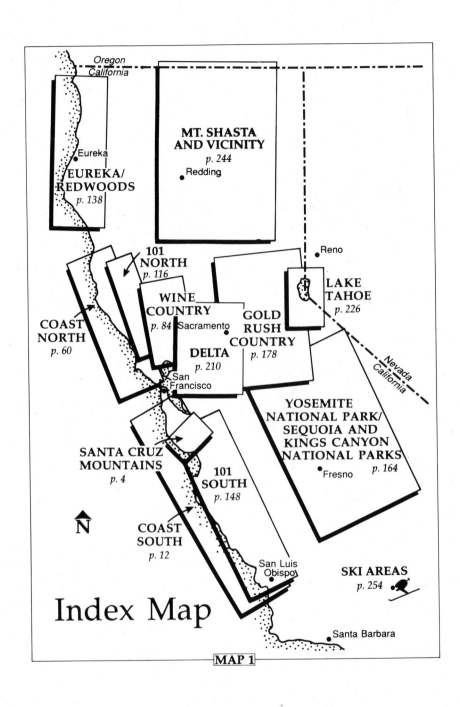

Oregon
California

MT. SHASTA
AND VICINITY
p. 244
• Redding

• Eureka

EUREKA/
REDWOODS
p. 138

101
NORTH
p. 116

• Reno

WINE
COUNTRY
p. 84 • Sacramento

LAKE
TAHOE
p. 226

COAST
NORTH
p. 60

GOLD
RUSH
COUNTRY
p. 178

DELTA
p. 210

Nevada
California

San
Francisco

YOSEMITE
NATIONAL PARK/
SEQUOIA AND
KINGS CANYON
NATIONAL PARKS
• Fresno *p. 164*

SANTA CRUZ
MOUNTAINS
p. 4

101
SOUTH
p. 148

N

COAST
SOUTH
p. 12

San Luis
Obispo

SKI AREAS
p. 254

Index Map

• Santa Barbara

MAP 1

Contents

Introduction

We residents of the Bay Area are fortunate to live within easy driving distance of an almost endless wealth of exciting vacation possibilities—the mountains, the ocean, the river, the snow. Our biggest recreational problem is deciding, from among the many possibilities, where we should go and what we should do.

The destinations in this book radiate out from the immediate San Francisco Bay Area. Most make good weekend trips, and all can easily be adapted to longer stays. (For information on San Francisco and Bay Area destinations, refer to my book *San Francisco Family Fun.*)

Because it is frustrating to discover after you're home that an area where you've just vacationed had an interesting attraction you didn't know about, and because it also isn't much fun to find out too late that there was a better or cheaper (depending on what you're after) lodging you could have booked into . . . or a restaurant you would have enjoyed trying, this book is designed so that you can quickly determine what is of special interest in the area you are planning to visit. Listings are selected based on the fact that they are in some way special—bargain rates, welcoming of families, aesthetically pleasing, historically interesting, etc. Phone numbers necessary for obtaining further information are included, and toll-free 800 numbers are provided when available. (I have found that writing for information is slow and unreliable, so I recommend that you instead always call for a brochure or to make a reservation.)

Parents especially need to have this information in advance. I know because one of the worst trips I ever experienced was the first trip my husband and I took with my first baby. I hadn't planned ahead. We took off for the Gold Rush Country and went where the winds blew us—just like before we were parents. That was a mistake. We wound up in a hotel that had no compassion for a colicky baby or his parents, and we ate a series of memorably bad meals. Now my husband and I can laugh about that trip, but at the time it wasn't funy. I know that fateful trip was what turned me into a travel writer. After that I never went anywhere without exhaustively researching beforehand. And truthfully I've never had a bad trip since that I can blame on lack of knowledge.

With all of this in mind, I've written this book to help make your trip-planning easier, allowing you to get the most out of a weekend away.

Guidelines For Interpreting Listings

This book is organized by geographical area. Each chapter has the following subsections:

A LITTLE BACKGROUND: historical and general background information about the area; what kinds of activities to expect.

VISITOR INFORMATION: address and phone number of Chamber of Commerce or Visitors Bureau.

GETTING THERE: the quickest, easiest driving route from San Francisco; scenic driving routes, other transportation options.

STOPS ALONG THE WAY: noteworthy places for meals or sightseeing.

ANNUAL EVENTS: the area's best events; in chronological order. When no phone number is listed, contact the Chamber of Commerce or Visitors Bureau for information.

WHERE TO STAY: select lodging facilities, listed alphabetically and including the following information when available: street address, toll-free 800 reservations number, area code and phone number, fax number for reservations; number of rooms; number of non-smoking rooms; price range per night for two people (see price codes below); months closed; policies regarding children (if there is a *children stay free in parents' room* policy; if facility is *unsuitable for children under a specified age*); if cribs are available; if no TVs are available; if kitchens, bathtubs, fireplaces, or wood-burning stoves are available; if any baths are shared; what recreational facilities are available: pool, hot tub, sauna, health club, exercise room, parcourse, tennis courts; if there is a complimentary breakfast (continental or full), a restaurant, room service; if pets are welcome.

   ♥ before a listing indicates facility is adult-oriented and inappropriate for children.

   $ = under $50, $$=$50-$99, $$$=$100-$149, $$$+=over $150

WHERE TO EAT: worthwhile restaurants, listed alphabetically and including the following information when available: address, phone number; meals served (B, L, D, SunBr), days open; price range (see price code below); availability of highchairs, booster seats, children's portions; if it is 100% non-smoking; if reservations are needed or accepted; credit cards accepted (see code below). Always call to confirm any information, as it frequently changes.

   ♥ before a listing indicates a quiet, romantic atmosphere.

   $ = inexpensive. Dinner for one adult might cost up to $12.

   $$ = moderate. Dinner for one adult might cost from $12 to $25.

   $$$ = expensive. Dinner for one adult might cost over $25.

   Projected costs are based on dinner prices and are exclusive of drinks, dessert, tax, and tip.

   Credit Cards: American Express (AE), MasterCard (MC), BankAmericard/Visa (V)

WHAT TO DO: activities and sights in the area that are of special interest, listed alphabetically and including the following information when available: address, phone number; days and hours open; admission fee. Note that some of these facilities are closed on major holidays. Always call to verify hours.

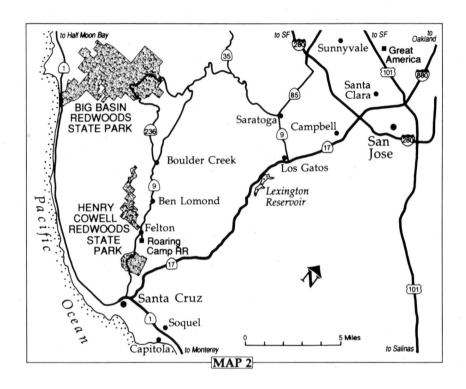

to Half Moon Bay

to SF

to SF

to Oakland

Sunnyvale

Great America

BIG BASIN REDWOODS STATE PARK

Santa Clara

Saratoga

Campbell

Boulder Creek

Los Gatos

San Jose

Lexington Reservoir

Pacific Ocean

HENRY COWELL REDWOODS STATE PARK

Ben Lomond

Felton

Roaring Camp RR

Santa Cruz

Soquel

0   5 Miles

Capitola

to Monterey

to Salinas

MAP 2

Santa Cruz Mountains

– Los Gatos/Saratoga –

A LITTLE BACKGROUND

Tucked in the lush, green Santa Cruz mountains, Los Gatos is known for its many antique shops. Nearby Saratoga is an even smaller and quieter town.

VISITOR INFORMATION

Los Gatos Chamber of Commerce *P.O. Box 1820 (50 University Ave.), Los Gatos 95031, 408/354-9300.*

Saratoga Chamber of Commerce *P.O. Box 161 (20460 Saratoga-Los Gatos Rd.), Saratoga 95070, 408/867-0753.*

GETTING THERE

Located approximately 60 miles south of San Francisco. Take Highway 101 to Highway 17 to the Los Gatos exit.

ANNUAL EVENTS

Paul Masson Summer Series *June-September; Saratoga, 408/741-5181; children under 5 not admitted.* The world's largest and the country's oldest winery-related music festival, this eclectic series of outdoor concerts has been held in its picturesque hilltop setting every year since 1958. A buffet dinner is available before most shows, and Paul Masson wines and champagnes are poured for tasting during intermissions.

WHERE TO STAY

Garden Inn of Los Gatos *46 E. Main St., Los Gatos, 800/888-8248, 408/354-6446, fax 408/354-5911; 28 rooms; 20 non-smoking rooms; $$; children under 10 free; cribs; some kitchens, bathtubs; heated pool (unavailable Nov-Apr); continental breakfast.* These rustic Spanish-style bungalows are in a quiet area just 2 blocks from Old Town. Complimentary use of a nearby health club is available to guests.

The Inn at Saratoga *20645 Fourth St., Saratoga, 800/543-5020, 408/867-5020, fax 408/741-0981; 46 rooms; 20 non-smoking rooms; $$$-$$$+; children under 18 free; cribs; some bathtubs; continental breakfast.* This recently built 5-story hotel combines an old-time Victorian feeling with modern luxurious amenities and a contemporary

5

decor. Set in a quiet canyon behind busy Highway 9, its rooms all face a forest of old eucalyptus through which winds gurgling Saratoga Creek. Afternoon wine and appetizers are served inside in the cozy lobby and outdoors on a sylvan patio. Families will appreciate that **Wildwood Park,** with its ample playground, is just across the creek.

La Hacienda Inn *18840 Saratoga-Los Gatos Rd., Los Gatos, 408/354-9230; 21 rooms; $$-$$$; children under 6 free; cribs; some kitchens, bathtubs, fireplaces; heated pool, hot tub; continental breakfast, restaurant, room service.* Tucked away from the main highway, this pleasant inn features a large lawn area and cozy, redwood-trimmed rooms with private patios.

Los Gatos Lodge *50 Saratoga Ave., Los Gatos, 800/231-8676, 408/354-3300, fax 408/354-5451; 123 rooms; 37 non-smoking rooms; $$; children under 12 free; cribs; some kitchens, fireplaces; all bathtubs; heated pool, hot tub; restaurant, room service; dogs welcome.* Located on attractive, spacious grounds, this modern 2-story motel provides a putting green and shuffleboard area. Complimentary use of a nearby health club is also available.

Sanborn Park Hostel *15808 Sanborn Rd., Saratoga, 408/741-0166.* This rustic building is constructed of logs and located in a secluded redwood grove in the area's foothills. It's a naturally fragrant, quiet spot with plenty of hiking trails, and a volleyball court and barbecue facilities are available to guests. Just down the road **Sanborn-Skyline County Park** offers campsites, picnic tables, and the **Youth Science Institute.** See also page 278.

WHERE TO EAT

The Chart House *115 N. Santa Cruz Ave., Los Gatos, 408/354-1737; D daily; $$-$$$; highchairs, booster seats, children's portions; reservations suggested; AE, MC, V.* Located inside a stately old Victorian mansion, this restaurant's menu features prime rib, steaks, and fresh seafood. All dinners include either a salad with homemade dressing or a soup, plus both hot sourdough and squaw breads.

The Good Earth *206 N. Santa Cruz Ave., Los Gatos, 408/395-6868; B, L, & D daily; $-$$; highchairs, children's menu; 100% non-smoking; AE, MC, V.* A good spot for a quick, light meal or snack, this restaurant's menu offers whole grain breads, organic beef, and a large selection of vegetarian items. Homemade soups, sandwiches, salads, hot entrees, omelettes, health-food shakes, and good-for-you desserts are also available. An extensive children's menu includes pancakes, noodles, a peanut butter and jelly sandwich, and several burgers.

Hobee's *14550 Big Basin Way, Saratoga, 408/741-1989; B, L, & D daily; $; highchairs, booster seats, children's portions; 100% non-smoking; MC, V.* Tasty, wholesome food, prepared with plenty of vegetables and tofu and served in a cheerful atmosphere in comfortable surroundings, is the secret to success here. The breakfast menu, which is available all day, offers a selection of omelettes and scrambles as well as items such as whole wheat pancakes, cinnamon-orange swirl French toast, and granola. Lunch and dinner bring on a salad bar, homemade soups, and a variety of sandwiches and hamburgers.

Mimi's Rooftop *in Old Town, Los Gatos, 408/354-5288; B & L daily, D W-Sat; $$; highchairs, booster seats, children's portions; 100% non-smoking; reservations suggested; AE, MC, V.* Anytime is a good time to dine outside on the veranda here, but the best time is at brunch when blintzes, apple pancakes, and egg dishes, served with superb homefries, are on the extensive menu. The lunch and dinner menu features soups, salads, sandwiches, crepes, and pastas. It is worth the wait for a railing-side table, because from there diners may look out into ancient oaks and down into a well-groomed topiary garden. Exotic coffees, ice cream sundaes, and desserts such as carrot cake and cheesecake with a pecan-walnut crust end the menu.

Pedro's Cabo Grill *316 N. Santa Cruz Ave., Los Gatos, 408/354-7570; L M-Sat, D daily, SunBr; $$; highchairs, booster seats, children's portions; reservations suggested; MC, V.* This popular spot features an authentic Mexican decor and serves huge portions of tasty Mexican dishes. Recommended menu items include chimichangas (deep-fried flour tortillas filled with spicy shredded beef and topped with guacamole and sour cream), quesadillas (large flour tortillas filled with Jack cheese and topped with guacamole and sour cream), and—the house specialty—a crab enchilada. There is often a wait to get in. Some people pass the time sipping margaritas and munching tortilla chips and salsa outside on the patio or inside in the cozy bar.

WHAT TO DO

Garrod Farms Stables *22600 Mt. Eden Rd., Saratoga, 408/867-9527; daily 8:30-4:30; horses $20/hour, ponies $8/half-hour.* Shetland ponies are available for children under 9 to ride; an adult must walk them with a lead rope. Anyone over 9 can ride the trails that roam over 200 acres.

Hakone Japanese Gardens *21000 Big Basin Way, Saratoga, 408/867-3438; M-F 10-5, Sat & Sun 11-5; by donation, $3/car on Sat & Sun.* Now a city park, this garden was originally constructed by a private citizen to typify a mid-17th century Zen garden. Now it is composed of four separate gardens: a Pond Garden, a Tea Garden, a Zen Garden, and a Bamboo Garden. Among its special features are a Japanese-style house built without nails or adhesives, a pond stocked with colorful koi, and an authentic Tea Ceremony room. It also boasts the largest collection of Japanese bamboo in the western world. Tea is served in the garden on summer weekends.

Los Gatos Museum *4 Tait St., Los Gatos, 408/354-2646; Tu-Sun 10-4; free.* Housed in a Spanish-style circa 1907 building, this small museum features exhibits on natural science and contemporary fine arts.

The tiny **Forbes Mill Museum** *(75 Church St., 408/395-7375)*, located in the remains of a flour mill dating from 1854, focuses on town history.

Montalvo Center for the Arts *15400 Montalvo Rd., Saratoga, 408/741-3421; daily 9-5; free. Guided tours Mar-Oct, Thur at 10, Sat at 10 & 1; $5.* Once the summer home of Senator James Phelan, this majestic Mediterranean-style estate is now the county center for fine arts. It also serves as a bird sanctuary. Self-guided nature trails wind through the 175-acre estate gardens. Performing arts events, some especially for children, are presented April through September in a natural outdoor amphitheater and indoor Carriage House.

Mountain Charley's *15 N. Santa Cruz Ave., Los Gatos, 408/395-8880; M-Sat 3pm-1:30am.* A live band performs nightly, making a visit to this gigantic, jumping saloon an exciting experience. Age minimum is 21.

Old Town *50 University Ave., Los Gatos, 408/354-6596; M-Sat 10-6, Sun 12-5.* Once the town elementary school, this attractive complex is now a series of interesting shops and restaurants. Free entertainment is often scheduled in an outdoor amphitheater.

Parks. The 12-acre **Oak Meadow Park** *(off Blossom Hill Rd., Los Gatos; 408/354-6809)* has picnic facilities, baseball diamonds, hiking trails, a 1910 hand-carved English clockwise carousel, a well-equipped playground with an authentic fire engine and airplane to climb on, and the **Billy Jones Wildcat Railroad** miniature steam locomotive *(Tu-Sun in summer, Sat & Sun rest of year).*

The 175-acre **Vasona Lake County Park** *(off Blossom Hill Rd., Los Gatos; 408/358-3741; 8-dusk; $3/car)* is dominated by a huge reservoir where visitors may rent rowboats and paddleboats, feed hungry ducks and seagulls, and fish. Visitors can also use the barbecue facilities and playground and visit the **Youth Science Institute** *(296 Garden Hill Dr., 408/356-4945; M-F 9-4:30, Sat in summer 12-4:30; free)* and its exhibits on water ecology and conservation.

Saso Herb Gardens *14625 Fruitvale Ave., Saratoga, 408/867-0307; Thur-Sat 9-2:30; free.* Taking advantage of the ideal climate for cultivating herbs, this nursery has one of the largest collections of organically grown culinary, medicinal, and ornamental herbs on the West Coast. Browse in its beautiful natural setting, or plan ahead to attend one of the workshops or free lecture tours.

WINERIES

Congress Springs Vineyards *23600 Congress Springs Rd./Highway 9, Saratoga, 408/741-2929; tasting daily 11-5.* Established in 1892, this winery is located at the end of a steep, woodsy back road. Picnic tables are available.

Mirassou Champagne Cellars *300 College Ave., Los Gatos, 408/395-3790; tasting daily 12-5; tours at 1:30 & 3:30.* High in the hills above town, this historic site was formerly occupied by the Novitiate Winery. All of the champagnes are field-pressed from night-harvested Monterey County grapes. A picnic area with a view of the town is situated just outside the stone cellar tasting room.

– San Lorenzo Valley –

A LITTLE BACKGROUND

Hidden in a dense redwood forest, this was once a popular resort area. The simple motels and cabins in the area are mostly relics left from that long ago heyday. Still, the abundance of trees, trails, and swimming holes, as well as reasonable prices, make the area a choice destination for bargain-hunting vacationers.

Traveling here is best done in daylight. Though the backroads are lightly traveled, they are also curvy and slow. And, of course, the forest scenery is part of the reason for coming here.

VISITOR INFORMATION

San Lorenzo Valley Chamber of Commerce *P.O. Box 67 (6257 Highway 9), Felton 95018, 408/335-5536.*

GETTING THERE

Located approximately 70 miles south of San Francisco. Take Highway 280 to Highway 84 to Highway 35 to Highway 9.

WHERE TO STAY

Ben Lomond Hylton Motel *9733 Highway 9, Ben Lomond, 408/336-2292; 21 rooms; 5 non-smoking rooms; $-$$; cribs; 1 kitchen, some bathtubs; heated pool (unavailable Nov-Mar).* These standard motel rooms are shaded by tall redwoods.

Fern River Resort *5250 Highway 9, Felton, 408/335-4412; 13 units; $-$$; 2-night minimum; children under 3 free; some kitchens, fireplaces.* These modern cabins are located on the river across from Henry Cowell Redwoods State Park. The 5-acre lot features a redwood-shaded outdoor recreation area with volleyball, tetherball, and Ping Pong, and guests have use of a private beach on the river.

Jaye's Timberlane Resort *8705 Highway 9, Ben Lomond, 408/336-5479; $$-$$$; 2-night minimum on weekends, 5-night minimum in summer; cribs; all kitchens; some fireplaces; heated pool (unavailable Nov-Apr).* These renovated cabins are scattered on spacious grounds shaded by redwoods.

Merrybrook Lodge *13420 Big Basin Way, Boulder Creek, 408/338-6813; 8 units; $$; 2-night minimum on weekends; cribs; some kitchens, fireplaces.* Tucked among towering redwoods, some of these cabins and motel units overlook a creek.

WHERE TO EAT

Heavenly Cafe *6250 Highway 9, Felton, 408/335-7311; B & L daily; $; highchairs, booster seats, children's portions; no reservations; no cards.* Located in a building dating from 1876, this cafe serves breakfast all day. Well-prepared bacon and eggs are on the menu, as are hot oatmeal, Belgian waffles, and biscuits and gravy. A selection of delicious muffins, for which the kitchen is well-known, is also available. Decor is simple: formica tables and wire-heart ice cream parlor chairs.

Scopazzi's Restaurant *13300 Big Basin Way, Boulder Creek, 408/338-4444; L W-Sat, D W-Sun; $$; highchairs, booster seats, children's portions; reservations suggested; AE, MC, V.* This spacious, rustic 1904 mountain lodge is known for its Italian meals. Cannelloni, veal scaloppine, and chicken cacciatore are on the menu along with fried prawns, pepper steak flambé, and quail en cocotte. Children should be pleased to see that this menu also offers a hamburger, a grilled cheese sandwich, and spaghetti.

♥**Tyrolean Inn** *9600 Highway 9, Ben Lomond, 408/336-5188; L & D Tu-Sun; $$; booster seat; reservations suggested; AE, MC, V.* Appearing as something right out of Germany's Black Forest, this family-operated restaurant prepares exquisite Austrian-German cuisine. An interesting assortment of imported beers is available, including a refreshing Weiss Bier, which is cloudy with yeast and served in a tall glass over a wedge of lemon. Entrees include sauerbraten and schnitzels, and desserts include a house-made fresh apple strudel and Black Forest cake. With 24 hours notice the kitchen will prepare any venison, hare, or duck specialty dish desired. In good weather lunch is available on a patio sheltered by mature redwoods. Dinner is served in a romantic, cozy dining room heated by two fireplaces.

Seven modestly-priced vintage housekeeping cottages, with warmly patinaed redwood paneling, are also available.

WHAT TO DO

Big Basin Redwoods State Park *21600 Big Basin Way, Boulder Creek, 408/338-6132; $5/car.* California's oldest state park, Big Basin has over 80 miles of hiking and nature trails. Self-guiding Redwood Trail leads to interesting redwoods such as the Animal Tree and the Chimney Tree, and a 10.3-mile trail leads to Berry Creek Falls. A Nature Lodge features related exhibits, and campfire programs are often scheduled. Campsites and 36 inexpensive tent cabins may be reserved.

Covered Bridge *off Graham Hill Rd., Felton.* Built over the San Lorenzo River in 1892, this redwood bridge has been restored to its original condition and can be walked on. A State Historical Landmark, it measures 34 feet high and is the tallest bridge of its kind in the U.S.

Hallcrest Vineyards *379 Felton Empire Rd., Felton, 408/335-4441; tasting and tours daily 11-5:30.* Situated upon a scenic hill, this winery boasts a good view of its half century-old vineyard and of Henry Cowell Redwoods State Park. The Estate White Riesling, for which the winery is noted, and the non-alcoholic premium varietal grape juice, which children are also welcome to sample, are of particular interest. A picnic area features an expansive lawn and tables shaded by oak trees; basic supplies are available for purchase during the summer.

Henry Cowell Redwoods State Park *101 N. Big Tree Park Rd., off Highway 9, Felton, 408/335-4598; daily 6am-sunset; $5/car.* A number of trails lead through this park's redwood groves; trail guides may be secured at the Nature Center. Campsites are available.

Highlands County Park *8500 Highway 9, Ben Lomond, 408/462-8300; daily dawn-dusk; $2/car in summer, free rest of year. Pool: 12-5 summer only, adults $2, under 17 $1.50.* The grounds of this old estate have been transformed into a park with pool, playground, two softball diamonds, three tennis courts, a volleyball court, and picnic tables. Nature trails lead to a sandy river beach.

Roaring Camp & Big Trees Narrow-Gauge Railroad *Graham Hill Rd., Felton, 408/335-4484; operates daily, call for schedule; adults $11, 3-15 $8.* This 6-mile, hour-long steam train ride winds through virgin redwoods and crosses over a spectacular trestle. About the time passengers start feeling a little restless, the train makes a

short stretch stop at Cathedral Grove—an impressive circle of tall, 800-year-old redwood trees said to have a 3,000-year-old root system! Another stop is made at Bear Mountain, where riders may disembark for a picnic or hike and then return on a later train. Remember to bring sweaters. Though this area enjoys warm to hot weather in the summer, it can get chilly on the train ride. Another train, the **Big Trees & Pacific Railway** *(adults $12.95, 3-15 $8.95)*, makes two trips each day between Roaring Camp and the Santa Cruz Boardwalk. The roundtrip excursion takes 2-1/2 hours.

An outdoor chuckwagon barbecue operates near the depot *(Sat & Sun 12-3, May-Oct)*, and the **Red Caboose Saloon** dispenses short order items. Be sure to save some tidbits for hungry ducks and geese in the lake.

Canvas tents on wooden platforms, like the ones used by mountain men in the late 1830s, are available for overnight stays. Each rents for $35 and can accommodate up to four people. Reservations are necessary.

Many special events are scheduled each year, including a **Civil War Encampment and Battles** and a chocolate **Easter egg hunt** for kids during spring vacation.

Swimming Holes.

Ben Lomond County Park *9525 Mill St., Ben Lomond, 408/462-8300; daily sunrise-sunset, summer only; free. Swimming Hole: adults $2, under 17 $1.50.* A sandy beach and good river swimming may be enjoyed at this dammed-up swimming hole. A playground and shaded picnic tables with barbecue facilities are also provided.

Junction Park *end of Middleton Ave., east of Highway 9, Boulder Creek; sunrise-sunset; 408/338-4144.* This swimming hole has both shallow and deep areas, plus a sandy beach. Picnic tables and barbecue facilities are in a shady area.

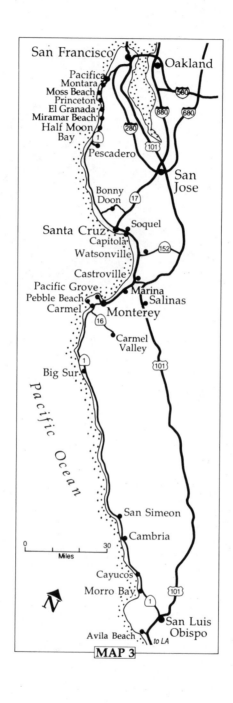

San Francisco

Oakland

Pacifica
Montara
Moss Beach
Princeton
El Granada
Miramar Beach
Half Moon
Bay

Pescadero

San
Jose

Bonny
Doon

Santa Cruz

Soquel

Capitola
Watsonville

Castroville

Pacific Grove
Pebble Beach
Carmel

Marina
Salinas

Monterey

Carmel
Valley

Big Sur

Pacific Ocean

San Simeon

Cambria

0   30
Miles

Cayucos
Morro Bay

Avila Beach
to LA

San Luis
Obispo

MAP 3

Coast South

– Highway 1 –

A LITTLE BACKGROUND

When the Bay Area is blazing with sunshine, this area can be disappointingly socked in with fog. And vice versa.

VISITOR INFORMATION

Half Moon Bay Coastside Chamber of Commerce *P.O. Box 188 (225 S. Cabrillo Hwy.), Half Moon Bay 94019, 415/726-5202.*

Coastside Harvest Trails *765 Main St., Half Moon Bay 94019, 415/726-4485.* For a free map to the area's farms, send a self-addressed, stamped legal-size envelope.

GETTING THERE

The trip down Highway 1 from San Francisco features a breath-taking, cliff-hugging ride along the Pacific Ocean. Half Moon Bay, with its restful farmland vistas, is located about 25 miles south.

ANNUAL EVENTS

Chamarita *May or June; in Half Moon Bay, 415/726-2729.* Held here for over 100 years, this Portuguese festival takes place seven weekends after Easter and includes a barbecue, parade, and carnival.

Art and Pumpkin Festival *October; in Half Moon Bay, 415/726-9652.* Children are invited to wear costumes and participate in the Great Pumpkin Parade. Rounding out the fun are pumpkin-carving and pie-eating contests, arts and crafts booths, a variety of pumpkin foods, and assorted on-going entertainment. Nearby pumpkin patches are open for picking.

WHERE TO STAY/WHERE TO EAT/WHAT TO DO

Pacifica

Seabreeze Motel *100 Rockaway Beach Ave., 415/359-3903; 20 rooms; $-$$; cribs; restaurant.* This is the place for a quick, inexpensive escape. Rooms are simple, but the beach is only a few steps away and a merry restaurant, **Nick's** *(415/359-3900;*

B, L, & D daily; $$; highchairs, booster seats; reservations suggested; AE, MC, V), is just next door.

Taco Bell *5200 Highway 1, 415/355-0591; L & D daily; $; highchairs, children's portions; no cards.* Located inside an attractive redwood building, this fast-food restaurant's exceptional beachfront location makes it worthy of a stop-in. Free entertainment is provided by always-present surfers in the ocean just outside.

Montara

Point Montara Lighthouse Hostel *on 16th St., off Highway 1, 415/728-7177; rooms for families and couples available.* This restored 1875 lighthouse is now the cliffside setting for a picturesque retreat. Lodging is in a modern duplex that was formerly the lightkeeper's quarters. Facilities include two kitchens, a laundry, a volleyball court, a private beach, an outdoor hot tub (fee), and bicycle rentals. A continental breakfast is available at additional charge. See also page 278.

Moss Beach

James Fitzgerald Marine Reserve *at the end of California Ave., off Highway 1, 415/ 728-3584; daily sunrise to sunset; free.* Excellent tidepooling may be enjoyed here. Usually some pools are accessible, with the occasional sea star or hermit crab caught by the tide. And because visitors are not permitted to remove anything, the sand is rich with shells and interesting natural debris. To see a large variety of specimens, visit when the tide is out. Naturalist-led walks are usually scheduled then on weekends. Call for times. Though the parking area may be deceptively warm and calm, the area by the ocean is usually windy and cold. Take wraps. Picnic tables are available near the parking lot.

El Granada

Village Green *89 Portola Ave., 415/726-3690; B, L, & tea Thur-Tu; $; highchairs, booster seats; 100% non-smoking; no reservations.* A touch of England is purveyed in this tiny, cozy, and cheery spot. Tea items are available all day. Cream tea includes two scones, jam, and wonderful sweet clotted cream. The tea plate consists of assorted finger sandwiches, savories, and sweets. Of course both are served with a pot of tea (or coffee) covered with a perky cozy. B&B accommodations are also available.

Miramar Beach

♥**Cypress Inn** *407 Mirada Rd., 800/83-BEACH, 415/726-6002, fax 415/726-1138; 8 rooms; 100% non-smoking; $$$-$$$+; children free; all fireplaces; some TVs, bathtubs; full breakfast, room service by arrangement.* Located on a quiet frontage road across the street from the ocean, this impressive inn is decorated with bright accents of Mexican folk art. Each of its rooms is on the ocean side, so guests can always hear the soothing sound of the ocean in the background, and each has a private balcony, ocean view, and fireplace. Many guests enjoy just sitting in their room and watching the brown pelicans dive for fish. To experience a bit of heaven, reserve the third-floor Las Nubes room. Its name meaning literally "the clouds," this penthouse room has a luxurious tiled bathroom with an over-size whirlpool tub, plus a bank of windows overlooking the ocean. Occupants want to stay forever. An afternoon tea, featuring exquisite hors d'oeuvres, is also included in the room rate.

Miramar Beach Inn *131 Mirada Rd., 415/726-9053; L M-Sat, D daily, SunBr; $$-$$$; highchairs, booster seats; reservations suggested; MC, V.* Seafood dinners and great ocean views are available here, and on Friday and Saturday nights live rock and roll is included free.

Bach Dancing and Dynamite Society *307 Mirada Rd., 415/726-4143; Sun 3pm; closed Jan, Sept, & Dec; adults $14, children 14-21 $10, 6-13 free.* Live jazz and classical music are performed at this beach house. The door opens at 3, and the music begins at 4:30. Arrive early as there are no advance reservations. A buffet, with a wine and juice bar, is available, and minors are welcome. Call for schedule.

Half Moon Bay

♥**San Benito House** *356 Main St., 415/726-3425; 12 rooms; $$-$$$; unsuitable for children under 10; no TVs; some bathtubs; some shared baths; sauna; continental breakfast, restaurant.* Upstairs, guest rooms feature vividly colored solid walls, high ceilings, and bathrooms with old-fashioned claw-foot tubs. Guests may stroll in the garden and, perhaps, indulge in some competition on the croquet lawn.

Downstairs, the charmingly decorated restaurant *(D Thur-Sun, SunBr; $$-$$$; highchairs, booster seats, children's portions; 100% non-smoking; reservations suggested; AE, MC, V)* invites romantic dining. The owner/chef makes use of fresh local produce and seafood in her accomplished preparation of California cuisine with a French country influence, and the kitchen is accomplished in producing delicious soups and French pastries. Dining reservations should be made when booking a room, as this cozy dining room is very popular with locals. A deli dispenses quick, inexpensive meals *(M-Sat 11-3)*, and a lively Western-style saloon *(daily from 4pm)* is the perfect spot for a nightcap.

A picnic can be put together by visiting the old-fashioned **Cunha's Country Store** *(Main St./Kelly Ave., 415/726-4071)*, which has been in the same building for over 50 years, and the **Half Moon Bay Bakery** *(514 Main St., 415/726-4841)*, which is still using its original brick ovens and is known for its French bread and Portuguese sweet bread. The bakery also makes its own donuts, and sandwiches are available to go.

The area's spectacular beaches are popular picnic destinations in summer. **Dunes Beach,** which is part of **Half Moon Bay State Beach,** is a personal favorite.

Whale-watching expeditions are scheduled January through April on Saturdays, Sundays, and some Fridays. They leave from Pillar Point Harbor in nearby Princeton-By-The-Sea. Sponsored by non-profit **Oceanic Society Expeditions** *(800/326-7491, 415/474-3385; $29-$32/person)*, each boat trip has a professional naturalist on board to educate participants about the whales and interpret their behavior. Children must be at least 5, and reservations are necessary.

Pescadero

Pigeon Point Lighthouse Hostel *Pigeon Point Rd., 415/879-0633; rooms for families and couples available.* Named after the first big ship that crashed on the rocks here, this scenic lighthouse, built in 1871, is the second tallest freestanding lighthouse in the U.S. Visitors are housed in adjacent bungalows, and a hot tub is available in the evenings. See also page 278.

Public **lighthouse tours** are available *(415/726-7000; Sun 10 to 3, also Sat in summer; reservations necessary)*, and excellent tidepools are located just to the north.

Duarte's Tavern *202 Stage Rd., 415/879-0464; B, L, & D daily; $-$$; highchairs, booster seats; reservations suggested for dinner; AE, MC, V.* Diners have been coming here since 1894 to enjoy drinks in the old-time bar and a homecooked meal in the cozy, casual coffee shop. Breakfast, served until 1 p.m. on Sundays, features giant buttermilk pancakes and outstanding omelettes—especially the garlic and olive oil-sauteed artichoke version—as well as more usual items. At either lunch or dinner try creamy artichoke heart soup, fresh artichoke hearts, fried oysters, homemade pie, and fresh applesauce. (Artichoke items are made with artichokes picked fresh in nearby fields.) Grilled fresh fish is available at dinner, and a popular fixed-price cioppino (seafood soup) feed is scheduled each Friday, Saturday, and Sunday night by reservation.

Año Nuevo State Reserve *New Year's Creek Rd., 415/879-0227; tours Dec-Apr; reservations necessary and must be made at least 10 days in advance (800/444-7275); $2/ person + $5/car.* Huge elephant seals return to this beach each year to mate and bear their young. It is the only elephant seal rookery on the U.S. mainland. Docent-guided tours, lasting 2-1/2 hours and covering 3 miles, take visitors close enough to observe the seals basking in the sun or sleeping. Usually that is the extent of the activity seen, but occasionally one of the weighty bulls (some weigh almost 8,000 pounds!) roars into battle with a challenging male. When picking a tour date note that the males arrive in December (when most of the battles occur), the females arrive in January, and the babies start being born in late January. Mating usually occurs in February, when the population is at its peak. Then the adult seals, and tourists, begin to leave, making March and April—when the weaned pups are still around—a somewhat quieter time to visit. An even quieter time is the rest of the year, when advance tickets aren't necessary. Call ahead for schedule. No food service is available at the reserve, and no drinking water is available along the tour trail.

Depending on the season, pick-your-own olallieberries, kiwi fruit, artichokes, pumpkins, or Christmas trees are waiting across the street at 476-acre, usually sunny **Coastways Ranch** *(415/879-0414; closed Jan-May & Aug-Sept).* This ranch has been farmed by the Hudson family since 1917. Call ahead for current information on crops, and bring along garden gloves to protect hands. Picnic facilities and snacks are available.

– Santa Cruz–

A LITTLE BACKGROUND

Close enough to San Francisco to visit just for the day, Santa Cruz has long been a popular summer destination. Weather is reliably clear and sunny, and the beach features fine sand and a gentle surf. In fact, it is a Very Southern California-style beach town. The beach people add to the simile with zinc on their noses, surfboards hanging out of their cars, and The Beach Boys blaring from their tapedecks. Why, even the police officers wear shorts!

The 1989 Loma Prieta earthquake wreaked havoc here. The damage is most noticeable along the popular Pacific Garden Mall, which continues to look like a disaster area.

VISITOR INFORMATION

Santa Cruz County Conference & Visitors Council *701 Front St., Santa Cruz 95060, 800/833-3494, 408/425-1234.*

GETTING THERE

Located approximately 80 miles south of San Francisco. Take Highway 101 or Highway 280 to Highway 17, or Highway 1 all the way.

ANNUAL EVENTS

West Coast Antique Fly-In and Air Show *May; in Watsonville, 408/724-3849.* An assortment of antique and classic planes, including some from World Wars I and II and some home-built models, provide an interesting air show. Always held on Memorial Day Weekend, this is the largest antique fly-in and air show on the West Coast.

Cabrillo Music Festival *July or August; held at locations in Santa Cruz County, 408/ 662-2701.* This is said to be one of the country's best small music festivals. The program includes a variety of classic and contemporary works as well as world premieres.

Brussels Sprout Festival *October; in Santa Cruz, at the Boardwalk, 408/423-5590.* Get ready to sample chocolate-covered sprouts, sprout water taffy, sprout chip cookies, and guacasprout dip . . . maybe even some sprout pizza and sprouts-on-a-stick. More conventional recipes, demonstrated by local restaurant chefs, are also available for tasting.

WHERE TO STAY

♥Babbling Brook Inn *1025 Laurel St., 800/866-1131, 408/427-2437, fax 408/427-2457; 12 rooms; 100% non-smoking; $$-$$$+; 2-night minimum on Saturdays; unsuitable for children under 13; some bathtubs, fireplaces; full breakfast, limited room service.* Shaded by tall redwoods, this secluded hillside inn was built as a log cabin in 1909. Room s were added through the years, and the inn was renovated in 1981. It is the oldest and largest B&B in the area and is on the National Register of Historic Places. The acre of beautfully landscaped grounds surrounding the inn features paths, covered footbridges, cascading waterfalls, a creek, and a gazebo. Complimentary wine and cheese are served beside the parlor fireplace each afternoon.

Casa Blanca Motel *101 Main St., 408/423-1570; 27 rooms; $$-$$$+; cribs; some kitchens, bathtubs, fireplaces; restaurant, limited room service.* Located across the street from the beach, this converted 1918 mansion features spacious, pleasantly decorated rooms. More rooms, boasting terraces and a country-style decor, are available in a newer 1950s annex.

Elegant steak and seafood dinners and a casual Sunday brunch are served in an adjoining restaurant *(408/426-9063; D daily, SunBr; $$-$$$; highchairs, booster seats, children's portions; reservations suggested; AE, MC, V)* that features the largest wine cellar in the county.

♥Chateau Victorian *118 First St., 408/458-9458; 7 rooms; 100% non-smoking; $$-$$$; unsuitable for children; no TVs; all fireplaces; 1 bathtub; expanded continental breakfast.* Built around the turn of the century, this B&B is only a block from the beach and Boardwalk. Attention to detail is displayed throughout. A favorite room is the L-shaped Lighthouse Room on the second floor. The inn's largest room, it is furnished with a large armoire, a queen-sized brass bed, and two very comfortable oversized rolled-arm chairs positioned on either side of the fireplace.

Dream Inn *175 W. Cliff Dr., 800/662-3838, 408/426-4330, fax 408/427-2025; 164 rooms; 41 non-smoking rooms; $$$-$$$$+; children under 12 free; cribs; all bathtubs; some* *kitchens; heated pool, hot tub; 2 restaurants, room service (special children's items).* This 10-story hotel is located right on the beach, and each room has a private balcony or patio overlooking the beach and ocean. The pool and hot tub are 1 story up from the sand and enjoy the same view.

Ocean Echo Motel & Cottages *401 Johans Beach Dr., 408/462-4192; 15 units; $-$$; 2-night minimum in summer; cribs; some kitchens, bathtubs.* Located a few miles south of the Boardwalk, these attractive units are on a private beach.

Santa Cruz Hostel *408/423-8304.* Located a short walk from downtown, this hostel operates in a converted Victorian house. See also page 278.

Motel Row. Many motels are located in the area surrounding the Boardwalk, including some inexpensive ones dating from the 1930s. Rooms are usually available at the last minute.

WHERE TO STAY NEARBY

Pajaro Dunes *2661 Beach Rd., Watsonville, 800/7-PAJARO, 408/722-9201, fax 408/728-7444; 125 units; 15 non-smoking units; $$$-$$$$+; 2-night minimum on weekends; cribs; all kitchens, bathtubs, fireplaces; 19 tennis courts.* Situated in the shoreline dunes, this private compound consists of condominiums, townhouses, and homes. Hiking and biking trails, jogging paths, and volleyball and basketball courts round out the recreational facilities. Bike rentals are also available.

WHERE TO EAT

Cocoanut Grove *400 Beach St., 408/423-2053; SunBr; $$; highchairs, booster seats, children's portions; reservations suggested; MC, V.* In the '30s and '40s this marvelous room was popular as a ballroom for big band dances. Now it is the scene of an opulent Sunday brunch. Since it is on the second floor, the dining room has wonderful views of the beach and ocean. On warm days, a domed-glass ceiling is opened to the fresh sea air. Among the array of foods are made-to-order omelettes (available until 11 a.m.). A buffet of fresh fruits, salads, relishes, cheeses, muffins, breakfast meats, and egg items is carefully maintained and available throughout. Topping it all off is a calorie-laden pastry table. Choice of drink is also included. Children are nicely accommodated, and dress varies from beach-casual to dressy.

The Crow's Nest *2218 E. Cliff Dr., 408/476-4560; L & D daily; $$; highchairs, booster seats, children's portions; reservations suggested in summer; AE, MC, V.* Fresh local seafood is the specialty here. Children are given a coloring menu and a prize from the treasure chest. Diners may be seated outdoors, protected by a glass windbreaker, and watch the yachts come and go from the **Santa Cruz Yacht Harbor.** Seals are also often observed frolicking close to shore.

Hobee's *740 Front St., 408/458-1212.* For description, see page 6.

Ideal Fish Restaurant *106 Beach St., 408/423-5271; D daily; $-$$; reservations suggested; AE, DC, MC, V.* Situated on the beach at the base of the Wharf, this popular old-time fish house features big windows overlooking the sand and nearby Boardwalk. Decorated with hefty ropes so as to make it resemble a ship's deck, the restaurant has a noisy, festive atmosphere. A bargain Early Dinner Special, with limited entree choices, is available daily from 4:30 to 6:30. The regular menu offers a wonderful made-from-scratch fresh snapper fish & chips served with a house-made tartar sauce. In addition to simple fish and shellfish items, the menu has saucy items (seafood Rockefeller), pastas (fettuccini Jambalaya), and steaks. Children's selections include fish as well as a grilled cheese sandwich and hamburger.

India Joze Restaurant *1001 Center St., 408/427-3554; L M-F, D daily, Sat & SunBr; $$; highchairs, booster seats, children's portions; reservations suggested; MC, V.* The day of the week determines the type of Asian cuisine found on this restaurant's exciting, exotic menu. Monday through Wednesday it's Mid-East Asian, Thursday and Friday it's East Indian, and Saturday and Sunday it's Indonesian. The pleasant dining area is light and airy, and live entertainment is scheduled some evenings. The kitchen is well-known for its splendid desserts, which may be enjoyed sans meal in an informal dining area outside the restaurant.

Each August the menu reflects the fact that the restaurant is the home of the **International Calamari Festival.** (Co-owners Beth Regardz and Joseph Schultz are co-authors of *The Calamari Cookbook.*)

Before or after a meal here, browsing is pleasant in the adjoining **Santa Cruz Art Center** shops.

Old Theatre Cafe *106 Walnut Ave., 408/426-0544; B, L, & D daily; $; highchairs, booster seats, children's portions; no cards.* This European-style coffee shop serves particularly good breakfasts. It's also well known for its German-Austrian bakery, which prepares such delights as Black Forest cake and Napoleons.

Santa Cruz Brewing Company/Front Street Pub *516 Front St., 408/429-8838; L & D daily; $; booster seats; MC, V.* Located downtown, this cheerful spot claims to be "the first brewery on California's central coast since Prohibition." It dispenses made-on-the-premises brews: an European-style Lighthouse Lager, a Lighthouse Amber, and a dark Pacific Porter. Children might like the root beer made from an old-time recipe. Like the brews, the pub food is made fresh on the premises and includes "spiedies" (grilled skewers of turkey), oyster shots (spicy oysters in a shot glass), beer bread (made from the spent grains of beer-making), and fish & chips (battered deep-fried snapper). All this, plus an assortment of sandwiches and "munchies."

WHAT TO DO

Beach & Boardwalk *400 Beach St., 408/423-5590; from 11am, daily June-Sept, weekends Oct-May, call for closing times; admission to Boardwalk free; individual fee for rides, all-day ride ticket $16.95; miniature golf $4.75-$5.75.* Fortunately, this is one beach boardwalk that has not degenerated over the years. Built in 1907, it was spiffed up a few years ago with a cheerful painting. Now the only boardwalk left on the West Coast and the oldest amusement park in California, it offers a variety of arcade games, fast-food stands (don't miss the salt water taffy and caramel apples at **Marini's**), and souvenir shops—plus 20 major rides and 7 kiddie rides. The half-mile-long concrete walkway parallels a clean, gorgeous beach. Thrill rides include the **Giant Dipper,** a rickety wooden roller coaster built in 1924 and rated by *The*

New York Times as one of the ten best in the country, and Logger's Revenge, a re-freshing water flume ride. An old-fashioned merry-go-round, built in New Jersey by Charles Looff in 1911 and the largest of the four remaining classic carousels in Northern California, features 70 hand-carved horses (all with authentic horsehair tails) and 2 chariots as well as its rare, original circa 1894 342-pipe Ruth band organ and a brass (now steel) ring toss—one of the few left in the country. Both the roller coaster and the carousel are now National Historic Landmarks, and the Boardwalk itself is a California Historic Landmark. All this and indoor miniature golf, too!

Bonny Doon Vineyard *2 Pine Flat Rd., Bonny Doon, 8 miles north of town, then 5 miles up the hill, 408/425-3625; tasting F-M 12-5:00, in summer W-M; tours by appointment.* The pleasant side trip taken to reach this winery follows a meandering country road to the tiny mountain town of Bonny Doon. Picnic facilities are available in a redwood grove, complete with a gurgling creek. Winery specialties include exotic Rhone-like Cuvees, a Muscat Canelli, and a Blanc de Noir of Pinot Meunier that is available only at the winery. A rich raspberry-flavored Framboise dessert wine makes delicious sipping,

Joseph M. Long Marine Laboratory *west end of Delaware Ave., 408/459-4308; Tu-Sun 1-4; free.* This marine research station for U.C. Santa Cruz features both a small aquarium of local sea life and a touching pool stocked with hermit crabs, sea stars, and sea anemones. Outside, the skeleton of an 86-foot-long blue whale makes an impressive display. (The whale washed ashore up the coast on Pescadero Beach in 1979.) Guided tours are usually available and include viewing the tanks where sea lions are housed for study. Research is conducted here on a variety of topics, including marine mammal behavior, fish diseases, and coral genetics.

Lighthouse Point *on West Cliff Dr.* **Seal Rock,** home to a herd of sea lions, is visible off shore from the small brick **Mark Abbott Memorial Lighthouse**, which now houses the unique **Santa Cruz Surfing Museum** *(408/429-3429; W-M 12-4; free).* Surfers can be viewed in action from nearby **Steamer Lane.**

Mission Santa Cruz *126 High St., 408/426-5686; M-F 2-5, Sat 12-5, Sun 11-2, call ahead to verify schedule; by donation.* The original mission, built in 1794, had a history of being destroyed. This half-size replica is built near the original mission site and houses a small museum.

Municipal Wharf *near the Boardwalk.* It is possible to either walk or drive to the end of this half-mile-long pier. Fishermen angle from the side, and seafood restaurants, snack stands, and picnic tables are scattered along its length. Seals may be fed through fishing holes at the end of the pier, and deep-sea fishing trips originate at concessions located here.

Mystery Spot *1953 Branciforte Dr., 3 miles north of town, 408/423-8897; daily 9:30-5; adults $3, 5-11 $1.50.* Located in a grove of redwoods, this small, quiet, cool spot measures only about 150-feet in diameter. Visitors are given a guided tour during which gravitational forces appear to be defied. Finding it can be a bit of a mystery, too.

Natural Bridges State Beach *north end of West Cliff Dr., 408/423-4609; daily 8am-sunset; $6/car.* Enjoy a picnic in the sun on the sandy beach, or in the shade at sturdy tables. All but one of the sandstone arches, after which the beach is named, have collapsed, but there are still plenty of tidepools to explore. Swimming in the ocean is not safe, but sometimes a lagoon forms where small children may safely wade.

From October through February large numbers of **monarch butterflies** make their winter home here. In fact, it is said to be the largest population of wintering monarchs on the West Coast. A 3/4-mile nature trail leads to good viewing points where they may be observed hanging in clusters on mature eucalyptus trees. Guided walks are also often scheduled. A Visitors Center *(daily 10-4)* displays informative exhibits.

Octagon County Historical Museum *118 Cooper St., 408/425-2540; M-Sat 12-5; free.* Exhibits inside this unusual building, constructed in 1882 and formerly the County Hall of Records, change regularly.

Pacific Garden Mall *Pacific Ave. between Water & Cathcart Sts.* These five landscaped blocks comprise downtown Santa Cruz. Once the park-like setting was home to a variety of boutiques, art galleries, and restaurants operating from within restored historic buildings. But the 1989 Loma Prieta earthquake turned the area into a disaster zone of destruction. While the city slowly repairs the damage, some businesses continue to operate. The **Bookshop Santa Cruz,** now located inside a canvas tent, is still great for browsing, and a pleasant courtyard behind it invites stopping for a relaxing snack break.

Santa Cruz City Museum *1305 E. Cliff Dr., 408/429-3773; Tu-Sat 10-5, Sun 12-5; adults $1.50, 14-18 50¢.* Located across the street from wonderful **Seabright Beach,** this museum displays the county's natural treasures. Exhibits include Indian relics, fossils, local wildlife specimens, an operating beehive, and a "touch tank" of live sea animals. Earthquake information is also provided.

Santa Cruz Mission State Historic Park *143 School St., 408/425-5849; W-Sun 10-4, daily in summer; adults $2, 12-18 $1.* One of the original mission buildings is housed in this 2-acre park, which is just a short walk from Mission Santa Cruz. Period crafts demonstrations are offered on Sundays; guided tours are also available then at 1 p.m.

University of California, Santa Cruz Campus *1156 High St., 408/459-0111; free parking Sat & Sun, M-F $3.* Get acquainted with this scenic campus by taking a self-guided walking tour. Maps are available at the Public Information Office *(408/459-2495).* Guided van/walking tours *(408/459-4008; M-F at 10:30 & 1:30; free; reservations required)* are also available, and free shuttle buses loop the campus daily.

The **Arboretum** *(408/427-2998; daily 9-4:30)* has an extensive collection of plants from Australia and New Zealand and of South African protea.

Wilder Ranch State Historic Park *1401 Old Coast Rd., off Highway 1, 2 miles north of town, 408/426-0505; W-Sun 10-4, daily in summer; tours on weekends; $6/car.* The perfect spot for a lazy day in the country, this 5,000-acre turn-of-the-century ranch complex invites visitors to bring along a picnic. Formerly a dairy, it was built in an arroyo, or valley, that protects it from whipping coastal winds and is reached via a short walk down from the parking lot. Visitors may inspect the owner's large Queen Anne Victorian home, an even older adobe, a bunk house, several barns, a chicken coop, and miscellaneous other structures. Plenty of live animals bring reality to the old buildings: horses, cows, sheep, goats, chickens, domestic turkeys, and guinea hens. Docents add to the atmosphere by dressing in old-fashioned garb.

The Old Cove Landing Trail provides a 2-mile nature walk. A self-guiding brochure is available at the trailhead. If all goes well, pond turtles, cormorants, and harbor seals might be sighted. A fern grotto is also on the itinerary.

– Capitola –

A LITTLE BACKGROUND

Dating back to 1861, this historic seaside resort was the state's first. Now it is an artsy-craftsy beach town. The lovely mile-long beach is sheltered between two bluffs and offers both swimming in calm ocean waters and wading in the fresh water of Soquel Creek. Be cautious, however, as sometimes that creek water isn't so fresh.

Fronting the beach, **The Esplanade** is lined with coffee houses and restaurants serving everything from hamburgers to lobster. Many have outdoor patios overlooking the beach.

Because it is such a popular spot, in the summer free shuttle buses are in service to take visitors from parking lots on Bay Avenue to the beach. Some shuttle bikes are also available for loan.

VISITOR INFORMATION

Capitola Chamber of Commerce *621-B Capitola Ave., Capitola 95010, 408/475-6522.*

GETTING THERE

Located approximately 5 miles south of Santa Cruz.

ANNUAL EVENTS

Begonia Festival *September; 408/476-3566.* Begun years ago as a way to make use of the beautiful blooms discarded by local begonia growers, who were interested only in the bulbs, this popular festival includes a sand castle contest, fishing derby, and nautical parade of flower-covered floats down Soquel Creek. Throughout the festival, the town's merchants and homeowners put on their own shows with begonia displays and decorations. (The only other begonia festival in the world is held in Ballarat, Australia.)

WHERE TO STAY

Capitola Inn *822 Bay Ave., 408/462-3004; 56 rooms; 12 non-smoking rooms; $$-$$$; children under 6 free; cribs; all bathtubs; some kitchens, fireplaces; heated pool, hot tub.* This tasteful, modern lodging facility operates a free shuttle bus to the beach daily in summer.

Capitola Venetian Hotel *1500 Wharf Rd., 800/332-2780, 408/476-6471; 20 units; $$$-$$$+; 2-night minimum on weekends; children under 2 free; cribs; all kitchens; some bathtubs, fireplaces.* This mini-village of charming stucco apartment units is located right on the beach. Some units have balconies and ocean views. Built in the 1920s, it is said to have been the first condominium complex in California.

Harbor Lights Motel *5000 Cliff Dr., 408/476-0505; 10 rooms; $$-$$$; children under 5 free; some kitchens, 1 fireplace.* This ordinary motel boasts an extraordinary location just across from the beach.

WHERE TO EAT

Mimi's Ice Cream Cart. In summer, be on the lookout for pretty Mimi pedaling her ice cream bike while peddling cold ice cream to hot and hungry tourists. It's been awhile since Mimi has been spotted. Hopefully she's still around and hasn't become just another wispy legend.

Shadowbrook *1750 Wharf Rd., 408/475-1511; L Sat & Sun, D daily; $$-$$$; highchairs, booster seats, children's menu; reservations suggested; AE, MC, V.* Located on the banks of Soquel Creek, this popular restaurant is said to be haunted by the man who built it as a summer home in 1917. Diners descend to the restaurant either by riding a bright red, self-operated cable car down a flower-laden hill from the street above, or by strolling down a winding path. The menu features prime rib and fresh fish as well as a variety of specials. Dinners include a choice of either spinach or Caesar salad or clam chowder, a fresh vegetable, and fresh sourdough bread. A jukebox provides music for dancing each evening.

WHAT TO DO

Antonelli Brothers Begonia Gardens *2545 Capitola Rd., Santa Cruz, 408/475-5222; daily 9-5; free.* Acres of indoor plants, ferns, and beautiful begonia baskets may be viewed and purchased here. Peak of bloom is August and September, but a good show may be enjoyed June through October. Picnic tables are available in the Hanging Begonia Room.

Bargetto Winery *3535 N. Main St., Soquel, 408/475-2258; tasting daily 10-5:30; tours M-F at 11 & 2.* This small family winery is known both for fruit wines, including olallieberry and apricot (a personal favorite), and excellent homemade wine vinegars. It also produces an unusual and authentic Mead (honey wine). Bring a picnic to enjoy on the rustic outdoor patio overlooking gurgling Soquel Creek.

– Monterey Peninsula –

A LITTLE BACKGROUND

Popular for years because of its proximity to San Francisco, this area (Monterey, Pacific Grove, and Carmel) is well-established as a vacation destination. A vast variety of overnight accommodations and restaurants is available. Once the off-season was the entire winter. Now, due to the area's immense popularity, there is no off-season. Reservations are essential for lodging as well as for most of the more popular restaurants.

GETTING THERE

Located approximately 40 miles south of Santa Cruz.

STOPS ALONG THE WAY

Giant Artichoke Restaurant *11261 Merritt St., off Highway 1, Castroville, 408/633-3204; B, L, & D daily; $; booster seats; no reservations; no cards.* Located in "the artichoke capital of the world," where three-quarters of the nation's artichokes are grown, this novelty restaurant makes a good rest stop. To find it, just look for the giant artichoke. Artichoke specialties include French-fried artichokes with mayonnaise dip, artichoke soup, artichoke salad, artichoke quiche, and artichoke cake. Other more standard short-order items are also on the menu.

– Monterey –

VISITOR INFORMATION

Monterey Peninsula Chamber of Commerce & Visitors & Convention Bureau *P.O. Box 1770 (380 Alvarado St.), Monterey 93942, 408/649-1770.*

ANNUAL EVENTS

Adobe House Tour *April; 408/649-7118.* This is a very popular self-guided walking tour of historic adobe homes and buildings.

Monterey Scottish Festival and Highland Games *July; 408/899-3864.* Celebrating everything Scottish, this event is described as being much like a three-ring circus. One ring features piping (as in bagpipes) and drumming contests, with massive pipe bands competing against each other. Another ring features unusual athletic events such as the Caber Toss (in which a huge pole is tossed end-over-end for accuracy) and Putting the Stone (in which a heavy stone is tossed). And another presents the Highland Dancing Championships, which today is participated in predominantly by females. Events, including several sheepdog demonstrations, run continuously.

Historic Automobile Races *August;* **Grand Prix** *October; both at Laguna Seca Racetrack in Salinas, 408/648-5111.* Originally held in Pebble Beach, the Historic Automobile Races demonstrate the abilities of a broad range of vintage sports and racing cars.

Castroville Artichoke Festival *September; in Castroville, 408/633-CHOK.* This is one of the state's oldest agricultural festivals. It was at this festival in 1947 that Marilyn Monroe was crowned the very first California Artichoke Queen.

Monterey Jazz Festival *September; 408/373-3366.* The oldest continuously presented jazz festival in the country, this well-known event usually sells out by the end of July.

Christmas in the Adobes and **La Posada** *December; 408/649-7111.* Adobes are decorated for the season and lit with luminaria and candles, and a candlelight parade re-enacts Mary and Joseph's search for a room in Bethlehem.

WHERE TO STAY

Casa Munras Garden Hotel *700 Munras Ave, 800/222-2446, 408/375-2411, fax 408/375-1365; 151 rooms; $$-$$$+; children under 12 free; cribs; some bathtubs, fireplaces, 1 kitchen; heated pool; restaurant.* The grounds are spacious, attractive, and peaceful at this large motel-like facility, and all rooms are furnished with brass beds.

Hyatt Regency Monterey *One Old Golf Course Rd., 800/228-9000, 408/372-1234, fax 408/375-3960; 575 rooms; 300 non-smoking rooms; $$$-$$$+; children under 18 free; cribs; all bathtubs; 2 heated pools, 2 hot tubs, exercise room, parcourse, 6 tennis courts (fee; 2 with night lights); restaurant, room service (special children's items).* Located on the outskirts of town, this quiet, luxurious resort is adjacent to the scenic **Old Del Monte Golf Course. Knuckles Historical Sports Bar** has 14 TVs tuned to sports action in a casual, peanut-shells-on-the-floor atmosphere. **Camp Hyatt,** an organized activity program for children, operates during holiday periods.

Monterey Marriott Hotel *350 Calle Principal, 800/228-9290, 408/649-4234, fax 408/372-2968; 341 rooms; 60 non-smoking rooms; $$$-$$$+; children under 15 free; cribs; all bathtubs; heated pool; hot tub, sauna, exercise room; 2 restaurants, room service (special children's items).* Located near the Wharf, this attractively designed hotel is built on the former site of the grand old Hotel San Carlos. At 10 stories, it is the tallest building in town, with quiet and tastefully appointed rooms. An attractive bar presents live jazz in the evening.

Monterey Peninsula Hostel *408/649-0375; summer only.* Accommodations consist of mattresses on the floor in a school gymnasium. See also page 278.

West Wind Lodge *1046 Munras Ave., 800/821-0805, 408/373-1337, fax 408/372-2451; 53 rooms; $$-$$$; children under 10 free; cribs; some kitchens, bathtubs, fireplaces; indoor heated pool, hot tub, sauna; continental breakfast.* Though the architecture of this motel is unpresumptious, its facilities are noteworthy.

Motel Row. Modern motel accommodations abound along Munras Avenue.

WHERE TO EAT

Abalonetti *57 Fisherman's Wharf, 408/373-1851; L & D Thur-M, daily in summer; $-$$; highchairs, booster seats, children's portions; AE, MC.* This tiny, unpretentious restaurant is named for a famous dish in which the squid is pounded until tender, breaded, and then sauteed in butter. So, not surprisingly, over half the menu is devoted to versions of the house specialty—calamari (squid). Other seafood and Italian dishes, as well as pizza, are also available, and there is a good view of Monterey Bay.

Casa Guttierez Mexican Restaurant *590 Calle Principal, 408/375-0095; L & D daily, Sat & SunBr; $; highchairs, booster seats, children's portions; reservations suggested on weekends; AE, MC, V.* Casa Guttierez was built by a young Mexican man for his bride in 1841—when Monterey was still part of Mexico. Fifteen children were raised by them here! Once inside this historic adobe it's easy to understand why it claims to be the funkiest Mexican restaurant in town. The special touch of recycling old Mexican newspapers as placemats is reminiscent of a Mexican roadhouse. Further recycling occurs on the patio, which is decorated with weathered hatch covers and timbers salvaged from Cannery Row's old sardine boats. Favorite menu items include a chispa (cheese and salsa on a flour tortilla), a huge tostada, a chile verde burrito, guacamole, and Mexican hot chocolate flavored with cinnamon and crushed almonds. Freshly fried tortilla chips and salsa accompany each meal.

Clock Garden Restaurant *565 Abrego, 408/375-6100; L M-F, D daily, Sat & SunBr; $$; booster seats, children's portions; reservations suggested for dinner; AE, MC, V.* Diners have a choice of sitting either inside this historic adobe, among a collection of antique clocks, or outside in a lovely courtyard garden. Weekend brunch features delicious hot bran muffins, orange marmalade served in a scooped-out orange shell, and frothy Ramos fizzes. Reservations are not taken then or for lunch, so be there when they open or expect a wait. The dinner menu features roasts, ribs, steak, and fresh seafood, and the kitchen's well-known Greek lemon soup.

Consuelo's *361 Lighthouse Ave., 408/372-8111; L & D daily, SunBr; $$; highchairs, booster seats, children's portions; reservations suggested; AE, MC, V.* Though it might be more appropriately located inside one of the area's historic adobes, this Mexican restaurant operates within an elegant 2-story Victorian mansion dating from

1886. Rooms in the house have been turned into semi-private dining areas, and the menu offers typical Mexican fare as well as a few more unusual items. A personal favorite is the flauta—a chewy flour tortilla filled with shredded beef, rolled, and then deep-fried and topped with a very good guacamole. Among the children's items are a soft quesadilla (sort of a Mexican grilled cheese sandwich) and a hamburger. Meals begin with two complimentary appetizers—a mixture of spicy carrots and peppers, and a giant crisp flour tortilla topped with melted cheese and served elegantly on a pedestal tray. Desserts include a piña colada and a Kahlua cheesecake as well as a more traditional flan. Olé!

Mark Thomas Outrigger *700 Cannery Row, 408/372-8543; L & D daily, SunBr; $$; highchairs, booster seats, children's portions; reservations suggested; MC, V.* Fresh local seafood dominates the menu, but a hamburger is also available. Diners are seated in a room featuring spectacular views of Monterey Bay. A comfortable bar juts out over the water and is a good spot to enjoy a potent tropical drink concoction and perhaps some—careful with this one—puu puus (appetizers). Live entertainment is scheduled on Friday and Saturday evenings.

Mike's Seafood Restaurant *25 Fisherman's Wharf, 408/372-6153; B, L, & D daily; $-$$; highchairs, booster seats, children's portions; reservations suggested at dinner; AE, MC, V.* Arrive before sundown to take advantage of the excellent bay views afforded from the tables of this busy and popular seafood restaurant. Steaks, hamburgers, and chicken are also on the menu.

♥The Sardine Factory *701 Wave St., 408/373-3775; D daily; $$$; highchairs, booster seats, children's portions; reservations suggested; AE, MC, V.* Once home to a canteen patronized by cannery workers, this building now houses an elegant, dimly-lit award-winning restaurant with five very different dining rooms and over 100,000 bottles of wine in its cellar. The kitchen offers continental-style fare and is known for its fresh seafood and well-aged beef. Special items include fresh abalone, chateaubriand, and a traditional osso buco. All dinners are accompanied by a plate of antipasto, breadsticks, and a highly acclaimed abalone cream bisque, and salads are presented with *chilled* forks. Children are welcome, but it would be unpleasant to be caught here with any whose behavior is unpredictable.

♥The Whaling Station Inn Restaurant *763 Wave St., 408/373-3778; D daily; $$$; highchairs, booster seats, children's portions; reservations suggested, AE, MC, V.* Situated inside a building that dates from 1929 and once housed a Chinese grocery store, this restaurant produces creative and delicious food. On one visit seafood selections included spicy barbecued Cajun prawns—the fresh, sweet, firm-fleshed kind that are so hard to find nowadays—and blackened fresh salmon. Entrees were served with a house salad consisting of Cajun-spiced walnuts resting on a bed of Belgian endive, spinach, and baby lettuce—all tossed with a sweet dressing fragrant with sesame oil. Steamed baby carrots and asparagus on a bed of purple cabbage accompanied the entrees, and a diamond of spicy polenta completed the plate. White veal chops, rack of lamb, and rib steak are among the non-seafood entrees. Desserts are made fresh in the kitchen each day, and an irresistible tray of them is presented at the end of each memorable repast.

Wharfside Restaurant *60 Fisherman's Wharf, 408/375-3956; L & D daily; $$; high-chairs, booster seats, children's portions; reservations suggested; AE, MC, V.* In the window downstairs it is possible to watch the various varieties of ravioli (meat and spinach, cheese, squid, salmon, shrimp, crab, lobster) being laboriously prepared. Dining takes place upstairs, where great views of the bay can be enjoyed. The menu is rounded out with other pastas and seafood, and there are plenty of reasonably-priced side orders that should please children.

WHAT TO DO

Allen Knight Maritime Museum *550 Calle Principal, 408/375-2553; Tu-F 1-4, Sat & Sun 2-4; free.* See ship models, bells, compasses, and related items, and learn about the area's naval history. (This museum is scheduled to move to Custom House Plaza.)

California's First Theater *Pacific/Scott, 408/375-4916; call for schedule and reservations; adults $7, 13-19 $5.50, under 13 $4.50.* Part of the Monterey State Historic Park, this building was once a saloon and boarding house for sailors. The first play was presented here in 1848, and the Troupers of the Gold Coast are still going strong. Nowadays the melodramatic shows and olios change periodically, but they are still presented in the tiny theater just like they were in the old days. Best seating for kids is on benches in the back.

Cannery Row. Once booming with sardine canneries, Cannery Row became a ghost town in 1945 when the sardines mysteriously disappeared from the area's ocean. Now this mile-long road houses restaurants, art galleries, shops, a **Bargetto Winery Tasting Room** (#700, 408/373-4053; daily 10:30-6), the **Spirit of Monterey Wax Museum** (#700, 408/375-3770; daily 9-9; adults $5.95, 13-18 $4.95, 6-12 $3.95), and the new **Monterey Bay Aquarium** (see page 32). The **Paul Masson Museum and Tasting Room** (#700, 408/646-5446; daily 10-6, in summer to 8) provides tastes along with a 180-degree view of the bay and a 10-minute video on the winery's history.

Reading John Steinbeck's *Cannery Row* gets visitors in the mood for visiting this historic street. Lee Chong's Heavenly Flower Grocery, mentioned in Steinbeck's novel, is now **The Cannery Row Shell Company** (#835), La Ida's Cafe is now **Kalisa's** (#851), and Doc's lab is now a private club (#800).

Just a block north of the aquarium, the **American Tin Cannery Outlet Center** (125 Ocean View Blvd., 408/372-1442; M-W & Sat 10-6, Thur & F 10-9, Sun 11-5) is worth the detour. Within its attractive industrial interior are some especially noteworthy outlets: Joan & David, Carole Little, Come Fly a Kite, Royal Doulton, and Corning-Revere.

Edgewater Packing Company 640 Wave St., 408/649-1899; open daily, restaurant from 7:30am, merry-go-round & shops from 11, closes at 11pm Sun-Thur, at 1am F & Sat. This family entertainment center has a game room, with both antique pinball machines and modern video games, and a candy shop stocked with cotton candy, caramel apples, and popcorn. It also has what might be the world's fastest merry-go-round. Built by Herschell-Spillman in 1905, it has 36 horses and 2 chariots.

Oscar's Emporia serves reasonably priced family-friendly food, and breakfast is available all day. Of special note are the ice cream concoctions and the substantial pie portions. The adjacent **Warehouse Restaurant** features seafood, fresh lobster, aged steaks, and Italian items such as ravioli, lasagna, fettucini, and spaghetti with various toppings. All dinners include a soup and salad bar. Also in this complex, **O'Kane's Irish Pub** serves inexpensive pub grub, and food prices are cut in half from 10 p.m. to midnight when ordered with a drink.

Bay Bikes (408/646-9090; daily 9-dusk; $6-$10/hour, $18/day) rents both 21-speed mountain bikes and multi-passenger Italian surrey bikes to ride on the spectacular waterfront **bike trail** that hugs the bay from Fisherman's Wharf to Lover's Point. Riders may also opt to take the 17 Mile Drive, drop the bike off at the Carmel branch of the shop, and take a taxi back.

El Estero Park Del Monte Ave./Camino El Estero/Fremont Blvd., 408/646-3860; open 10-dusk. Enjoy hiking and bike trails and a lake filled with hungry ducks. Paddle boats and canoes may be rented, and children may fish from boats. Located by the lake on Pearl Street, **Dennis the Menace Playground** features some colorful play equipment designed by Hank Ketchum—creator of *Dennis the Menace* and a former resident of the area. Notable are a hedge maze with a corkscrew slide in its center, a long suspension bridge, and an authentic Southern Pacific train engine to climb on. Picnic tables and a snack concession are available.

Fisherman's Wharf. Lined with restaurants and shops, the Wharf also offers some inexpensive entertainment. Sometimes an organ grinder greets visitors at the entrance, his friendly monkey anxious to take coins from children's hands. Free-loading sea lions hang out around the wharf pilings. Toss them a fish (available at the bait shops), and they will put on a show. A **diving bell** provides a 30-foot plunge into the water for a fish's-eye view of Monterey Bay. Several businesses offer bay cruises and deep-sea fishing expeditions.

Jacks Peak County Park *25020 Jacks Peak Park Dr., off Highway 68 going toward Salinas, 408/372-8551; 10-8 daily, 9-5 in winter; $1-$2/car.* This 525-acre park has 8 miles of trails and a variety of picnic areas. Follow the nature trail up to Jacks Peak for a great view of Monterey Bay, Carmel Bay, and the valley.

Monterey Bay Aquarium *886 Cannery Row, 408/648-4888; daily 10-6; adults $9.75, 3-12 $4.50.* Built on the site of what was once the Row's largest sardine factory, this spectacular $55 million facility is one of the nation's largest seawater aquariums. Well-arranged and architecturally interesting, it provides a close-up view of the underwater habitats and creatures of Monterey Bay—an area known for its spectacular and varied marine life. Among the more than 100 galleries and exhibits is one that displays a 3-story-high kelp forest in what is the tallest exhibit tank in the world. Another displays the area's playful sea otters. More than 6,500 fish, mammal, bird, invertebrate, and plant specimens are on display, and almost all are native to Monterey Bay. Don't miss the special walk-through aviary of shorebirds or the bat ray petting pool. Children especially enjoy the Touch Pool, where they can handle a variety of sea stars and other tidepool life. Both a fast food cafeteria and a pricier restaurant are available inside; picnic tables are provided outside.

Monterey Bay Kayaks *693 Del Monte Ave., 800/649-5357, 408/373-KELP; M-F 10-6, Sat & Sun 8:30-6; $48/4-hour tour.* Observe sea lions and otters up close near Fisherman's Wharf and along Cannery Row. Tours, guided by marine biologists, include a half-hour of safety instruction, and no experience is necessary. Kayaks hold two people. Children must be at least 4-1/2 feet tall. Smaller children may be accommodated in a triple kayak with two adults. Call for details on more extensive and demanding trips.

Monterey Peninsula Museum of Art *559 Pacific St., 408/372-7591; Tu-Sat 10-4, Sun 1-4; free.* Located downtown, this museum exhibits regional art and photography. Important artists of the Monterey Peninsula, including Ansel Adams and Edward Weston, are well represented. The strong graphics collection includes works by Rembrandt, Manet, and Picasso

An extension, the historic **La Mirada adobe,** features beautiful gardens, antique furnishings, and more works of art. It is open for tours.

Monterey State Historic Park *525 Polk St., 408/649-7118; daily 10-4; adults $4, 6-17 $2, individual buildings $2.* Part of the California State Park System, this park consists of 14 historical sites and preserved adobes. The fee includes admission to all of the buildings (gardens are free) and includes guided tours of the very special **Stevenson House** (said to be haunted by a forelorn woman dressed in black), **Cooper-Molera Adobe** (a 2-acre complex with chickens, sheep, carriages, and visitor center), **Larkin House, Casa Soberanes, Pacific House,** and **Custom House.** Picnic facilities are available.

Operating from the Pacific House, **California Heritage Guides** *(10 Custom House Plaza, 408/373-6454; M, Tu, & F at 2; adults $2.75, 6-16 $1; reservations suggested)* provides guided walking tours through Monterey's historic area. Customized tours and tours to other areas are also available.

Western Hang Gliders *1 Reservation Rd., Marina, 408/384-2622.* For those longing to take up hang-gliding, this is the place to do it. Located on the dunes east of town, this school offers a 3-hour beginning course with five flights for $75. Reservations are recommended.

– Pacific Grove –

VISITOR INFORMATION

Pacific Grove Chamber of Commerce *P.O. Box 167 (Forest/Central Aves.), Pacific Grove 93950, 408/373-3304.*

ANNUAL EVENTS

Each year in early October hundreds of thousands of stunning orange and black **monarch butterflies** return to Pacific Grove to winter on the needles of favored local pine trees. They migrate all the way from western Canada and Alaska and stay until March, when they again fly north.

Somewhat of a mystery is how they find their way here each year since, with a lifespan of less than a year, no butterfly makes the trip twice. It is, in fact, the great grandchildren of the prior year's butterfly visitors that return. Somehow the monarchs program a genetic message into their progeny, which then return to these same trees the following fall and repeat the cycle.

Reacting to the weather somewhat as does a golden poppy, monarchs prefer to flutter about on sunny days between the hours of 10 a.m. and 4 p.m. In fact, they can't fly when temperatures drop below 55 degrees. So on cold and foggy days, which are quite common in this area, they huddle together with closed wings and are often overlooked as dull pieces of bark or dead leaves. On cold days observers must be careful where they step: Monarchs that have dropped to the ground to sip dew off the grass may be resting there, having found it too cold to fly back to their perch.

During early March the butterflies can be observed mating. Watch for females chasing males in a spiral flight. (Males are recognized by a characteristic black dot on their wings.) When a female finds a male she likes, they drop to the ground to mate. Literally standing on his head at one point, the male, while still mating, then lifts the female back to a perch in a tree, where they continue mating for almost an entire day!

Butterfly nets should be left at home. To discourage visitors from bothering these fragile creatures, Pacific Grove has made molesting a butterfly a misdemeanor crime carrying a $1000 fine.

To celebrate the annual return of the butterflies, the town of Pacific Grove, also known as Butterfly Town U.S.A., has hosted a **Butterfly Parade** every October since 1938. Completely non-commercial, this delightful parade provides the low-key pleasure of viewing local grade school children marching down the street dressed as butterflies. Traditional bands and majorette corps from local schools also participate. Weather always cooperates: This parade has never been rained on.

For more information on the monarchs, contact the non-profit Friends of the Monarchs organization *(P.O. Box 51683, Pacific Grove 93950, 408/375-0982).* Largely behind the successful purchase by the city of the area by Butterfly Grove Inn, the group continues to work on behalf of the butterflies. To get a child's packet of information on the monarch (stories, a coloring page, etc.), send a request and $1 for postage and handling.

Each April there is a **Victorian Home Tour.** Children under 12 are not permitted.

WHERE TO STAY

Andril Fireplace Cottages *569 Asilomar Blvd., 408/375-0994; 15 units; $$; 1-week minimum in summer; children under 5 free; cribs; all kitchens, bathtubs, fireplaces; hot tub; pets welcome.* These woodsy cottages make for very comfortable lodging, especially for longer stays. The pine-paneled cottages surround a shady courtyard furnished with picnic tables, and it is just a 1-block walk to the ocean.

Asilomar Conference Center *800 Asilomar Blvd., 408/372-8016; $$; children under 2 free; cribs; all bathtubs; some kitchens, fireplaces; heated pool; full breakfast, dining room.* Though this 105-acre facility is used mainly as a conference grounds, it is part of the California State Parks system. When underbooked, rentals are made available to the general public. Reservations may not be made more than a month in advance; last-minute accommodations are often available. In Spanish the word asilomar means "refuge by the sea," and, indeed, the grounds are located in a quiet, scenic area just a short walk from the ocean. Both guests and non-guests are welcome to participate in inexpensive, family-style conference meals at 7:30, noon, and 6; reservations are not necessary.

Butterfly Grove Inn *1073 Lighthouse Ave., 408/373-4921; 28 rooms; $-$$$; 2-night minimum on weekends; some kitchens, bathtubs, fireplaces; heated pool, hot tub; small dogs welcome.* This attractive complex offers a choice of either suites in a vintage house or regular motel rooms. Located on a quiet side street, it is adjacent to a 2.7-acre grove of Monterey Pine trees particularly favored by the monarchs. Though the threat of developing this area has loomed for several years, it was recently decided that the town of Pacific Grove will purchase the lot. The area will be protected as a butterfly habitat, and the public will continue to have access.

Centrella Hotel *612 Central Ave., 800/233-3372, 408/372-3372, fax 408/372-2036; 26 rooms; 100% non-smoking; $$-$$$+; children under 12 free; cribs; some TVs, bathtubs, fireplaces; some shared baths; full breakfast.* This restored turn-of-the-century Victorian has won awards for its interior decor. Rooms are furnished with antiques and feature Laura Ashley wallpapers and fabrics, and some bathrooms have claw-foot tubs. Suites on the third floor are particularly nice. Families with children under 12 are accommodated only in the more expensive cottage suites, each of which has a fireplace and private garden.

♥**The Gosby House Inn** *643 Lighthouse Ave., 408/375-1287; 22 rooms; $$-$$$; no TVs; some bathtubs, fireplaces; some shared baths; continental breakfast.* Located in the heart of the town's shopping area, this Queen Anne Victorian features a charming rounded corner tower and many bay windows. Built in 1887 by a cobbler from Nova Scotia, it is now an historic landmark. Noteworthy features include particularly attractive wallpapers, a well-tended garden, and an assortment of stuffed bears and bunnies that welcome guests throughout the inn (all are available for purchase). A complimentary tea is served in the parlor each afternoon.

For a hopelessly romantic getaway, make dinner reservations at **Gernot's Victoria House Restaurant** *(649 Lighthouse Ave., 408/646-1477)*. Located just next door, in another restored Victorian, this lovely dining room offers a continental menu with selections such as wienerschnitzel and wild boar Bourguignonne.

♥**Seven Gables Inn** *555 Ocean View Blvd., 408/372-4341; 14 rooms; 100% non-smoking; $$-$$$+; 2-night minimum on weekends; unsuitable for children under 12; no TVs; all bathtubs; full breakfast.* Located across the street from the ocean, this elegant yellow Victorian mansion was built in 1886. Rooms and cottages all have ocean views and are decorated with fine European and American antiques. High Tea is served each afternoon.

Motel Row. Numerous motels are located at the west end of Lighthouse Avenue and along Asilomar Boulevard.

WHERE TO EAT

Bay Cafe *589 Lighthouse Ave., 408/375-4237; B & L daily; $; highchairs, booster seats; no cards.* The all-American menu here includes plate-size pancakes, house-baked meats, and made-from-scratch mashed potatoes with homemade gravy.

Just next door, the **Grove Pharmacy** is worth a visit for its collection of butterfly-related souvenirs.

Cascade Cafe *602 Lighthouse Ave., 408/372-7006; B & L daily; $; highchairs, booster seats; AE.* This small, comfortable cafe specializes in old-time home cooking. They bake their own pies, cakes, and cookies, and a different homemade soup is available every day. Lots of specialty coffees are also on the menu.

♥**Old Bath House** *620 Ocean View Blvd., 408/375-5195; D daily; $$$; highchairs, booster seats; reservations suggested; AE, MC, V.* Continental cuisine is served here amid an elegant Victorian decor, and every table has a splendid view of Monterey Bay. Entrees include roast rack of lamb, Australian lobster in pastry, and mesquite-grilled prawns with wild boar sausage. Divine desserts, such as mocha-almond cheesecake and cream puffs filled with French vanilla ice cream and topped with hot fudge sauce, are made in the restaurant's own pastry kitchen.

Tinnery *631 Ocean View Blvd., 408/646-1040; B, L, & D daily, SunBr; $$; highchairs, booster seats, children's portions; AE, MC, V.* Located at Lover's Point, this comfortable, casual restaurant offers outstanding views of the bay. Breakfast is particularly pleasant, with omelettes, egg dishes, and strawberry pancakes on the menu. The eclectic international dinner menu includes appetizers such as nachos and deep-fried zucchini, and entrees such as tempura prawns, pasta primavera, and prime rib.

WHAT TO DO

Butterfly Viewing. The densest clusters of monarchs occur in the pine grove located behind the Butterfly Grove Inn. Another good viewing spot is the west side of **George Washington Park,** along Melrose Street south of Pine Avenue.

Lover's Point *626 Ocean View Blvd.* Located at the southern tip of Montery Bay, this park holds a chunky granite statue honoring the monarch butterfly. It offers a pleasant beach for sunbathing and wading, and a grassy picnic area with barbecue pits.

Pacific Grove Museum of Natural History *165 Forest Ave., 408/648-3116; Tu-Sun 10-5; free.* The natural history of Monterey County is told here through exhibits of marine and bird life, native plants, shells, and Indian artifacts. Butterfly-related exhibits include photographs and displays, as well as an informative 20-minute videotape. The life history of the monarch is portrayed in drawings, and during the summer larvae are often on view. Milkweed—the only plant on which the female monarch will lay her eggs—attracts many butterflies to a native plant garden outside the museum.

Each year during the third weekend in April this tiny museum sponsors a **Wildflower Show.** As many as 500 varieties are displayed.

Point Piños Lighthouse *on Asilomar Blvd., about 2 blocks north of the end of Lighthouse Ave., 408/648-3116; Sat & Sun 1-4; free.* The Coast Guard gives guided tours of this oldest continuously operating Pacific Coast lighthouse. It was built in 1855 out of granite quarried in the area. Doc's Great Tide Pool, from Steinbeck's *Cannery Row,* is located here. The area surrounding the lighthouse is a good spot to walk, picnic, and observe sea otters.

Poor Man's 17-Mile Drive. There is no charge for taking this scenic 4.2-mile drive that passes rugged seascapes and some impressive Victorian homes. Begin at Ocean View Boulevard and 3rd Street. At Point Piños, turn left on Sunset Drive. Tidepooling is good in several spots, and from April to August beautiful lavender ice plant cascades in full bloom over the rocky beach front.

– Carmel –

A LITTLE BACKGROUND

A well-established weekend destination, Carmel is best known for its abundant shops, cozy lodging, and picturesque white sand beach.

It is also known for the things that it doesn't have. No street signs, streetlights, electric or neon signs, jukeboxes, parking meters, or buildings over 2 stories high are allowed in town. No sidewalks, curbs, or house numbers are found in the residential sections. These absent items help Carmel keep its small-town feeling.

Do be careful. Eccentric laws in the town make it illegal to wear high-heeled shoes on the sidewalks, throw a ball in the park, play a musical instrument in a bar, or dig in the sand at the beach other than when making a sandcastle.

It seems that almost every weekend some special event is scheduled in the area, making available lodging perpetually scarce. It is important to make accommodation reservations far in advance, especially for the quainter lodgings.

VISITOR INFORMATION

Carmel Business Association *P.O. Box 4444 (San Carlos/5th, next to the Hog's Breath Inn), Carmel 93921, 408/624-2522.*

Tourist Information Center *P.O. Box 7430 (Mission/5th), Carmel 93921, 408/624-1711.* This private agency provides helpful information and makes lodging reservations.

ANNUAL EVENTS

AT&T Pebble Beach National Pro-Am *January; in Pebble Beach, 800/541-9091.* This was formerly known as the Bing Crosby Golf Tournament.

Carmel Bach Festival *July; 408/624-1521.* Held annually since 1937, this festival varies its highlights from year to year. Candlelight concerts are usually presented in the town's picturesque mission, and a special children's concert is always scheduled.

Concours d'Elegance *August; in Pebble Beach, 408/649-2724.* Car buffs don their dressiest summer attire for a stroll over the spacious lawn at the Lodge at Pebble Beach, where this elegant affair is held. Classic vintage and antique automobiles are displayed.

WHERE TO STAY

Carmel River Inn *Highway 1 at the bridge, 408/624-1575; 43 units; $$-$$$; 2-night minimum on weekends; children under 12 free; some kitchens, bathtubs, fireplaces; heated pool.* Located on the outskirts of town on the banks of the Carmel River, this lodging facility stretches over 10 acres. Guests have a choice of motel rooms or individual cottages.

The Cobblestone Inn *Junipero/8th, 408/625-5222; 24 rooms; $$-$$$+; children under 3 free; cribs; all gas fireplaces; 1 bathtub; full breakfast.* Located only 2 blocks from the main shopping street, this charming inn is filled with teddy bears. They await guests in fanciful poses. They decorate the large lounge/dining area. And should one capture a heart, they are all available for adoption by purchase. The spacious guest rooms are furnished with country-style pine furniture and iron-frame beds. Shutters provide privacy, refrigerators are stocked with complimentary cold drinks, and fireplaces constructed with large river rocks provide atmosphere and warmth. In the morning all guests are greeted with a newspaper at their door, and breakfast may be enjoyed either outside on a sunny slate-and-brick-paved courtyard filled with English flowers blooming in stone containers, or inside with the bears. Two bicycles are available for guests to borrow.

Colonial Terrace Inn *San Antonio/13th, 408/624-2741; 25 rooms, 3 non-smoking rooms; $$-$$$+; 2-night minimum on weekends; cribs; some kitchens, bathtubs, fireplaces;*

continental breakfast. In business since 1925, this crisply attractive lodging is located in a quiet residential area just 1 block from the beach.

The Green Lantern *7th/Casanova, 408/624-4392; 19 units; $$-$$$; children under 5 free; cribs; some bathtubs, fireplaces; continental breakfast*. Operating as an inn since 1926, this pleasant group of rustic multi-unit cottages is located on a quiet side-street just a few blocks from the village and 2 blocks from the beach.

Highlands Inn *on Highway 1, 4 miles south of town, 800/682-4811, 408/624-3801, fax 408/626-8105; 142 units; $$$+; children under 18 free; cribs; all fireplaces; some bathtubs, kitchens; heated pool, 3 hot tubs; 2 restaurants, room service (special children's items)*. Located on the scenic outskirts of town, this inn was built on its spectacular cliffside setting in 1916. It was extensively remodeled in 1984. The contemporary-style accommodations are luxurious, and guests may choose between lanai rooms and cottages. It is the perfect choice for a self-indulgent splurge. Upon check-in children are given a special amenities bag filled with goodies, and all rooms are equipped with a VCR.

Hamburgers are on the menu at the **California Market** and may be enjoyed outside on a balcony overlooking the rugged coastline.

The Homestead *Lincoln/8th, 408/624-4119; 12 rooms; $$; 2-night minimum on weekends; some kitchens, bathtubs, fireplaces*. Painted a cheery rust red, this home-turned-inn provides a variety of interesting rooms. It features a lovely garden and is conveniently located on a quiet corner lot just a few blocks from the village.

Lamp Lighters Inn *Ocean/Camino Real, 408/624-7372; $$-$$$; children under 5 free; cribs; some bathtubs, 1 kitchen, 1 fireplace; full breakfast*. This enclave has both charming rooms and gingerbread-style cottages . Conveniently located between the village and the ocean, it very well might fulfill guest's fairytale fantasies. Several cottages accommodate families; one known as the "Hansel and Gretel" has a special sleeping loft for kids. Accommodations in an annex, located 1 block closer to the beach, are a little less expensive.

La Playa Hotel *Camino Real/8th, 800/582-8900, 408/624-6476, fax 408/624-7966; 80 units; $$$-$$$+; children under 12 free; cribs; all bathtubs; some kitchens, fireplaces; heated pool; restaurant, room service*. This luxury 3-story, Mediterranean-style hotel is conveniently located just 2 blocks from the beach and 4 blocks from town. Taking up an entire block, it is the largest hotel, as well as the only full-service resort hotel, in Carmel. The beds in the thick-walled rooms all have rustic carved headboards sporting the hotel's mermaid motif, and the beautifully maintained grounds are always abloom with colorful flowers. Recently a group of spacious cottages, situated a block closer to the ocean, were added to the property.

Lincoln Green Inn *Carmelo/15th, 408/624-1880; 4 units; $$$; 2-night minimum on weekends; cribs; all kitchens, bathtubs, fireplaces; pets welcome*. Located on the outskirts of town, just a few blocks from where the Carmel River flows into the ocean, this cluster of comfortable English housekeeping cottages features living rooms with cathedral-beamed ceilings and stone fireplaces.

The Lodge at Pebble Beach *on 17-Mile Drive, Pebble Beach, 800/654-9300, 408/624-3811, fax 408/626-3725; 161 rooms; 4 non-smoking rooms; $$$+; 2-night minimum on* *weekends; cribs; all bathtubs, fireplaces; heated pool, children's wading pool, sauna, 14 tennis courts (fee); 3 restaurants, room service.* Complete luxury and the best of sporting facilities await guests here. Golfers may enjoy playing some of the best courses in the country. Horse rentals and equestrian trails are nearby, as are jogging and hiking trails and a parcourse.

Non-guests are welcome to stop in and enjoy the spectacular ocean view over a drink or meal. Try the **Club XIX** at lunch, when diners may sit on a terrace overlooking both the 18th hole and the ocean while enjoying bistro fare.

Normandy Inn *Ocean/Monte Verde, 800/343-3825, 408/624-3825; 48 units; 24 nonsmoking units; $$-$$$+; 2-night minimum on weekends; children under 12 free; cribs; some kitchens, bathtubs, fireplaces; heated pool (unavailable Jan-Mar); continental breakfast.* Conveniently located on the town's main shopping street, this inn features an attractive half-beamed Normandy style of architecture. The comfortably appointed rooms are decorated in French country style, and the pool is invitingly secluded.

Pine Inn *Ocean/Monte Verde, 800/228-3851, 408/624-3851, fax 408/624-3030; 49 rooms; $$-$$$+; 2-night minimum on weekends; children under 12 free; cribs; all bathtubs; 1 fireplace; restaurant, room service (special children's items).* Decorated in an elegant Victorian style, this inn opened in 1889 and just might be the oldest in town. It is conveniently located in the center of town.

♥**San Antonio House** *San Antonio/7th, 408/624-4334; 4 rooms; 100% non-smoking; $$$; 2-night minimum on weekends; unsuitable for children under 12; all fireplaces; some bathtubs; continental breakfast.* This attractive guest house offers large rooms, a lovely garden, and a location in a quiet residential area just 1 block from the beach.

♥**Sea View Inn** *Camino Real/12th, 408/624-8778; 8 rooms; 100% non-smoking; $$-$$$; 2-night minimum on weekends; unsuitable for children under 12; no TVs; some bathtubs; some shared baths; continental breakfast.* Located 3 blocks from the beach, this converted 3-story Victorian home offers pleasantly appointed rooms. Guests are served tea and sherry in the afternoon and wine in the evening.

♥**The Stonehouse Inn** *8th/Monte Verde, 408/624-4569; 6 rooms; 100% non-smoking; $$-$$$; 2-night minimum on weekends; unsuitable for children under 12; no TVs; all shared baths; full breakfast.* Built by local Indians in 1906, this rustic stone country house is close to the village. The original owner often entertained well-known artists and writers, and the antique-furnished rooms are now named in honor of some of those guests.

Sundial Lodge *Monte Verde/7th, 408/624-8578; 19 rooms; $$-$$$+; 2 night minimum on weekends; unsuitable for children under 5; some bathtubs, kitchens; continental breakfast, restaurant.* Located just 1 block from the center of town, next to City Hall (known for awhile as "Clint's Place"), this charming 2-story hotel is built around a flower-filled brick courtyard. Tea and sherry are served to guests in the afternoon.

♥**Vagabond House Inn** *4th/Dolores, 800/262-1262, 408/624-7738; 11 rooms; $$-$$$; 2-night minimum on weekends; unsuitable for children under 12; some bathtubs, kitchens, fireplaces; continental breakfast; pets welcome.* This English Tudor-style building features cozily furnished rooms that open off a quiet, rustic, flower-bedecked courtyard.

WHERE TO EAT

Birgit & Dagmar *Dolores/7th, 408/624-3723; B & L daily, D Sat & Sun; $; 100% non-smoking; no reservations; no cards.* Previously known as the Swedish Restaurant, this charming spot is a favorite for breakfast. A large window allows diners to view the busy sidewalk traffic, and a fireplace warms the tiny dining room. Portions are generous, and most items are served with toasted homemade breads. Swedish pancakes with wild lingonberries—a relative of the American cranberry that grows only in Scandinavia's northern forests—are a specialty of the house and memorably delicious. Breakfast items are also available at lunch.

Across the street, tiny **Picadilly Park** invites relaxing contemplation with its benches, flower garden, and goldfish pond.

Carmel Bakery *Ocean/Lincoln, 408/626-8885; daily 6:30am-9:30pm.* Caramel apples, Cookie Monster cupcakes, and both alligators and turtles made of marzipan bread are just a few of the delicacies available at this popular bakery. Also particularly good are the apricot log pastries, wild blueberry scones, and focaccia with spicy pepper topping. Pastries and drinks may be enjoyed on the premises or while walking the boutique-laden streets.

Clam Box Restaurant *Mission/5th, 408/624-8597; D Tu-Sun; $$; closed most of Dec; highchairs, booster seats, children's portions; no reservations; MC, V.* Customers wait as happily as clams in the constant line to get seated in this tiny, cozy restaurant. That's because they know they're going to enjoy themselves once they get a table. The menu is predominantly seafood, but a hamburger is also available.

Cottage of Sweets *Ocean/Lincoln, 408/624-5170; daily 10-6.* Among the sweet surprises in this charming candy cottage are imported chocolates, diet candy, gourmet jelly beans, and taffy.

At **The House of Hansel and Gretel** *(6th/Lincoln, 408/624-3125; daily 10-5)* they still make ribbon candy by hand. Honeycomb, chocolate-covered caramels, and assorted flavors of hard candies made with natural flavorings are also available.

♥**Creme Carmel Restaurant** *San Carlos/7th, 408/624-0444; D daily; $$-$$$; reservations suggested; MC, V.* The owner/chef of this charming, quiet little dining room prepares some very interesting cuisine. One dinner enjoyed here featured an appetizer of shitake mushroom-tarragon soup with bass quenelles, unusual local produce (including Roman broccoli—a cross between broccoli and cauliflower), delicate charbroiled mahi-mahi topped with an orange-cilantro sauce and presented beautifully on an oversized plate, and a dessert of puff pastry filled with vanilla bean ice cream, warmed strawberries bursting with old-time flavor, and a touch of cassis liqueur.

Em Le's *Dolores/5th, 408/625-6780; B & L daily; $; highchairs, booster seats; no cards.* Cozy and always crowded, this casual spot offers a large variety of breakfast items. Favorites include buttermilk waffles, in a choice of light or dark bake, and wild blueberry pancakes. Pleasant views of sidewalk traffic and counter seating add to the low-key Carmel charm.

Hog's Breath Inn *San Carlos/5th, 408/625-1044; L M-Sat, D daily, SunBr; $$; highchairs, booster seats, children's portions; no reservations; AE, MC, V.* Owned by actor, director, and former mayor of Carmel Clint Eastwood, this rustic, secluded spot exudes a casual, cozy atmosphere. Redwood burl tables and comfortable, colorful, and appropriate director's chairs are scattered outdoors under a gigantic, rambling old oak tree. Guests are warmed by fireplaces and heaters when the temperature chills, and seating is also available inside. The brunch menu offers eggs Benedict, omelettes, and plain eggs served with homemade blueberry muffins and homefried potatoes. Lunch features wonderful homemade soups, salads, sandwiches, and a weighty Dirty Harry Burger served on a good-for-you whole wheat bun. It is perfectly acceptable to stop in just for a drink. Hot drinks and simple drinks tend to be best.

Jack London's *San Carlos/5th, 408/624-2336; L & D daily, SunBr; $-$$; booster seats; V.* Even locals come here to enjoy the excellent bar drinks and cozy bistro atmosphere. Kids are welcome and can order fancy non-alcoholic drinks. Specialties include individual-size pizzas, a variety of hamburgers, and deep-fried calamari. Fresh fish selections change daily. Rich, velvety pasta carbonara Milano and a New York steak round out the eclectic menu. Dinner entrees come with a generous house salad topped with ranch dressing.

♥**La Boheme Restaurant** *Dolores/7th, 408/624-7500; D daily; closed most of Dec; $$; 1 booster seat, children's portions; 100% non-smoking; no reservations; MC, V.* Cozy and colorfully decorated, this charming petite cafe offers no menu choices. It serves just one three-course fixed-price dinner each evening. (A vegetarian entree is always an available option.) Soup and entree change each evening, so it is a good idea to call ahead for the night's menu. The French and Italian country-style dishes are served informal family-style. One dinner enjoyed here began with a large, crisp salad accentuated with olives and substantial slices of ham, salami, and cheese. Then came a perfectly seasoned cream of broccoli soup, followed by a main course of pork loin with a cream sauce flavored with juniper berries. Strawberries Romanoff cost additional and made a refreshing, light dessert.

Mediterranean Market *Ocean/Mission, 408/624-2022; daily 9-6.* This well-stocked delicatessen offers freshly marinated artichoke hearts, sandwich meats, cheeses, skinny French baguettes, exotic beers, wines, bottled waters, and soft drinks. Caviar is also available, as are picnic baskets to carry it all away in.

Popular **Wishart's Bakery** *(408/624-3870; daily 6:30am-9pm)*, a branch of the Carmel Bakery, is located practically next door.

The beach is the perfect destination for a pleasant picnic.

♥**Patisserie Boissiere** *Mission/Ocean, 408/624-5008; B F-Sun, L daily, D W-Sun; $$; reservations suggested; AE, MC, V.* The menu at this elegant little gem offers homemade soups as well as more substantial entrees. Though it would be hard to do so, don't overlook the pastries and desserts: lemon cheesecake, chocolate whiskey cake, zabaglione, and plenty more.

Rocky Point *12 miles south of town on Highway 1, 408/624-2933; L & D daily; $$-$$$; highchairs, booster seats, children's portions; reservations suggested; MC, V.* Take a scenic drive down the coast toward Big Sur, and stop here for a charcoal-broiled steak or fresh seafood dinner. The spectacular view is included in the steep menu prices. Sandwiches and hamburgers are on the lunch menu, making it a relative bargain.

Scandia *Ocean/Lincoln, 408/624-5659; B, L, & D daily; $$; highchairs, booster seats, children's portions; reservations suggested; AE, MC, V.* Pretty and pink is the dining room at this old standby. A bargain Early Bird dinner, served from 4 to 6:30, comes with kavli flatbread and a French baguette, homemade soup or salad, and fresh vegetables. Entree choices then include fresh fish, prepared in exemplary manner, and traditional Danish meatballs (frikadeller). Children's portions are a choice of hamburger steak or linguine marinara. Though children are welcome, they don't fit in well in the evening, when the atmosphere is quite romantic.

Thunderbird Bookshop *3618 The Barnyard, 408/624-9414; L daily, D Tu-Sun; $-$$; highchairs, booster seats, children's portions; reservations suggested; MC, V.* Dine among world-famous authors in this combination bookstore/restaurant. Sandwiches and hamburgers are available at lunch, full meals at dinner, coffee-and during the off hours.

The **Barnyard** shopping center is filled with unusual shops worthy of a browse. Don't miss **Succulent Gardens** *(408/624-0426)* with its rare and unusual varieties of flowering cacti and succulents.

Tuck Box English Tea Room *Dolores/Ocean, 408/624-6365; fax 408/624-5079; B, L, & afternoon tea W-Sun; $; booster seats; 100% non-smoking; no reservations; no cards.* Featuring fairytale architecture and verily reeking of quaintness, this tiny dining room can be quite difficult to get seated in. If ever it is without a long line in front, go! Seating is also available on a tiny outdoor patio. The limited breakfast menu offers simply prepared eggs served with delightful fresh scones and a choice of either homemade olallieberry preserves or orange marmalade. At lunch sandwiches, salads, and omelettes are available along with Welsh rarebit and a daily entree special. Afternoon tea features scones, pies, delicious English trifle, and, of course, plenty of hot English tea.

WHAT TO DO

Bay Bikes II *Lincoln/5th, 408/625-BIKE; daily 9-dusk.* For description, see page 31.

Carmel Beach *at the foot of Ocean Ave., 408/626-1255.* Known for its white powdery sand and spectacular sunsets, this world-famous beach is a choice spot for a refreshing walk, a picnic, or flying a kite. Swimming is unsafe.

The **Great Sand Castle Contest** *(408/624-2522)* is held here each September or October, depending on the tides.

Mission San Carlos Borromeo del Rio Carmelo *3080 Rio Rd., 1 mile south of town off Highway 1, 408/624-3600; M-Sat 9:30-4:30, Sun 10:30-4:30, services on Sun; by donation.* Father Junipero Serra, who established this mission in 1770, is buried here at the foot of the altar. A museum displays Indian artifacts, mission tools, and recreations of both the original mission kitchen and California's first library. A courtyard garden, featuring a restful pond stocked with colorful koi, accents the cemetery where over 3,000 mission Indians are buried. A **fiesta** is held each year on the last Sunday in September.

Across the street, 37-acre **Mission Trail Park** *(408/624-3543; daily dawn-dusk; free)* has several hiking trails. The broad Serra Trail is an easy uphill hike. Doolittle Trail goes further on for great views of the bay and a visit to the 1929 Tudor **Flanders Mansion,** where it is possible to tour the grounds and stroll through the **Lester Rowntree Arboretum.**

Pebble Beach Equestrian Center *Portola Rd./Alva Ln., Pebble Beach, 408/624-2756; group rides daily at 10 & 2, $30/person; reservations required; riders must be 12 or older.* It's strictly English saddles here. Escorted rides follow the extensive bridle trails that wind through scenic Del Monte Forest, around the legendary **Spyglass Hill Golf Course,** and over the sand dunes. Lessons are available.

Point Lobos State Reserve *3 miles south of town off Highway 1, 408/624-4909; daily 9-dusk; $6/car.* Described as "the greatest meeting of land and water in the world," Point Lobos provides the opportunity to see the rustic, undeveloped beauty of the Monterey Peninsula. The flat-topped, gnarled-limbed Monterey cypress trees are native to just the 4-mile stretch between here and Pebble Beach, and sea otters are often spotted in the 1,250-acre reserve's protected waters. Self-guiding trails are available, and guided ranger walks are scheduled daily in summer. Dress warmly and bring along binoculars, a camera, and maybe a picnic, too.

17-Mile Drive *at Pebble Beach exit off Highway 1, between Carmel and Monterey, 408/ 649-8500; daily; $6/car.* The scenery along this world-famous drive is a combination of showplace homes, prestigious golf courses, and raw seascapes. Sights include the **Restless Sea,** where several ocean crosscurrents meet; **Seal and Bird Rock,** where herds of sea lions and flocks of shoreline birds congregate; the **Pebble Beach Golf Course,** one of three used during the annual AT&T National Pro-Am Tournament; and the landmark **Lone Cypress** clinging to its jagged, barren rock base. Picnic facilities and short trails are found in several spots.

Consider splurging on lunch or dinner at one of the three ocean-view restaurants (one is a reasonably-priced coffee shop) at the elegant Lodge at Pebble Beach (see page 40). With reservations, the gate fee is waived.

Point Lobos State Reserve

Special Shops.

Dansk II *(Ocean/San Carlos, 408/625-1600; daily 10-6)* offers bargain prices on discontinued items and seconds from their expensive line of kitchen accessories. Charming **Peter Rabbit & Friends** *(Lincoln/Ocean, 408/624-6854; M-Sat 10-5, Sun 11-5)* specializes in delightful Beatrix Potter-illustrated items.

Thinker Toys *(Ocean/Mission, in Carmel Plaza, 408/624-0441; M-Sat 9:30am-9pm, Sun 10-6)* offers an exciting selection of puppets, dolls, workbooks, and puzzles. This is where to bring the kids to select a souvenir. An annex to this store, located in another part of the shopping center, houses a large inventory of model trains. Also in this shopping center, **Come Fly a Kite** *(408/624-3422; daily 10-5)* is where to pick up a kite. Then head for the beach—the perfect spot to launch it.

Tor House *26304 Ocean View Ave., 408/624-1813; tours F & Sat, on the hour 10-3; adults $5, teenagers $1.50-$3.50; reservations required; children must be at least age 12.* Poet Robinson Jeffers built this medieval-style house and tower retreat out of huge granite rocks hauled up from the beach below. He did much of the work himself and was of the opinion that the manual labor cleared his mind and that, as he put it, his "fingers had the art to make stone love stone." All of his major works and most of his poetry were written while he lived with his wife and twin sons on this craggy knoll overlooking Carmel Bay.

– Carmel Valley –

A LITTLE BACKGROUND

Reliably sunny and peaceful, Carmel Valley is often overlooked by visitors to the Monterey Peninsula. That's a shame, because it is a wonderful place to relax, and it's only a few miles from Carmel. Lodgings, restaurants, and shops dot Highway 16/Carmel Valley Road along its 15-mile stretch into the hub of town.

VISITOR INFORMATION

Carmel Valley Chamber of Commerce *P.O. Box 288, Carmel Valley 93924, 408/659-4000.*

Carmel Valley Reservations *7 Crossroads Mall, Carmel 93923, 800/422-7634, 408/624-5434.*

WHERE TO STAY

Carmel Valley Inn *Carmel Valley Rd., 800/541-3113, 408/659-3131; 46 rooms; 5 non-smoking rooms; $$-$$$; children under 18 free; cribs; some bathtubs; solar-heated pool (unavailable Nov-Mar), hot tub; 7 clay tennis courts (2 with night lights); restaurant, room service; pets welcome.* Surrounded by lush green foothills, the unpretentious rooms here open onto large grassy expanses that invite children to romp. No amenities basket or cable TV await guests, but coffee is available in the lobby each morning. Cars are parked away from the rooms, and there are no bellhops—

meaning it is very quiet and money is to be saved on tipping. Facilities include an enclosed whirlpool hot tub available by reservation, a horseshoe pit, and a naturally-stocked frog pond.

♥**John Gardiner's Tennis Ranch** *Carmel Valley Rd., 408/659-2207; 14 rooms; $1,600-$1,700/person; rate includes lodging, meals, and tennis instruction; closed Mar-Nov; adults only; some kitchens, bathtubs, fireplaces; 2 pools (1 heated), hot tub, sauna, 14 tennis courts.* Begun by John Gardiner in 1957, this legendary tennis retreat has been visited by three presidents (Nixon, Ford, and Reagan). The 5-day clinics run Sunday through Friday and include approximately 25 hours of instruction. Most are set up for mixed doubles; several are just for women. And with 14 courts and only 14 guest rooms, there is never any waiting. When guests aren't on the courts, they're usually either relaxing on the private patio of their luxurious cottage, admiring the extensive flower gardens, or satisfying their worked-up appetites with a sumptuous meal. Low-cal diets haven't been discovered here yet. Meals include items such as "angel fluff" pancakes for breakfast, souffles for lunch, and beef Wellington or fresh fish with popovers for dinner.

Quail Lodge Resort & Golf Club *8205 Valley Greens Dr., 800/682-9303, 408/624-1581, fax 408/624-3726; 100 units; 10 non-smoking units; $$$+; children under 13 free; cribs; all bathtubs; some fireplaces; heated pool, hot tub, 4 tennis courts; restaurant, room service; dogs welcome.* These lakeside cottages and rooms are located on the serene 850-acre grounds of the **Carmel Valley Golf & Country Club**—formerly the site of the Carmel Valley Dairy. Guests may make use of hiking trails and visit 11 lakes that are also wildlife sanctuaries. Attracting a classy crowd, the resort's parking lot has been witnessed holding a DeLorean and several Ferraris at the same time.

The dressy **Covey Restaurant** offers an eclectic menu—shrimp with coconut milk curry and broiled mango, Maine lobster, sweetbreads with morels—and a restive view of the 18-hole golf course.

Tassajara Zen Mountain Center *415/431-3771; 29 units; 100% non-smoking; $$$+; rate includes 3 vegetarian meals; 2-night minimum on weekends; closed Sept-Apr; number of children permitted is controlled; cribs; no TVs; some fireplaces; some shared baths; hot springs pool, steam rooms. Day use: 408/659-2229; $8-$12/person; reservations essential.* Owned by the Zen Center of San Francisco, this traditional Zen Buddhist monastery is located deep in the Ventana Wilderness and is home to 50 monks. Getting there requires a 14-mile drive down a steep dirt road (a four-wheel-drive or stick-shift is stongly advised), but overnight guests have the option of arranging a ride in on a four-wheel-drive "stage." The famous hot mineral springs are semi-enclosed in a Japanese-style bathhouse. Men's and women's baths and steam rooms are separated, and swimsuits are optional. More activities include hiking, river wading, and picnicking. Guests stay in simple wooden or stone cabins with no electricity. Lighting is provided by kerosene lamps. And this isn't a place to sleep in. Bells go off at 5:30 a.m. to announce meditation time for any guests who would like to participate. Getting a reservation can be difficult. It is best to call early for overnight stays; reservations open in mid-February. Day visits should also be booked well in advance; reservations open on April 25. Day guests should bring their own towels and food.

WHERE TO EAT

The Iron Kettle *in White Oak Plaza, in Carmel Valley Village, 408/659-5472; B, L, & afternoon tea; $; no cards.* Operating inside the Old Milk House, an historical landmark built in 1890 that was once an overnight stop for passengers on the Salinas-Tassajara stage, this homey and cute restaurant also offers patio seating. At breakfast it's homemade granola, oatmeal, scones, and egg dishes; at lunch it's simple sandwiches. Afternoon tea is served until 4 and features olallieberry and blueberry scones with homemade jam.

Wagon Wheel Coffee Shop *in Valley Hills Shopping Center, Highway 16/Valley Greens Dr., 408/624-8878; B & L daily; $; no reservations; no cards.* Extremely popular with locals, this spot is usually packed. Tables are tiny, but portions are generous. Breakfast seems to be the busiest meal and is served until the 2 p.m. closing time. The menu then includes omelettes, eggs Benedict, oatmeal, assorted styles of pancakes, and fresh-squeezed orange juice. A late breakfast permits chowing-down more than enough grub to satisfy a tummy until dinner. The hamburgers, French fries, and homemade beans are also reputed to be very good.

WHAT TO DO

Chateau Julian Winery *8940 Carmel Valley Rd., 408/624-2600; tasting M-F 8:30-5, Sat & Sun 11-5; tours daily at 10:30 & 2:30.* While their parents are busy tasting Chardonnay and Merlot, the two varietals this winery is noted for, children may partake of juice and crackers. A garden patio invites picnicking.

Garland Ranch Regional Park *off Carmel Valley Rd., 8 miles from Highway 1, 408/659-4488; daily dawn-dusk; free.* Running along the banks of the Carmel River, this park boasts more than 3,000 acres. Self-guided hiking trails lead up into the mountains, and a Visitors Center provides orientation.

– Big Sur –

A LITTLE BACKGROUND

Big Sur is such a special place that many people who have been here don't feel generous about sharing it. However, facilities are so limited that it's hard to imagine it getting overrun with tourists. Except, perhaps, in the thick of summer, when the weather is best.

The town of Big Sur seems to have no center. It stretches along Highway 1 for 6 miles, offering a string of amenities. Then, as one continues driving south, the highway begins a 90-mile stretch of some of the most spectacular scenery in the U.S.

Note that the river's bottom here is rocky. Bring along waterproof shoes for wading.

VISITOR INFORMATION
Monterey Peninsula Chamber of Commerce. See page 26.

GETTING THERE
Located approximately 25 miles south of the Monterey Peninsula.

WHERE TO STAY
Big Sur Lodge *off Highway 1, 408/667-2171; 62 rooms; $$-$$$; 2-night minimum on weekends; no TVs; some kitchens, bathtubs, fireplaces; heated pool; restaurant (May-Sept only).* Located in Pfeiffer-Big Sur State Park, this facility offers modern motel rooms scattered throughout spacious, grassy grounds where deer are often seen grazing. Rooms close to the pleasant pool area seem most desirable. Guests have access to the state park's facilities (see page 52). A casual, reasonably-priced restaurant serves meals all day.

Esalen Institute *off Highway 1, 408/667-3000; pool, hot tubs.* Located on a breathtaking crest above the ocean, this legendary educational facility offers lodging and dining in conjunction with its workshops. Space is open to the general public when the facility is underbooked. Then a bed space runs $65 to $115 per person per day and includes three meals. Special family rates are available. Some will want to be forewarned, others informed, that nude bathing is de rigueur in the hot tubs and swimming pool.

Self-exploration workshops include massage, Rolfing, vision improvement, etc. Call for further information and a copy of the workshop catalogue.

New Camaldoli Hermitage *off Highway 1, 408/667-2456, 408/667-2341; $30/person; includes 3 meals.* Solitary, silent, non-directed retreats, in the Catholic tradition of the Benedictine order, are offered here and are open to people of all faiths. Guests come to this quiet 800-acre wildlife and wilderness preserve to meditate, read, rest, and pray. Chapel services are available for those who wish to participate, and each room has an ocean view.

A gift shop *(daily 8:30-11 & 12:30-5:30)* sells fruitcake and datenut cake made by the resident Camaldolese monks.

Ripplewood Resort *on Highway 1, 408/667-2242; $-$$; children under 12 free; some kitchens, fireplaces; restaurant.* Rustic, pleasantly decorated redwood cabins are located both above and below the highway. The ones below are in a dense, dark grove of redwoods and are only a stone's throw from the Big Sur River. A cafe serves breakfast and lunch.

♥**Ventana-Big Sur Country Inn Resort** *off Highway 1, 800/628-6500, 408/667-2331, fax 408/667-2419; 60 rooms; $$$+; 2-night minimum on weekends; unsuitable for children under 18; all bathtubs; some kitchens, fireplaces; 2 heated pools, hot tub, sauna; continental breakfast, restaurant.* The striking, clean-lined architecture of this resort has won awards, and the restaurant, which serves lunch and dinner, is known for its accomplished California-style cuisine. The spectacular secluded location in the hills 1,200 feet above the ocean makes this facility a good choice for a restive, revitalizing, and hedonistic retreat. Clothing is optional in the Japanese hot baths located adjacent to the pools. But, alas, all rooms are equipped with color TVs. Campsites are available at an adjacent facility.

WHERE TO EAT

Deetjen's Big Sur Inn *on Highway 1, 408/667-2378; B & D M-Sun; $-$$$; highchairs, booster seats, children's portions; reservations suggested for dinner; no cards.* For aesthetic pleasure it's hard to beat lingering over breakfast at this Norwegian-style inn—especially when it's raining outside and the table is situated in front of the fireplace. The mellow, rustic, and informal setting of this inn is a complementary background to the fresh, simple, and wholesome foods produced by its kitchen. Dinner is more expensive and sedate, and children don't fit in well then.

Rustic, casual lodging is also available in cabins located amidst a forest of redwoods and firs. They are usually booked up far in advance.

Glen Oaks Restaurant *on Highway 1, 408/667-2623; D daily; $$; highchairs, booster seats, children's portions; 100% non-smoking; reservations suggested; MC, V.* Classical music and fresh flowers greet diners inside this charming log cabin-like building. The eclectic menu prepared by the owner/chef includes a variety of salads and pastas as well as bouillabaisse, mesquite-grilled steak and fish, and several vegetarian entrees.

Nepenthe *on Highway 1, 408/667-2345; L & D daily; $$; highchairs, booster seats; no reservations; AE, MC, V.* Located at the top of a cliff 808 feet above the ocean and offering a breathtaking view of the coastline, this famous restaurant was designed by a student of Frank Lloyd Wright. It is an elaboration of a cabin that was bought in 1945 from Rita Hayworth and Orson Welles. When the weather is mild, lunchers may dine outside on a casual terrace. The menu features simple food such as steak, fresh seafood, roasted chicken, homemade soup, and a very good hamburger. It is also possible to stop in at the bar for just a drink. The atmosphere has mellowed since the days when then-Senator John F. Kennedy was said to have been turned away because he wasn't wearing shoes. Now it seems to be living up to the promise of its name, which refers to a mythical Egyptian drug that induced forgetfulness and the surcease of sorrow.

Cafe Amphora *(408/667-2660)*, located downstairs, serves medium-priced brunch and lunch items on a patio featuring the same striking view. On a warm afternoon it is an especially choice spot to enjoy a refreshing cold drink and an excellent pastry.

The classy **Phoenix** gift shop provides pleasant browsing before or after dining.

WHAT TO DO

Big Sur is so non-commercial that there is little to list in this section. Visitors can look forward to relaxing, swimming in the river, picnicking on the beach, or taking a hike through the woods. Look out for poison oak, and bring along a good book.

Pfeiffer Beach. Watch for unmarked Sycamore Canyon Road on the west side of Highway 1. This narrow road begins about 1.7 miles south of Fernwood Resort and winds for 2 lovely miles to a beach parking lot. The only easily accessible public beach in the area, it features striking rock formations and arches carved out by the very rough surf. Visitors may wade in a stream that meanders through the sandy beach but should stay out of the turbulent ocean. If it all looks vaguely familiar, it may be because this is where Elizabeth Taylor and Richard Burton acted out some love scenes in *The Sandpiper.*

Pfeiffer-Big Sur State Park *on Highway 1, 408/667-2315; $6/car.* Activities at this 821-acre park include hiking (among the many trails is a half-mile nature trail), river swimming, and ranger-led nature walks and campfires. There is also an open meadow that is perfect for playing baseball or throwing a frisbee. Facilities include picnic tables, a restaurant, and a store, and campsites are available.

Point Sur State Historic Park *off Highway 1, north of town, 408/625-4419; Sat at 10 & 2, Sun at 10; adults $2, 6-12 $1.* The **Point Sur Lightstation** that is the center of this park was built in 1889. It is now open for strenuous 2-1/2-hour guided tours that include a half-mile hike and a 300-foot climb. Tours are not recommended for small children. Because parking is limited, only the first 15 cars to arrive can be accommodated.

– San Simeon/Cambria –

A LITTLE BACKGROUND

Located in the small town of San Simeon on the wind-blown coast south of Big Sur, the spectacular **Hearst Castle** is perched atop La Cuesta Encantada (the enchanted hill). It was designed by architect Julia Morgan and is filled with art treasures and antiques gathered from all over the world. Though considered by William Randolph Hearst to be unfinished, the castle contains 38 bedrooms, 31

bathrooms, 14 sitting rooms, a kitchen, a movie theater, 2 libraries, a billiard room, a dining hall, and an assembly hall! Exotic vines and plants grace the lovely gardens, and wild zebras, tar goats, and sanbar deer graze the hillsides—remnants of the private zoo that once included lions, monkeys, and a polar bear.

Before 1958 visitors could get no closer than was permitted by a coin-operated telescope located on the road below. Now maintained by the State of California as an Historical Monument, the castle is open to the public. Five tours are available; all include a scenic bus ride up to the castle.

Tour 1 is suggested for a first visit and includes gardens, pools, a guest house, and the main floor of the castle.

Tour 2 covers the upper floors of the castle, including Mr. Hearst's private suite, the libraries, a guest duplex, the kitchen, and the pools.

Tour 3 covers the 36-room guest wing, and includes the pools and a guest house.

Tour 4 stresses the gardens and is a behind-the-scenes tour. It includes the elegant 17-room Casa del Mar guest house and the pools. It is available only from April through October.

The **Evening Tour** combines highlights of the daytime tours and additionally features volunteers in period dress—helping to bring the magnificent surroundings to life. This tour is available only in the spring and fall.

Reservations for the castle tours are essential and may be made by calling 800/444-7275. Tickets may also be purchased at the castle after 8 a.m. on the day of the tour, but often none are available. And when they are available, they are usually sold out before noon. The charge for each of the four day tours is $14 for adults, $8 for children age 6 through 12; evening tours are $25 for adults, $13 for children.

Note: Children under 6 are free only if they sit on their parent's lap during the bus ride. Tours require walking about 1/2 mile and climbing approximately 300 steps; comfortable shoes are advised. Strollers are not permitted. Tours take approximately 2 hours. Picnic tables and a snack bar are available near the Visitor Center.

VISITOR INFORMATION

San Simeon Chamber of Commerce *P.O. Box 1 (9511 Hearst Dr.), San Simeon 93452, 800/845-8945, 805/927-3500.*

Cambria Chamber of Commerce *767 Main St., Cambria 93428, 805/927-3624.*

GETTING THERE

Located approximately 75 miles south of Big Sur.

For a more leisurely trip try the train package offered by Key Holidays *(11390 S. Main St. #312, Walnut Creek, 510/945-8938).* Via train is the way guests used to travel to the castle in its heyday. Invitations then always included train tickets. Today travelers can still relax and enjoy the scenery while Amtrak's Coast Starlight transports them to San Luis Obispo. From there, after seeing the local sights, they are transported via bus for a tour of the coast, a stop in Cambria, and on to San Simeon for the night. The next day participants are bused to the famed castle for a guided tour, then down scenic Highway 1 for a stop in the fishing village of Morro Bay, and then back to San Luis Obispo for the train trip back. The package does not include meals. Rates vary, and special rates are available for children. Call for details.

ANNUAL EVENTS

Christmas at the Castle *December.* During the entire month the castle is lighted and decorated in splendid fashion for the Christmas holidays.

WHERE TO STAY

Cambria Pines Lodge *2905 Burton Dr., Cambria, 800/445-6868, 805/927-4200, fax 805/927-4016; 120 units; 22 non-smoking units; $$; children under 3 free; cribs; some bathtubs, fireplaces; indoor heated pool, hot tub; restaurant.* Located on a pine-covered hill above town, this spacious lodging facility features both lodge rooms and cabins. A volleyball area is available to guests, and a nature trail leads into the village.

Cavalier Inn *9415 Hearst Dr., San Simeon, 800/826-8168, 805/927-4688, fax 805/927-0497; 90 rooms; 10 non-smoking rooms; $$-$$$; cribs; all bathtubs; some fireplaces; 2 heated pools, hot tub, exercise room; restaurant, room service; pets welcome.* The only ocean-front resort in the area, this modern lodging facility features rooms with ocean views. Some rooms also have private patios, and all rooms are equipped with a VCR.

♥Pickford House *2555 MacLeod Way, Cambria, 805/927-8619; 8 rooms; 100% non-smoking; $$-$$$; unsuitable for children; all claw-foot bathtubs; some fireplaces; full breakfast.* Though this inn was built in 1983, it is far from modern in feel and boasts rooms bearing the names and personalities of eight silent film stars. Notable among them is the Valentino Room, which is furnished with dark-wood antiques and has a great view. Breakfast features the traditional Danish pancake fritters known as aebleskivers.

WHERE TO EAT

The Brambles Dinner House *4005 Burton Dr., Cambria, 805/927-4716; D daily, SunBr; $$-$$$; highchairs, booster seats, children's portions; reservations suggested; AE, MC, V.* Located inside an 1874 English-style cottage with Victorian decor, this homey restaurant provides cozy booths and a special Family Dining Room. The restaurant is known for its prime rib, traditional Yorkshire pudding, and fresh salmon barbecued over an oakpit. Steaks and fresh seafood are also available, as are a hamburger and English trifle.

Sebastian's General Store/Patio Cafe *422 San Simeon Rd., San Simeon, 805/927-4217. Store: daily 8:30-6. Cafe: B & L daily; closed Nov-Mar; no reservations; no cards.* Built in 1852 and moved to its present location in 1878, this store is now a State Historical Landmark. Inexpensive short-order items are served in the outdoor cafe.

In winter watch for **monarch butterflies** congregating in the adjacent eucalyptus and cypress trees.

WHAT TO DO

The Pewter Plough Playhouse *824 Main St., Cambria, 805/927-3877; shows F & Sat; tickets $8.* Plays and art films are scheduled year-round in this intimate theatre.

The Soldier Factory *789 Main St., Cambria, 805/927-3804; daily 10-5.* An ideal souvenir stop, this shop offers everything from an inexpensive unpainted pewter animal to a dearly-priced and elaborately-painted Alice in Wonderland chess set. Assorted sizes and styles of pewter soldiers from various wars are also for sale, and the owner's private collection of toy soldiers is on display. The majority of items are designed, molded, and cast on the premises.

William Randolph Hearst State Beach *San Simeon; daily 8am-sunset; $6/car.* In addition to providing a very nice swimming beach, this park has a 640-foot-long fishing pier. No license is required to fish from the pier.

– Morro Bay –

A LITTLE BACKGROUND

A huge volcanic rock, visible from just about everywhere in town, is the reason Morro Bay is sometimes called "the Gibraltar of the Pacific." The rock stands 576 feet high and is now a State Monument. Peregrine falcons, an endangered species, nest at the top.

Commercial fishing is this small, picturesque town's main industry. Albacore and abalone are the local specialties, and they frequently show up on restaurant menus.

Lodgings often fill up on weekends, so reservations should be made well in advance.

VISITOR INFORMATION

Morro Bay Chamber of Commerce *895 Napa #A-1, Morro Bay 93442, 800/231-0592, 805/772-4467.*

GETTING THERE

Located approximately 30 miles south of San Simeon.

WHERE TO STAY

Blue Sail Inn *851 Market Ave., 800/336-0707, 805/772-2766; 48 rooms; 10 non-smoking rooms; $$; cribs; all bathtubs; some fireplaces; hot tub.* This streamlined modern motel is centrally located, allowing guests to walk to restaurants. The hot tub area has a view of Morro Rock, as do most of the rooms.

The Inn at Morro Bay *800/321-9566, 805/772-5651; 96 rooms; 48 non-smoking rooms; $$-$$$+; children free; cribs; some bathtubs, fireplaces; heated pool; restaurant, room service.* Located at the southern end of town in Morro Bay State Park, this small resort provides a quiet, restful spot to spend the night. Some of the rooms have lovely bay views. A golf course and heron rookery are located adjacent.

WHERE TO EAT

Dorn's Original Breakers Cafe *801 Market Ave. 805/772-4415; B, L, & D daily; $$; highchairs, booster seats; reservations suggested; no cards.* This casual restaurant features a great bay view and is especially pleasant at breakfast. The menu then offers a choice of hearty breakfasts, plus novelty items such as chocolate chip pancakes with chocolate syrup. The dinner menu features fresh local fish and an award-winning Boston clam chowder.

The Great American Fish Company *1185 Embarcadero, 805/772-4407; L & D daily; $$; highchairs, booster seats, children's portions; no reservations; MC, V.* Located a short, scenic stroll from the center of town, this restaurant provides a comfortable, casual atmosphere and good views of the rock. The extensive menu includes mesquite-grilled fresh fish and shark, as well as deep-fried fresh local prawns and Monterey squid. A steak and hamburger are also available. Most dinners come with garlic bread, a vegetable, and a potato.

Rose's Landing *725 Embarcadero, 805/772-4441; L & D daily; $$-$$$; highchairs, booster seats, children's portions; reservations essential; AE, MC, V.* The best view here is from the downstairs bar. However, the upstairs restaurant has decent views from most of the tables, and that is where the food is. Seafood, steak, and pasta dominate the menu. Complete dinners include the house-specialty seafood chowder, a salad, either a baked potato or rice pilaf, a vegetable, and sourdough bread.

WHAT TO DO

Clam Digging. Go for it! World-famous Pismo clams may be dug up on the beach just about anywhere.

Coleman Park *Embarcadero Rd./Coleman Dr., east of Morro Rock.* Children are sure to enjoy this idyllic playground in the sand.

Fishing. The pier is a prime spot for fishing. Chartered fishing boats are also available.

Giant Chess Board *Embarcadero/Front, 805/772-1214 x226.* At the base of this 44-step stairway is one of the two largest chess boards in the U.S. (The other is in New York City's Central Park.) The redwood chess pieces stand 2- and 3-feet high and weigh from 18 to 30 pounds—making a game here physical as well as mental exercise. From noon to 5 p.m. each Saturday the Morro Bay Chess Club sponsors games on the giant 16- by 16-foot concrete board; the general public is welcome to challenge. Except for the hours mentioned above, the board is available to the public daily from 8 to 5. Reservations must be made by filling out an application at the Recreation Office. Call for details.

Morro Bay Aquarium *595 Embarcadero, 805/772-7647; daily from 9, closing time varies; adults $1, 5-11 50¢.* This teeny, tiny aquarium is a draw for the gift shop located in front. However, the price is right, and over 300 live marine specimens may be observed. Some preserved specimens are also displayed, and very noisy seals beg to be fed.

Morro Bay State Park *at the southern end of town, 805/772-2560.*
   Bird Sanctuary. Following a trail through the marsh and hills allows for the possiblity of catching glimpses of over 250 species of birds. This is said to be the third largest bird sanctuary in the world.
   Heron Rookery. No one is allowed inside the rookery, which is one of the last where the Great Blue Heron may be found, but the herons may be viewed from an observation area.
   Museum of Natural History *on State Park Rd., 805/772-2694; daily 10-5; adults $2, 6-12 $1.* Situated on a scenic perch over the bay, this museum presents lectures, slide shows, and movies about the wildlife and Indian history of the area. Guided tours are sometimes available. In the winter, inquire about walks to see the **monarch butterflies** that congregate in nearby eucalyptus groves.

The Shell Shop *590 Embarcadero, 805/772-8014; daily 9:30-5, to 7 in summer.* The perfect souvenir stop, this shop has the largest selection of sea shells on the West Coast and offers them at bargain prices.

Tiger's Folly II *1205 Embarcadero, 805/772-2257; daily June-Sept, Sat & Sun Oct-May, call for schedule; adults $6, 5-12 $3.* The 1-hour harbor cruise aboard this sternwheeler requires no reservation, but the special Sunday champagne brunch cruise does.

WHAT TO DO NEARBY

Avila Beach *20 miles south of town off Highway 101.* This tiny, old-fashioned beach community is a great place to watch surfers and to swim in a generally mild surf.

Cayucos *6 miles north of town on Highway 1.* This pleasant little beach town has a string of inexpensive motels. It also boasts both a fine beach with a gentle surf and a 400-foot fishing pier where equipment rentals are readily available. Good meals and overnight lodging may be had at **The Way Station** *(78 N. Ocean, 805/995-1227),* a 19th century traveler's rest stop once again functioning as such.

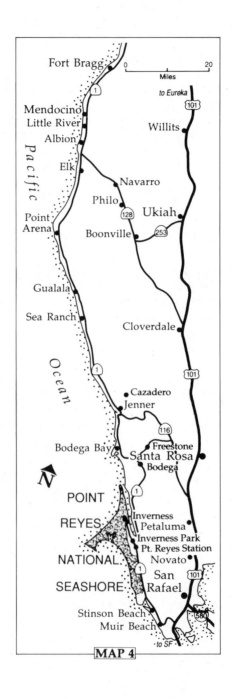

MAP 4

Coast North

– Highway 1 –

VISITOR INFORMATION

Redwood Empire Association *785 Market St., 15th floor, San Francisco 94103-2022, 415/543-8334.* Information on the counties north of San Francisco can be obtained Monday through Friday from 9 to 5. A *Visitor's Guide* is $2 by mail, free if picked up in person.

GETTING THERE

From San Francisco, take Highway 101 to Highway 1 north.

A WORD OF CAUTION

The rocky cliffs and beaches along the coast are scenic and beautiful. In their awe, people sometimes forget that they are also dangerous. It is tempting to stand at the edge where the surf is pounding, but people have been washed out to sea doing just that. Don't be one of them. Be careful. Stay on trails. Obey posted signs. And take special care not to let children run loose.

WHERE TO STAY/WHERE TO EAT/WHAT TO DO

Muir Beach

♥**The Pelican Inn** *10 Pacific Way, 415/383-6000; 7 rooms; 1 non-smoking room; $$$+; cribs; 1 bathtub; full English breakfast; restaurant.* Built in 1979, this replica 16th century English Tudor offers snug rooms furnished with English antiques, canopied beds, and oriental carpets.

Elegant pub fare is served in the restaurant at lunch, and tea service is always available. Continental meals are served in the evenings. The inn is closed to non-guests on Mondays.

Green Gulch Farm *on Highway 1 just before town, 415/383-3134.* Reached via a sharp downhill turnoff, this Zen retreat offers public meditation programs on Sundays. Visitors are also welcome then to take informal afternoon walks in the organic garden, which supplies the herbs and vegetables for Green's Restaurant in San Francisco.

Overnight lodging is available in a peaceful Japanese-style guest house *($$)*, and guests may take their meals with the permanent residents.

Muir Beach. Reached by turning onto a leafy, blackberry-lined lane located just south of the Pelican Inn, this popular beach is unsafe for swimming. However, it is excellent for sunbathing and people-watching, and picnic tables are available.

Muir Woods National Monument *off Highway 1, on Panoramic Highway, 415/388-2595; daily 8-sunset; free.* Located just off Highway 1 and enveloping 560 acres, this fragrant virgin redwood forest has 6 miles of walking trails. Among them are an easy paved Main Trail; seven more-challenging unpaved trails lead away from the crowds. Naturalist John Muir, for whom the forest was named, said of it, "This is the best tree lover's monument that could be found in all the forests of all the world." Because over one million people come here each year, only a visit early or late in the day provides the hope of some solitude. And no matter what time of year it is, visitors are advised to bring along warm wraps. The dense forest lets in very little sunlight, and the weather is usually damp, foggy, and cold. Discovery Packs, which invite children to explore nature, may be borrowed free from the Visitors Center. Picnicking is not permitted, but a snackbar dispenses simple foods.

Slide Ranch. See page 281.

Stinson Beach

♥**Casa del Mar** *37 Belvedere Ave., 415/868-2124; 4 rooms; 100% non-smoking; $$$-$$$+; 2-night minimum on Sat; unsuitable for children under 6; children 6-13 free; no TVs; full breakfast.* Perched on a hill above town, this peachy-colored stucco Mediterranean-style structure has two rooms with great views of the ocean and two with views of Mount Tamalpais—the inn's back yard. Its terraced garden was planted in the 1930s and was used as a teaching garden by the U.C. School of Landscape Architecture in the '70s. Now the owner tends to it and invites guests to also pinch and prune, should the mood strike them. The house itself was recently completely rebuilt. Wonderful breakfasts, sometimes prepared with ingredients from the garden, greet guests in the morning in a sunny dining area.

Steep Ravine Cabins *1 mile south of town, 800/444-7275, 916/323-2988; 10 units; $; no TVs; all wood-burning stoves.* Perched on a rocky bluff overlooking the ocean, within **Mount Tamalpais State Park,** each of these primitive cabins dates from the 1930s and sleeps up to four people. Running water is available, but no electricity or shower facilities. Guests must provide their own bedding, cooking equipment, and light source. Paths lead down to the beach.

Stinson Beach Grill *3465 Highway 1, 415/868-2002; B, L, & D daily; $-$$; booster seats; reservations suggested for dinner; AE, MC, V.* Overlooking Highway 1, this in-

formal grill has an eclectic menu offering everything from hamburgers to osso bucco. In between are a Greek salad, an impeccably fresh salmon with tomato-basil sauce, and a spicy blackened snapper. A large variety of complementary beers from micro-breweries are also available.

Audubon Canyon Ranch *4900 Highway 1, 3-1/2 miles north of town, 415/868-9244; Sat, Sun, & holidays mid-March through mid-July; by donation.* Situated on picturesque **Bolinas Lagoon** just north of town, this 1,000-acre ranch is a non-profit project sponsored by the four Bay Area Audubon Societies. It is open only during the breeding season.

In 1991 seven breeding pairs of Great Blue Herons (measuring 4 to 5 feet tall and with a wingspan of nearly 6 feet), four pairs of snowy egrets, and 100 pairs of Great Egrets nested noisily in the tall redwood trees located in the ranch's Schwarz Grove. Approximately 60 other bird species also make their home here, making this a birdwatcher's paradise. Nests contain an average of two to five eggs, which incubate for about 28 days. Once hatched, baby birds, covered in fluffy down, waddle about their nests while waiting for their parents to return from gathering a meal of fish and crustaceans in nearby Bolinas Lagoon. (Baby egrets fly at 7 weeks of age, herons at 9 weeks.)

A self-guiding nature trail, and several other scenic trails of varying length and challenge, lead to Henderson Overlook. There, visitors may rest on benches and observe these graceful birds as they court, establish a pecking order, build their nests, and begin rearing their young. Telescopes are available, and a Ranch Guide is on hand to interpret and assist.

Exhibits in the **Display Hall** museum, a converted milking barn left from the days when the ranch was a dairy, give visitors more detailed information about the birds as well as about the geology and natural history of the area. Nearby, a stream-side, sod-roofed **Bird Hide** is designed so observers can see out, but birds can't see in. Its feeders attract a variety of unsuspecting birds, including many colorful hummingbirds. A picnic area, from which the nesting site may be viewed, provides a scenic spot to relax and enjoy a leisurely lunch in peaceful surroundings.

Point Reyes Station

Holly Tree Inn *3 Silverhills Rd., 415/663-1554; 6 units; 100% non-smoking; $$$-$$$+; 2-night minimum on weekends; cribs; no TVs; some kitchens, bathtubs, fireplaces; full breakfast.* Tucked away in its very own valley just beneath the Inverness Ridge, this rustic B&B offers four attractively appointed rooms and a spacious cottage with a wood-burning stove, a stereo and tapes, and a claw-foot tub. A stream runs picturesquely through the property, and an informal playground with a wooden plank swing invites children to play.

A rustic cottage, perched right on Tomales Bay and featuring a solarium with a hot tub, is also available.

♥**Manka's Inverness Lodge** *Callender Way/Argyle, Inverness, 415/669-1034; 8 units; $$-$$$+; children free in cabins; some kitchens, bathtubs, fireplaces; restaurant.* This rustic old Arts and Crafts-style hunting lodge dates from 1917. It was the first place in town with a phone, and it served as a speakeasy in the 1940s. Both cozy lodge rooms and larger cabin units are available. Room 1 is equipped with fresh flowers and old books and boasts both a large weathered deck overlooking Tomales Bay and a claw-foot tub. It also features a large four-poster bed made with whole logs. Sleepers climb a stepstool, then sink into peaceful slumber upon its featherbed and under its fluffy down comforter.

Local game is often on the dinner menu, prepared by a chef hailing from

Berkeley's famed Chez Panisse and served in the inn's intimate dining room nightly except Wednesday. Breakfast is optional, inexpensive, and not to be missed. Served fireside in the lobby, one such gustatory extravaganza featured eggs scrambled with local goat cheese and hand-gathered mushrooms, a side of toasted herb bread, and both homemade rhubarb puree and blood orange marmalade.

Point Reyes Hostel *415/663-8811; a room for families is available.* Formerly a ranch house, this hostel offers both a kitchen and outdoor barbecue for preparing meals. Two cozy common rooms with wood-burning stoves are also available to guests. See also page 278.

Reservations Services. For information on the area's B&Bs call:
    Coastal Lodging of West Marin *415/663-1351.*
    Inns of Point Reyes *415/663-1420.*
    Seashore Bed & Breakfasts of Marin *415/663-9373.*

Chez Madeleine *10905 Highway 1, 415/663-9177; D Tu-Sun; highchairs, booster seats; reservations suggested on weekends; MC, V.* Featuring a casual, noisy atmosphere, this restaurant is reminiscent of those found in the French countryside where children blend in and seem to belong. Indeed, the menu offers both escargot and a hamburger. One meal enjoyed here began with a wonderful light celery soup topped with red bell pepper puree. The main course, a brochette of impeccably fresh salmon, scallops, and prawns with beurre blanc, was served with rice and a sweet carrot puree. Dessert was a Grand Marnier souffle.

Knave of Hearts Bakery *12301 Sir Francis Drake Blvd., Inverness Park, 415/663-1236; Tu-Sun 8-5.* Unexpectedly, this unpretentious, tiny spot is home to an outstanding bakery. The owner/husband makes almost everything himself and serves it up, too! Among the goodies are a moist, light chocolate cake, a wonderful poppyseed cake, and a kid-pleasing blueberry pastry. The owner/wife prepares the noteworthy breads and decorates the fruit tarts. A small counter overlooks picturesque farmland. If that isn't entertaining enough, there's always the possibility of browsing through a copy of the Pulitzer Prize-winning local newspaper—*The Point Reyes Light.*

Station House Cafe *11180 Highway 1, 415/663-1515; B, L, & D daily; $$; highchairs, booster seats, children's portions; 100% non-smoking; reservations suggested in summer; AE, MC, V.* Menu choices in this casual, popular spot include sandwiches, light and inexpensive entrees, and pricier daily specials that always feature fresh fish and local shellfish. Reasonably-priced desserts such as carrot cake, apple and pecan pies, and Cocolat truffles are also available. Truly all stages of hunger can be satisfied here at the same table. Additionally, service is fast and unpretentious.

Johnson's Drakes Bay Oyster Company *1717 Sir Francis Drake Blvd., Inverness, 415/669-1149; Tu-Sun 8-4:30.* A visit to this scenically situated enterprise allows viewing the various stages of the oyster farming process. Oysters are available for purchase.

Llunch with a Llama. *Camelid Capers, 415/669-1523; adults $45-$60, 6-12 $35-$50, under 6 free, bring-your-own picnic $25/$10; half-day trip with mini breakfast or lunch*

$30/person; reservations required. These llama-chàperoned picnic hikes take place within Point Reyes National Seashore. The llamas carry in the picnic supplies and set the pace. Since they are definitely not in a hurry, the hike is leisurely. The picnic food—items such as salmon pâté, aram sandwiches, and Peruvian purple potato salad—is wonderful and the guide/proprietor is considerate—he carries in on his own back the llamas' alfalfa lunch.

Point Reyes National Seashore *west of Olema, 415/663-1092; daily 9-5; free.* Known for its beaches and hiking trails, this area has plenty of other interesting things for visitors to do. Many activities are clustered around the Park Headquarters. A Visitor Center houses a working seismograph and a variety of nature displays. The **Morgan Horse Ranch,** where pack and trail animals for the national parks are raised and trained, is adjacent. A short walk away **Kule Loklo,** a replica Miwok Indian village, has been re-created using the same tools and materials as the Indians themselves originally used.

Trails beginning near the headquarters include the self-guided Woodpecker Nature Trail, the .6-mile-long self-guided Earthquake Trail, which follows the San Andreas fault and passes the epicenter of the 1906 quake, and the popular 4.1-mile Bear Valley Trail, which winds through meadows, fern grottos, and forests before ending at the ocean. The area has over 70 miles of equestrian trails, and horses may be rented at a nearby stable. Also, mountain bikes are permitted on some trails, and walk-in backpacking campsites are available by reservation.

Further away from the headquarters is the 1870 **Point Reyes Lighthouse,** where winds have been recorded blowing at 133 miles per hour—the highest rate in the continental U.S. The bottom line is that it can get mighty windy, cold, and wet at this scenic spot. The lighthouse, reached by maneuvering 300 steps down the side of a steep, rocky cliff, is a popular spot in winter for viewing migrating grey whales.

Drake's Beach offers easy beach access and has a great little short-order cafe.

Bodega Bay

Bodega Bay Lodge *103 Highway 1, 800/368-2468, 707/875-3525; 78 rooms; 8 non-smoking rooms; $$$-$$$+; children under 12 free; cribs; all bathtubs; some fireplaces; solar-heated pool, hot tub, sauna, exercise room; continental breakfast, restaurant, room service.* Situated on the southern end of town, overlooking the wetlands marsh and sand dunes of **Doran Park,** this rustically attractive modern motel features rooms with stunning ocean views. A wonderful whirlpool hot tub is sheltered from the elements by glass walls, but its ceiling is open to the possibility of a light mist or rain providing a cooling touch. Bicycles are available for guests to borrow, and golfing may be arranged at an adjacent 18-hole course.

A convenient ocean-view restaurant serves elegant dinner fare prepared with the best local ingredients: fresh Tomales Bay oysters on the half shell, Petaluma escargot with Enfant Riant truffle butter, rack of Sonoma lamb with olive-basil Zinfandel glacé and minted Sebastopol apples. The restaurant is open nightly, and reservations are required. Delectable box lunches—packed with such goodies as marinated local fresh vegetables, herb-stuffed Petaluma game hens, and croissant sandwiches filled with Valley Ford lamb—are also available.

♥**Schoolhouse Inn** *17110 Bodega Lane, Bodega, 5 miles inland from town, off Highway 12, 707/876-3257; 4 rooms; 100% non-smoking; $$; unsuitable for children under 10; no TVs; full breakfast.* Used as the school building for Hitchcock's film *The Birds*, this classic Victorian structure dates from 1874. It was used as a school until 1961. Now a B&B, the four former classrooms serve as guest rooms, with blackboards adorning their walls and school desks serving as end tables. Breakfast is served upstairs in a Victorian parlor, affording great views of the area. A video of *The Birds* is available for viewing should the mood strike.

The Tides Wharf Restaurant *835 Highway 1, 707/875-3652; B, L, & D daily; $$; highchairs, booster seats, children's portions; reservations suggested; AE, MC, V.* Always crowded, this popular spot offers a bargain breakfast and serves it until noon. Lunch and dinner menus, both nearly the same in content and cost, offer an extensive selection of seafood entrees. Fish is prepared rare, as is currently trendy, so those who prefer it flaky should specify that when ordering. A tasty tartar sauce is freshly made, and the dungeness crab cocktail, though made with frozen crab, is delicious. Complete dinners come with either a wonderful potato-rich New England clam chowder or a green salad with shrimp garnish as a starter, a vegetable, and sourdough bread. Less expensive seafood items such as fish & chips and deep-fried clam strips are available, as are fried chicken and steak for those who don't care for fish. In addition to fish & chips, the children's menu offers a hamburger, hot dog, and grilled cheese sandwich. (One kid was overheard here saying, "It's a really good hamburger for a *nice* restaurant.") Desserts, such as chocolate velvet and raspberry-almond tortes, and coffees are also available. Because most tables afford sweeping views of Bodega Bay, it is worthwhile planning around having a meal here before sunset.

Upscale rooms with ocean views are available across the street at **The Inn at the Tides** *(800/541-7788, 707/875-2751).*

Fisherman's Festival *held annually in April; 707/875-3422.* This festival's highlights are a traditional parade of colorfully decorated commercial fishing boats and a Blessing of the Fleet, but bathtub races, stunt kite demonstrations, and a juried art show are also part of the fun.

Goat Rock State Beach *off Highway 1, 4 miles south of Jenner, 707/865-2391.* Located where the Russian River flows into the ocean, this beach is popular with harbor seals. March is the beginning of **pupping season,** when Seal Watch volunteers are on hand to interpret and answer questions for viewers. Seeing the baby seals, many people are tempted to get closer, but visitors should stay at least 50 yards away. When pups are born they depend on the mother's milk for the first 48 hours. During that critical period the mother will often go out to feed, and newborn pups are left by themselves. If a mother finds humans around her pup when she returns, she will abandon it. Seals hang around this area in large numbers through July. Then the population thins out until the following March.

Driftwood collecting is encouraged because pile-ups of wood debris are a po-

tential fire hazard to the town. Note that swimming in the ocean is hazardous due to sleeper waves and riptides.

♥**Osmosis** *209 Bohemian Highway, Freestone, 5 miles east of town, 707/823-8231, fax 707/874-3702; daily 9-8; enzyme bath & blanket wrap $42, with massage $100; reservations required; unsuitable for children.* Long popular in Japan, the enzyme bath available here is something like a mud bath—only lighter and more fragrant. It is said to improve circulation, break down body toxins, and relieve stress. The experience begins with a soothing cup of enzyme tea enjoyed in a tranquil tea garden. Then bathers, either nude or in a swimsuit, are submerged for 20 minutes in a hot mixture of Hinoki cedar fiber, rice bran, and over 600 active plant enzymes that naturally generate heat. This is followed by a blanket wrap or massage.

Sea Horse Stables *2660 Highway 1, 707/875-2721; daily 10-4; horses $20/hour, ponies $5/10 minutes; reservations advised.* Guided trails rides, and pony rides for kids, are available at this guest ranch. Several picnic tables and a barbecue area are provided, and a bunk house can accommodate two couples or a family for overnight lodging.

Jenner

Murphy's Jenner Inn *10400 Highway 1, 707/865-2377; 11 units; 100% non-smoking; $$-$$$; 2-night minimum on weekends; children under 3 free; no TVs; some kitchens, bathtubs, wood-burning stoves; continental breakfast, restaurant; pets welcome with damage deposit.* Tucked into a curve in the highway at the point where the Russian River runs into the Pacific Ocean, this inn offers a choice of cabins, lodge rooms, or private homes. Three rooms in the River House get unobstructed views of the estuary and share a hot tub. A communal lounge is kept cozy by an antique wood-burning stove and offers guests a library filled with books and games.

Salt Point Lodge *23255 Highway 1, 17 miles north of town, 707/847-3234; 16 rooms; $-$$$; 2-night minimum on weekends; cribs; some wood-burning stoves; hot tub, sauna; restaurant.* Located across the street from the Pacific Ocean, this motel provides a large expanse of lawn dotted with a swing and tether ball equipment.

A small restaurant features ocean views and serves breakfast, lunch, and dinner. The dinner menu is both ambitious and expensive, offering selections made with local oysters, fresh fish, chicken, and beef, plus a variety of tempting house-made desserts.

♥Timber Cove Inn *21780 Highway 1, 14 miles north of town, 707/847-323l; 47 rooms; $$-$$$+; 2-night minimum on Saturdays; unsuitable for children; no TVs; some bathtubs, fireplaces; restaurant.* Perched on a rocky seaside cliff, this inn offers many rooms with magnificent ocean views and some with sunken tubs and private hot tubs. A tall Bufano sculpture, which acts as a landmark, juts above the lodge, and the lobby bar and restaurant feature a dramatic Japanese-modern style of architecture and ocean views.

♥Timberhill Ranch *35755 Hauser Bridge Rd., Timber Cove-Cazadero, 19 miles northeast of Jenner, 707/847-3258; 15 units; $$$+; 2-night minimum; unsuitable for children; all refrigerators, fireplaces; heated pool (summer only), hot tub, 2 tennis courts; full breakfast, restaurant.* Modern cedar-log cottages, with private decks and luxurious amenities, offer a quiet retreat on this 80-acre working ranch. A six-course gourmet dinner in the dining room and full breakfast brought to the room are included in the room rate. Non-guests may visit for lunch or dinner but need a reservation.

Fort Ross State Historic Park *19005 Highway 1, 11 miles north of town, 707/847-3286; daily 9-4:30; $5/car.* Built by Russian and Alaskan hunters in 1812 as a trading outpost, this historic fort has been authentically restored by the state. The compound consists of two blockhouses equipped with cannons, a small Russian Orthodox chapel, two commandant's houses, and a barracks. Picnic tables are available. Outside the gates, on a picturesque bluff at the edge of the ocean, visitors can sometimes mingle with a flock of grazing sheep; a path there leads down to the beach. An architecturally striking Visitors Center is located adjacent to the parking area.

Living History Days, which allow visitors to step back in time to 1836, are held periodically. Then, soldiers perform musket drills and fire cannons, candlemakers demonstrate their skills, and a blacksmith pounds at his forge.

Kruse Rhododendron State Reserve *on Kruse Ranch Rd., 22 miles north of town, 707/847-3221.* Best known for its spring floral display, this park has 5 miles of hiking trails that take visitors over picturesque bridges and through fern-filled canyons.

Salt Point State Park *25050 Highway 1, 20 miles north of town, 707/847-3221.* A popular spot with skin divers, this park is also choice for a walk along the beach. Stump Cove has an easy, short trail down to its scenic beach. Campsites are available.

The Sea Ranch

Homes. *Rams Head Realty and Rentals, 707/785-2427; 120 units; $$-$$$+; 2-night minimum; cribs; some kitchens, bathtubs, fireplaces; pets welcome in some homes.* Stunningly beautiful wind-swept coastal scenery is the backdrop for the luxury vacation homes situated in this development. Each home is unique. For example, The Admiral's Retreat, built in the 1970s, is an older home that has recently been upgraded. Its huge octagonal dining room looks out to the ocean. The bathroom has a spa-sized Jacuzzi tub and a TV, and the kitchen is well-appointed for preparing gourmet vacation meals. The spectacular oceanfront Monette House, only 5 years old, has three bedrooms. Its special highlight is a hot tub in an enclosed room with sliding glass doors opening to the sights and sounds of the ocean. Rustic hike-in cabins are also available.

Guests may use all the facilities at the nearby lodge, mentioned below, and there are hiking and jogging trails as well as a children's playground. A 9-hole golf course, designed in the Scottish manner by Robert Muir Graves, may be played at extra charge.

Lodge. *60 Sea Walk Dr., 800/732-7262, 707/785-2371; 20 rooms; 16 non-smoking rooms; $$$-$$$+; 2-night minimum on weekends May-Oct; children under 5 free; cribs; no TVs; all bathtubs; some wood-burning stoves; heated pool, sauna, 4 tennis courts, parcourse; restaurant.* At this rustic modern facility each room has an ocean view and either one or two queen-size beds. Two rooms have private courtyards with hot tubs.

Gualala

Named for an Indian word that is pronounced wha-LA-la and means "water coming down place," this town is located in a banana-belt of regularly warm weather. The area's many celebrity property owners include singer Kris Kristofferson and comedian Robin Williams.

Mar Vista Cottages *35101 Highway 1, 707/884-3522; 12 units; $$; crib; no TVs; all kitchens; some fireplaces; hot tub; pets welcome.* These cottages are just a short walk from a sandy beach with a gentle surf. Two ponds and an assortment of geese and ducks are located on the 9-acre grounds.

♥The Old Milano Hotel *38300 Highway 1, 707/884-3256; 9 units; 100% non-smoking; $$-$$$+; 2-night minimum on Sat; unsuitable for children under 16; some kitchens, bathtubs, fireplaces; some shared baths; hot tub; full breakfast, restaurant, room* *service.* Built originally in 1905 as a railroad rest stop and pub, this elegantly refurbished cliffside Victorian hotel is now listed in the National Register of Historic Places. A garden cottage and a converted caboose—complete with upstairs brakeman's seats where occupants may enjoy watching the sun set—are available in addition to the hotel rooms. An expansive ocean view is enjoyed from the cliff-top hot tub.

Serenisea *36100 Highway 1, 800/331-3836, 707/884-3836; 21 units; 3 non-smoking units; $$-$$$; 2-night minimum on weekends; children under 1 free; all kitchens; some bathtubs, fireplaces; pets welcome in some units.* These oceanfront cabins and houses are located on a scenic bluff. Some have private hot tubs, and one has a private sauna.

♥St. Orres *36601 Highway 1, 707/884-3303; 18 units; $$-$$$+; 2-night minimum on weekends; unsuitable for children; some kitchens, bathtubs, fireplaces; some shared baths; hot tub, sauna; full breakfast, restaurant.* Built of weathered wood, in a Russian style of architecture featuring onion-domed turrets, this unusual inn offers both rooms and detached cabins.

A memorable fixed-price, three-course dinner is served in the inn's striking 3-story-tall dining room. Game such as boar, guinea hen, and pheasant is often on the menu.

♥Whale Watch *35100 Highway 1, 800/WHALE-42, 707/884-3667; 18 rooms; 100% non-smoking; $$$+; 2-night minimum on weekends; unsuitable for children; no TVs; some kitchens, bathtubs, fireplaces; sauna; full breakfast.* Perched on an oceanside cliff, this dramatic contemporary-style lodging facility offers plenty of peace and quiet. All rooms have private decks and coastal views, and eight have two-person whirlpool bathtubs. Breakfast is served in the room each morning.

Point Arena

Point Arena Lighthouse *at the end of Lighthouse Rd., 2 miles off Highway 1, 707/882-2777; daily 11-2:30, in summer to 3:30; adults $2, under 13 50¢.* Originally built in 1870, this lighthouse was destroyed in the '06 quake and then rebuilt. It was finally automated in 1976. Visitors may take a self-guided tour of the museum, which is filled with old photos and features a whale-watching room. Then it's a 145-step climb (equivalent to 6 stories) up the 115-foot light for a guided tour of the tower.

Those who want to stay the night can book one of the bargain three-bedroom, two-bath lightkeeper's homes located adjacent.

Elk

♥Harbor House *5600 Highway 1, 707/877-3203; 10 units; 100% non-smoking (except in dining room); $$$-$$$+; 2-night minimum on weekends; unsuitable for children under 15; no TVs; some bathtubs, fireplaces; dinner & full breakfast included.* Built entirely of redwood in 1917, this lovely inn has six rooms and four cottages. Meals are served in a beautifully appointed dining room with a spectacular ocean view. A path leads to a private beach where guests may sun, explore tidepools, and gather driftwood.

– Mendocino –

A LITTLE BACKGROUND

Mendocino provides a rejuvenating, quiet escape from the hectic pace of city life. Now an Historical Monument, this tiny artists' colony is built in a pastel Cape Cod-style of architecture and exudes the feeling that it belongs to a time past. Visitors can really slow down their systems by parking their cars for the duration of a visit. It is easy to get anywhere in town via a short walk.

Visitors are advised that Mendocino has a limited water supply and should be careful not to waste water when in town. Also, there is a Volunteer Fire Department with an alarm that has been known to go off in the middle of the night. Resembling the scream of an air raid siren, it can be quite startling—even when a person is aware of what it is.

The night life here is of the early-to-bed, early-to-rise variety. Consider this itinerary: dinner out, a stroll through town, a nightcap at the Mendocino Hotel or Sea Gull Inn, and then off to bed.

Make lodging reservations as far in advance as possible; in-town lodging is limited and popular.

VISITOR INFORMATION

Fort Bragg-Mendocino Coast Chamber of Commerce *P.O. Box 1141 (332 N. Main St.), Fort Bragg 95437, 800/726-2780, 707/961-6300.*

Anderson Valley Chamber of Commerce *P.O. Box 275, Boonville 95415.*

GETTING THERE

Located approximately 150 miles north of San Francisco. Take Highway 101 to Highway 1, or Highway 101 to Highway 128 to Highway 1.

ANNUAL EVENTS

California Wine Tasting Championships *July; in Philo, 707/877-3262.* Held at **Greenwood Ridge Vineyards,** this unique and potentially stupefying event includes good food, live music, and a chocolate-tasting contest. Advance registration is required for participation in the novice, amateur, and professional wine tasting competitions.

Mendocino Music Festival *July; 707/937-2044.* A variety of performances—including orchestra, chamber music, opera, and jazz—are presented in a small oceanside tent in Mendocino Headlands State Park. Master classes are scheduled, and free pre-concert lectures educate the audience about the music being performed.

STOPS ALONG THE WAY

Note that in Boonville the townspeople speak an unusual dialect known as "Boontling." For example, public telephones are labeled "Buckey Walter," quail are called "rookie-to."

PICNICS. On the drive to Mendocino, a picnic makes a good lunch stop. Several wineries off Highway 101 have picnic facilities (see page 135). More picnic spots are situated along Highway 128—a route that passes an 11-mile corridor of redwoods known as the "tunnel to the sea." In Boonville look for **Indian Creek City Park,** located just east of town, and the **Masonite Corporation Demonstration Forest,** just past Navarro.

For picnic supplies, stop in Boonville at the **Boont Berry Farm** *(13981 Highway 128, 707/895-3576; daily 10-6).* This health food store has a cozy, old-fashioned atmosphere and is well-stocked with deli items, locally-grown organic produce, pastries, breads (including the town's famous Bruce Bread), and homemade ice cream.

The **Anderson Valley Historical Museum** *(Highway 128/Anderson Valley Way, 707/895-3207; F-Sun 1-4, from 11 in summer; free),* an old-fashioned one-room red schoolhouse located just west of town, is also a worthwhile stop.

RESTAURANTS. The casual **Buckhorn Saloon** *(14081 Highway 128, Boonville, 707/895-BEER; L & D Thur-Tu; MC, V)* has an airy dining room overlooking the scenic countryside. Its inexpensive menu features snack items—such as nachos, spicy chicken wings, and piroshki—as well as fish & chips and several kinds of hamburgers and deli sandwiches. Breads, soups, and desserts are homemade.

Beers, brewed directly beneath the pub, include Poleeko Gold (light ale), High Rollers (wheat beer), Boont Amber (ale), Deependers Dark (porter), and Barney Flats (oatmeal stout). Fresh lemonade and an apple spritzer, made with local apple juice and sparkling mineral water, are also available.

WINERIES. The **Kendall-Jackson Winery** (*5500 Highway 128, Philo, 707/895-3232; tasting daily 11-5, in summer 10-6; tours by appt.*) is located atop a scenic hill just west of Boonville. Across the street, **Navarro Vineyards** (*5601 Highway 128, Philo, 800/537-9463, 707/895-3686; tasting daily 10-5; tours by appt.*) operates in a striking modern facility. Known for its varied Gewurztraminers, the winery offers tastes of varietal grape juices to children. Both wineries have attractive picnic areas.

The **Roederer Estate** (*4501 Highway 128, Philo, 707/895-2288; tasting F-M 11-4; tours by appt.*) boasts state-of-the-art methode champenoise winemaking facilities and a tasting room with beautiful valley views.

LODGING. Among the more interesting accommodations in this area is the **Highland Ranch** (*18941 Philo-Greenwood Rd., Philo, 707/895-3600; 11 units; $$$+; 2-night minimum; cribs; no TVs; all fireplaces; unheated pool (unavailable Nov-Mar), 2 tennis courts; full breakfast, lunch, & dinner included; restaurant for guests only; pets welcome*). Guests can enjoy the rural pleasures of fishing, swimming, and canoeing in three ponds, as well as horseback riding at no additional charge. Lodging is in modern redwood cabins with fireplaces, and all meals are included.

Situated on a former sheep ranch, the 1912 **Toll House Inn** (*15301 Highway 253, Boonville, 707/895-3630, fax 707/895-3632; 5 rooms; 100% non-smoking; $$$-$$$+; closed in Jan; unsuitable for children under 12; no TVs; some bathtubs, fireplaces; hot tub; full breakfast, restaurant*) offers quiet B&B accommodations.

WHERE TO STAY IN TOWN

Hill House of Mendocino *10701 Palette Dr., 800/422-0554, 707/937-0554, fax 707/937-1123; 44 rooms; $$$-$$$+; cribs; all bathtubs; some fireplaces; restaurant.* Located on a scenic hill above the village, this lodging facility was built in 1978. It has become famous as the setting for many of the early episodes of the TV series *Murder, She Wrote*. Because of this Hollywood connection, it attracts many stars as patrons. Rooms are spacious and furnished comfortably with brass beds and lace curtains.

♥**Joshua Grindle Inn** *44800 Little Lake Rd., 707/937-4143; 10 units; 100% non-smoking; $$-$$$; 2-night minimum on weekends; unsuitable for children; no TVs; 1 bathtub, some fireplaces; full breakfast.* Situated on 2 acres at the edge of town, this small inn was built in 1879 by the town banker. It has a New England country atmosphere, and Early American antiques furnish every room. Rooms are in the main house, a cottage, and a water tower.

MacCallum House Inn *45020 Albion St., 707/937-0289; 20 rooms; 100% non-smoking; $$-$$$+; 2-night minimum on weekends; cribs; no TVs; some kitchens, bathtubs, fireplaces; some shared baths; continental breakfast, restaurant.* Built in 1882 by William H. Kelley for his newlywed daughter, Daisy MacCallum, this converted Victorian home was one of the first B&Bs in the area. Its attractively decorated rooms are furnished with antiques, many of which belonged to the original owner.

Accommodations are also available in newer structures adjacent to the house. The ten rooms in the house itself tend to be best suited to couples and parents with just one child. A continental breakfast is served buffet-style in two magnificent dining rooms in the main house. Guests are greeted with the morning paper and a crackling fire in two fireplaces built of smooth river stone.

In the evening an independent restaurant operation serves elegant seafood and game entrees in the dining rooms. Light dinners and snacks are available across the hall in the cozy **Grey Whale Bar,** also operated by the restaurant. Interesting drinks include Daisy's Hot Apple Pie (a blend of apple cider, Tuaca, cinnamon, and whipped cream) and a non-alcoholic Velvet Rabbit (a frothy mix of cream, grenadine, and strawberries served elegantly in a brandy snifter).

Mendocino Hotel & Garden Suites *45080 Main St., 800/548-0513, 707/937-0511, fax 707/937-0513; 51 rooms; 2 non-smoking rooms; $$-$$$+; some bathtubs, fireplaces; some shared baths; 2 restaurants, room service.* Built in 1878, this hotel has been renovated in Victorian style. Its small rooms combine modern convenience with 19th century elegance. Modern cottages, with luxurious suites featuring canopied beds and marble bathrooms, provide additional lodging behind the hotel. They are located amidst almost an acre of well-tended gardens.

A casual, greenhouse-like cafe serves both breakfast and lunch. Dinner is available in a more formal dining room (*$$$; highchairs, booster seats, children's portions; 100% non-smoking; reservations suggested; AE, MC, V*) furnished in old-fashioned oak. Fresh seafood and meat entrees are on the a la carte menu. Starters include a French onion soup and a very good Caesar salad, and the dessert tray always includes deep-dish olallieberry pie with homemade ice cream—the house specialty. The hotel's bar is a good spot to stop and enjoy a fancy drink among beautiful specimens of stained glass and oriental carpets.

♥**Mendocino Village Inn** *44860 Main St., 800/882-7029, 707/937-0246; 12 rooms; 100% non-smoking; $$-$$$; 2-night minimum on weekends; unsuitable for children under 10; no TVs; some bathtubs, fireplaces; some shared baths; full breakfast.* Built in 1882, this Queen Anne Victorian home is known as "the house of the doctors" because it was originally built by a doctor, and then bought in turn by three more doctors. All the cozy rooms are decorated with antiques and contemporary art.

Sea Gull Inn *44594 Albion St., 707/937-5204; 9 rooms; $-$$; 2-night minimum on weekends; some TVs, bathtubs; continental breakfast.* Built in 1877 as a town house, this rustic, non-cutesy inn has a casual, friendly atmosphere. A mature garden, with giant fuchsias and a century-old rosemary bush, surrounds the inn. The breakfast includes hot beverages and muffins from the **Mendocino Cookie Co.**

Sears House Inn *44840 Main St., 707/937-4076; 8 units; 4 non-smoking units; $$; 2-night minimum on weekends; no TVs; some kitchens, bathtubs, fireplaces; some shared baths; continental breakfast; pets welcome.* Guests here have the choice of staying in an 1870 Victorian house, in a cottage, or in a converted water tower. In the morning, a breakfast basket is delivered to each room.

♥**Whitegate Inn** *499 Howard St., 707/937-4892; 6 rooms; 100% non-smoking; $$-$$$; 2-night minimum on weekends; unsuitable for children under 13; no TVs; some bathtubs,* *fireplaces; full breakfast.* Built in 1880, this tasteful Victorian home has been refurbished and is decorated with antiques.

WHERE TO STAY NEARBY

♥**Fensalden Inn** *33810 Navarro Ridge Rd., Albion, 7 miles south of town, 707/937-4042; 8 rooms; 100% non-smoking; $$-$$$; 2-night minimum on weekends May-Dec; unsuitable for children under 7; some kitchens, bathtubs, fireplaces; full breakfast.* Originally a stagecoach way station in the 1860s, this B&B sits atop 20 tree-lined acres of headland meadow. Rooms are in both the large main house and in a separate house built around an 1890s water tower.

Heritage House *5200 Highway 1, Little River, 4 miles south of town, 800/235-5885, 707/937-5885; 74 units; $$$-$$$$+; closed Dec & Jan; children under 3 free; some bathtubs, fireplaces; full dinner & breakfast included, restaurant.* Located on a craggy stretch of coast with magnificent ocean views, this inn offers a luxurious escape from city living. Guests are housed in rooms and cottages furnished with antiques. If it all looks familiar, it may be because it's been seen before in the movie *Same Time Next Year*, which was filmed here.

Male guests are encouraged to dress in jacket and tie for meals served in the elegant cliffside dining room. Non-guests are welcome to make dinner reservations.

Little River Inn *7750 Highway 1, Little River, 2 miles south of town, 707/937-5942; 55 units; 4 non-smoking units; $$-$$$+; 2-night minimum on weekends; children under 14 free; cribs; some TVs, kitchens, bathtubs, fireplaces; 2 tennis courts (night lights); restaurant.* Built in 1853, this house became an inn in 1929 and now offers a choice of cozy attic rooms, cottages, and standard motel units. Most have ocean views. A 9-hole golf course is on the property, and the restaurant is open for breakfast and dinner.

Mendocino Coast Reservations *1001 Main St., 800/262-7801, 707/937-5033; 60 units; some non-smoking units; $$-$$$; 2-night minimum, 1-week in July & Aug; cribs; all kitchens; some bathtubs, fireplaces; dogs welcome in some units.* This vacation home rental service arranges lodging in studios, cabins, cottages, inns, and estate homes located on the Mendocino coast. Some units are oceanfront, some have ocean views, and some have private hot tubs.

Stanford Inn by the Sea *on Comptche-Ukiah Rd., Mendocino, 800/331-8884, 707/937-5615; 26 rooms; 100% non-smoking; $$$+; 2-night minimum on Sat; cribs; all fireplaces; some kitchens, bathtubs; indoor heated pool, hot tub, sauna; continental breakfast; pets welcome.* Located on the outskirts of town, upon a bluff overlooking a scenic llama farm and duck pond, these modern luxury rooms are decorated with antiques, fresh flowers, and the work of local artists. Bicycles are available for guests to borrow.

WHERE TO EAT

Cafe Beaujolais *961 Ukiah St., 707/937-5614; B, L, & D Thur-M, Sat & SunBr; closed Jan & Feb; $$; highchairs, booster seats, children's portions; 100% non-smoking; reserva-*

tions suggested; no cards. The highly acclaimed breakfasts served in this converted Victorian home include light crepes filled with ricotta and topped with strawberry sauce, omelettes with unusual fillings (one combines sautéed eggplant, greens, and goat cheese), and homemade cashew granola. A large selection of specialty coffees is also available, as is steamed almond milk—a favorite item with many children. Lunch includes innovative entrees and sandwiches as well as two popular desserts—panforte di Mendocino and a buttercream caramel bar sundae. Daily "heart healthy specials" are on the menus, and a basket of toys is on hand to entertain restless children.

Eight-inch pizzas, topped with both the unusual (barbecued chicken, Mexican carnitas) and usual (salami) and baked in a wood-fired brick oven, are available from an adjacent building dubbed **The Brickery.** Wonderful breads, including a dense Austrian sunflower bread and an unusual hazelnut bread, are also available by the loaf, and informal outdoor dining can be enjoyed on a deck in the garden.

Dinner is more formal affair, with seatings at 6:15 and 9:30, and is unsuitable for children.

Should anyone get anxious for some of these homemade goodies when they return home, a mail-order brochure is available. It offers especially wonderful spicy gingersnaps and panfortes.

Mendocino Bakery *on Lansing St., 707/937-0836; daily 8-7; $.* The perfect spot for a light lunch, this super bakery dispenses tasty homemade soup and thick-crusted pizza warm from the oven. A hunk of the fragrant, moist gingerbread makes a memorable dessert, as do the chewy cinnamon twists and chocolate chip-oatmeal "cowboy" cookies. The bakery also presents an assortment of breads and breakfast pastries—all made without mixes or preservatives. Everything is exceptional.

Next door, the **Mendocino Chocolate Company** *(10483 Lansing St., 800/722-1107, 707/937-1107)* dispenses delicious candies.

Mendocino Ice Cream Co. *45090 Main St., 707/937-5884; F & Sat 8am-9pm, Sun-Thur 8-6, in summer daily 8-9; $.* People wait in long lines to get the 1/4-pound ice cream cones scooped up here. And, indeed, the award-winning ice cream is delicious—especially the Black Forest flavor made with rich chocolate ice cream infused with chocolate chips and cherry bits. The foot-long hot dogs are pretty good, too. Sodas and sandwiches round out the menu, and wooden booths are available for seating.

Sea Gull of Mendocino *10481 Lansing St., 707/937-2100; B, L, & D daily; closed first week of Feb; $$; highchairs, booster seats, children's portions; no reservations; no cards.* The specialty here is fresh food prepared simply. Breakfast items are especially good and include eggs, pancakes, and hot oatmeal. The premier choice on the dinner menu is any of the fresh local fish items, which include a cioppino and gumbo. A cheeseburger, steak sandwich, and several chicken entrees are also available. Dinners come with homemade soup or green salad, fresh vegetable, baked potato or rice pilaf, and crusty French bread.

The upstairs **Top of the Gull Lounge** usually has live music in the evening and is a good spot for an Irish coffee nightcap.

WHAT TO DO

Beachcombing. Follow down to the beach the little path behind the church on Main Street. While there, make a **kelp horn** by cutting the bulb off the end of a long, thin piece of fresh bull kelp. Rinse out the tube in the ocean so that it is hollow. Then wrap it over one shoulder, and blow through the small end. The longer the tube, the greater the resonance.

Catch A Canoe & Bicycles, Too *on Comptche-Ukiah Rd., 707-937-0273, 707/937-5615; daily 9:30-5:30; $10+/hour; reservations recommended.* Drifting down calm Big River affords the opportunity to picnic in the wilderness, swim in a secluded swimming hole, and observe a variety of wildlife. Canoe rentals include paddles and life jackets. Bicycle rentals are also available.

Current local events. Check the postings in the entryway to the Sea Gull restaurant.

Ford House Visitor Center *735 Main St., 707/937-5397; daily 11-4; free; strollers not permitted.* Inside this historic 1854 home is an interpretive center focusing on the cultural and natural history of the area. During whale-watching season, a short orientation film is presented. Information on interpretive programs held at nearby **Mendocino Headlands State Park** can also be obtained here then. (December through April whales migrate close to shore and can sometimes easily be seen from the headlands "breaching"—jumping out of the water.) In good weather, a picnic at tables provided in the backyard offers a spectacular ocean view.

Kelley House Museum *45007 Albion St., 707/937-5791; F-M 1-4; adults $1.* A gigantic cypress tree grows in the front yard of this home built by William H. Kelley (Daisy MacCallum's father) in 1861. The restored first floor displays a collection of photos from the 1800s, as well as changing exhibits of local artifacts and private collections.

Mendocino Art Center *45200 Little Lake St., 707/937-5818; daily 10-4; free.* Three galleries are open for browsing. Picnic tables are provided in the courtyard garden, and informal snacks are sold in the lobby. Activities related to fine arts and crafts are scheduled year-round, and theatre performances are presented from March through December, Thursday through Sunday.

Russian Gulch State Park *on Highway 1, 2 miles north of town, 707/937-5804; daily dawn-dusk; $5/car.* A protected beach, a waterfall, and a blowhole are among the features at this rustic park. Picnic tables and campsites are available.

Van Damme State Park *8125 Highway 1, Little River, 2 miles south of town, 707/937-5804; daily dawn-dusk; $5/car.* Among the interesting features in this 2,069-acre park is a canyon filled with ferns and a 1/3-mile Bog Trail leading to a large area of skunk cabbage. Picnic facilities and campsites are available.

An unusual **Pygmy Forest** *(follow Little River Airport Rd. approximately 3 miles inland to the parking lot),* where stunted trees grown in leached soil, has a short boardwalk trail. A brochure describing the various types of trees is available at the trailhead.

Wind & Weather *on Albion St., 707/937-0323; daily 10-5.* Located inside a picturesque old water tower, this tiny specialty shop sells barometers, weather vanes, sundials, and other paraphernalia for measuring the weather. Don't miss it.

– Fort Bragg –

GETTING THERE
Located approximately 15 miles north of Mendocino.

ANNUAL EVENTS
World's Largest Salmon Barbecue *July; 707/964-2313, 707/964-6598.* In addition to feasting on king salmon, participants can look forward to music, dancing, a variety of educational salmon displays, and a fireworks show over the ocean. Proceeds benefit the non-profit Salmon Restoration Association and assist them in restocking Northern California salmon runs.

WHERE TO STAY
Colonial Inn *533 E. Fir St., 707/964-9979; 8 rooms; 4 non-smoking rooms; $$; closed part of Oct & part of spring; some TVs, bathtubs, fireplaces.* Located in a quiet residential area, this huge 1912 woodframe home was turned into a guest house in 1945. It features tastefully decorated rooms, one of which has a huge fireplace. A public tennis court is just 1 block away.

DeHaven Valley Farm *39247 Highway 1, Westport, 10 miles north of town, 707/961-1660; 8 units; 100% non-smoking; $$-$$$; 2-night minimum on weekends; children un-*

der 6 free; some bathtubs, fireplaces; some shared baths; hot tub; full breakfast. Romance and family fun are both available here. For romance, request the cozy Valley View room and enjoy its private bathroom, small corner fireplace, and view of the valley. The spacious Eagle's Nest, with its Franklin stove and huge windows overlooking the valley, is another winner. With kids in tow, opt for one of the two cottages. One teenager who stayed here actually uttered, "Mom, you did right. This place is great!" A cozy communal living room in the traditional Victorian farmhouse is the gathering spot for afternoon refreshments. It holds a grand piano for self-entertainment and a TV with a large video library. Guests are welcome to play with the many resident cats and to walk the goats—although sometimes the goats seem to be walking the guests. Also, the tidepools of **Westport Union Landing Beach** await just across the highway, and a hilltop hot tub offers views of the valley and ocean. Delicious, intimate four-course dinners are available to guests by reservation.

The Grey Whale Inn *615 N. Main St., 800/382-7244, 707/964-0640; 14 rooms; 100% non-smoking; $$-$$$+; 2-night minimum on Sat; some TVs, kitchens, bathtubs, fireplaces; full breakfast.* Originally built as a hospital, this stately redwood building was converted to an especially spacious inn in 1976. Some of the pleasantly decorated rooms have a private deck, some have good ocean views that permit viewing the whale migration, and one has a whirlpool bathtub for two. A large communal guest area is equipped with a TV, fireplace, pool table, and plenty of board games. An elaborate breakfast is served buffet style and sometimes includes a wonderful concoction of fresh bananas and blueberries mixed with a light cream cheese sauce. A relaxing stay here can be just what the doctor ordered.

Pine Beach Inn *16801 Highway 1, 4 miles south of town, 707/964-5603; 51 rooms; $$; cribs; some kitchens, bathtubs; 2 tennis courts; continental breakfast (Nov-Mar only), restaurant (Apr-Oct only).* This motel complex is located on 12 acres of private land. Facilities include a private beach and cove.

Motel Row. Three traditional motels on the northern end of town offer good value and an extraordinary beachfront location.
    Beachcomber Motel *1111 N. Main St., 800/400-SURF, 707/964-2402; $$-$$$+.*
    Hi-Seas Beach Motel *1201 N. Main St., 707/964-5929; $$.*
    Ocean View Lodging *1141 N. Main St., 707/964-1951; $-$$.*

WHERE TO EAT

Cap'n Flint's *32250 N. Harbor Dr., 707/964-9447; L & D daily; $; highchairs, booster seats, children's portions; no reservations; no cards.* Popular with locals, the menu here offers various kinds of fish & chips, clam chowder, and the house specialty— deep-fried shrimp wontons made with a tasty cream cheese filling. Hamburgers, hot dogs, sandwiches, and unusual mixed wine drinks are also available. Though the decor consists of well-worn, mismatched furniture, the view of picturesque **Noyo Harbor** is excellent.

Egghead Omelettes of Oz *326 N. Main St., 707/964-5005; B & L daily; $; highchairs, booster seats, children's portions; 100% non-smoking; no reservations; no cards.* This cheerful, popular, and tiny diner serves a large variety of big omelettes. Regular breakfast items and an assortment of sandwiches are also available. Families will appreciate the privacy afforded by enclosed booths, and children's portions are available upon request.

The Restaurant *418 N. Main St., 707/964-9800; L Thur-F, D Tu-M, SunBr; closed during Mar; $$; highchairs, booster seats, children's portions; 100% non-smoking; reservations suggested; MC, V.* In completely unpretentious surroundings, this restaurant serves good food at reasonable prices. The eclectic menu changes regularly, but the emphasis is on fresh local seafood and vegetarian items. A recent lunch menu offered a variety of sandwiches, plus a hamburger, Philly cheesesteak, chicken flauta, vegetable chili, and several salads and soups. Desserts were a chocolate shortcake with fresh berries and cream, a house-made ice cream, and a lemon tart. Dinner entrees that night included Thai-style shrimp in green curry sauce, Denver lamb riblets with sweet & sour glaze, and chicken breast Amalfi topped with lemony arugula.

WHAT TO DO

Downtown Shopping. A walk along Main and Laurel Streets allows a look at some of the town's most interesting shops. Stop in at the **Mendocino Chocolate Company** at 542 Main *(707/964-8800; daily 10-5:30)* for hand-dipped chocolates and truffles. Duck down Laurel Street to **Round Man's Smoke House** at #137 *(800/545-2935, 707/964-5954)* for smoked meats and salmon. Across the street at #136, the informal **Laurel Deli & Desserts** *(707/964-7812; M-F 7:30-5)* dishes up homemade soups and sandwiches, as well as gigantic blackberry muffins and delicious pies. Back on Main Street stop in at #362, the **Northcoast Artists Gallery** *(707/964-8266; M-Sat 10-6, Sun 10-3)*, where the works of local artists are displayed and available for sale. Just a bit futher down at #330, **Carol Hall's Hot Pepper Jelly Company** *(707/961-1422; M-Sat 10-5:30, Sun 10:30-5)* dispenses charming doily-topped jars of their delicious pepper jelly as well as many other local food products.

The Fort Bragg Footlighters Gaslite Gaities *248 Laurel St., 707/964-3806; W & Sat at 8pm, summer only; $7/person; reservations suggested.* Gay Nineties music and nonsense highlight a program that appeals to all ages.

Georgia-Pacific Tree Nursery *90 W. Redwood Ave., 707/964-5651; daily; free.* Visitors here get a view of 4 million seedling trees. A nature trail and picnic tables are available. Sawmill tours are given in summer; call for details.

Guest House Logging Museum *343 N. Main St., 707/961-2825; W-Sat 10-4, Sun 10-1, Apr-Oct only; $1.* Get a sense of this area's history by viewing the old logging photos and artifacts on display inside this beautifully restored 1892 mansion that was constructed entirely of redwood. A steam donkey is among the displays in the manicured gardens.

Jughandle State Reserve *on Highway 1, 3 miles south of town, 707/937-5804; daily dawn-dusk; free.* A unique self-guided nature trail takes hikers through an **ecological staircase** consisting of five wave-cut terraces that demonstrate how plants and soils affect one another. During the 5-mile, 3-hour walk, the terrain changes from grass-covered headlands, to a pine and redwood forest, to a pygmy forest filled with full-grown trees measuring only 1 to 2 feet tall. Wear sturdy shoes, and bring water and a lunch.

Mendocino Coast Botanical Gardens *18220 Highway 1, 2 miles south of town, 707/ 964-4352; daily 9-5, Oct-Mar 9-4; adults $5, under 12 free.* Enjoy a self-guided tour through 47 acres of flowering plants. This garden is known for its rhododendrons, fuchsias, and native California plants. It also boasts a major collection of heathers, succulents, ivies, and old heritage roses. Picnic facilities are available.

Ricochet Ridge Ranch *24201 Highway 1, 707/964-7669; daily by appt. at 10, 12, 2, & 4; $23/hour; riders must be 6 or older.* Equestrian excursions vary from by-the-hour guided rides on the beach to week-long trips that make nightly stops at inns. They include treks on Fort Bragg's **Ten Mile Beach** and in Mendocino's majestic redwood forests. Catered trips, camping expeditions, and private tours can also be arranged. Pony rides are available for children under 6.

Skunk Train/California Western Railroad *foot of Laurel St., 707/964-6371; schedule varies; round trip: adults $23, 5-11 $11, under 5 free if they don't occupy a seat; reservations suggested.* This train gets its name from the fact that the original logging trains emitted unpleasant odors from their gas engines, allowing them to be smelled before they were seen. In addition to gas engines, the Skunk Train is also pulled by steam and diesel engines. The train travels through dense redwood forest, through deep mountain tunnels, and over many bridges and trestles on its run between Fort Bragg and Willits, where there is a stopover for lunch. Stops are also made along the way to deliver mail. A half-day trip is also available.

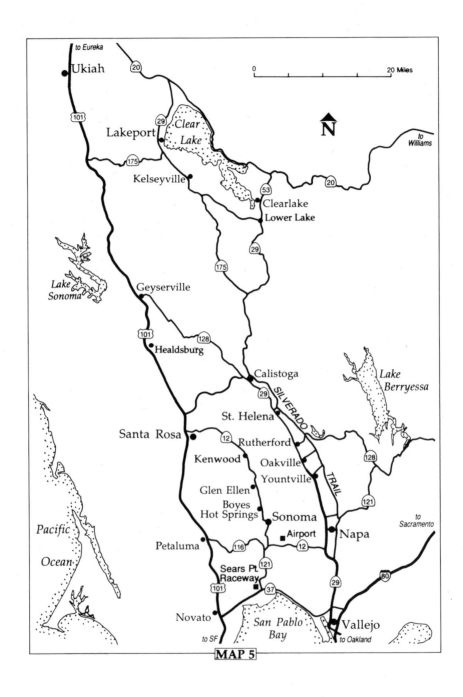

to Eureka

Ukiah

20

0   20 Miles

N

to Williams

101

29

Lakeport

Clear Lake

175

Kelseyville

53

Clearlake

20

Lower Lake

29

175

Lake Sonoma

Geyserville

101

128

Healdsburg

Calistoga

29

SILVERADO

Lake Berryessa

St. Helena

Santa Rosa

12

Rutherford

Kenwood

Oakville

128

Yountville

TRAIL

Glen Ellen

121

Boyes Hot Springs

Sonoma

Pacific

Airport

Napa

to Sacramento

Ocean

Petaluma

116

12

Sears Pt. Raceway

121

101

37

80

29

Novato

San Pablo Bay

Vallejo

to SF

to Oakland

MAP 5

Wine Country

A LITTLE BACKGROUND

California's first wineries were appendages of the 21 Franciscan missions that were built a day's ride (by horseback) from each other in a chain reaching from San Diego to Sonoma. The wine was produced by the missions for sacramental use. Eventually the church gave up producing wine, and the art passed into the realm of private enterprise.

Presently Sonoma County and Napa County are literally erupting with new small family wineries. Winemaking is becoming a hobby with many city folks who have bought themselves modest vineyard retreats.

The most popular route for wine tasting in this area is along Highway 29 between Oakville and Calistoga. When visiting this stretch of highway, which is heavily concentrated with wineries, the problem is to remain selective in tasting. Experts suggest not planning to taste at more than four wineries in one day.

Young children can be difficult on a winery tour. Out of courtesy to the other tour participants (a noisy child interferes with the guide's presentation), parents might consider having a member of their party stay with the children while the others go on a tour. Or visit a winery with a self-guided tour. Most wineries allow tasting without taking a tour. It's a nice idea to bring along some plastic wine glasses and a bottle of grape juice so the children can "taste," too.

Many wineries have picnic areas. An ideal itinerary is to tour a winery, taste, and then purchase a bottle of a pleasing wine to drink with a picnic lunch.

A new wrinkle in the pleasure of wine tasting is that many wineries now charge for tasting. Charges range from 25 cents to $5. Sometimes the charge permits tasters to keep their glass as a souvenir, and sometimes the charge is applied to a wine purchase. Tasting fees tend to be imposed by smaller wineries with more expensive vintages, and their purpose seems to be to keep the less serious tasters away.

Some tasting rooms will provide vertical tastings, which portray the aging process of a varietal, and cross tastings, which show the different results that varied treatment of the same grapes can cause. To arrange a special tasting, call ahead.

Because the Wine Country is so close to the Bay Area, this trip can easily be made into a 1-day adventure.

VISITOR INFORMATION

Wine Institute *425 Market St. #1000, San Francisco 94105, 415/512-0151.*

– Sonoma –

VISITOR INFORMATION

Sonoma Valley Visitors Bureau *453 First St. East, Sonoma 95476, 707/996-1090.*

GETTING THERE

Located approximately 45 miles north of San Francisco. Take Highway 101 to Highway 37 to Highway 121 to Highway 12.

ANNUAL EVENTS

World Pillow Fighting Championship *July; in Kenwood, 707/833-2440.* This very serious all-day competition takes place on a greased pipe positioned over a muddy morass into which losers, and sometimes winners, are buffeted.

Valley of the Moon Vintage Festival *September; 707/996-2109.* Begun in 1887 as a celebration of the harvest, this old-time event kicks off in the historic Barracks each year with an evening tasting of elite Sonoma Valley wines. Daytime events include a Blessing of the Grapes, several parades, and a re-enactment of the Bear Flag Revolt. (During the revolt American soldiers seized the town from General Vallejo, taking down the Mexican flag and raising the bear flag—which later became California's state flag.) Messy grape stomping competitions, in which one person stomps and the other holds a bottle under the spicket, are also part of the fun.

WHERE TO STAY

El Dorado Hotel *405 First St. West, 800/289-3031, 707/996-3030; 25 rooms; $$-$$$; cribs; some bathtubs; heated pool; continental breakfast, restaurant; small dogs welcome.* Built in 1843, this historic inn was recently gutted and remodeled with plenty of Mexican pavers tiles and beveled glass. Each of the modern rooms contains hand-made furnishings such as iron four-poster beds and big mirrors softened by rustic twig frames. A split of wine greets guests upon arrival.

♥Sonoma Hotel *110 W. Spain St., 707/996-2996; $$-$$$; unsuitable for children under 12; no TVs; some bathtubs; some shared baths; continental breakfast, restaurant.* Dating from the 1870s, when it was the town theater, this 3-story hotel is located on the town square. Rooms are furnished in carefully selected turn-of-the-century antiques, and private bathrooms feature claw-foot tubs.

    The restaurant specializes in hearty country fare and serves lunch and dinner in the dining room. An old-fashioned bar adjoins.

♥Sonoma Mission Inn & Spa *18140 Highway 12, Boyes Hot Springs, 3 miles north of town, 800/862-4945, 707/938-9000; 170 rooms; 80 non-smoking rooms; $$$$-$$$+; 2-night minimum on Sat; children under 14 free; cribs; all bathtubs; some fireplaces; 2 heated pools, 2 hot tubs, sauna; 2 tennis courts (fee for night lights); restaurant, room service.* Built in 1927, this sedate luxury resort features pink adobe architecture. All rooms are equipped with a VCR and a cooling old-fashioned ceiling fan. Though children are welcome, this is an adult-oriented resort. Children under 18 are not allowed in the well-equipped, full-service spa, but in summer they are permitted in one of the pools.

WHERE TO EAT

Big 3 Cafe *18140 Highway 12, Boyes Hot Springs, 3 miles north of town, 707/938-9000; B, L, & D daily; $$; highchairs, booster seats, children's portions; 100% non-smoking; reservations suggested; AE, MC, V.* Operated by the Sonoma Mission Inn, this spacious, casual dining room offers seating at tables and in comfy booths. The restaurant is well-known for its breakfasts, and at lunch and dinner the menu features northern Italian fare as well as sandwiches, soups and salads, wonderful hamburgers, and trendy pizzas.

Feed Store Cafe & Bakery *529 First St. West, 707/938-2122; B, L, & D daily; $-$$; highchairs, booster seats, children's portions; MC, V.* Located in a former feed store on the town plaza, this restaurant makes use of fresh local produce, meats, and cheeses. Absolutely not to be missed at lunch are the big, beer-batter-dipped, deep-fried onion rings. They go magnificently with one of the sandwiches or hamburgers. A variety of salads made from local greens is also available, and a different hearty homemade soup is offered every day. A rotating selection of desserts prepared by the restaurant's award-winning bakery includes fresh fruit pies, old-fashioned chocolate cake, lemon torte, and carrot cake. Before departing, stop at the bakery for take-home supplies.

Piatti *405 First St. West, 707/996-2351; L & D daily; $$; booster seats, children's portions; 100% non-smoking; reservations suggested; MC, V.* Located on the main floor of the El Dorado Hotel, this appealing restaurant is perfect for a Wine Country dining experience. In good weather, diners may be seated at heavy marble tables outside on a rustic tiled patio dominated by a majestic old fig tree. But the large inside dining room is inviting, too. The menu of deliciously innovative Italian cuisine changes regularly, and there are always several daily specials and a risotto. A variety of unusual pizzas are baked in a wood-burning oven, and most of the pastas are made by hand in the kitchen. Piatti oil, a delicious dipping sauce for bread (made with virgin olive oil, balsamic vinegar, salt, pepper, garlic, red pepper flakes, and chopped parsley) is served gratis upon request. Both local and imported Italian wine varietals are available by the glass, and trendy tiramisu is always on the dessert menu.

PICNIC PICK-UPS

Lainie's Cuisine to Go *678 W. Napa St., 707/996-5226; Tu-Sat 11-8.* Call ahead and have a picnic waiting for pick-up, or stop in at this tiny take-out and make on-the-spot selections. Perhaps an artichoke and rice salad or a jicama tabbouleh with mint dressing. Most definitely a foccacia round topped with carmelized onions and, of course, a cappuccino brownie. It seems that everything is wonderful, making it worth the drive to the outskirts of town.

Sonoma Cheese Factory *2 W. Spain St., 800/535-2855, 707/996-1931; daily 8:30-5:30.* This crowded shop stocks hundreds of cheeses (including their famous varieties of Sonoma Jack made from old family recipes), cold cuts, salads, marvelous marinated artichoke hearts, and Frank Sinatra's favorite cheesecake (made in Santa Rosa). Sandwiches are made to order. A few tables are available inside; more are outside on a shaded patio. The workings of the cheese factory may be observed through large windows in the back of the shop.

Sonoma French Bakery *468 First St. East, 707/996-2691; W-Sat 8-6, Sun 7:30-noon, closed last 2 weeks of Aug.* This renowned bakery makes both sweet and sourdough French breads that are so delicious people are willing to wait in a long line to purchase them. The Basque baker, hailing from the French Pyrenees, makes the bread s without yeast. Flutes, rolls, croissants, gateau Basque bread, French and Danish pastries, and cream puffs are just a few of the other delights available.

Sonoma Sausage Company *453 First St. West, 707/938-8200; daily 10-5.* Over 70 kinds of lunch meats and sausage—including hot beer sausage, Nurnberger bratwurst, smoked Hawaiian Portugese sausage, and Kalbs leberwurst—are available here. They're all made with Old World techniques from 100 percent meat (no fillers), and some are smoked and ready to eat. German potato salad, sauerkraut, and herb bread are also available.

WHAT TO DO

Depot Park Museum *270 First St. East, 707/938-9755; W-Sun 1-4:30; adults 50¢, 10-18 25¢.* Operated by volunteers from the Sonoma Historical Society, this tiny museum is housed in the restored Northwestern Pacific Railroad Depot and features changing historical and railroad exhibits.

Adjacent **Depot Park** has a playground and picnic area. A bicycle path, which follows the old railroad tracks, originates here.

Sonoma Plaza. This town square, the largest in the state and a National Historic Landmark, was designed by General Vallejo in 1834 for troop maneuvers. Basically an old-fashioned park, it is great for picnics and has a playground and a tiny duck pond. City Hall, which is located here, acts as the Tuscany County Courthouse on TV's *Falcon Crest.*

Sonoma State Historic Park *located off the Plaza along Spain St., 707/938-1578; daily 10-5; adults $2, 6-12 $1.* This extensive park preserves structures dating from the early 1800s, when General Vallejo, founder of Sonoma, was Mexico's administrator of Northern California. The 2-story whitewashed adobe **Barracks,** which once housed Vallejo's soldiers, now contains historical exhibits. Vallejo drilled his soldiers across the street in what is now the town square.

Next door and across the street from the Barracks is the re-created **Mission San Francisco Solano.** Founded in 1823 and the most northerly and last in the chain of California missions, this historic site has been through a lot. It was burned to the ground twice, was the victim of an Indian uprising, and was seriously damaged in the '06 quake. Then it went through a period of being used as a saloon, as a winery, and even as a hennery. Currently it exhibits a permanent collection of watercolors depicting each of California's 21 missions. The paintings were done in 1903 by Chris Jorgensen, who traveled from mission to mission via horse and buggy. An impressive old prickly pear cactus forest graces the mission courtyard, and the chapel is said to host a ghost.

General Vallejo's home, a Victorian Gothic with its original furnishings, is located 1 mile east. Shaded picnic tables and another giant prickly pear cactus garden are found here.

Sonoma Traintown Railroad *20264 Broadway, 707/938-3912; daily in summer 10:30-5, weekends rest of year; adults $2.60, 2-16 $1.90.* A miniature steam train winds through 10 acres during the 20-minute ride here. It passes through forests and tunnels and crosses both a 70-foot double truss bridge and a 50-foot steel girder bridge. During a 5-minute stop at a miniature mining town, where the train takes on water, riders enjoy the pleasures of a petting zoo inhabited by sheep, birds, and miniature horses. Picnic facilities are available.

Toscano Hotel *20 E. Spain St., 707/938-0510; tours on Sat & Sun 1-4, M 11-1; by donation.* This beautifully restored mining-era hotel was built in 1858.

Vasquez House *129 E. Spain St., in El Paseo de Sonoma, 707/938-0510; tours W-Sun 1-5; by donation.* Built in 1856, this refurbished woodframe house features a tearoom where visitors may relax over homemade pastries and a pot of tea.

WHAT TO DO NEARBY

Aeroschellville *23982 Arnold Dr., at the airport off Highway 121, 2 miles north of Sears Point Raceway, 707/938-2444; daily 9-5:30; $60-$130; reservations suggested.* An aerobatic ride in an authentic 1940 Stearman biplane, once used to train World War II combat pilots, is said to "top any rollercoaster ever built." Calmer scenic rides are also available, and old and antique planes may be viewed at the airport.

Jack London State Historic Park *2400 London Ranch Rd., Glen Ellen, 8 miles north of town off Highway 12, 707/938-5216; daily 9-dusk, museum 10-5; $5/car.* Located in the **Valley of the Moon,** this 800-acre park contains the ruins of Jack London's 26-

room **Wolf House** (reached via a pleasant 1/2-mile trail), his grave, and **The House of Happy Walls**—a museum built in his memory by his widow. It was all given to the state by London's nephew. (London, who wrote 191 short stories and 51 books, was once one of the highest paid authors in the country.)

Guided 1- and 2-hour horse rides, some with a picnic included, are available within the park. For information and reservations contact the **Sonoma Cattle Company** *(707/996-8566; riders must be 8 or older; $20/hour, $30/2 hours)*.

To get in the mood for this trek, read a London classic such as *The Call of the Wild* or *Martin Eden*. Or on the way to the park stop at the **Jack London Bookstore** *(14300 Arnold Dr., 707/996-2888; daily 10:30-5)*, where the owner can provide assistance in selecting a London title.

Morton's Warm Springs *1651 Warm Springs Rd., Kenwood, 10 miles north of town, 707/833-5511; May-Sept only, call for schedule; adults $3.50-$5, 2-11 $3-$4*. Two large pools and one toddler wading pool are filled each day with fresh mineral water averaging 86 to 88 degrees. Lifeguards are on duty. Facilities include picnic tables and barbecue pits, a snackbar, a large grassy area for sunbathing, a softball field, horseshoe pits, a basketball court, and two volleyball courts. A special teenage rec room is equipped with a juke box, Ping Pong tables, and pinball machines, and dressing rooms and lockers are also available. There are a few rules: no cutoffs in the pools; no glass allowed.

Sears Point International Raceway *Highways 37/121, 800/870-RACE, 707/938-8448; Feb-Nov only, call for schedule & ticket prices, under 12 free*. This is where to go to see car races. Facilities include a 2.52-mile course with 12 turns and a 1/4-mile drag strip. Concession stands dispense fast food, and an assortment of grassy hillsides provide perfect picnic perches.

Wine Country Wagons *Kenwood, 707/833-2724; $40/person; May-Oct only; reservations required*. Take a ride through the vineyards in a horse-drawn carriage. After traveling down a scenic back country road to the 110-year-old ranch house that is the meeting point, participants board their vehicle—perhaps a new Amish carriage with a surrey top or maybe a larger antique wagon. Life slows down as the wagon rolls bumpily along back roads and vineyard trails, pulled by the clip-clopping hooves of Belgian draft horses.

Stops are made at **Kenwood Vineyards and Winery** for tasting, at the not-yet-open **Kunde Estate Winery** for a look-see, and at the **Smothers Brothers Tasting Room** (see page 92). Then a stop is made at **Jake's Delicatessen** *(405 Warm Springs Rd., Kenwood, 707/833-1350; daily 8-7)* to pick up the superb picnic goods (delicious fried chicken, freshly baked breads, and unbelievably good cookies) for a picnic in a woodsy area known as the Magic Ring, located at the back of the proprietor's ranch.

WINERIES

Buena Vista Winery *18000 Old Winery Rd., 800/926-1266, 707/938-1266; tasting daily 10-5; tour daily at 2, in summer also at 11am*. Founded in 1857, this is California's oldest winery. A wonderful picnic area features tables shaded by stately old eucalyptus trees growing on the banks of a tiny brook. After tasting wines in the welcoming old Press House (don't miss the nutty Dry and Cream Sherrys, which are available only at the winery), select a bottle for a picnic outside. If kids are along, purchase a chilled bottle of Gewurztraminer grape juice for them. A variety of picnic supplies are also available in the winery's shop. Visitors park among the grapevines and take a short, pleasant walk in.

Chateau St. Jean Vineyards and Winery *8555 Highway 12, Kenwood, 10 miles north of town, 800/332-WINE, 707/833-4134; tasting daily 10-4:30; self-guided tour 10:30-4.* Built in 1975, this winery specializes in white varietals. The tasting room is in a 1920s chateau, and the grassy, shaded picnic area sports fountains and several fish ponds.

Gloria Ferrer Champagne Caves *23555 Highway 121, 707/996-7256; tasting daily 10:30-5:30, fee $2.50-$3.50/glass; tours 11-4, on the hour.* Located back from the highway atop a hill, this thoroughly modern winery provides tasters with views across the vineyards. In cooler weather, tasters may gaze from inside, warmed by a large fireplace.

Gundlach-Bundschu Winery *2000 Denmark St., another entrance is on Thornsberry Rd., 707/938-5277; tasting daily 11-4:30; no tours.* Located in the back-country, off a winding road about 3 miles from the plaza, this pioneer winery was established in 1858. Now the great-great grandson of German founder Jacob Gundlach's partner continues the tradition. Jim Bundschu and his winemakers produce wines they like to drink themselves—wines with intense varietal character. White wines tend to be dry and flavorful, reds dark and complex. Unique to the winery, the Kleinberger varietal, which is a kind of Riesling, is produced by vines brought over in 1860. It is sold only at the winery. Picnic tables are perched on a small hill overlooking a pond and the vineyards. When leaving, be sure to take the alternate road out. Each route provides different scenery.

Hacienda Winery *1000 Vineyard Lane, 707/938-3220; tasting daily 10-5; tours by appt.* Built in a Spanish Colonial style of architecture, this small winery has a charming tasting room. It is known for its Chardonnays and Pinot Noirs, and its Antares and Vintage Port are available only at the winery. Wine glasses may be borrowed to use during a picnic at one of the inviting tables shaded by giant oak trees.

Sebastiani Vineyards *389 Fourth St. East, 800/888-5532, 707/938-5532; tasting daily 10-5; tours daily 10:30-4.* This winery has been owned continuously by the same family since 1904—longer than any other in the country. It is best known for its Symphony and Pinot Noir Blanc, which are available only at the winery. While here, take time to view the world's largest collection of carved oak wine casks and a display across the street featuring an extensive collection of Indian mortars and pestles. A pleasant picnic area is also available.

Smothers Brothers Wine Store *9575 Highway 12, Kenwood, 707/833-1010; tasting daily 10-4:30, fee 25¢-50¢/taste; no tours.* Many people stop here just to see if Tommy is around. (Dick is no longer involved with the winery.) For those after the label's cachet, it is worth knowing that Smothers Brothers Wines are available only from this wine store. Yo-yos are also available for purchase, and a small shaded area is equipped with picnic tables.

Viansa Winery *25200 Arnold Dr., off Highway 121, 2 miles south of town, 707/935-4700; tasting and self-guided tours daily 10-5.* Built on top of a hill commanding magnificent views of the area, this winery opened in 1990. Owned by Sam Sebastiani and his wife Vicki (and named by merging the first two letters of their first names), this beautifully crafted Tuscan-style winery building was inspired by a monastery near Farneta, Italy. Noteworthy wines include the Barbera Blanc, a light blush wine perfect for picnics and sold only at the winery, and, of course, the Cabernet Sauvignons. They can be tasted in the state-of-the-art tasting room that features a magnificent "wall of wines" behind the tasting bar.

The combination tasting room/food hall is designed after one in Lucca, Italy, and the extraordinary food offerings almost overshadow the wines. Using Vicki's recipes, the kitchen staff prepares wonderful things packaged for picnics: country pâté, torta rustica, hot-sweet mustard, foccacia bread, a triple chocolate chunk cookie, tiramisu. Some of the items make use of produce from the winery's adjacent vegetable garden. On nice days, picnics may be enjoyed at the tables located outside on a knoll providing a panoramic view of the Sonoma and Napa Valleys. On cooler days, tables are available inside. Other goodies from the food hall include porcini mushroom tomato sauce (made with Viansa Cabernet Sauvignon) and spiced figs (made with Sonoma black mission figs and Viansa Cabernet Sauvignon using Vicki's grandmother's recipe).

The winery welcomes children and provides them with a complimentary souvenir balloon.

– Yountville –

VISITOR INFORMATION

Yountville Chamber of Commerce *P.O. Box 2064, Yountville 94599, 707/944-0904.*

GETTING THERE

Located approximately 60 miles north of San Francisco. Take Highway 101 to Highway 37 to Highway 121 to Highway 12 to Highway 29.

WHERE TO STAY

Bordeaux House *6600 Washington St., 800/677-6370, 707/944-2855; 6 rooms; $$-$$$; all bathtubs, fireplaces; continental breakfast.* This ultra-modern inn features a curved red-brick exterior and lush French- and English-style gardens.

Inn at Napa Valley *1075 California Blvd., Napa, 800/433-4600, 707/253-9540; 205 units; 123 non-smoking units; $$$-$$$$+; children under 12 free; cribs; all kitchens, bathtubs; indoor heated pool, hot tub, sauna; full breakfast, restaurant (fall only), room service (special children's items).* Originally part of the nation-wide chain of Embassy Suites, this lodging is now part of the Crown Sterling Suites chain. Each suite has a bedroom, front room with hide-a-bed, and kitchenette. Further amenities include two TVs and complimentary evening drinks. Breakfast is the all-you-can-eat variety with eggs cooked to order, bacon, sausage, pancakes, fried potatoes, toast, fresh fruit, muffins, cereals, and beverages. It may be enjoyed either in a pleasant indoor atrium or outside by a pond inhabited with ducks and both black and white swans.

♥Magnolia Hotel *6529 Yount St., 800/788-0369, 707/944-2056; 12 rooms; 100% non-smoking; $$-$$$$+; 2-night minimum on weekends Apr-Nov; some bathtubs, fireplaces; full breakfast; heated pool (unheated Nov-Apr), hot tub.* Located in the center of town, this rustic 3-story building was built as a hotel in 1873. Rooms, some of which are located in several adjacent buildings, are decorated with Victorian antiques. Guests are greeted with a complimentary decanter of Port in their room and may order from a wine cellar stocked with over 12,000 bottles.

Napa Valley Lodge *Highway 29/Madison, 800/368-2468, 707/944-2468; 55 rooms; 28 non-smoking rooms; $$$-$$$$+; cribs; all bathtubs; some fireplaces; heated pool, hot tub, sauna, exercise room; continental breakfast.* Located on the outskirts of town, this Spanish-style motel is across the street from a park and playground. Each room has a private patio or balcony.

Napa Valley Railway Inn *6503 Washington St., 707-944-2000; $$-$$$$+; 2-night minimum on weekends; children under 7 free; no TVs; some bathtubs.* Railroad enthusiasts are sure to enjoy a night in a brass bed at this unusual lodging facility. Three cabooses and six railcars—authentic turn-of-the-century specimens sitting on the original town tracks—have been whimsically converted into comfortable suites complete with private bath, sitting area, and skylight. Guests are greeted with a chilled bottle of wine.

Should hunger strike, the town's original depot, now a hamburger haven known as **The Vintage Cafe,** is just a few steps away.

Silverado Country Club and Resort *1600 Atlas Peak Rd., Napa, 15 miles south of town, 800/532-0500, 707/257-0200; 280 units; 25 non-smoking units; $$-$$$+; children under 14 free; cribs; all kitchens, fireplaces; some bathtubs; 1 heated pool, 7 unheated pools, hot tub, sauna, 23 tennis courts (fee/3 with night lights); 3 restaurants, room service (special children's items).* Once part of General Vallejo's Rancho Yajome, this 1200-acre resort is now the largest tennis complex in Northern California. Its heart is a gracious 1875 mansion, where guests are greeted and registered and within which are the resort's two restaurants. Though all accommodations are in individually-owned condominiums, the location, architectural style, and decor of each vary. Some units are available on the grounds adjacent to the mansion. Staying in one of these allows an easy walk to most of the facilities. Larger condos, some opening right onto the golf course, are further away and require a drive of 1 or 2 miles. Facilities include jogging trails, and two 18-hole golf courses designed by Robert Trent Jones, Jr.

The romantic **Royal Oak** restaurant offers a surf & turf menu and a classic Caesar salad, prepared table-side. A complimentary chocolate fondue dessert and choice of cordial from a vast collection is included with each entree. A casual **Bar & Grill** serves breakfast all day, as well as lighter fare such as salads and hamburgers.

Vintage Inn *6541 Washington St., 800/351-1133, 707/944-1112, fax 707/944-1617; 80 rooms; 60 non-smoking rooms; $$$-$$$+; 2-night minimum on Sat Apr-Nov; cribs; all bathtubs, fireplaces; heated pool, hot tub, 2 tennis courts; continental breakfast.* This attractive modern lodging facility is centrally located next to Vintage 1870. In summer, bicycles are available for guests to rent.

WHERE TO EAT

The Diner *6476 Washington St., 707/944-2626; B, L, & D Tu-Sun; closed last 2 weeks in Dec; $; highchairs, booster seats, children's portions; 100% non-smoking; no reservations; no cards.* This unpretentious spot offers counter seating as well as tables and booths. California-ized Mexican specialties enhance the cafe menu, and all items are made with quality ingredients. Breakfast choices include the house specialty of crispy cornmeal pancakes served with smoky links, as well as potato pancakes, homemade sausage patties, and old-fashioned oatmeal. At lunch it's hamburgers, sandwiches, and soda fountain treats, among them an unusual buttermilk shake said to taste like liquid cheesecake. Dinners include an excellent flauta entree and, in season, a dessert cobbler made with fresh apricots and blackberries and topped with a scoop of vanilla ice cream.

♥**Domaine Chandon** *1 California Dr., 800/236-2892, 707/944-2892; L daily May-Oct, D W-Sun; $$$; 100% non-smoking; reservations suggested; AE, MC, V.* The spacious, elegant dining room at this winery is lovely, but in good weather the terrace is the premier spot to be seated. Chef Philippe Jeanty, who has been with the restaurant since it opened, prepares an innovative California-style menu that reflects his French Champagne heritage. Dishes are designed especially to complement the winery's sparkling wines. Specialties include home-smoked red trout, oven-roasted eggplant soup, and mussels steamed in Pinot Meunier. The dessert selection is exciting and extensive. In addition to the winery's own sparkling wines, available by the glass, the wine list includes still varietals from neighboring vintners. Men are required to wear jackets at dinner. See also page 98.

♥**The French Laundry** *6640 Washington St., 707/944-2380; D W-Sun; closed part of Jan; $$$; reservations essential; no cards.* This attractive old stone building was indeed once a French laundry. With only one seating, the dining pace is leisurely, and a stroll in the garden between courses is encouraged. The kitchen specializes in freshly prepared, innovative cuisine and serves a fixed-price *($46)* five-course dinner with a choice of appetizer and dessert. For example, one dinner menu featured sorrel soup, duckling with curry glaze, a green salad, and cheeses. The appetizer choices were an artichoke with garlic mayonnaise, cold sliced veal with salsa verde, smoked tuna and potatoes on arugula, or shrimp in beer with red pepper sauce. Dessert choices were coffee pot de creme, peach ice cream with fruit, plum cobbler, or raspberries in a chocolate meringue. The wine list features only the best local vintages.

Mustards *7399 Highway 29, 707/944-2424; L & D daily; $$; booster seats; reservations essential; MC, V.* The best place to be seated at this popular bar and grill, where tables are set with crisp white nappery, is the cool, screened porch. The atmosphere is casual and chic and the menu imaginative. Selections include soups, salads, and sandwiches (a winning grilled ahi tuna with basil mayonnaise, a good hamburger) as well as entrees such as barbecued baby backribs, mesquite-grilled Sonoma rabbit, and marinated skirt steak. Fresh fish specials are also available. The thin, light onion rings are superb, and homemade ketchup can be ordered to go with them. Garlic lovers will be pleased with a roasted head to spread on their complimentary baguette. Varietal wines are available by the glass. Rich desserts, among them a good bread pudding, and specialty coffees invite lingering.

The **Cosentino Winery** (*7415 St. Helena Highway, 707/944-1220; tasting daily 10-5, $2 fee, applies to purchase or keep tasting glass; self-guided tour*) is located just next door. Built in 1990, this winery is known for producing the country's first designated Meritage wine. Referred to as The Poet, this wine is composed of a wonderful blend of Cabernet Sauvignon, Cabernet Franc, and Merlot. It is pleasant to reserve a picnic lunch from Mustards to enjoy at the winery's bocce ball court-side tables.

Ristorante Piatti *6480 Washington St., 707/944-2070; L & D daily; $$; reservations essential.* This is the original Piatti. For description, see page 88.

WHAT TO DO

Hot Air Balloon Rides. Tour the Napa Valley via hot air ballon. Trips average 1 hour in the air; altitude and distance depend on which way the wind blows.

Adventures Aloft (*6525 Washington St., in Vintage 1870, 707/255-8688; $165; reservations necessary*) includes a before-flight continental breakfast, an after-flight champagne brunch celebration, and a flight certificate.

Napa Valley Balloons *(6795 Washington St., 800/253-2224, 707/253-2224; $165, children under 8 $82.50)* offers a similar experience, plus balloon pins and photos of the launch or landing.

Napa Valley Wine Train *1275 McKinstry St., Napa, 800/427-4124, 707/253-2111; daily; closed 1st week in Jan; $29; reservations required.* This leisurely 36-mile excursion lasts 3 hours and takes passengers through the heart of the Wine Country. Unfortunately, passengers can't get off to visit any wineries. At additional charge, passengers are served Saturday or Sunday brunch ($22), lunch ($22-$25), or dinner ($45) on board. They dine in opulent dining cars outfitted with the refined pleasures of damask linen, bone china, silver flatware, and etched crystal. A special car for families with young children is added on weekends. The fare is $20, with children under 8 riding free, and an inexpensive a la carte menu is available.

Vintage 1870 *6525 Washington St., 707/944-2451; daily 10-5:30.* This lovely old brick building, a former winery, now houses a number of interesting specialty shops and restaurants. Antique wine glasses can be purchased at the **Golden Eagle Bazaar.** The **Yountville Pastry Shop,** an European-style bakery, offers breads, fancy pastries, and tiny quiches as well as coffee. **Cooks' Corner Deli** has picnic supplies, **Gerhards Sausage Kitchen** a variety of fresh sausages made without nitrates (which can be packed on ice to travel), and **The Chocolate Tree** ice cream concoctions and delicious homemade candies. The 15-minute **Napa Valley Show,** which follows the seasons in the vineyards with slides and music, is offered daily in the Keith Rosenthal Theatre. Hot air balloons can often be viewed from the children's play area outside.

Wild Horse Valley Ranch *at end of Coombsville Rd., Napa, 20 miles southeast of town off Highway 121, 707/224-0727; W-M 8-5; reservations necessary; riders must be at least age 8.* Two-hour trail rides ($25) are scheduled three times daily. Rope-led ponies ($9/half-hour, $12/hour) are available for children under 8.

WINERIES

Chateau Potelle Winery *3875 Mt. Veeder Rd., Napa, 707/255-9440; tasting Thur-M 12-5; no tours.* Reached via a scenic back country road that was just recently paved, this winery features a picnic area with tables overlooking the vineyards. (To get to the winery, which is about 3.5 miles from Oakville, take the Oakville Grade west and turn left on Mt. Veeder Road.)

Domaine Chandon *1 California Dr., 707/944-2280; daily May-Oct, W-Sun Nov-Apr; tasting 11-6, fee; tours 11-5:30.* This attractive French-owned winery specializes in sparkling wines produced by the traditional methode champenoise. It is reached by crossing a wooden bridge spanning a scenic duck pond surrounded by beautiful grounds. Built with stones gathered on the site, its arched roofs and doorways were inspired by the caves in Champagne, France. For tasting, visitors are seated at tiny tables covered with French floral cloths in the **Vins Le Salon.** Sparkling wine may be purchased by the glass, and a variety of sparkling wine cocktails are also available. Complimentary bread and cheese are provided to help keep things steady. Children are allowed in the salon and can order mineral water or orange juice. See also page 95.

The Hess Collection Winery *4411 Redwood Rd., Napa, 707/255-1144; tasting daily 10-4, fee $2.50; self-guided tours; gallery admission free.* Located on the slopes of Mt.

Veeder, off a road that winds first through the suburbs and then through scenic woods, this unusual winery is owned by Swiss entrepreneur Donald Hess. Here he grows grapes in rocky soil on steep, terraced hillsides and turns them into premium wines. Built in 1903, the winery was also the original Napa Valley home for the Christian Brothers. Extensively remodeled, it features its original stone walls and a stunning 13,000-square-foot art gallery. The gallery's eclectic collection holds 130 contemporary paintings and sculptures, including works by Robert Motherwell and Frank Stella as well as an absolutely stunning 129-foot by 114-foot portrait by Swiss artist Franz Gertsch entitled "Johanna II." At various points in the galleries, portholes look into rooms where steel fermentation tanks and bottling machines are located. Visitors may also view a 12-minute narrated slide presentation of the winemaking operations. The winery is known for its Chardonnay and Cabernet Sauvignon, and its Mt. Veeder Estate Merlot is available for purchase only at the winery. Valser mineral water from Switzerland is provided to children accompanying their tasting parents.

THE SILVERADO TRAIL

Stretching approximately 60 miles from Napa to Calistoga, this scenic route offers a quieter, less-crowded wine tasting experience. The wineries described here are listed in sequential order, beginning in Napa.

Pine Ridge Winery *5901 Silverado Trail, 707/253-7500; tasting daily 11-4, fee $2.50, applies to purchase or keep tasting glass; tours at 11 & 4, also at 10:15 & 2:15 by appt.* The tiny tasting room here is a pleasant place to sample the premium Cabernets produced by this winery's Stags Leap regional grapes. A pleasant picnic area is situated under a young grove of tall pines; two board swings await the kiddies.

Rutherford Hill Winery *200 Rutherford Hill Dr., Rutherford, 800/726-5226, 707/963-7194; tasting daily 10-4:30, fee $3, keep tasting glass; tours daily at 11:30, 12:30, 1:30, 2:30, and 3:30.* Visitors pass through massive 15-foot-tall doors as they enter the tasting room here. The tour includes seeing the most extensive wine-aging cave system in the U.S. A sylvan hillside picnic area, with spacious tables sheltered by old oaks and a pleasant view of the valley, beckons across the street from the tasting room.

Mumm Napa Valley *8445 Silverado Trail, Rutherford, 707/963-3434; tasting daily 10:30-6, fee $3.50/flute; tours hourly 10:30-4:30.* In good weather tasters may sample Brut Prestige and Blanc de Noirs while sitting under umbrellas on a patio that provides a magnificent view of the valley's vineyards.

– St. Helena –

VISITOR INFORMATION

St. Helena Chamber of Commerce *P.O. Box 124 (1080 Main St.), St. Helena 94574, 800/767-8528, 707/963-4456.*

Note: St. Helena Highway, Main Street, and Highway 29 are all the same road.

GETTING THERE

Located approximately 15 miles north of Yountville via Highway 29.

ANNUAL EVENTS

Napa Valley Wine Auction *June; events held throughout the valley, 707/963-5246.* Though tickets run $800 per couple, this 4-day event usually sells out early. Its popularity may be explained by the fact that many winemakers open their homes and wineries to unique public events in the interest of helping to raise money for local health centers. For example, one year the Rutherford Hill Winery hosted a refined candlelight dinner in their hillside caves, while Stag's Leap Wine Cellars hosted a festive Greek dinner and dancing extravaganza in their courtyard. A Friday night Vintner Dinner and Saturday afternoon auction take place at the lush Meadowood Resort.

Robert Mondavi Summer Festival *July & August; in Oakville, 707/963-9617.* Ah, the pleasure of sitting on the grass, surrounded by vineyards and rolling foothills, while listening to great jazz. The entertainers (who in the past have included Ella Fitzgerald, Al Hirt, and the Preservation Hall Jazz Band—on the same bill!) probably enjoy the dusk concerts as much as their audience. After an intermission featuring wine and cheese tasting, the concerts conclude under the stars. Picnics are encouraged, and catered picnics are available by advance reservation. Ticketholders may begin selecting seats at 4:30. The winery's retail shop remains open until 7, when the concerts begin.

This winery also hosts a **Great Chefs at the Robert Mondavi Winery** series each year. Both 1-day and weekend-long formats are scheduled. The $750 and up fee includes meals and cooking classes, plus demonstrations by world-famous chefs. Call for current details.

WHERE TO STAY

♥**Ambrose Bierce House** *1515 Main St., 707/963-3003; 3 rooms; 100% non-smoking; $$-$$$; 2-night minimum on Sat; unsuitable for children under 12; no TVs; some bathtubs; continental breakfast.* Named after the witty author who wrote *The Devil's Dictionary* and whose life was portrayed in the movie *The Old Gringo*, this 1872 house was once Ambrose Bierce's home. One pleasantly decorated room is named after Eadweard Muybridge, who is known as the "father of the motion picture" and who was a friend of Bierce's. The room holds two interesting artifacts—an 1897 Eastman Kodak No. 2 Hawk-eye camera and a Smith and Wesson No. 2 that is just like the one Muybridge used in 1874 to shoot his wife's lover. Located at the northern end of town, the inn is within convenient walking distance of shopping and dining.

El Bonita Motel *195 Main St., 800/541-3284, 707/963-3216; 41 rooms; 7 non-smoking rooms; $-$$$; 2-night minimum on weekends; cribs; some kitchens, bathtubs; heated pool, hot tub, sauna; continental breakfast; some pets welcome.* Featuring an art deco decor, this motel has a shaded, grassy pool area and offers an alternative to classy, cutesy, and expensive Wine Country lodgings.

Harvest Inn *One Main St., 800/950-8466, 707/963-WINE; 54 rooms; $$$-$$$+; 2-night minimum on weekends; cribs; all bathtubs; some fireplaces; 2 heated pools, 2 hot tubs; continental breakfast; small dogs welcome.* Situated on a 21-acre working vineyard, this modern English Tudor-style inn has beautifully landscaped grounds. Rooms are furnished with antiques.

♥La Fleur *1475 Inglewood Ave., 707/963-0233; 5 rooms; 100% non-smoking; $$$; 2-night minimum on weekends; unsuitable for children under 12; no TVs; all fireplaces; some claw-foot bathtubs; full breakfast.* Set back from the main highway, this Queen Anne Victorian B&B is real quiet. An extensive rose garden invites relaxing, and each of the spacious rooms features a different decor. Breakfast is served in a cheery solarium with vineyard views, and sometimes guests are able to see hot air balloons floating above.

It's just a short stroll through the flower garden to the tiny **Villa Helena Winery** *(1455 Inglewood Ave., 707/963-4334; tasting & tours by appt.)* located next door. Call ahead to alert the owner, a former metallurgical engineer from Los Angeles, so that he can be in his office to assist with tasting his Chardonnays and unusual Viognier white varietal. He also provides what he calls "the shortest tour in the Napa Valley."

Meadowood Resort & Hotel *900 Meadowood Lane, 800/458-8080, 707/963-3646; 98 units; $$$+; 2-night minimum on weekends; children under 12 free; cribs; some kitchens,*

bathtubs, fireplaces; 2 heated pools, 6 tennis courts (fee); 2 restaurants, room service. This luxury resort allows guests an escape from reality. A variety of cabins provide plenty of privacy and are scattered throughout the property. Facilities on the 256 acres of lush, wooded grounds include a 9-hole golf course, a children's playground, two professional-size croquet lawns, and 3 miles of hiking trails.

The resort also operates a **Wine School.** A package that includes classes, winery tours, meals, and lodging is available.

♥**Villa St. Helena** *2727 Sulphur Springs Ave., 707/963-2514; 3 rooms; $$$-$$$+; 2-night minimum on weekends; unsuitable for children under 12; no TVs; some bathtubs, fireplaces; continental breakfast.* Movie stars reputedly know how to live: in style, in comfort, in seclusion. This Mediterranean-style inn, situated on a 20-acre country estate, offers all of these things. Perhaps that is why it is easy to believe the rumors bandied about regarding past guests. *BIG* names from the heyday of Hollywood. After passing through a closed, privacy-preserving gate, guests follow a scenic, winding back country road, arriving in a large gravel area fronting the estate's arched garages. Once inside the villa, it is a surprisingly long walk, over expanses of shining Mexican terra cotta tile that appear to go on forever, to the three spacious bedchambers. A bottle of Robert Pepi Sauvignon Blanc and a jar of tasty, precious pickled quail eggs—prepared on the premises from eggs laid by the villa's own quail flock—await to refresh. This roomy retreat is unpretentiously furnished in eclectic period furniture and features a comfortable library in the west wing, a very large breakfast room/solarium and living room in the center area, and a formal dining room (not used by guests) in the east wing. The three wings surround a grassy center courtyard, which abuts a landscaped hillside and boasts a large, inviting pool. Nights here are very, very quiet.

♥**The Wine Country Inn** *1152 Lodi Lane, 800/473-3463, 707/963-7077; 24 rooms; $$-$$$+; 2-night minimum on some rooms; unsuitable for children under 13; no TVs; some fireplaces (usable Oct-Apr only); solar-heated pool, hot tub; continental breakfast.* Built in the style of a New England inn, without a lot of fuss and frill, this attractive, quiet lodging is located back from the main highway on top of a small country hill. Rooms are decorated with floral wallpapers and tasteful antiques, and many have views of the surrounding vineyards and hills. A filling breakfast, served on attractive handmade crockery, includes homemade granola and breads.

WHERE TO EAT

♥**Auberge du Soleil** *180 Rutherford Hill Rd., Rutherford, 800/348-5406, 707/963-1211; B, L, & D daily; $$$; highchairs, children's portions; 100% non-smoking inside; reservations suggested; AE, MC, V.* Located just off The Silverado Trail, this elegant French restaurant has plush inside seating as well as more rustic outside seating on a veranda overlooking the valley. Fresh local ingredients are used in the preparation of such items as seared ahi tuna with creamy polenta, olive oil, and balsamic vinaigrette, or sauteed duck liver with wild mushrooms, huckleberries, and bok choy. Sandy Walker was the architect, Michael Taylor the interior designer.

A luxury resort is attached. Call for more information.

Brava Terrace Restaurant *3010 St. Helena Highway N., 707/963-9300; L & D daily; $$; MC, V.* On warm afternoons and evenings this spot's casual deck seating, amid trees and a gurgling creek, is highly desirable. A great hamburger shares the menu along with a cassoulet (made with green lentils imported from Puy, France) and both a pasta and risotto du jour. Desserts include an apple-raisin strudel with Tahitian vanilla bean cream and a chocolate chip creme brulee. Coffees and dessert wines are also available.

Gillwoods *1313 Main St., 707/963-1788; B & L daily, D F-Sun July-Nov; $; highchairs, booster seats; 100% non-smoking.* This comfortable downtown cafe is known for its breakfasts. All kinds of egg dishes and an assortment of three-egg omelettes are on the menu, as is preservative-free Mother Lode bacon and toasted home-baked bread. And then there's corned-beef hash, buttermilk pancakes, French toast, hot cereals, and granola. Beginning at 11 a.m., soups and sandwiches are also available.

Rizza Oriental Cafe *1420 Main St., 707/963-7566; L & D M-Sat; $; booster seats; 100% non-smoking; MC, V.* Owned and operated by chef Hiro Sone of Terra, this less formal spot serves an eclectic menu of Asian dishes. Absolute winners include gyoza (sauteed and steamed Japanese pork dumplings), satay (grilled Indonesian-style skewered beef), and Chinese chicken salad. All are flavorful and distinctive. Roasted barley iced tea makes a refreshing drink, and a large chunk of moist ginger cake, made with fresh ginger, is not to be missed for dessert.

♥**Terra** *1345 Railroad Ave., 707/963-8931; D W-M; closed mid-Feb to mid-Mar; $$$; 100% non-smoking; reservations suggested; MC, V.* Fronted by planter boxes filled with gorgeous flowers, this trendy spot has a stone-walled, cave-like interior and offers a cool respite from the area's often warm weather. Menu selections offered by owner/chef Hiro Sone, formerly of Spago in Los Angeles, are unusual and flavorful and change periodically: radicchio salad tossed with a balsamic vinaigrette and lots of Parmesan; grilled sea bass with a fennel-tomato ragout and lemon-herb butter sauce; salmon with red chili-coriander sauce; sumptious fresh fruits topped with crème frâiche.

Tra Vigne *1050 Charter Oak Ave., 707/963-4444; L & D daily; $$; reservations suggested; MC, V.* Situated in a rustic stone building, with a stunning high-ceilinged room that is furnished with both comfortable tables and booths, this popular restaurant specializes in northern Italian cuisine. Outside seating, which is quite desirable on warm days, is available on a stone patio that was once part of the now defunct St. Helena Winery. A round of crusty bread and some olive oil for dipping are provided to enjoy while perusing the menu. Pastas and pizzas share the menu with fresh fish, meats, and poultry. The antipasti items and daily specials are often intriguing, the sandwiches can be exquisite, and the desserts include such goodies as fresh fruit gelato and biscotti with sweet wine. Wine varietals are available by the glass and include both local and Italian selections.

Stop in next door at the **Merryvale Vineyards** *(1000 Main St., 707/963-7777; tasting daily 10-5:30, $3 fee, applies to purchase; no tours)* to do some tasing. A courtyard, with a soothing fountain and bocce ball court, are situated at the tasting room entrance.

PICNIC PICK-UPS

The Model Bakery *1357 Main St., 707/963-8192; Tu-Sat 7-5:30.* Among the great breads baked in an old-fashioned brick oven here are pain de campagne (half-wheat, half-sourdough), sour rye, crusty sourdough, and both sweet baguettes and rounds. Then there are croissants stuffed with either ham and cheese or spinach and Feta cheese, wedges of Brie, and pizza by the slice. Chocolate chocolate chip cookies, oatmeal-raisin cookies, and biscotti make pleasing desserts, and coffee and espresso drinks are also available. A few tables are provided for on-the-spot indulgence.

Napa Valley Olive Oil Manufacturing Co. *835 McCorkle Ave. (Charter Oak/ Allison), 707/963-4173; daily 8-5.* Everything needed for a picnic is available here: cheese, sausage, olives, bread sticks, focaccia, biscotti. This Old World-style Italian deli also offers a variety of pastas, sauces, and dried mushrooms, plus its own cold-pressed olive oil and homemade red wine vinegar—all placed helter-skelter in barrels and on make-shift tables. It's really quite unusual. A picnic area is provided outside.

Oakville Grocery *7856 Highway 29, Oakville, 707/944-8802; daily 10-6.* Everything needed to put together a fantastic gourmet picnic can be found here. Select from a large variety of mustards, vinegars, jams, fresh fruits, imported beers, mineral waters, natural juices, cheeses, and other deli items, as well as smoked poissons, cornichons, sausages, and a large assortment of enticing desserts. If the choice seems overwhelming, call 48 hours in advance to order a pre-packed picnic box.

Pometta's Deli *7787 Highway 29, on Oakville Grade, Oakville, 707/944-2365; W-Sat 10-6, Sun 10-4.* Located just off busy Highway 29, this down-home-style deli has been operating here since 1952. Known for its wine-marinated barbecued chicken, it also offers a limited selection of made-to-order sandwiches, homemade salads, and cold soft drinks. Informal indoor and outdoor seating is available.

WHAT TO DO

Bale Grist Mill State Historic Park *3369 Highway 29, 3 miles north of town, 707/963-2236; daily 10-5; $5/car.* Reached via a shaded, paved stream-side path, this grist mill ground grain for farmers from the 1840s through the turn of the century. The damp site and slow-turning millstones were reputedly responsible for the exceptional cornmeal produced here. Now interpretive displays are located inside the gable-roofed mill house, and the 36-foot diameter water wheel has been restored to full operation. Corn and wheat are ground at 1 and 4 p.m. on weekends and are available for purchase. Picnic tables are provided in several shaded areas.

Dansk Factory Outlet *801 Main St., 707/963-4273; daily 10-6.* For description see page 47.

Lake Berryessa *take Highway 128 east, 707/966-2111.* This man-made lake is over 25 miles long, 3 miles wide, and has 165 miles of shoreline. Boats and water-skis may be rented, and the swimming and fishing are excellent. Camping and lodging facilities are also available.

The Silverado Museum *1490 Library Lane, 707/963-3757; Tu-Sun 12-4; free.* This museum contains over 8,500 pieces of Robert Louis Stevenson memorabilia. There are paintings, sculptures, and manuscripts as well as his childhood set of lead soldiers. Consider a family read-in of *A Child's Garden of Verses* or *Treasure Island* before or after this visit. The modern stucco library building, situated on the edge of a scenic vineyard, also contains the **Napa Valley Wine Library.**

WINERIES

Beaulieu Vineyard *1960 St. Helena Highway, Rutherford, 707/963-2411; tasting & tours daily 10-5.* Founded in 1900 by Frenchman Georges deLatour, this winery is known for its Cabernet Sauvignons and Chardonnays. A $3.75 fee is charged for a special tasting of old wines.

Beringer Vineyards *2000 Main St., just north of town, 707/963-4812; tours every half-hour, daily 9:30-4; free tasting follows tour.* Established in 1876, this winery's Visitor Center is located in a beautiful oak-paneled, stained-glass-laden reproduction of a 19th century German Tudor mansion known as the Rhine House. Its tour is considered to be one of the most historically informative. The winery is noted for its Chardonnays and Cabernet Sauvignons, and its best vintages may be tasted in the Founder's Room for a $2 to $3 per sample tasting fee. Unfortunately, picnicking is not permitted on the beautifully landscaped grounds.

Christian Brothers *2555 Main St., just north of town, 707/963-0763; tasting Thur-M 10-5, fee $2; self-guided tour.* This magnificent landmark winery building is constructed of locally quarried volcanic stone. **Brother Timothy's corkscrew collection,** which consists of over 1,800 corkscrews, is on display. The winery is known for its Zinfandels, Cabernet Sauvignons, and Chardonnays.

Freemark Abbey *3022 St. Helena Highway N., 707/963-9694; tasting daily 10-4:30, fee $5, applies to wine purchase or keep tasting glass; tour at 2.* The large, lodge-like tasting room here has oriental carpets covering its hardwood floor. Comfortable furniture arranged around a fireplace invites leisurely sampling. The winery is noted for its Chardonnays and Cabernet Sauvignons. A picnic area is provided to purchasers of wine.

Next door, **Hurd Beeswax Candles** *(3020 St. Helena Highway N., 707/963-7211; daily 10-5)* operates in an old stone building constructed in 1896. The factory is open to view, and an active beehive, hidden behind two wooden window covers, can be observed.

Spring Mountain Vineyards *2805 Spring Mountain Rd., 707/963-5517; tasting daily 10-4:45; tours by appt. (weekdays at 10:30 & 2:30, weekends 10:30); grounds tour daily 11-4, on the hour, $4/person.* Located off the main highway on a scenic back road, this winery is known for the Victorian manor house made famous in the opening scenes of TV's *Falcon Crest.* The house, a private residence, is not included on the grounds tour, but its exterior can be viewed from the tasting room. The winery is known for its pricey Chardonnays and Cabernet Sauvignons, but a bonus with some of the less expensive bottlings is a label sporting a picture of the celebrity house. Unfortunately, no picnicking is allowed on the scenic, spacious grounds.

Vichon Winery *1595 Oakville Grade, Oakville, 707/944-2811; tasting daily 10-4:30; tours Sat & Sun at 11, 1, & 3.* After driving about a mile up this scenic side road off busy Highway 29, visitors are greeted by an informal tasting room and shaded picnic tables with a beautiful vineyard view.

V. Sattui Winery *1111 White Lane, 707/963-7774; tasting & self-guided tour daily 9-5.* Established in the North Beach area of San Francisco in 1885, this winery was shut down during Prohibition, then re-established in St. Helena in 1976. Family-owned for four generations, the current winemaker is the great-grandson of founder Vittorio Sattui. V. Sattui wines are sold only at the winery. The Johannisberg Rieslings and Cabernet Sauvignons that they are best known for may be tasted in the stone winery building featuring 3-foot-thick walls and chiseled archways. Picnic supplies are available in a well-stocked deli that claims to have the largest selection of international cheeses on the West Coast. Plenty of oak-shaded picnic tables are provided on a 2-acre picnic grounds.

– Calistoga –

A LITTLE BACKGROUND

Often referred to as "the Hot Springs of the West," Calistoga sits on top of a hot underground river. The town's name originated from a combination of California and Saratoga—a spa area in New York. More of the town's history is to be discovered in *The Silverado Squatters* by Robert Louis Stevenson.

Calistoga is enjoying a renaissance as a popular weekend and summer retreat. Its many unpretentious spas are geared to helping visitors relax, unwind, and get healthy in pools filled from hot springs. Most offer services such as mud baths, steam baths, and massages, and many make their mineral pools available for day use for a small fee.

While here, don't miss taking a **mud bath,** one of life's great experiences. The mud is prepared using a mixture of volcanic ash (collected from nearby Mount St. Helena), peat moss, and naturally heated mineral water. After a period of nude immersion, the bather takes a mineral bath and a steam bath, and then, swaddled in dry blankets, rests and cools. Ahhh. (Note that pregnant women, people with high blood pressure or heart conditions, and children under 14 are cautioned against taking mud baths.)

VISITOR INFORMATION

Calistoga Chamber of Commerce *1458 Lincoln Ave., Calistoga 94515, 707/942-6333.*

GETTING THERE

Located approximately 10 miles north of St. Helena via Highway 29.

WHERE TO STAY

Calistoga Spa Hot Springs *1006 Washington St., 707/942-6269; 57 units; $$; 2-night minimum on weekends; cribs; all kitchens; 3 hot spring pools, hot tub, exercise room.* This conveniently located, unpretentious, and particularly family-friendly spa offers both motel rooms and cottages, all of which open onto the pool area. Three mineral water pools are available: a 100-degree soaking pool, an 83-degree swimming pool, and a 90-degree children's wading pool. Mud baths, mineral baths, steam baths, and massage are available.

Dr. Wilkinson's Hot Springs *1507 Lincoln Ave., 707/942-4102; 42 rooms; 18 non-smoking rooms; $-$$; 2-night minimum on weekends; cribs; some kitchens; 1 indoor heated pool, 2 outdoor heated pools, hot tub, steam room.* Operated by the Wilkinson family, this pleasant spa features an indoor 104-degree mineral pool with a view of the nearby foothills, a cooler 92-degree outdoor mineral pool, and a refreshing 82-degree outdoor swimming pool. Pools are not open to non-guests. Mud baths, mineral baths, steam baths, and massage are available, and a separate facial salon offers an assortment of treatments. Lodging is in motel units. Cottages that are unsuitable for children are also available nearby.

Indian Springs Spa & Resort *1712 Lincoln Ave., 707/942-4913; 17 units; $$-$$$; 2-night minimum on weekends; cribs; all kitchens, bathtubs; some fireplaces; heated mineral water pool, children's wading pool.* Built on the site of the town's first resort (which was built in 1860 by Sam Brannan—California's first Gold Rush millionaire), this resort is where Robert Louis Stevenson vacationed in 1880 and is said to have written part of *The Silverado Squatters*. The spa facilities include an Olympic-size

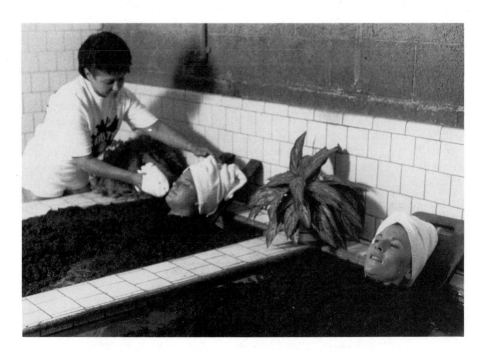

swimming pool filled with 90-degree geyser mineral water; it is open to non-guests for day use *(adults $7-$15, children $5-$7)* and is especially popular with children. Accommodations are 1930s housekeeping cottages. Croquet, a children's playground, and loaner bicycles are available to guests.

Mountain Home Ranch *3400 Mountain Home Ranch Rd., 6 miles from town, 707/942-6616; 14 units; $$-$$$; 2-night minimum in July & Aug; closed Dec & Jan; cribs; no TVs; some kitchens, bathtubs, fireplaces; unheated pool (unavailable Nov-Apr), 1 tennis court; continental breakfast & restaurant (Sept-June only).* Guests at this informal rural spot stay in their choice of modern cabins with either a private deck or porch, lodge rooms, or rustic cabins (summer only) for which they provide their own bedding and linens. Summer activities include swimming, hiking, and fishing. Rates are higher in summer and include both breakfast and dinner.

♥**Mount View Hotel** *1457 Lincoln Ave., 707/942-6877; 33 rooms; $$-$$$+; 2-night minimum on weekends May-Oct; cribs; some bathtubs; heated pool, hot tub, sauna; continental breakfast, 2 restaurants.* This beautifully restored hotel, built in 1918 and decorated in a '30s art deco style, is a National Historic Monument. Nine themed suites are furnished in period pieces, and three private cottages have their own decks and hot tubs. An upscale European-style spa offers a variety of treatments, and packages are available.

The main restaurant serves breakfast, lunch, and dinner daily and offers an imaginative menu of California cuisine as well as spectacular desserts. In good weather mesquite barbecues are held in the attractive outdoor pool area, and live music is often scheduled in the classy chrome-and-black decorated lounge. Special events centered around food and wine are held regularly. Call for more information.

WHERE TO EAT

All Seasons Cafe and Wine Shop *1400 Lincoln Ave., 707/942-9111; L Thur-Tu, D Thur-M, Sat & SunBr; $$-$$$; highchairs, booster seats; reservations suggested; MC, V.* Call the day before for a custom wine-tasting picnic luncheon. Items to consider include rum-soaked lady fingers, house-smoked chicken, and homemade pickled watermelon rind, plus obscure cheeses and interesting housemade salads and ice creams. Or dine in on an entree item such as black pepper noodles with olives and smoked chicken, or on a dessert such as strawberry-rhubarb pie with homemade ice cream.

Calistoga Inn *1250 Lincoln Ave., 707/942-4101; B, L, & D daily; $$-$$$; highchairs, booster seats; reservations suggested; MC, V.* The specialty here is simply-prepared seafood, and the menu changes daily. Consider grilled catfish with tomatoes and garlic, grilled thresher shark with red bell pepper sauce, or ceviche of barracuda. Duck, veal, steak, and pastas are often on the menu, as are irresistable desserts such as Santa Rosa plum sorbet or raspberries with chocolate crème fraîche. In warm weather diners are seated outside on a patio overlooking the Napa Valley River.

An informal brew pub operating in the bar area offers five house brews—one of them a Pilsner-style lager (the house specialty)—and hearty, inexpensive pub food.

Modest, inexpensive lodging with shared baths is available upstairs. Several sets of adjoining rooms are suitable for families.

Cinnabar Cafe *1440 Lincoln Ave., 707/942-6989; B, L, & D daily; $-$$; highchairs, booster seats, children's portions; reservations suggested; AE, MC, V.* Attractive and unpretentious, this spot serves reasonably priced, honest food. Breakfast is the expected items plus 19 kinds of three-egg omelettes, sauteed fresh boned trout, buttermilk or buckwheat pancakes, and homemade granola. Lunch includes homemade soups and breads and a large variety of sandwiches and hamburgers. Dinner is a pricier selection of fresh fish, lobster, and prime rib.

Silverado Restaurant *1374 Lincoln Ave., 707/942-6725; B, L, & D F-W; $$; highchairs, booster seats, children's portions; MC, V.* Comfortable booths with views of the sidewalk parade combine with fresh and tasty food to make this a pleasant dining spot. Lunch is informal, with a menu of hamburgers, sandwiches, soups, and desserts as well as a large selection of non-alcoholic drinks and alcoholic fruit daiquiris. Dinner is more upscale and features updated American classics and mesquite-grilled items. The lighter bar menu is available all day and features items such as nachos, pizza, and hamburgers, and regional beers are on tap.

The Village Green Cafe *1413 Lincoln Ave., 707/942-0330; B & L daily; $; highchairs, boosters seats; no cards.* This place seems like it has been around almost forever. It has an informal, unpretentious atmosphere, with comfortable booths and counter seating. Short-order items dominate the menu: hamburgers, fried chicken, spaghetti, homemade French fries with the skins still on, design-your-own-omelettes, homemade pies, ice cream fountain goodies. Half-orders are available for children.

WHAT TO DO

Bothe-Napa Valley State Park *3801 St. Helena Highway, 707/942-4575; daily 8-dusk; $5/car. Pool: summer only; adults $3, under 18 $1.* Swimming in a naturally heated pool is a favorite activity at this lovely park, but picnicking and hiking are also popular. Campsites are available.

Calistoga Gliders *1546 Lincoln Ave., 707/942-5000; daily 9-5:30, to 7:30 Oct-May; $79/1 person, $99/2; reservations suggested on weekends.* The 20-minute glider ride/sightseeing trip covers approximately 10 miles. Longer flights are also available.

Old Faithful Geyser *1299 Tubbs Lane, 707/942-6463; daily 9-5, to 6 in summer; adults $4, 6-11 $2.* Located in the crater of an extinct volcano, this idyllic site is home to one of only three geysers in the world that erupt regularly and merit the name Old Faithful. (The other two are in Yellowstone National Park in Wyoming and on North Island in New Zealand.) It erupts approximately every 40 minutes and shoots 350-degree water 60 feet into the air. The show lasts from 3 to 4 minutes. Plenty of picnic tables and a snack bar are available.

Once in a Lifetime Balloon Co. *800/659-9915, 707/942-6541, fax 707/942-5770; $165/person; reservations required.* Because the winds will almost certainly carry it over the scenic vineyards, the northern end of the valley is said to be the best area to take off in a hot air balloon These 1-hour flights take off between 5 and 7 a.m. and include a champagne brunch at the Cinnabar Cafe.

Petrified Forest *4100 Petrified Forest Rd., 4 miles west of town, 707/942-6667; daily 10-5; adults $3, 4-11 $1.* A self-guided 1/4-mile path leads through this unusual forest. Open to the public since 1870, it contains petrified redwood trees that are over 3 million years old and as long as 126 feet. Facilities include a small museum and picnic tables.

Sharpsteen Museum and Sam Brannan Cottage *1311 Washington St., 707/942-5911; daily 12-4, in summer 10-4; free.* This exceptionally well-designed museum displays an elaborate and extensive diorama of Calistoga as it appeared in 1865—when Sam Brannan opened the town's first spa and began its career as a resort area. The beautifully furnished cottage displays the style in which wealthy San Franciscans lived when they vacationed here in the late 1800s. A working model of the Napa Valley Railroad is also displayed.

Smith's Mount St. Helena Trout Farm *18401 Ida Clayton Rd., 14 miles from town, 707/987-3651; Sat & Sun 10-6, Apr-Aug; closed Sept-Mar.* All ages can enjoy fishing on this lake. Poles and bait are free. The charge for fish caught is determined by size, and cleaning and packaging are included. Do call for directions.

WINERIES

Chateau Montelena Winery *1429 Tubbs Lane, 707/942-5105; tasting daily 10-4, fee; tours at 11 & 2, reservations required.* This winery, which is noted for its Chardonnays and Cabernet Sauvignons, can be difficult to find. Do call for directions. Crayons and paper are provided to entertain antsy children while their parents sample wines in the stone tasting room.

Reservations are necessary to use the winery's unusual island picnic area in Jade Lake. Two islets, reached via footbridge, hold miniature picnic pagodas. The lake features a berthed Chinese junk and is populated with ducks, swans, and geese .

Clos Pegase *1060 Dunaweal Lane, 707/942-4981; tasting daily 10:30-5, fee $3, keep tasting glass; tours by appt.* Because of its stark stucco architecture, this winery opened in 1987 amid much controversy. There were those who liked it and those who didn't. (It is interesting to note that its Post-Modern design was the winner in a contest sponsored by the San Francisco Museum of Modern Art.) Surrounded by young vineyards, with tall, thin cypress trees lining an outdoor walkway, it has a surreal quality.

Named after Pegasus, the winged horse of Greek mythology that gave birth to wine and art, the winery appropriately displays a collection of fine art within its caves. Among the treasure trove are ancient vineyard tools, rare free-blown wine bottles, carafes, and glasses dating from the 3rd century B.C. to the present.

Sterling Vineyards *1111 Dunaweal Lane, 707/942-3344; tasting and self-guided tour daily 10:30-4:30; gondola ride: adults $5, under 16 free.* Accessible to the public only via a 4-minute gondola ride, this winery was built to resemble a Greek monastery. It features a stunning and unusual white stucco, cubist style of architecture. Spectacular views of the Napa Valley are provided throughout the self-guided winery tour. For tasting, visitors are seated at tables either in a spacious interior room or on an outdoor terrace, and each adult is given a $2 credit toward the purchase of Sterling wines. A picnic terrace with a wonderful view is available.

– Clear Lake –

A LITTLE BACKGROUND

Spring-fed Clear Lake is the largest fresh-water lake that is totally within California. (Lake Tahoe is partially in Nevada.) It measures 25 miles by 8 miles. The 70-mile drive around the perimeter takes 2-1/2 to 3 hours.

From the 1870s into the early 1900s, this area was world-famous for its health spas and huge luxury resort hotels. Then, for various reasons, it fell into a state of disrepair and slowly lost its acclaim. Now it is basically a reasonably-priced family resort area.

Lake County's first traffic light was installed in 1982, and there are still no parking meters. And in 1990 Lake County was deemed by the California Air Resources Board to be the only area in the state that met air quality standards for all pollutants—meaning it has the cleanest air in California!

Clear Lake is situated on volcanic terrain, which gives it an unusual physical appearance and a profusion of hot springs. The Pomo Indians, who lived in this area many years ago, had a legend that predicted when there is no snow on 4,200-foot Mount Konocti in April, the volcano will erupt. Those who heed legends should check the April snowfall before making vacation plans.

VISITOR INFORMATION

Lake County Visitor Information Center *875 Lakeport Blvd., Lakeport 95453, 800/ LAKESIDE, 707/263-9544.*

GETTING THERE

Located approximately 50 miles north of St. Helena via Highway 29. This scenic route goes through the heart of the Wine Country. The rolling hills are strewn with blooming wild flowers during the spring, and with brilliantly colored foliage during the fall. Make the drive during daylight; this winding two-lane road is tedious and dangerous to drive at night, and, of course, the lovely scenery cannot be enjoyed then.

An alternate route follows Highway 101 north to Highway 175 east.

ANNUAL EVENTS

Summer Concert Series *June-August; held in **Library Park** in Lakeport and **Austin Park** in Clearlake.* A little bit of everything is on the bill at this casual, free event. In the past the mostly-California bands have included Joe Louis Walker and Country Joe and the Fish.

WHERE TO STAY

Jules Resort *14195 Lakeshore Dr., Clearlake, 707/994-6491; 18 units; $-$$; 1 week minimum in July & Aug; cribs; all kitchens; 1 fireplace; heated pool (unavailable Nov-Mar), hot tub, sauna; pets welcome.* Lodging here is in pleasant old cabins. Facilities include a lakefront pool, private beach, fishing pier, and launching ramp. This place is so popular in the summer that it is necessary to book at least 1 year in advance!

The super **Jules Miniature Golf** course, which is owned by the resort, is just across the street.

Konocti Harbor Resort & Spa *8727 Soda Bay Rd., Kelseyville, 800/862-4930, 707/ 279-4281; 250 rooms; $$-$$$; children under 12 free; cribs; some kitchens, bathtubs; 2 heated pools (unavailable Nov-May), 2 wading pools, 8 clay tennis courts (fee/night lights); 2 restaurants.* Nestled in the shadow of Mount Konocti on the rim of the lake, this beautifully landscaped resort enjoys a superb setting. Reminiscent of luxury resorts in Hawaii, it is a lot easier to reach and much less expensive. The list of facilities is extensive: tennis courts and pro lessons, a children's playground, a recreation room, a jogging trail, feature films, a bar with live music in the evenings, a paddlewheel boat cruise, a miniature golf course, and a marina that rents equipment for fishing, water-skiing, and paddleboating. The resort even has its own gas station! Babysitting can usually be arranged, and tennis, golf, and fishing packages are available. A health spa offers an indoor pool and hot tub, a sauna and steam room, and all kinds of services.

The dining room has stunning lake views, offers an innovative American menu, and is comfortably equipped for children. A coffee shop serves more informal meals.

A **Concert by the Lake** series that is operated much like a casino show, with both dinner and cocktail seatings, brings in big names each summer.

Skylark Motel *1120 N. Main St., Lakeport, 800/675-6151, 707/263-6151; 45 rooms; 5 non-smoking rooms; $-$$; children under 1 free; cribs; some kitchens, bathtubs; heated pool (unavailable Oct-May).* These modern motel units are located lakefront. The spacious, well-maintained grounds feature an expansive lawn, swings, and a wading area in the lake.

WHERE TO STAY NEARBY

Wilbur Hot Springs Health Sanctuary *near intersection of Highways 16 & 20, 25 miles east of the lake, 22 miles west of Williams, 916/473-2306; 20 rooms; 100% non-smoking; $$; 2-night minimum on weekends; unsuitable for children under 3; no TVs; some shared baths; pool, 4 hot tubs. Day use: $10/person; reservations necessary.* Soaking in one of the four tubs filled with hot sulphurous springwater and then plunging into the cool water of the outdoor pool are the main activities here. Clothing is optional. The ambitious are also welcome to take walks in the surrounding forested hills. Lodging is available in both private rooms and dormitory-style shared rooms. Evening light is provided by kerosene lamps, heat by wood-burning stoves. A parlor provides a pool table and piano for entertainment, and guests prepare their own meals in a large communal kitchen.

WHERE TO EAT

Konocti Klines' Oak Barrel *6445 Soda Bay Rd., Kelseyville, 707/279-0101; D W-Sun; $$; highchairs, booster seats, children's portions; reservations suggested; no cards.* Reached by driving along a scenic rural road, this cozy, antique-furnished restaurant is a delightful surprise. The specialty of the house is fresh seafood. A chalkboard menu announces a wide variety of entrees, each of which is served with a delicious bowl of homemade soup and an exotic salad of mixed lettuces. Steak and chicken entrees are also available. Fish & chips are an option for children, and local wine varietals may be ordered by the glass. For dessert, the homemade pear and walnut cake is not to be missed.

Park Place *50 Third St., Lakeport, 707/263-0444; L & D daily; $-$$; highchairs, booster seats, children's portions; 100% non-smoking; reservations suggested; MC, V.* Located lakefront and across the street from Library Park, this cafe offers incredible views from its outdoor rooftop dining area. For starters, don't miss the magnificent bruchetta—a baguette topped with pesto and sundried tomatoes and then grilled.

The menu boasts a large selection of pastas, all made fresh daily. Several kinds of tortellinis and raviolis are available, as are fresh fish, steaks, and hamburgers.

WHAT TO DO

Fishing, hunting, swimming, boating, rock hunting, golfing, and water-skiing are the big activities here. Fishing is the biggest. The lake is reputed to be the best bass fishing spot in the West—maybe even the best in the entire country. The lake's nutrient-rich waters are credited with producing plenty of 10-pounders, and the lake record is a 17.52-pounder!

Lakefront public parks and beaches are located in Lakeport and Clearlake.

Anderson Marsh State Historic Park *on Highway 53 between Lower Lake & Clearlake, 707/994-0688; W-Sun 10-5; $2/car*. Acquired by the state in 1982, this 940-acre park contains an additional 470 acres of tule marsh. It also holds an 1855 ranch house, where a docent dispenses information, and a partially reconstructed Pomo Indian village. Tree-shaded picnic tables are provided.

A **Blackberry Festival,** featuring a variety of entertainment and homemade blackberry pie, is held annually in August.

Clear Lake State Park *5300 Soda Bay Rd., Kelseyville, 3.5 miles northeast of town, 800/ 444-7275, 707/279-4293*. Located on the shores of the lake, this park offers swimming, fishing, picnic facilities, campsites, and miles of hiking trails—including the 1/4-mile Indian Nature Trail and the 3-mile Dorn Nature Trail. A Visitor Center provides a slide show introduction to the area and a Touch Corner for children. Displays include local wildlife dioramas, a native fish aquarium, and exhibits on the area's Pomo Indian history.

Homestake Mining Company Tour *26775 Morgan Valley Rd., 15 miles southeast of Lower Lake, 800/525-3743, 707/263-9544; F at 11am, 1st & 3rd Sat at 11am, May-Oct only; free; reservations suggested; strollers not permitted*. Visitors to this modern gold mine are treated to a 1-1/2-hour guided bus tour of the **McLaughlin Gold Mine.**

WINERIES

Both of these wineries are located just off of Highway 29:

Kendall-Jackson Winery *700 Matthews Rd., Lakeport, 707/263-5299; tasting daily 11-5; no tours*. This premium winery is known for its Zinfandels and Chardonnays. A large grassy area beckons kids to play, and a picnic arbor overlooking the vineyards is invitingly situated among shady walnut trees.

Konocti Winery *on Thomas Dr., Kelseyville, 707/279-8861; tasting M-Sat 10-5, Sun 11-5; tours by appt*. Specialties here are Fume Blancs and Cabernet Francs. A grassy picnic area with tables is available to visitors.

A **Harvest Festival,** featuring grape-stomping contests, is scheduled each year on the second weekend of October.

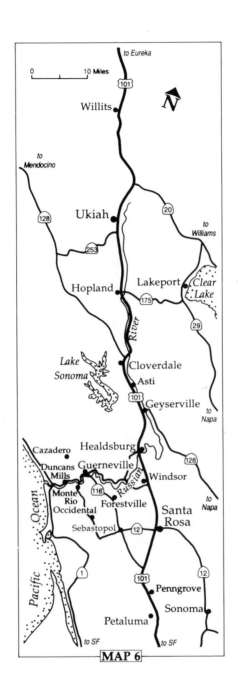

MAP 6

101 North

– Petaluma –

A LITTLE BACKGROUND

Located less than an hour's drive north of San Francisco, Petaluma offers an old-fashioned small town atmosphere. Perhaps this is why it was chosen as the filming location for both *American Graffiti* and *Peggy Sue Got Married*. In fact, director Francis Coppola is quoted as saying, "You can find any decade you want somewhere in Petaluma."

It's pleasant to spend a day here, just walking around the downtown area. Noteworthy among the numerous antique shops is the gigantic collective-run **Old Mill Antiques** located in **The Great Petaluma Mill** shopping complex.

Once known as the World's Egg Basket, this area still produces plenty of eggs but is currently better known as a dairy center.

VISITOR INFORMATION

Petaluma Area Chamber of Commerce *215 Howard St., Petaluma 94952, 707/762-2785.*

GETTING THERE

Located approximately 50 miles north of San Francisco. Take Highway 101 all the way.

ANNUAL EVENTS

Butter & Egg Days *April; 707/762-9348.* In the past the parade that kicks off this celebration has been populated with giant papier-mâché cows, huge dairy trucks converted into floats, and plenty of children dressed as chickens. Other events have included the Cutest Little Chick in Town Contest (when the imaginative costumes of those marching chickens, limited to ages 1 through 8, are judged), an Egg Toss, and a Team Butter Churning Contest. The next day the **Petaluma Antique Street Fair** takes place on a street that is blocked off to traffic.

Ugly Dog Contest *June; 707/763-0931.* Just one of the many events scheduled at the annual **Sonoma-Marin Fair**, this good-spirited contest has three divisions: Pedigree Class, Mutt Class, and Ring of Champions.

Petaluma River Festival *August; 707/762-5331.* Once home to the third busiest river in the state, the town celebrates its steamboat heyday with an old-fashioned pancake breakfast and boat rides galore. Usually the *Alma*, an 1891 scow schooner that is usually berthed at San Franciso's Hyde Street Pier, is on hand for tours and sea chantey sing-alongs led by park rangers.

Petaluma River Festival

Petaluma Summer Music Festival *August; 707/763-8920.* This festival features diverse musical events that appeal to all ages. Many are scheduled in locations of historical interest. Most events have an admission charge, but free concerts in the park are also scheduled.

Wrist Wrestling Contest *October; 707/778-0210.* Begun in a local bar, this contest became a world's championship in 1962. Anyone can pay the $25 entry fee and vie for the titles of righthanded and lefthanded heavyweight, middleweight, lightweight, featherweight, and bantamweight.

WHERE TO STAY

Quality Inn *5100 Montero Way, 800/221-2222, 707/664-1155; 110 rooms; 60 non-smoking rooms; $$-$$$; children under 19 free; cribs; some kitchens, bathtubs; heated pool (unavailable Oct-Apr), hot tub, sauna; continental breakfast; dogs welcome.* Located on the outskirts of town, this is a link in a chain known for its attractive Cape Cod-style of architecture and comfortable, modern rooms. A generous buffet breakfast of hot drinks, pastries, cereals, and fresh fruit is served in the lobby.

WHERE TO EAT

McNear's Saloon & Dining House *23 Petaluma Blvd. N., 707/765-2121; L & D daily; $-$$; highchairs, booster seats, children's portions; AE, MC, V.* Located inside the historic 1886 McNear Building, this casual restaurant and sports bar serves an extensive eclectic menu. Diners can get great bar food, such as spicy buffalo wings and beer-batter mushrooms, as well as house-made soups, salads, sandwiches, hamburgers, barbecued chicken and ribs, pastas, and steaks. Happy Hour, from 5 to 6 p.m. daily, is a great time to visit for a drink and complimentary snacks. Kids have their own Happy Hour then, too, and get a free soft drink and game token with their dinner. On fair weather days, windows are opened wide in the front dining area near the sidewalk, allowing for pleasant people-watching.

Steamer Gold Landing *1 Water St., 707/763-6876; L & D daily; highchairs, booster seats, children's portions; reservations suggested; AE, MC, V.* This restaurant features a comfortable, spacious dining room, with brick walls and operating fireplaces. The dinner menu offers an assortment of beautifully prepared fresh fish items (including a superb baked salmon), prime rib and steaks, and several salads and pastas. Dinners include both an excellent spinach salad topped with a warm, sweet vinaigrette dressing and a perfectly prepared baked potato with all the trimmings. Specials are available before 7 p.m., and an assortment of wine varietals are available by the glass. A children's menu offers a choice of hamburger, steak, fish, chicken, or grilled cheese. Desserts vary daily. One of the best is an unusual, flaky-crusted cherry-blackberry pie.

WHAT TO DO

The Creamery Store *711 Western Ave./Baker St., 707/778-1234; tours every hour, M-Sat 11-3; free.* Tours of the cheese-making operation here, which processes the milk from thousands of area cows, begin with viewing a brief video. They include a visit to the cheese plant, where the cheese-making process is observed, and to the aging cooler. A gift shop purveys over 600 cow-themed items. But the best souvenir just might be "squeaky cheese"—mild, chewy fresh cheese curds. Because it is highly perishable and not aways available, it is truly a rare treat.

Eagle Ridge Winery *111 Goodwin(e) Ave., Penngrove, just north of town, 800/892-8463, 707/664-WINE; tasting daily 11-4; self-guided tours.* Claiming to have the first tasting room north of San Francisco that is open to the public, this picturesque hilltop winery is an historic landmark. Formerly a dairy, the pasture has been converted into a vineyard. Known for its offbeat wines, the winery produces a late-harvest Zinfandel and a rare Ehrenfelser varietal—a cross between Riesling and Sylvaner grapes. This winery was the first commercial vineyard to plant the grape in the U.S. and is the only one currently making Ehrenfelser wine. Ehrenfelser is also the only wine in the country produced in a blue bottle. A picnic area shaded by a grape arbor overlooks the vineyards, and limited picnic supplies are available for purchase in the tasting room.

Marin French Cheese Company *7500 Petaluma-Point Reyes Rd. (also known as Red Hill Rd.), 707/762-6001; sales room daily 9-5; tours daily 10-4, on the hour; free.* Located way out in the country, this cheese factory has been operated by the Thompson family since 1865. By now, they have perfected the art of making Camembert cheese. They also make good Brie, schloss, and breakfast cheeses. Tours take visitors through the factory and explain how these special cheeses are produced, and cheeses are sampled at the end. Picnic supplies are available in an adjoining store, where these house cheeses are on sale along with salami, French bread, sandwiches, crackers, soft drinks, juices, and ice cream. Two large grassy areas, one with a large pond, beckon for picnics. Some picnic tables are also available.

Petaluma Adobe State Historic Park *3325 Adobe Rd., 707/762-4871; daily 10-5; adults $2, 6-11 $1.* Once part of the 66,000-acre estate of General Vallejo, this rancho has been restored to reflect life as it was in 1840. The living quarters, a weaving shop, and a blacksmith shop are on the self-guided tour. A pony may be viewed in its rustic enclosure, and roosters, chickens, sheep, and a goat run free. Shady picnic spots with tables are located by Adobe Creek, which is often dry. Because of fire regulations, no barbecuing is permitted.

Special events include **Sheep Shearing/Kids Day** (first Sunday in May), **Living History Day** (third Saturday in May), and **Old Adobe Day Fiesta** (second Sunday in August).

– Santa Rosa –

VISITOR INFORMATION

Sonoma County Convention & Visitors Bureau *10 Fourth St., Santa Rosa 95401, 707/575-1191.*

Sonoma County Farm Trails *P.O. Box 6032, Santa Rosa 95406, 707/586-FARM.* For a free copy of this organization's map of local farms that sell directly to the consumer, send a stamped, self-addressed legal-size envelope. The map pinpoints the location of u-pick farms, as well as of farms that sell more unusual items such as fresh rabbits and pheasants, herbs, mushrooms—even feather pillows and earthworms.

GETTING THERE

Located approximately 10 miles north of Petaluma via Highway 101.

ANNUAL EVENTS

Scottish Gathering and Games *September; 415/897-4442.* The oldest and largest gathering of the clans outside of Scotland, this event features a variety of competitions—including the popular **Caber Tossing Championships**, in which a piece of wood the size of a telephone pole is tossed end-over-end for accuracy.

WHERE TO STAY

Doubletree Hotel *3555 Round Barn Blvd., 800/528-0444, 707/523-7555; 247 rooms; 44 non-smoking rooms; $$-$$$+; children under 18 free; cribs; all bathtubs; some refrigerators; heated pool, hot tub; restaurant, room service.* Sprawled across one of the few hills in town, the facilities at this comfortable modern motel include a 7.5-mile jogging trail. Golf and tennis facilites are just 1 mile away.

Flamingo Resort Hotel & Fitness Center *2777 4th St./Highway 12, 800/848-8300, 707/545-8530, fax 707/528-1404; 135 rooms; 85 non-smoking rooms; $$-$$$+; 2-night minimum in summer; children under 12 free; cribs; all bathtubs; heated pool, children's* *wading pool, hot tub, health club (fee), 5 tennis courts; restaurant, room service.* When this spacious, unpretentious resort was originally built, it was out in the country. Now, in the midst of urban sprawl, it provides all the comforts of a full-service resort. Guests get the convenience of a motel—parking just outside their room; not having to walk through a lobby—with the amenities of a hotel—a piano bar with live entertainment and dancing; express check-out. Facilities include shuffleboard, Ping Pong, and a lighted jogging path. The Olympic-size pool is heated year-round, and the state-of-the-art health club features sauna and steam rooms, basketball and volleyball courts, and massage service. A variety of packages are available.

♥**Hotel La Rose** *308 Wilson St., 800/LAROSE-8, 707/579-3200, fax 707/579-3247; 49 rooms; $$; cribs; some bathtubs; continental breakfast on Sat & Sun, restaurant, room service.* Conveniently located in Railroad Square, this tasteful hotel was built in 1907 of cut stone quarried from the area now known as **Annadel State Park.** It combines turn-of-the-century charm with modern conveniences. Rooms are stylishly decorated and furnished with English country antiques, and many on the top floor feature pitched ceilings. Some rooms have private balconies, and a communal sundeck is available for relaxation. Shoes left outside the door in the evening are polished and returned by dawn.

A self-service **High Tea,** consisting of an array of homemade sweets and savories prepared by the hotel's pastry chef, is available to both guests and non-guests *(Tu-F 3-5; $5).* Entertainment is provided by the hotel's player piano.

Vintners Inn *4350 Barnes Rd., 800/421-2584, 707/575-7350, fax 575-1426; 44 rooms; $$$-$$$+; 2-night minimum Mar-Nov; children under 6 free; cribs; all bathtubs; some fireplaces; hot tub; continental breakfast, restaurant, room service.* This elegant country inn is surrounded by a 50-acre working vineyard. Located in three separate buildings, the rooms are all decorated with European antiques.

The highly acclaimed **John Ash & Co.** *(707/527-7687)* restaurant is located adjacent.

WHERE TO EAT

Bull Moose Saloon & Pizza Co. *1529 Farmers Lane, in Farmers Lane Plaza, 707/575-8553; L & D daily; $; highchairs, booster seats; AE, MC, V.* Enjoy a tasty pizza or calzone (pizza turnover) in a friendly atmosphere. A variety of sandwiches, a salad bar, and a good selection of beers round out the menu. Comfy wooden booths are great when kids are in tow, and a juke box and pool table provide entertainment.

The Good Earth *610 Third St., 707/523-3060; B, L, & D daily; $-$$; highchairs, booster seats, children's portions; 100% non-smoking; MC, V.* This attractive modern dining room features tall ceilings and comfortable seating. A guitar player entertains each evening. For menu description, see page 6.

Peter Rabbit's Chocolate Factory *2489 Guerneville Rd./Fulton Rd., 800/4R-CANDY, 707/575-7110; Tu-Sat 10-6.* Located on the outskirts of town, in a building that belies the cute name, this candy store is worth seeking out. Visitors can usually observe some yummy or other being whipped up on huge marble slabs located adjacent to the retail area. Among the over 120 goodies produced are nut brittles, salt water taffy, and caramel corn that seems to get better with age. There are even chocolate-dipped prunes. Should addiction occur, everything is available by mail order.

Thursday Night Market *on Fourth & B Sts., 07/539-0345; Thur 5-8, May-Sept only; free.* At this festive event, local restaurants serve up inexpensive portions of barbecued turkey legs, sausage, kebobs, burgers, and oysters along with salads, calzone, chili, and burritos. Farmers are also on hand with fresh produce, arts and craftspeople display their wares, and plenty of street entertainers do their thing.

Willie Bird's Restaurant *1150 Santa Rosa Ave., 707/542-0861; B, L, & D daily; $-$$; highchairs, booster seats, children's portions; AE, MC, V.* This casual restaurant celebrates Thanksgiving every day by serving their own tasty, natural brand of turkey in varied forms. Try the Willie Bird Special—the traditional turkey feast— or something more unusual, such as turkey scallopini or turkey sausage. Children's portions include a turkey hamburger and turkey hot dog. Plenty of non-turkey items are also available.

WHAT TO DO

Howarth Memorial Park *Summerfield Rd., access from Sonoma Ave. & Montgomery Dr., 707/524-5169. Rides: Feb-Oct Sat & Sun 11:30-5, in summer Tu-Sun; 75¢-$1.* There is something for everyone in this scenic park. Children especially enjoy the playground, miniature train ride, animal farm, pony rides, and merry-go-round. But there are also paddleboat, rowboat, and sailboat rentals on Lake Ralphine, plus hiking trails and tennis courts.

Luther Burbank Home & Gardens *Santa Rosa/Sonoma Aves., 707/524-5445; gardens open daily; museum & house tours Apr-Oct only, W-Sun 10-3:30; gardens & museum free; house tours: adults $1, under 12 free.* During his 50-year horticultural career, Luther Burbank developed over 800 new plants. This memorial garden displays many of his achievements, including a plumcot tree, the ornamental Shasta daisy, and a warren of spineless cacti. (He also developed the Santa Rosa plum and elephant garlic.) Burbank is buried here in an unmarked grave. Tours of his greenhouse and modified Greek Revival-style home, which retains its original furnishings, last 1/2 hour. The adjacent **Carriage House Museum** offers annual exhibits that relate to Burbank's life and work.

Once In a Lifetime Balloon Co. *800/659-9915, 707/578-0580.* For description, see page 109.

Railroad Square *centered at Fourth/Davis Sts.; 707/578-8478.* Now a national historic district, this area is filled with antique stores, restaurants, and specialty shops.

The **Daily Planet** *(Fifth/Davis Sts., 707/578-1205)* presents live comedy and dancing in the evenings. Patrons must be age 21 or older.

Redwood Empire Ice Arena *1667 W. Steele Lane, 707/546-7147; open daily, call for schedule; adults $6.50, 12-17 $6, under 12 $5.50, skate rental $1.50.* Built in 1969, this ice skating rink has been called "the most beautiful ice arena in the world." Since it is owned by cartoonist Charles Schulz, the Alpine decor is unexpected. However, the fast-food coffee shop does have a few stained-glass windows depicting Snoopy.

Located adjacent, **Snoopy's Gallery and Gift Shop** *(707/546-3385; daily 10-6)* purveys the largest selection of *Peanuts* merchandise in the world. Cuddly Snoopys are available in sizes ranging from 4 inches to 5 feet. Copies of original *Peanuts* columns, matted and framed, are also available. Above the shop is a small museum containing Schulz's awards and some of his favorite drawings, as well as an assortment of other interesting items. Schulz also has an office on the premises and is frequently sighted by skaters.

Each December the rink is converted into a theater for a special **Christmas Show,** when Snoopy always makes an appearance on ice skates. Some ice-side tables are available, and tickets sell out fast *(707/546-3385).*

Robert L. Ripley Memorial Museum *492 Sonoma Ave., 707/576-5233; W-Sun 11-4, closed Nov-Feb; adults $1.50, 7-17 75¢.* Believe it or not, Robert Ripley was born, raised, and buried in Santa Rosa! Dedicated to his memory, this museum displays a wax reincarnation of Ripley as well as some of his original drawings and personal effects. A few oddities mentioned in his columns are also displayed, including stuffed Siamese twin calves and a 45-inch white rhinoceros horn that some suspicious types claim is actually wood. The museum is located inside the **Church of One Tree,** which was built in 1873 from the wood of a single redwood tree!

The beautifully landscaped gardens of **Julliard Park** are just outside. A self-guided tour of the park's unusual trees may be enjoyed with the help of a brochure available at the museum.

Sonoma County Museum *425 Seventh St., 707/579-1500; W-Sun 11-4; adults $1, 13-19 50¢.* Located inside the city's beautifully restored 1910 post office building, this museum exhibits material relating to the county's history.

Victorian Homes. Driving along MacDonald Avenue, which is located in the older part of town, allows the viewing of lovely Victorian mansions.

– Guerneville/Russian River –

A LITTLE BACKGROUND

Once upon a time, in the '20s and '30s, this was a summer resort area favored by wealthy San Franciscans who traveled here by ferry and train. Then it faded in popularity and became a pleasant and uncrowded retreat. Today, slowly recovering from a state of decay, it is regaining its former popularity. The atmosphere is easy going, and it is acceptable to dine anywhere in casual clothing.

Guerneville, the hub of the Russian River resort area, is surrounded by many smaller towns. There are numerous public beaches, but many more are privately owned. Also, there are some unofficial nude beaches. Inquire in town about how to find, or avoid, them.

VISITOR INFORMATION

Russian River Region Visitors Center *P.O. Box 255 (14034 Armstrong Woods Rd.), Guerneville 95446, 800/253-8800, 707/869-9009.*

Russian River Wine Road Map *P.O. Box 46, Healdsburg 95448, 800/648-9922, 707/ 433-6782.* This free map provides details on wineries stretching from Forestville to Cloverdale.

GETTING THERE

Located approximately 15 miles west of Santa Rosa. Take Highway 12 west to Highway 116. For a more scenic route take the River Road exit just north of Santa Rosa and follow it west.

ANNUAL EVENTS

Russian River Wine Road Barrel Tasting *March; 707/433-6782.* Participants are permitted to get behind the scenes in winemaking and sample special wines that aren't normally available for tasting.

Slug Fest *March; 800/253-8800, 707/869-9009.* Celebrating the versatility of the region's ubiquitous banana slug, which absolutely thrives in the damp winter climate, this unusual festival features the Slug Sprint, in which kids under 12 race their pet gastropods, and the Slug-Off Recipe Contest, in which past entries have included Upslime Down Cake and Slugghetti. A Super Slug weigh-in adds to the fun.

Apple Blossom Festival *April; in Sebastopol, 707/823-3032.* Scheduled each year to occur when the area's plentiful apple orchards are snowy white with blossoms, this festival includes a parade down Main Street and plenty of booths purveying apple-related crafts and foods.

Bohemian Grove *last 2 weeks of July.* Many of the world's most powerful political, military, and corporate leaders meet at this 2,700-acre private resort. The public is not invited.

Gravenstein Apple Fair *August; in Sebastopol, 707/544-GRAV.* Held on and off since the turn of the century, this old-time country fair is staged amid the large, shady oak trees and rolling hills of **Ragle Ranch Park.** The fair specifically celebrates the flavorful, crisp, early-ripening Gravenstein apple that is indigenous to the area and well-known for making the best juices and pies. In fact, this area is known as the world's Gravenstein capital. Fun at the fair is of the "down home" variety, with opportunities to taste apples, observe bee-keepers in action, and pet a variety of farm animals. Apples, and related foods and products, are available for purchase directly from farmers.

Russian River Jazz Festival *September; 707/869-3940.* Music festivals don't get much more casual than this one. Audience members can actually float in the placid river on an inner tube while listening to a range of jazz. It's a good idea to pack a picnic basket, but food and drink are available for sale. (Note that no bottles are permitted.)

WHERE TO STAY

♥**Applewood** *13555 Highway 116, 707/869-9093; 10 rooms; 100% non-smoking; 2-night minimum on weekends; unsuitable for children under 21; some bathtubs; heated pool (May-Oct only), hot tub; full breakfast.* Built in 1922 as a private home, this Mission Revival-style mansion is now a county historical landmark. Formerly known as The Estate, it is situated on 6 acres and features an idyllic pool area surrounded by mature vineyards and tall pine trees. The hot tub is wonderful at night, especially when all the stars are out. Public tennis courts, located adjacent to the property, are reached via a short walk through a valley still populated with some of the apple trees that once comprised an orchard. The inn's decor is tasteful and unfussy, and rooms are spacious and comfortable, with aesthetically pleasing touches such as down comforters, fragrant apple soap, and apple-green walls and towels. Some rooms have private patios or balconies overlooking the vineyards and peaceful pastures beyond.

Breakfast is simple, yet special—perhaps a sectioned grapefruit topped with a perfect red maraschino cherry, followed by beautifully presented eggs Florentine prepared with tender baby spinach fresh from the inn's own garden. On warm days it can be enjoyed outdoors by the pool. Enticing fixed-price four-course dinners, prepared by the inn's creative owners and available only to guests, are served on Monday, Wednesday, and Saturday evenings.

Creekside Inn & Resort *16180 Neeley Rd., 800/776-6586, 707/869-3623; 15 units; 6 non-smoking rooms; $-$$; children under 2 free; cribs; some TVs, kitchens, bathtubs, fireplaces; some shared baths; unheated pool (unavailable Nov-Apr); continental breakfast (B&B rooms only).* Located a short stroll from town, just across the historic town bridge, this quiet resort dates back to the '30s. Guests are offered a choice of lodgings. The main house operates as a B&B, with six rooms sharing two bathrooms. Nine modernized housekeeping cottages feature attractive half-timbered exteriors. The Tree House is one of the nicest and derives its name from the fact that trees may be observed from every window. RV spaces are also available. Facilities include a large outdoor pool area with a barbecue, horseshoe pit, pool table, Ping Pong table, croquet lawn, and lending library. When rains are normal, Pocket Canyon Creek provides the soothing sound of running water as it meanders through the property.

Johnson's Beach & Resort *16241 First St., 707/869-2022; 10 rooms; $; 1-week minimum; closed Nov-Apr; some kitchens.* These old-time hotel rooms are adjacent to the river. They are rented for stays of less than 1 week on a first-come, first-served basis. Campsites are also available. Facilities include two rustic wooden swings, a large tire sandbox, pool and Ping Pong tables, and access to one of the best-equipped beaches in the area. A snack bar and both boat and beach paraphernalia rentals are available.

Ridenhour Ranch House Inn *12850 River Rd., 707/887-1033; 8 rooms; 100% non-smoking; $$-$$$; 2-night minimum on Sat; some TVs, bathtubs, wood-burning stoves; hot tub; full breakfast.* Built of redwood in 1906, this canary-yellow ranch house was built by the first settlers in the area on 960 acres of land. Decorated with English and American antiques, the house has six guest rooms. Two more are available in an adjacent cottage dating from 1934. Recreational facilities include a hot tub that is pleasantly situated beneath sheltering trees, a badminton area, and a croquet lawn. Secluded beaches may be reached via a short walk down a lane lined with blackberry bushes.

An expansive breakfast is prepared each morning in a restaurant-style kitchen by the Austrian owner-chef, who warns his guests, "If you don't eat well in the morning, you don't look well at the wineries." So he offers wonderful treats such as homemade Gravenstein applesauce and fruit preserves, gigantic croissants, a fruit smoothie with a touch of brandy from the neighboring Korbel winery, a wonderfully light bread pudding, and some sort of egg dish—perhaps eggs Florentine—made with eggs collected from the ranch's own hens. Fresh cookies and sherry are always available in the living room, which is also well-equipped with games and reading matter. A wonderful four-course dinner is served on some evenings. It is highly recommended and available only to ranch guests, who must reserve their spot in advance.

♥**Rio Villa Beach Resort** *20292 Highway 116, Monte Rio, 4 miles west of town, 707/ 865-1143, fax 707/865-0115; 12 rooms; $$-$$$; unsuitable for children under 12; some kitchens; hot tub; continental breakfast.* Some of the rooms at this peaceful spot have private balconies with river views. Guests can relax on a large deck area surrounded by manicured grounds overlooking the river. River access is available.

Riverlane Resort *16320 First St., 707/869-2323; 12 units; $-$$$; 2-night minimum on weekends; children under 1 free; cribs; all kitchens; some fireplaces; heated pool (unavailable Oct-Apr), hot tub.* Located by the river, this pleasant enclave of cabins offers a private beach and recreational equipment.

Village Inn *20822 River Blvd., Monte Rio, 4 miles west of town, 707/865-2304; 22 rooms; $-$$$; 2-night minimum on weekends July-Sept; some rooms suitable for children; children under 2 free; some TVs, kitchens, bathtubs; some shared baths; continental breakfast, restaurant, room service.* Built as a summer home in 1906, this rustic structure was turned into a hotel in 1908 and has remained one ever since. A worthy claim to fame is that *Holiday Inn*, starring Bing Crosby, was filmed here. Lodging facilities vary from small sleeping rooms to suites with a riverfront deck.

In summer the restaurant serves a popular Sunday brunch outdoors on a pleasant deck overlooking the river, and live music is sometimes scheduled in the evening.

House Rentals. Call the Visitors Center for the names of realty companies that rent private homes to vacationers.

WHERE TO EAT

Burdons *15405 River Rd., 707/869-2615; D Thur-M; closed in Jan; $$; booster seats, children's portions (ask server); reservations suggested on weekends; MC, V.* The American-Continental menu here features reliably well-prepared steaks, chops, and prime rib—the house specialty. Diners will also find pastas and fresh local fish on the menu, as well as a particularly tender rack of lamb featuring tiny chops garnished with green mint sauce and a side of creamy scalloped potatoes. All dinners come with homemade soup and a crisp tossed green or spinach salad. Dessert choices, which change daily, sometimes include a wonderful strawberry short-cake made with tasty berries, a homemade biscuit, and the lightest whipped cream imaginable. Further enhancing the dining experience, the walls of the simple dining room are decorated with the chef's colorful, whimsical paintings.

Cazanoma Lodge *1000 Kidd Creek Rd., Cazadero, 13 miles west of town, 707/632-5255; L, D, & SunBr Thur-Sun, also W in summer; closed Dec-Feb; $$; highchairs, booster seats, children's portions; 100% non-smoking; reservations suggested; AE, MC, V.* Nestled between two creeks in a protected valley, this 1926 lodge is reached via a 1 mile-long dirt road. German specialties—barbecue spareribs, several schnitzels, a sausage platter with sauerkraut—are on the menu along with American fare. But the really unusual item here is **catch-your-own-trout.** That's right. Customers here have the option of catching it themselves from a well-stocked spring-fed trout pond—to make sure it's *really fresh.* For the unimpressed, the kitchen will do the job with a net. The dining room offers great views of the tanquil forest setting, and in warm weather a large deck under the redwoods is irresistible. Live music is usually scheduled on weekends.

Moderately-priced cabins and lodge rooms are also available. Among the amenities on the 147 acres are a man-made waterfall, a swimming pool, and 2 miles of hiking trails.

Mom's Apple Pie *4550 Gravenstein Highway N., Sebastopol, 10 miles south of town, 707/823-8330; L & D daily; $; 1 highchair; no cards.* Located near the intersection of Highways 12 and 116, this little lunch counter is worth a stop for some homemade soup and pie. Fried chicken and sandwiches are also available.

The Occidental Two *in Occidental, 10 miles south of town.* Both of these restaurants serve bountiful multi-course, family-style Italian dinners. They have highchairs, booster seats, and a reasonable plate charge for small children. Prices are moderate, and inexpensive ravioli and spaghetti dinners with fewer side dishes are also available. Reservations are suggested at prime dining times during the summer. Both accept American Express, MasterCard, and Visa. People come to these restaurants to eat BIG. Picking a favorite can prove fattening.

Negri's *(3700 Main St., 707/823-5301)* starts with a steaming bowl of minestrone soup, rounds of moist salami, and a hunk of crusty Italian bread. Then come more plates bearing pickled vegetables, marinated bean salad, creamy large-curd cottage cheese, and a salad tossed with Thousand Island dressing. When tummies begin to settle, the homemade ravioli arrives—stuffed with spinach and topped with an excellent tomato-meat sauce. Then the entree arrives: a choice of crispy, moist fried chicken, saucy duck, or grilled porterhouse steak. (Seafood entrees are available on weeknights.) Entrees are served with a side of thick French fries and heavy zucchini pancakes. Then come the doggie bags. For those with room, apple fritters are available at additional charge.

In operation since 1876, the **Union Hotel** *(3703 Main St., 707/874-3555)* seats 500 people in three enormous dining rooms and on an outdoor patio. Simplicity seems to be the key to its success. The entree choice is limited to baked chicken, chicken cacciatora, duck, or steak. Side dishes include an antipasto plate of marinated kidney beans, cheese, and salami, plus minestrone soup, a delicious salad with light Thousand Island dressing, chewy homemade ravioli, zucchini fritters, potatoes, a fresh vegetable, and bread and butter. Dessert—apple fritters, spumoni ice cream, or apple pie—and coffee are extra.

River Inn Restaurant *16377 Main St., 707/869-0481; B, L, & D daily; closed Oct-Apr; $-$$; highchairs, booster seats, children's portions; 100% non-smoking; no reservations; no cards.* Extensive menu choices at breakfast include crisp cream waffles, thin Swedish pancakes, perfect French toast, omelettes, oatmeal, and fresh fruit. At lunch and dinner, just about everything imaginable is available. All this in a casual, noisy coffee shop atmosphere with comfy booths.

Russian River Vineyards Restaurant *5700 Highway 116, Forestville, 800/486-5844, 707/887-1562: L M-Sat, D daily, SunBr; closed M & Tu in winter; $$; highchairs, booster seats, children's portions; 100% non-smoking; reservations suggested; AE, MC, V.* In good weather, diners are seated outdoors in an attractive area shaded by grape arbors and umbrellas. In colder weather, tables are available inside an attractive old farm house. Greek dishes are the house specialty, but extensive use is made of local ingredients, and a hamburger is on the lunch menu. A large selection of the winery's own vintages are available by the glass. This is the only family-owned and -operated winery/restaurant in the state.

A stop at the tiny tasting room operated by the **Topolos at Russian River Vineyards** *(707/887-1575; tasting daily 10:30-5:30; tours by appt.)* is recommended. Of special interest are the Zinfandels and the unusual, rich Alicante Bouschet. Children are served sparkling apple cider while their parents taste.

WHAT TO DO

Armstrong Redwoods State Reserve *17000 Armstrong Woods Rd., Guerneville 707/ 869-2015; daily 8-dusk; $5/car.* A Visitors Center orients hikers to the trail system within this park. A free parking lot is located there, just outside the toll gate. There is no charge to those who park their cars and walk in.

The **Armstrong Woods Pack Station** *(707/887-2939)* offers half-day trail rides ($35) and full-day lunch rides ($70). One- and two-night pack trips ($300-$350) are also available April through October. Riders must be age 10 or older, and reservations are required.

Three miles further—at the end of a narrow, steep, winding road—**Austin Creek State Recreation Area** has 20 miles of hiking trails, as well as rustic camping facilities and four hike-in campsites.

Duncans Mills *on Highway 116, 10 miles west of town.* Once a lumber village, this tiny town is now home to a collection of shops, a deli, a restaurant, a riverside campground with private beach, and a stable where horses may be rented.

J's Amusements *16101 Neeley Rd., 707/869-3102; daily in summer, weekends Sept & Mar-June; closed in winter; $1.25-$3.50/ride.* Various kiddie rides and entertainments await the family in search of cheap thrills. Among them are a rickety mini-roller coaster, a tilt-a-whirl, and a waterslide.

Kozlowski Farms *5566 Highway 116 N., Forestville, 7 miles southeast of town, 707/ 887-2104; daily 9-5.* This scenic farm has 50 acres of apple trees and 15 acres of assorted berries. In season the produce may be purchased in bulk. Homemade juices, berry vinegars, wine jellies, and both flavorful berry jams and apple butter made without sugar are available year-round at the farm's barn outlet. A mail-order catalogue is also available.

Pet-A-Llama Ranch *5505 Lone Pine Rd., Sebastopol, 707/823-9395; Sat & Sun 10-4; free, feed 25¢.* Spread over 15 acres, this ranch is home to a herd of about 20 llamas. They love being petted and love it even more when someone purchases a cup of feed for them. Picnic tables are set up under trees adjacent to their pens. The farm-house's garage doubles as a crafts shop, purveying items handmade with llama wool (shawls, blankets, hats). Sometimes the fleece collected from a favorite llama is also available, and spinning wheels and drop spindles are displayed.

Swimming. Anywhere along the banks of the Russian River is bound to be nice to lay a blanket. A prime spot is under the **Monte Rio bridge,** where parking and beach access are free. Another choice spot is **Johnson's Beach** (see page 125). Ca-noe and paddle boat rentals and snack stands are available at both. The riverbed and beaches are covered with pebbles, so waterproof shoes are advised.

A good game to play with children here is "Find the Twin Clam Shells." Be prepared with a special prize for the kid who finds the most intact pairs.

Western Hills Nursery *16250 Coleman Valley Rd., Occidental, 707/874-3731; W-Sun 10-5; free.* Located in the hills behind town, this commercial nursery seems more like a botanical garden. Customers may meander along a path that leads past a lily pond and areas featuring California natives.

WINERIES

Korbel Champagne Cellars *13250 River Rd., 3 miles east of town, 707/887-2294; tasting daily 10-4; tours daily 10-3, on the hour; rose garden tours May-Nov only, daily at 11, 2, & 3:30.* The nation's oldest producer of methode champenoise champagne, this century-old winery also produces brandy and wine. Eight kinds of champagne may be tasted, and chilled splits, as well as minimal deli supplies, are available for impromptu picnics.

The grounds are landscaped with beautifully maintained flower gardens, and an **Antique Rose Garden,** faithfully restored to its turn-of-the-century beauty, is filled with old-time flowers such as coral bells, primroses, and violets, plus more than 200 varieties of roses. Among the rare roses are the original Burbank Tea Rose, the Double Musk rose celebrated in Shakespeare's plays, and the true Ambassa-dor, which was once thought to be extinct.

Mark West Winery *7000 Trenton-Healdsburg Rd., off River Rd., Forestville, 7 miles southeast of town, 800/888-9921, 707/544-4813; tasting daily 10-5; tours by appt.* Located off the beaten path, back in some scenic vineyards and up on a little hill, this winery can be difficult to find. Consider calling ahead for directions. Known now for its use of only organic grapes, the winery produces an unusual dry Gewurz-traminer. Children are treated to organic grape juice while their parents taste. Pic-nic tables are provided on a shaded lawn, and some deli items are available for purchase.

Just behind the tasting room, **California Carnivores** *(7020 Trenton-Healdsburg Rd., 707/838-1630; daily 10-4, Apr-Nov; by appt. Dec-Mar; free)* operates an unusual business out of a greenhouse. Over 350 varieties of insect-eating plants are raised, fed, and sold here. They include inexpensive Venus Fly Traps as well as more exotic varieties—one of which resembles the star of the movie *The Little Shop of Horrors.* According to the *New York Times* it is "a botanical museum." The *San Francisco Examiner* calls it an "arresting assemblage."

– Healdsburg –

VISITOR INFORMATION

Healdsburg Area Chamber of Commerce *217 Healdsburg Ave., Healdsburg 95448, 800/648-9922, 707/433-6935.*

GETTING THERE

Located approximately 20 miles northeast of Guerneville via Highway 101.

ANNUAL EVENTS

Antique Apple Tasting *Sept-Oct; at the* **Sonoma Antique Apple Nursery** *(4395 Westside Rd., 707/433-6420; nursery open Tu-Sat 9-4:30, Jan-Mar only; by appt. rest of year).* Lacking the fanfare of most special events and definitely not an apple festival, the aim of this tasting is to give customers the opportunity to sample what the fruit of a tree they purchase will taste like. Among the varieties usually presented for tasting are the sweet, crisp Stayman Winesap and the spicy, flavorful, but not very pretty Spitzenburg—said by some to be the best tasting apple of all time. Some potted trees are available for purchase on the spot, and orders are taken for bareroot trees for February delivery.

WHERE TO STAY

♥**Camellia Inn** *211 North St., 800/727-8182, 707/433-8182; 9 rooms; 100% non-smoking; $$-$$$; 2-night minimum on Sat; children under 2 free; no TVs; some bathtubs, gas fireplaces; heated pool (unavailable Nov-Apr); full breakfast.* Situated just 2 blocks from the town square, this 1869 Italianate Victorian townhouse offers a quiet retreat. The grounds surrounding the inn are planted with over 50 varieties of camellia, some of which were given to the original owner by Luther Burbank. Staying in theme, each room is named for a variety of camellia. The tastefully furnished, high-ceilinged Royalty Room boasts an antique Scottish high bed with a ceiling-hung canopy and stepstool. Originally the home's dining room, it also features an unusual ornate antique brass sink fitting. Several rooms have whirlpool bathtubs for two. An afternoon out by the oak-shaded, villa-style pool area is unbelievably relaxing. A buffet breakfast is served in the dining room, where guests are seated at a large claw-foot mahogany table.

Dry Creek Inn *198 Dry Creek Rd., 800/222-5784, 707/433-0300; 102 rooms; 50 non-smoking rooms; $-$$; children under 12 free; cribs; all bathtubs; heated pool (unheated*

Nov-Mar), hot tub; continental breakfast, restaurant; dogs welcome. Part of the Best Western chain, this attractive modern motel has some rooms with waterbeds. All rooms have a complimentary bottle of wine awaiting their occupants.

♥**Madrona Manor** *1001 Westside Rd., 800/258-4003, 707/433-4231, fax 707/433-0703; 21 rooms; some fireplaces; pool; full breakfast.* Featuring an unusual mansard roof, this majestic 3-story mansion is situated off a sideroad that runs through rural vineyards. An imposing archway frames the long driveway leading up to the 8-acre estate. Built in 1881 as a country retreat, it is now a protected historic site operating as an inn. Five of the rooms are furnished with furniture original to the house, and a public music room boasts a square rosewood piano.

For dinner, guests just stroll to the elegant dining room where chef Todd Muir, formerly of Berkeley's Chez Panisse, prepares wonderfully complex dishes and often uses produce from the estate's own gardens and orchards. A fixed-price six-course dinner is $50 per person. One dinner enjoyed here featured a delicious soft shell crab tempura and a peachy dessert sampler of peach shortcake, peach crisp, and peach ice cream. Featuring local Sonoma wines, the wine list actually has a table of contents!

PICNIC PICK-UPS

Downtown Bakery and Creamery *308-A Center St., 707/431-2719; M & W-Sat 7-5:30, Sun to 3:30; closed first 2 weeks in Jan.* Co-owner Lindsey Shere did time in the kitchen at Berkeley's renowned Chez Panisse. She also wrote the best-selling cookbook *Chez Panisse Desserts.* So the exceptional breads, pastries, and ice creams produced in her kitchen here are not a complete surprise. When available, the focaccia, sticky buns, fruit turnovers, and fig newtons are not to be missed. And on warm Wine Country days, it is a pleasure to indulge in one of the shop's old-fashioned milk shakes or sundaes.

Dry Creek General Store *3496 Dry Creek Rd., 707/433-4171, fax 707/433-0409; daily 7-7, to 9 in summer.* Claiming to be "the best deli by a dam site!," this old-fashioned general store/deli is located by a dam site (the Warm Springs Dam) and it sure does dispense good picnic fare! Sandwiches are made to order, and there are plenty of homemade salads and garnishes.

The Salame Tree Deli *304 Center St., 707/433-7224; M-Sat 8-7, Sun 9-6; AE, MC, V.* Sandwiches are made-to-order at this well-stocked old-time deli. A seating area is available for those who prefer to eat on the spot.

WHAT TO DO

Swimming.
　　Healdsburg Memorial Pool *1024 Prince Ave., 707/431-3326; daily 1:30-5:30; adults $1.50, 6-17 75¢, under 6 50¢.* They keep the water warm here—between 80 and 90 degrees—and there is a wading pool for young children.
　　Healdsburg Veterans Memorial Beach *13839 Old Redwood Highway, 707/433-1625; 7am-8pm; $3/car.* This is a choice spot to swim in the warm Russian River, which in summer has an average water temperature of 70 to 75 degrees. A lifeguard is on duty from 10, and canoe and inner tube rentals are available. Facilities

include a diving board, children's wading area, a picnic area with barbecues, and a snack bar. Sunbathers have a choice of a large sandy beach or a shady lawn area.

Timber Crest Farms *4791 Dry Creek Rd., 707/433-8251; M-F 8-5, Sat 10-4.* The high-quality dried fruits available here are made without sulfur, preservatives, or additives. The usual are available as well as the unusual—tropical starfruit, black Bing cherries, mission figs. A bottled mixture of Dried Tomato Spice Medely is wonderful on crackers. Depending on the time of year, it is possible to observe the fruit being harvested or prepared for packaging.

W.C. "Bob" Trowbridge Canoe Trips *20 Healdsburg Ave., 800/640-1386, 707/433-7247; check-in daily 8-12:30, Apr-Oct only; $32/canoe/ day, dinner $6-$6.75; reservations necessary.* Trips are unguided, and children must be at least 6. The canoe fee includes life jackets, paddles, and canoe transport. An after-canoeing barbecue takes place from 4 to 7 each weekend and includes steak or chicken, vegetable, baked beans, salad, garlic bread, and beverage. Trowbridge has five other rental sites along the river.

Westside Farms *7097 Westside Rd., 7 miles south of town, 707/431-1432; daily 10-5 in Oct, by appt. rest of year.* This family farm is open every day in October for its annual **Pumpkin Festival**. Hayrides are free then, and a variety of farm animals are on hand. In addition to several varieties of pumpkins, both Indian corn

and gourds are available for purchase. A self-service stand usually has jars of pop-corn and fresh fertile brown eggs for sale, too.

Windsor Waterworks & Slides *8225 Conde Lane, Windsor, 6 miles south of town, 707/838-7760; M-F 11-7, Sat & Sun 10-8, June-Aug; closed Sept-May; adults $10.95-$11.95, 2-13 $9.95-$10.95, waterslides $2.50/half-hour.* Among the features of the four 400-foot waterslides here are tunnels, 360-degree turns, and a 42-foot drop. Children must be at least 48 inches tall to ride the slides. In addition, there are swimming pools, a wading pool, volleyball courts, a snack bar, and shaded picnic facilities.

WINERIES

Dry Creek Vineyard *3770 Lambert Bridge Rd., 3 miles west of Highway 101, 707/433-1000; tasting daily 10:30-4:30; no tours.* Known for its Fume Blancs and Chenin Blancs, this winery has a cool, shady picnic area under an umbrella formed by old pine and maple trees. When tasting, be sure to sample the winery's spicy Fume Blanc mustard.

A good time to visit is during the annual **Open House** held in June. That's the time to bring a picnic and celebrate the season with live music and wine tasting. Children are not permitted. Call for current details.

Foppiano Vineyards *12707 Old Redwood Highway, 707/433-7272; tasting daily 10-4:30; self-guided tour.* Visitors here are welcome to take a self-guided tour through the Chardonnay, Cabernet Sauvignon, and Petite Sirah vineyards. The tour takes about 30 minutes, and a free explanatory brochure is available in the tasting room.

Hop Kiln Winery *6050 Westside Rd., 707/433-6491; tasting daily 10-5; no tours.* This unique winery is reached by taking a quiet back road through miles of scenic vineyards. Wine tasting occurs inside a landmark 1905 hops-drying barn, once used to supply San Francisco breweries. Known for its big Zinfandels, the winery also produces unique Big Red and A Thousand Flowers blends. Two appealing picnic areas are available. One overlooks a duck pond and vineyards; the other is situated in the shade of a gigantic kadota fig tree planted in 1880.

Piper Sonoma *11447 Old Redwood Highway, 707/433-8843; tasting daily 10-5, Jan-Mar F-Sun only, fee $3; self-guided tours.* Celebrated for its French-style champagnes, the lines of this ultra-modern winery are softened with attractive landscaping and a lily pond. A stop here allows killing the proverbial two birds with one stone. Park once, taste twice: The following winery is located just across the way.

Rodney Strong Vineyards *11455 Old Redwood Highway, 800/678-4763, 707/431-1533; tasting daily 10-5; tours every hour.* While the adults sample the winery's Chardonnays and Cabernet Sauvignons, children may indulge in some grape juice or soda. Picnic tables are available.

Simi Winery *16275 Healdsburg Ave., 707/433-6981; tasting daily 10-4:30; tours at 11, 1, & 3.* This friendly tasting room provides samples of both reserve and non-reserve wines. An inviting shady picnic area is situated under some ancient redwoods.

– Geyserville –

GETTING THERE

Located approximately 8 miles north of Healdsburg via Highway 101.

ANNUAL EVENTS

Fall Colors Festival *October; 707/857-3745.* The whole town celebrates the end of the grape harvest with a parade and festival.

WHERE TO STAY

♥**The Hope-Merrill House** *21253 Geyserville Ave., 800/825-4BED, 707/857-3356; 12 rooms; 100% non-smoking; $$-$$$; 2-night minimum on weekends; children under 1 free; no TVs; some bathtubs, fireplaces; some shared baths; heated pool (unavailable Oct-Apr); full breakfast.* This Eastlake Stick Victorian dates from 1870 and is exquisitely restored to that period with antique furnishings. It even has authentically duplicated Bradbury & Bradbury silk-screened wallpapers. In fact, the owner's restoration efforts won a first place award from the National Trust for Historic Preservation. When the temperature permits, a dip in the attractively situated pool beckons, and in the morning a full breakfast is served in the formal dining room.

Should this lovely inn be booked, try the charming Queen Anne Victorian **Hope-Bosworth House** located across the street. Under the same ownership, these two houses share facilities.

A special two-part package is available for wannabe winemakers. Participants check in at harvest time in September for a round of grape picking and pressing, plus, of course, some tasting and dining. They return in the spring for a bottling and labeling session, plus, of course, more tasting and dining, and then depart with three cases of their own wine sporting personalized labels. Call for details.

WHERE TO EAT

Chateau Souverain *400 Souverain Rd., Independence Lane exit off Highway 101; closed first 2 weeks in Jan. Restaurant: 707/433-3141; L & D W-Sat, SunBr; $$-$$$; highchairs, booster seats; 100% non-smoking; reservations suggested; AE, MC, V. Winery: 707/433-8281; tasting in cafe W-Sun 10:30-5; no tours.* In addition to tasting, this winery features a first-rate restaurant. Overlooking the scenic Alexander Valley, the restaurant presents a menu of refined cuisine designed to complement the all-Sonoma County wine list. The winery's own vintages are available by the glass. In good weather diners are seated outdoors. A more casual cafe serves a less expensive menu of salads, focaccia pizzas, and sandwiches. Live entertainment is provided on weekends.

WHAT TO DO

Lake Sonoma *3333 Skaggs Springs Rd., 707/433-9483.* This scenic spot hosts all manner of water activities—fishing, boating, water-skiing, swimming. A Visitors Center *(Thur-M 10-5; free)* displays the area's wildlife and provides a self-guided tour through a **fish hatchery**. When the salmon run here, usually from November through April, they may be observed using a man-made fish ladder.

WINERIES

Geyser Peak Winery *22281 Chianti Rd., 1 mile north of town at Canyon Rd. exit off Highway 101, 800/225-WINE, 707/857-9426; tasting daily 10-5; tours by appt.* Shaded patio picnic tables overlook Alexander Valley. While parents are tasting wines, children are treated to grape juice and balloons.

Lake Sonoma Winery *9990 Dry Creek Rd., 707/431-1550; tasting daily 10-5; tours by appt.* Featuring a gorgeous view of the Dry Creek Valley, this winery is known for its Cabernet Sauvignons and Merlots. It is the only winery in the country that produces the rich Zinfandel-like Cinsault varietal. Tasters are welcome to picnic on the porch overlooking the vineyards, and on weekends grills are always fired up and waiting to barbecue.

Trentadue Winery *19170 Geyserville Ave., 707/433-3104; tasting daily 10-5; tours by appt.* Don't miss a picnic here in the welcoming shade of a spacious grape arbor. Known for its spicy red Carignane and red muscat Aleatico, which is available only at the winery, this small family enterprise also sells picnic supplies in its tasting room.

– Hopland –

VISITOR INFORMATION

Hopland Chamber of Commerce *P.O. Box 677, Hopland 95449, 707/744-1171.*

GETTING THERE

Located approximately 25 miles north of Geyserville via Highway 101.

WHERE TO EAT

The Cheesecake Lady *13325 S. Highway 101, 800/CAKE-LADY, 707/744-1441; B & L daily; $; children's portions; 100% non-smoking; MC, V.* This factory services restaurants and hotels throughout Northern California. Visitors are welcome to observe it in operation. In the cafe over 30 different desserts are available, along with premium Double Rainbow ice cream and drinks from an espresso bar. Cheesecakes can be shipped anywhere in the country through the mail order division.

The Hopland Brewery *13351 S. Highway 101, 707/744-1361, 707/744-1015; L & D daily; $; highchairs; MC, V.* Opened in 1983, this microbrewery was the first brewpub in California since Prohibition. Ales are unpasteurized and unfiltered. Try a Blue Heron Ale (like English bitter) or a sweeter Red Tail Ale. Seating is either inside the 100-year-old brick pub room, featuring vintage stamped tin walls, or outside in a pleasant beer garden, where children can play in a large sandbox while adults sip suds in shade provided by hop vines. The simple, tasty pub food includes juicy hamburgers on whole wheat Boonville Bruce bread, house-made beer sausages, salads, and chips with salsa or guacamole.

The **Mendocino Brewing Company brewhouse** is located out back. Tours are available with 24-hour notice.

– Ukiah –

GETTING THERE

Located approximately 15 miles north of Hopland via Highway 101.

WHERE TO STAY

Orr Hot Springs *13201 Orr Springs Rd., 707/462-6277; 13 units; 100% non-smoking; $-$$$; 2-night minimum on Sat; children under 3 free; no TVs; communal kitchen; some wood-burning stoves; unheated spring water pool, 4 hot tubs, sauna.* In the 1800s, when this mineral springs resort was built, patrons reached it via stagecoach. Its natural rock swimming pool is filled with cool mineral spring water. Several underground springs are tapped to fill four porcelain Victorian tubs in an 1863 bath house, where bathing suits are optional. A gas-fired sauna features a stained-glass window and a clear skylight. Guests sleep either in cabins or in a dormitory and must bring their own food. Campsites and day use rates are also available.

Montgomery Redwoods State Park, which offers two loop trails for hiking, is just 1 mile down the road.

Vichy Springs Resort *2605 Vichy Springs Rd., 3 miles east of Highway 101, 707/462-9515; 14 units; $$$; 100% non-smoking; no TVs; some kitchens, fireplaces, wood-burning stoves; unheated pool (unavailable Nov-Apr), hot tubs; continental breakfast.* Founded in 1854, this 700-acre B&B resort was named after the famous French springs dis-

Mark Twain taking the waters

covered by Julius Caesar. It is said to have the only naturally carbonated mineral baths in North America. In its heyday the resort attracted guests from San Francisco, who had to endure a day's journey to get here—by ferry across the Bay, by train to Cloverdale, then by stagecoach to the resort. They came in search of the curative powers attributed to the waters found here. Among the famous guests were writers Mark Twain, Jack London, and Robert Louis Stevenson, and presidents Ulysses S. Grant, Benjamin Harrison, and Teddy Roosevelt. The resort's 130-year-old concrete "Champagne" tubs, filled with tingling 90-degree naturally carbonated water, are situated in a shady area overlooking a creek. Swimsuits are required. Guests may hike to a 40-foot-tall waterfall, mountain bike over dirt roads, and swim in a non-chlorinated Olympic-size pool. Picnic lunches may be arranged, and the resort's own bottled Vichy Springs Mineral Water is available. Non-guests are also welcome to use the facilities (*$25/person/day*).

WHAT TO DO

Grace Hudson Museum and **Sun House** *431 S. Main St., 707/462-3370; W-Sat 10-4:30, Sun 12-4; tours of Sun House on the hour, 12-3; suggested donation $2/person, $5/family.* Named for the prominent painter who specialized in doing portraits of the area's Pomo Indians, this museum displays Indian games, musical instruments, and baskets as well as some of Ms. Hudson's personal paraphernalia.

Her six-room home, the California Craftsman-style Sun House, is adjacent to the museum. Built of redwood in 1911, it still has most of its original furnishings. Picnic facilities are available in a park area within the 4-1/2-acre complex.

– Willits –

GETTING THERE

Located approximately 25 miles north of Ukiah via Highway 101.

WHERE TO STAY

Emandal Farm *16500 Hearst Rd., 16 miles northeast of town, 800/262-9597, 707/459-5439; open for 1-week stays during Aug, weekends in spring and fall; rates vary according to age and include 3 meals/day; cribs; communal bathrooms.* On weekend visits to this 1,000-acre working farm, guests arrive for Friday night dinner. Families are assigned a table for the weekend and then spend some blissful hours there chowing down superb home cooking prepared with the farm's own organically grown produce. Days are filled with leisurely activies—perhaps a short hike down to a sandy beach on the magnificent Eel River for a swim, or maybe a hike up the steep mountain behind the barn to Rainbow Lake. Some folks just doze in the hammocks outside each of the rustic one-room redwood cabins dating from 1916. Others get involved with the farm chores: milking the goats, collecting eggs, feeding the pigs.

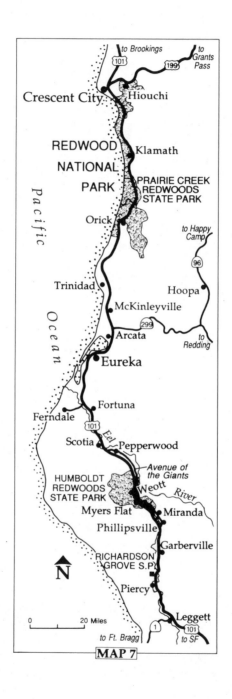

to Brookings
101
to
Grants
Pass
199

Crescent City Hiouchi

REDWOOD
NATIONAL
PARK

Klamath

PRAIRIE CREEK
REDWOODS
STATE PARK

Pacific

Orick

to Happy
Camp
96

Trinidad

Hoopa

McKinleyville

Ocean

299

Arcata

to
Redding

Eureka

Fortuna

Ferndale
101

Scotia Pepperwood

Avenue of
the Giants

HUMBOLDT
REDWOODS
STATE PARK

Eel

Weott

River

Myers Flat Miranda

Phillipsville

Garberville

RICHARDSON
GROVE S.P.

N

Piercy

0   20 Miles

Leggett

1

101

to Ft. Bragg

to SF

MAP 7

– Eureka/Redwoods –

A LITTLE BACKGROUND

Ambitious logging activity has, over time, changed the scenery here quite a bit. The best of the remaining virgin redwoods are in this area's state parks, all of which were established in the 1920s.

Eureka is known as "the coolest city in the nation." The average temperature in July ranges from 52 to 60 degrees. In January it drops to between 41 and 53 degrees. The average annual rainfall is 39 inches, and fog is heavy even in summer.

The winter off-season is an uncrowded (and cold) time to visit the north coast redwood country around Humboldt Bay. Visitors then should pack warm clothing and kiss the sunshine good-bye as they prepare to enjoy the stunning beauty of this quiet, foggy area.

Eureka and nearby Arcata are both known for their well-preserved Victorian homes. Arcata, a smaller town and home to Humboldt State University, also has an old-fashioned town square.

VISITOR INFORMATION

Eureka/Humboldt County Convention & Visitors Bureau *1034 Second St., Eureka 95501, 800/338-7352, 707/443-5097.*

The Greater Eureka Chamber of Commerce *2112 Broadway, Eureka 95501, 800/ 356-6381, 707/442-3738.*

GETTING THERE

Located approximately 130 miles north of Willits and approximately 280 miles north of San Francisco via Highway 101.

ANNUAL EVENTS

World Championship Great Arcata to Ferndale Cross Country Kinetic Sculpture Race *May; 800/GET-RACE, 707/725-3851.* In this unusual competition, artistic people-powered sculptures race 38 miles over dunes and rivers from Arcata to Ferndale. It is always held on Memorial Day Weekend.

WHERE TO STAY

♥**Carter House** *1033 3rd St., 707/445-1390; 6 rooms; 100% non-smoking; $$-$$$+; unsuitable for children; no TVs; 1 fireplace; some shared baths; full breakfast.* Looking a bit ominous on its bare corner lot, this weather-darkened redwood home was built in 1982. A re-creation of the 1884 design of two San Francisco architects, it is all sweetness and light inside. Contemporary paintings and ceramics by local artists are on display throughout, and all are available for purchase. Evening wine and hors d'oeuvres are served in a pleasant parlor, and at bedtime cookies and cordials appear. Dinner is available in the dining room on weekends by reservation.

Across the street, the even newer **Hotel Carter** *(301 L St., 707/444-8062)* provides tasteful lodging amenable to families. Some of the rooms there have kitchens and fireplaces, and they all have color TVs and bathtubs. A restaurant, with highchairs and booster seats, and room service are also available.

The Eureka Inn *518 7th St., 800/862-4906, 707/442-6441, fax 707/442-0637; 105 rooms; 15 non-smoking rooms; $$-$$$; children under 16 free; cribs; some kitchens, bathtubs, fireplaces; heated pool, hot tub, 2 saunas; 2 restaurants, room service; dogs welcome.* Built in English Tudor style in 1922 and now a National Historic Landmark, this is *the* place to stay. It is within easy walking distance of Old Town attractions. An elaborate series of Christmas events is scheduled here each December.

Motel Row. Last-minute accommodations can usually be found along both 4th Street and Broadway.

WHERE TO EAT

Lazio's Seafood Restaurant *327 2nd St., in Old Town, 707/443-9717; L & D daily; $$; highchairs, booster seats, children's portions; no reservations; MC, V.* Fresh local seafood is the specialty here. It's usually crowded, so expect a short wait.

Samoa Cookhouse *on Cookhouse Dr. (from Highway 101 take Samoa Bridge to end, turn left on Samoa Blvd., take first left turn), 707/442-1659; B, L, & D daily; $$; highchairs, booster seats, children's portions; no reservations; AE, MC, V.* Originally built by the Georgia-Pacific Corporation to feed its loggers, this is the last surviving cookhouse in the West. There is no menu. Just sit down and the food starts arriving. The hearty, delicious family-style meals are served at long tables in three large, noisy dining halls. Though the menu changes daily, a typical lunch might consist of marinated three-bean salad, homemade soup, fresh baked bread with butter, assorted jams and honey, coleslaw, scalloped potatoes, deep-fried cod with tartar sauce, mixed vegetables, coffee or tea, and butterscotch pudding topped with whipped cream. A fantastic value! Most items are prepared with fresh ingredients. The only item served that is not included in the fixed price is milk.

After dining, visitors can wander through a logging mini-museum. Freshly-baked loaves of bread and toy logging trucks are available for purchase and make good souvenirs. To work off some calories or to work up an appetite, many diners enjoy walking along the area's driftwood-strewn beaches. To find them, follow one of the unmarked turnoffs from Samoa Boulevard.

Tomaso's Tomato Pies *216 E St., 707/445-0100; L M-Sat, D daily; $-$$; highchairs, booster seats; no reservations; AE, MC, V.* Menu items in this casual spot include a square Sicilian-style pizza with whole wheat crust, spinach pies, calzone, homemade soups, and hot pasta items. Portions run large, and delicious homemade breadsticks are served with all meals. For dessert there are cakes, a variety of coffees, and hot chocolate made with real milk. A dumbwaiter, which delivers orders to the loft dining area, provides free entertainment.

WHAT TO DO

Carson Mansion *2nd/M Sts.* Built in 1885, this is said to be the most photographed house in the United States and is the "queen" of Victorian architecture. It now houses a private club and may be viewed only from the exterior.

Clarke Memorial Museum *240 E/3rd Sts., 707/443-1947; Tu-Sat 12-4; by donation.* An important collection of local Indian baskets and ceremonial regalia is on display here along with an extensive collection of 19th century regional artifacts and pioneer relics. The palatial 1912 building is also the background for displays of antique weapons and Victorian furniture and decorative arts.

Covered Bridges *take Highway 101 south to Elk River Rd., then follow Elk River Rd. to either Bertas Rd. (2 miles) or Zanes Rd. (3 miles).* These two all-wood covered bridges were constructed in 1936.

Dolbeer steam donkey

Fort Humboldt State Historic Park *3431 Fort Ave., 707/445-6567; W-Sun 9-5; free.*
This was U.S. Grant's headquarters in 1854. The hospital, which dates to 1863, has
been restored and is now used as a museum. Exhibits within the park include some
locomotives, a restored logger's cabin, and displays of pioneer logging methods.
An excellent view of Humboldt Bay makes this a nice spot for a picnic.

At the annual **Steam Donkey Days,** held in April, there are logging demonstrations and the steam donkeys are operated.

Humboldt Bay Harbor Cruise *foot of C St., 707/445-1910; daily at 1, 2, 4, & 7; adults*
$15, children $10. The 75-minute cruise aboard the tiny *M/V Madaket*, which once
ferried workers to the lumber mills across the bay in Samoa, allows a view of the
bustling activity and native wildlife of the bay. Built in 1910 in Fairhaven, California, it is the oldest operating passenger vessel in the U.S. and has the smallest
licensed bar in the state. A cocktail cruise sails at 5:30, and a Sunday brunch cruise
sails at 11; both have an additional charge.

Old Town *1st/2nd/3rd Sts. from C to G Sts.* This waterfront area consists of restored
commercial and residential buildings. Many restaurants, boutiques, and antique
shops are now located here.

Because flowers don't grow well in the area due to the lack of sunshine, the
late artist Romano Gabriel constructed a folk art garden from vegetable crates. It
is now known as the **Romano Gabriel Sculpture Garden** *(315 Second St).* On the
other hand, across the street in the courtyard at Imperiale Square a gardener man-

ages to defy the weather by growing a forest of giant, colorful flowers in containers.

Sequoia Park Zoo *Glatt/W Sts., 707/442-6552; Tu-Sun 10-5, May-Sept to 7; free.* The backdrop for this combination zoo/playground/picnic area is a 52-acre grove of second-growth redwoods. Hiking trails, gardens, and a duck pond are also within the zoo, and a petting zoo is open during the summer.

101 South of Town

Ferndale *15 miles south of town.* This entire town is composed of well-preserved and restored Victorian buildings. A State Historical Landmark, it is also an artists' colony and is filled with antique shops, galleries, restaurants, and B&Bs. Just south of town is **Cape Mendocino**—the most westerly point on the continental U.S.

♥**The Gingerbread Mansion** *400 Berding St., Ferndale, 800/952-4136, 707/786-4000; 9 rooms; 100% non-smoking; $$$-$$$+; unsuitable for children under 10; no TVs; some bathtubs, fireplaces, wood-burning stoves; continental breakfast.* Originally built in 1899 as a doctor's home, this carefully restored Victorian mansion has gables and turrets and is painted a cheery peach and yellow. Rooms are furnished with Victorian antiques, and one suite features antique "his" and "hers" claw-foot tubs perched toe to toe on a raised platform. Guests are pampered with bathrobes and bubble bath, and coffee or tea is left outside rooms before breakfast. Bicycles painted to match the house are available for loan, an afternoon tea is served in the four guest parlors, and hand-dipped chocolates announce bedtime.

Pacific Lumber Company Mill Tour *125 Main St., Scotia, 27 miles south of town, 707/764-2222; M-F 8-10:30am & 12-2:30pm, closed weeks of July 4th and Christmas; free.* Take a self-guided tour through the world's largest redwood lumber mill. Get a pass for the hour tour in the old Greek Revival-style First National Bank building, which is now a logging museum. Scotia is one of the last company-owned lumber towns in the United States.

Scotia Inn *106 Mill/Main Sts., Scotia, 707/764-5683; 11 rooms; 100% non-smoking; $-$$$; children under 2 free; cribs; all bathtubs; continental breakfast, restaurant.* The hotel that stood on this site in 1888 accommodated travelers waiting for the stagecoach south. The current hotel, built in 1923, greets guests with a magnificent lobby featuring walls of burnished redwood. Rooms are furnished with antiques, and bathrooms feature claw-foot tubs. A splurge on the Bridal Suite is worthwhile because of its impressive private Jacuzzi room. Dinner and Sunday brunch are served in grand style in the dining room.

Demonstration Forest *on Highway 101, 5 miles south of Scotia; daily 8-4, summer only.* To educate the public about modern forestry practices and to permit the public to see how a forest grows back after harvest, the Pacific Lumber Company has set up self-guided tours through a part of its forest that was harvested in 1941. Picnic tables are available.

The Avenue of the Giants.

   Humboldt Redwoods State Park *2 miles south of Weott, 707/946-2311; M-F 9-5; $4/car.* Millions of years ago, when dinosaurs roamed the earth, gigantic redwood forests were plentiful. After the Ice Age, the redwood survived only in a narrow 500-mile strip along the northern coast of California. Before the logging days on the north coast, it is estimated the area contained 1-1/2 million acres of redwoods. Now only 100,000 acres remain—most preserved by the State Park System. Approximately half of these huge old trees are found in Humboldt Redwoods State Park, home of the Avenue of the Giants.

   The Avenue of the Giants, which is actually the old Highway 101, begins just south of Pepperwood. It continues on for 26 miles to Phillipsville, where it rejoins

the busy newer Highway 101. This breathtaking route parallels the freeway and the Eel River and winds through grove after grove of huge redwoods.

Unusual sights along this unique stretch of road are numerous. Near Myers Flat, the **Shrine Drive-Thru Tree,** which is not part of the state park, has a circumference of approximately 64 feet and provides the opportunity to take an unusual picture. The **Children's Forest,** located across the south fork of the Eel River, is a 1,120-acre memorial to children. **Williams Grove** features picturesque picnic and swimming sites on the river. The 13,000-acre **Rockefeller Forest**—the world's largest grove of virgin redwoods—is near Weott. Also referred to as "the world's finest forest," it features hiking trails leading to the Flatiron Tree, the Giant Tree, and the 356-foot Tall Tree. Campsites are available.

Richardson Grove State Park *(707/247-3318, 8 miles south of Garberville)* also has campsites.

Lodging facilities are scattered along the route. A few of the best are listed here in the order found when driving south to Piercy:

Miranda Gardens Resort *6766 Avenue of the Giants, Miranda, 707/943-3011; 16 units; $-$$$+; cribs; some kitchens, bathtubs, fireplaces; heated pool (unavailable Nov-Apr), 2 tennis courts; pets welcome.* Lodging here is a choice of either motel rooms or cottages. A children's playground and plenty of outdoor games—croquet, shuffleboard, and horseshoes—are available.

Benbow Inn *445 Lake Benbow Dr., Garberville, 65 miles south of town, 707/923-2124; 55 rooms; 100% non-smoking; $$-$$$+; closed Jan-Mar; unsuitable for infants; some TVs, fireplaces; restaurant.* This magnificent English Tudor inn, built in 1926, features blooming English gardens, rooms furnished with antiques, a majestic communal room with fireplace and library, an elegant dining room, and a cozy taproom bar. Facilities include a putting green, a 9-hole golf course, lawn games, bicycle rentals, and a private beach and lake. A complimentary tea is served each afternoon, and classic films are scheduled each evening.

Hartsook Inn *900 Highway 101, Piercy, 75 miles south of town, 707/247-3305; 62 units; $-$$; cribs; no TVs; some kitchens, bathtubs; restaurant; pets welcome.* These cottages are scattered in a majestic 30-acre redwood setting adjoining Richardson Grove State Park. Guests may swim in the Eel River and have the use of a children's playground, lawn games, and a lounge with games, movies, and a fireplace.

Confusion Hill *75001 N. Highway 101, Piercy, 707/925-6456; daily 10-5. House: adults $2.50, 6-12 $1.25. Train: Apr-Sept only; adults $2.50, 3-12 $1.25.* At this spot water runs uphill, appearing to defy gravity, and a train takes passengers on a ride through a tree tunnel to the crest of a hill in the redwoods.

Eel River Redwoods Hostel *70400 Highway 101, Leggett, 90 miles south of town, 707/925-6469.* This 40-bed facility is located on the scenic Eel River. See also page 278.

Drive-Thru Tree Park *67402 Drive-Thru Tree Rd., Leggett, 707/925-6363; daily dawn-dusk; $3/car.* Most average-size cars can squeeze through the hole in this 315-foot high, 21-foot diameter redwood tree. Bring a camera. Nature trails and lakeside picnic areas are available.

101 North of Town

Trinidad 23 *miles north of town*. In addition to the following lodgings and attractions, this scenic fishing village has a lighthouse and a very nice beach.

Bishop Pine Lodge *1481 Patrick's Point Dr., 707/677-3314; 13 units; $-$$; cribs; some kitchens, bathtubs; exercise room; pets welcome*. These cozy, secluded cabins are situated among redwoods. A playground, complete with a rustic treehouse, is on the spacious, well-maintained grounds, and the helpful owner knows where to find both the Roosevelt elk and the best restaurants.

The Lost Whale *3452 Patrick's Point Dr., 707/677-3425; 6 rooms; 100% non-smoking; $$-$$$; 2-night minimum on weekends & every night in summer; children under 3 free; cribs; no TVs; some bathtubs; some shared baths; hot tub; full breakfast*. Located on 4 acres of coastal property, this Cape Cod-style inn features four spacious suites with spectacular ocean views. It's actually possible to wake up to the sound of sea lions barking out on Turtle Rock. It's also possible to watch migrating whales while eating breakfast out on the deck. Guests may walk down a scenic, wooded trail to the inn's private beach, and Patrick's Point State Park is just down the road. In the afternoon, guests are served Sherry and home-baked pastries. Children, who are especially well cared for here, can look forward to picking berries, fantasizing in a playhouse, frolicking on a playground, and feeding the inn's bunnies and goats. Two of the suites have special sleeping lofts for children.

Patrick's Point State Park *4150 Patrick's Point Dr., 6 miles north of Trinidad, 707/677-3570; $5/car*. **Agate Beach** is reached via a steep, winding trail with lots of stairs. The Octopus Trees Trail passes by Sitka spruces, whose odd roots cause them to resemble octopi. This 632-acre park is also home to an authentic Yurok Indian village and a small museum. Campsites are available.

Teloniches Marine Lab *707/677-3671*. Part of Humboldt State University, this research facility has a small aquarium exhibit and a "petting pool" that are open to the public. A 30-minute lab tour is available by reservation.

Redwood National Park *Visitor Centers in Orick (40 miles north of town), Crescent City, and Hiouchi, 707/464-6101; daily 8-5; free*. This magnificent national park encompasses 110,000 acres and three state parks. Ranger-led interpretive programs are scheduled daily June through August. During the summer, horses may be rented for rides on scenic equestrian trails and for overnight pack trips. Inquire at the Visitors Center about summer ranger-guided kayak float trips on the Smith River. Also ask there about borrowing Family Adventure Packs, to aid in explorations with children, and about the summer Field Seminars program that offers in-depth, day-long natural history programs.

In summer a **shuttle bus** *(707/488-3461; daily June-Aug, call for schedule and suggested donation)* takes visitors to a trailhead leading to the Tall Trees Grove, which contains the world's tallest tree (367.8 feet) as well as the second, third, and fifth tallest trees. The entire excursion takes about 4 hours, and the walk covers 3.2 miles. The rest of the year it is an 8-1/2-mile walk each way.

Prairie Creek Redwoods State Park *on Highway 101, 46 miles north of town, 707/488-2171; daily 9:30-5; $5/car*. The 8-mile unpaved gravel road to **Gold Bluffs Beach** and **Fern Canyon,** where a short and easy trail awaits, passes through a

beautiful forest into an area of fern-covered cliffs. This 14,000-acre park tends to be foggy and cold and is a refuge for one of the few remaining herds of native **Roosevelt elk.** Campsites are available.

Redwood Hostel *14480 Highway 101, Klamath, 60 miles north of town, 707/482-8265; 1 family room.* This northernmost link in the California coast hostel chain is located within the national park boundaries. Located in the historic circa 1890s **DeMartin House,** it has 30 beds, a full kitchen, and spectacular ocean views. See also page 278.

Requa Inn *451 Requa Rd., Klamath, 707/482-8205; 10 rooms; 100% non-smoking; $$; closed Nov-Mar; unsuitable for children under 8; no TVs; some bathtubs; full breakfast.* Comfortable, pleasantly decorated rooms are available at this restored historic hotel dating from 1914. The dining room is open only to guests and features a surf & turf menu. Fishermen particularly favor this location, which is at the scenic mouth of the Klamath River and in the center of Redwood National Park, just 30 miles south of the Oregon border.

Trees of Mystery *15500 Highway 101, Klamath, 800/638-3389, 707/482-2251; daily dawn-dusk; adults $5.50, 6-12 $2.75.* Visitors to this grove of redwoods are greeted by a 50-foot-tall Paul Bunyan and a 32-foot-tall Babe. Then they pass through a tunnel made from a hollowed-out log and visit a well-maintained group of unusual trees. And at the **End of the Trail Indian Museum** they may peruse a large collection of Indian artifacts. Two snack bars and picnic facilities are available.

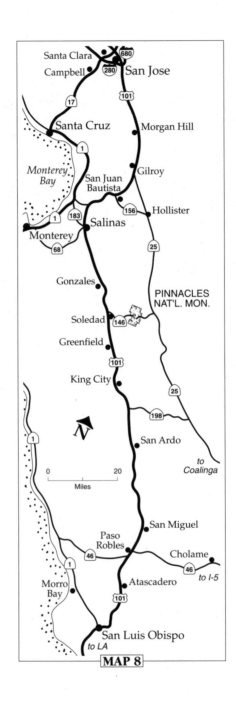

MAP 8

101 South

– San Jose –

A LITTLE BACKGROUND

Currently touting itself as the "capital of Silicon Valley" (a title that seems valid considering that 24 of the area's largest computer companies have headquarters or divisions here), the country's eleventh-largest city and California's third-largest, and oldest, San Jose—having been founded as a Spanish pueblo in 1777—receives relatively little attention for its attractions. But that seems to be changing as the city concentrates on revitalizing its downtown area. Now visitors to the city center can enjoy its many cultural offerings as well as its reliably mild climate.

VISITOR INFORMATION

San Jose Convention & Visitors Bureau *P.O. Box 6299 (333 W. San Carlos St. #1000), San Jose 95150, 800/SAN-JOSE, 408/295-9600, fax 408/295-3937.*

GETTING THERE

Located approximately 50 miles south of San Francisco. Take Highway 101 all the way.

WHERE TO STAY

Fairmont Hotel *170 S. Market St., 800/527-4727, 408/998-1900; 541 rooms; 180 non-smoking rooms; $$-$$$+; children under 18 free; cribs; all bathtubs; some fireplaces; heated pool (unavailable Nov-Apr), sauna, exercise room; 2 restaurants, room service.* Built on the site of what was California's capitol building from 1849 to 1851, this luxury highrise hotel is located within convenient walking distance of all the downtown attractions.

Pruneyard Inn *1995 S. Bascom Ave., Campbell, 800/582-4300, 408/559-4300; 116 rooms; 58 non-smoking rooms; $$-$$$+; children under 13 free; cribs; some kitchens, bathtubs, fireplaces; heated pool, hot tub, exercise room, parcourse; full breakfast.* One of only three hotels in the western U.S. that is located in a shopping center, this tastefully decorated hotel is adjacent to the attractive **Pruneyard** shopping complex. In spite of the location, it manages to provide a secluded feeling. Turndown service is included, and some rooms have VCRs and access to an extensive video library.

WHERE TO EAT

Gordon Biersch Brewery Restaurant *33 E. San Fernando St., 408/294-6785; L & D daily; $-$$; highchairs, booster seats; reservations suggested; AE, MC, V.* Located downtown, this upscale restaurant offers pleasant patio dining as well as seating in a spacious, airy dining room overlooking the stainless steel brew tanks. The eclectic menu changes regularly and features salads, sandwiches, and individual pizzas as well as more serious entrees and desserts. In addition to three styles of house-made beer, the menu offers a selection of varietal wines and coffees. A wonderful sourdough pumpernickel bread from a Santa Cruz bakery is served gratis. Live jazz is performed outdoors on Sunday afternoons from 2 to 5 p.m., and a variety of music is scheduled on Wednesday evenings and some Monday evenings; a cover is charged.

The Old Spaghetti Factory *51 N. San Pedro, 408/288-7488; L M-F, D daily; $; high-chairs, booster seats, children's portions; MC, V.* Oodles of noodle selections await spaghetti connoisseurs here. There is spaghetti with regular marinara sauce, with mushroom sauce, with white clam sauce, and with meat sauce. For those who can't make up their minds, there is spaghetti with a sampler of sauces. Meatballs, spinach tortellini, and baked chicken are also available. Complete dinners come with bread, salad, drink (coffee, tea, or milk), and spumoni ice cream. Housed in what was once the warehouse for the *San Jose Mercury News*, the restaurant features a variety of interesting spots to be seated: an antique barber's chair in the bar, within a restored streetcar, on a brass bed converted into a booth.

WHAT TO DO

Children's Discovery Museum *180 Woz Way, 408/298-5495; Tu-Sat 10-5, Sun 12-5; adults $6, kids $3, parking $2-$4.* Children ages 3 through 13, for whom this museum was designed, are sure to be entertained. Located in **Guadalupe River Park,** the striking lavender-colored building housing what is the largest children's museum in the West was designed by Mexico City architect Ricardo Legorreta. Fortunately he included plenty of places for adults to sit and watch while their kids have a great time—doing everything from making a tortilla from scratch, to blowing gigantic bubbles, to climbing on a full-size fire engine. A snack bar serves inexpensive things that kids like to eat: hot dogs, hamburgers, peanut butter and jelly sandwiches.

Steve Wozniak, of Apple Computer fame, sponsored the Jesse's Clubhouse exhibit named in honor of his son. And the street the museum is located on, Woz Way, is named for guess who?

The Gaslighter Theater *400 E. Campbell Ave., Campbell, 408/866-1408; F & Sat at 8; adults $13, under 13 $11.* A staff member says that this cozy theater is located "in lovely downtown Campbell—Santa Clara County's fastest growing ghost town." And, indeed, at night this seems to be the only show in town. After being greeted in the street and at the door by the exhuberant cast, the whole family has fun inside hissing the villain and cheering the hero—while munching on, and throwing, complimentary popcorn. The two-part shows are not at all subtle, making them great for school-age children. Shows include both a melodrama (such as *Ignorance Isn't Bliss* or *No Mother to Guide Her)* and a vaudeville performance featuring dancing, singing, and comedy.

Golfland *976 Blossom Hill Rd., across from Oakridge Mall, 408/225-1533; call for schedule. Golf: adults $4.75, under 12 $3.50, M Family Night $2.75. Waterslide: 10 rides $3.75, 20/$5.75, all-day golf & waterslides $10.95. Other locations: 855 El Camino/Wolf, Sunnyvale, 408/245-8434; 1199 Jacklin Rd./I-680, Milpitas, 408/263-6855.* Two 18-hole miniature golf courses, a video room filled with 130 of the latest games, and three waterslides make this a fun family outing.

Great America *on Great America Parkway, off Highway 101 & Highway 237, Santa Clara, 408/988-1800; call for schedule; closed Nov-Feb; $22.95, 3-6 $11.45.* There's no question about it. The thrill rides here are spectacular, and the roller coasters are great shocking fun. Then there are the Yankee Clipper and Logger's Run flume

rides, the double-decker carousel with modern fiberglass animals, the antique carousel with wooden animals built by the Toboggan Company of Philadelphia in 1918, and the Triple Wheel—the world's first triple-arm Ferris wheel. Smurf Woods and Fort Fun feature special rides and activities for children under 12. The world's largest indoor movie screen and three live shows round out the fun.

Kelley Park.

Happy Hollow Park and Zoo *Keyes/Senter Rds., 408/292-8188; M-Sat 10-5, Sun 11-6; adults $2.50, 2-14 $2, parking $3.* Children through age 8 love this mini-theme park. Spacious and shady, it offers a satisfying combination of kiddie rides and zoo animals. A small roller coaster and several other rides cost extra, but a concrete maze and playground equipment are included with admission. Puppet shows are scheduled daily, and picnic tables are available. Zoo animals include shetland ponies and a pygmy hippo, and there is a small seal pool and bird enclosure. For small change, children can hand-feed animals in a petting area. The **Kelley Park Express Train** *(irregular schedule; $1/person)* can be boarded just outside the zoo. It makes stops at the following sites:

Japanese Friendship Garden *408/294-4706; daily 10-5:30; free.* Patterned after the Korakuen Garden in San Jose's sister city of Okayama, this 6-1/2-acre garden includes four heart-shaped lakes populated with rare Koi.

San Jose Historical Museum *1600 Senter Rd., 408/287-2290; M-F 10-4:30, Sat & Sun 12-4:30; adults $2, 6-17 $1.* This 25-acre, ever-growing complex contains over 25 relocated and reconstructed historic homes and business buildings. It depicts San Jose as it was in the 1890s. Refreshments are available in **O'Brien's Ice Cream and Candy Store**—the first place to serve ice cream and sodas west of Detroit.

Mirassou Winery *3000 Aborn Rd., (East Capitol Expressway exit off Highway 101), 408/274-4000; tasting M-Sat 10-5, Sun 12-4; call for tour schedule.* This area's Wine Country may be sampled by taking a freeway ride into the suburbs. Grapevines announce the winery entrance. At this location since 1937, this winery is operated by its fifth generation, making Mirassou the country's oldest winemaking family (since 1854). A broad selection of premium wines may be sampled in a spacious tasting room.

Special events are scheduled regularly: cooking classes; Sunday brunches and sunset dinners featuring refined, elegant menus. An **American Pops Concert and Fireworks Display** is held annually on the Fourth of July.

Museum of Innovation *145 W. San Carlos, 408/279-7150; Tu-Sun 10-5; adults $6, 6-18 $4.* Formerly called "The Garage," this small interim museum was originally named in whimsical reference to the garages in which many Silicon Valley inventions had their humble beginnings—the most famous being the personal computer developed by Steve Jobs and Stephen Wozniak in their garage. The nickname was dropped in favor of something more befitting the major science and technology museum it will become when its new home is completed in 1996. A whimsical audio-kinetic sculpture by George Rhoads is located just outside the entrance. Called The Imaginative Chip, it is a Rube Goldberg-style object made with billiard balls moving through a maze of familiar objects and is meant to represent the movement of information in an integrated circuit chip. Inside, the museum focuses on what is being done currently at local computer companies. Exhibits allow visitors to see how silicon chips are produced, to design a bike, and meet to Vanna the spelling robot. A guided tour is highly recommended. They are scheduled regularly and may also be requested on the spot. Volunteer "Explainers" are also on hand to answer questions, and video and newspaper clippings provide enlightening background information. A winning souvenir is Silicon Valleyopoly, available in the gift shop. Visitors may sample the game's pleasures in the Info Lounge, where they are also welcome to relax with professional journals and computers hooked up to electronic information lines. A snack bar is also available.

Raging Waters *2333 S. White Rd., (Capitol Expressway/Tully Rd.), 408/238-9900; daily 10-7, June-Aug; closed Sept-May; $15.50, under 42" $11.50, after 3pm $9.95, parking $1.* Located in **Lake Cunningham Regional Park,** this water-oriented amusement park claims to have the fastest waterslides this side of the Rockies. Sliders can reach speeds up to 25 miles per hour and can be dropped 6 stories into a catch-pool below. In addition to the waterslides, there is an inner tube ride, a sled ride, a rope swing, and a myriad of other water activities. Among the amenities are 40 lifeguards, free changing rooms and showers, and inexpensive lockers. Where else can a family find such good, clean fun? Note that foods and beverages may not be brought into the park. Food service is available, and a public picnic area is provided just outside the main gate.

Rosicrucian Egyptian Museum *1342 Naglee Ave., 408/947-3636; daily 9-5; adults $6, 7-15 $3.50; strollers not permitted.* This museum houses the largest exhibit of Egyptian, Babylonian, and Assyrian artifacts on the West Coast. Highlights of the collection include mummies, fine jewelery, and a full-size reproduction of a 4,000-year-old rock tomb. The surrounding 7.5-acre park is stunningly adorned with exotic trees and flowers and unusual Egyptian statuary.

The adjacent **Rosicrucian Planetarium Science Center** *(408/947-3638; call for schedule; adults $3, 7-15 $1.50, under 5 not admitted)* presents shows daily.

San Jose Flea Market *1590 Berryessa Rd., between Highways 680 & 101, 408/453-1110; W-Sun dawn-dusk; free; $3 parking fee Sat & Sun.* Said to be the largest in the world, this flea market features over 2000 vendors spread out over 120 acres. In addition, there are more than 35 restaurants and a 1/4-mile-long produce section. A variety of free entertainment is also provided.

San Jose Museum of Art *110 S. Market St., 408/294-2787; W-Sun 10-5, Thur to 8pm; adults $4, students $2, under 12 free, free admission on Thur.* Holding a collection of primarily contemporary American art, this unusual part 1892 Romanesque/part 1991 stark modern sandstone building is said to serve as a metaphor for contemporary art's ties to tradition.

Winchester Mystery House *525 S. Winchester Blvd., 408/247-2101; tours daily 9:30-4, longer in summer; adults $12.95, 6-12 $6.50; strollers not permitted.* The story goes that Sarah Winchester, heir to the $20 million Winchester rifle fortune, believed that to make amends for a past wrong-doing she had to build additions to her circa 1884 Victorian mansion continuously, 24-hours-a-day. Her eccentric ideas resulted in some unusual features: asymmetrical rooms, narrow passageways, zig-

zag stairwells, and doors opening into empty shafts. The tour takes in 110 of the 160 rooms, climbs more than 200 steps, and covers almost a mile.

The **Winchester Historical Firearms Museum,** which holds one of the largest collections of Winchester rifles on the West Coast, provides an interesting way to pass time while waiting for the tour to begin. Food service is available, and picnic tables are provided in a courtyard. A self-guided tour of the 6 acres of Victorian gardens, which are sprinkled liberally with fountains and statues, is also included with admission.

Spooky flashlight **Halloween Tour**s are scheduled annually in October.

– Morgan Hill –

GETTING THERE

Located approximately 20 miles south of San Jose via Highway 101.

WHERE TO EAT/WHAT TO DO

The Flying Lady Party Restaurant *15060 Foothill Rd., (Tennant exit east off Highway 101), 408/779-4136; L W-Sat, D W-Sun, SunBr; $-$$; highchairs, booster seats. Museums: by donation.* This family-owned and -operated enterprise offers the unique opportunity of dining beneath six full-size aircraft, including a reproduction of the Wright Brothers Flyer. Additionally, over 100 scale model planes continuously "fly" overhead on a 451-foot-long converted dry cleaners rack. Upon request, diners are provided with a written guide that helps identify each of the scale models. Lunch, an especially good time for families, is a cafeteria-style buffet. Selections, prepared from scratch in the restaurant's huge kitchen and bakery, include a variety of salads, sandwiches, hot entrees, the kitchen's famous honey-baked ham, breads, fruits, desserts, and beverages. Sunday brunch is enhanced by live Dixieland jazz, and on Friday and Saturday nights there is live music and dancing.

But the fun doesn't stop there. Hundreds of colorful flags from the owner's collection decorate the property. All countries are represented—even some that no longer exist. Located on 200 acres of former dairy land, the complex also houses a public 18-hole golf course and a wedding chapel. The **Wagons to Wings Museums** are also here. The former displays horse-drawn wagons in a barn. The latter displays antique planes (a red Stinson, a green bi-wing Sopwith Camel, a World War II P-51 Mustang, and a 1929 TWA Ford tri-motor airplane that starred in the opening scenes of *Indiana Jones and the Temple of Doom*) and cars in an airplane hangar the size of a football field.

– San Juan Bautista –

A LITTLE BACKGROUND

Once the largest city in central California, this town is now a sleepy remnant of that time. It's hard to believe that at one time seven stage lines operated out of the town and that there were numerous busy hotels and saloons. Now there are just a few Mexican restaurants, boutiques, and antique shops.

VISITOR INFORMATION

San Juan Bautista Chamber of Commerce *P.O. Box 1037 (402-A Third St.), San Juan Bautista 95045, 408/623-2454.*

GETTING THERE

Located approximately 25 miles south of Morgan Hill. Take Highway 101 south, then Highway 156 east.

ANNUAL EVENTS

Early Days at San Juan Bautista *July; 408/623-4881.* Visitors see re-enactments of 19th century townspeople performing everyday tasks, such as tortilla-making and baking bread in a hornito oven. The restored Plaza Hotel's famous bar is opened for business, and sometimes a Santa Maria-style barbecue is held in the mission's olive grove.

La Virgen del Tepeyac *December; 408/623-2444.* This early California folk opera is presented in the mission by El Teatro Campesino, a local acting company. Also scheduled are a candlelight tour of the mission and **La Posada**—a procession through the city streets in which Mary and Joseph are portrayed seeking shelter.

WHAT TO DO

Fremont Peak State Park *on San Juan Canyon Road, 11 miles from town, 408/623-4255, observatory 408/623-2465; daily 8-sunset; $5/car.* A popular destination for picnickers and hikers, this park's summit is an easy 15-minute climb from the parking area. An astronomical observatory with a 30-inch reflecting telescope is open to the public twice each month. Call for schedule. Campsites are available.

San Juan Bautista State Historic Park *408/623-4881; daily 10-4:30; adults $2, 6-12 $1; mission only, by donation.* This is the main attraction in town. Located within the park, **Mission San Juan Bautista** was founded in 1797. It is the fifteenth in the chain of 21 California missions and has the largest church. The park's assortment of restored buildings allows visitors to see what life was like in this area in the early 1800s. The **Castro Adobe** sits on the plaza in a picturesque area perfect for picnicking. If everything looks familiar, it may be because it was a major location in the Hitchcock movie *Vertigo.*

WHERE TO EAT

Jardines de San Juan *115 Third St., 408/623-4466; L & D daily; $-$$; highchairs, booster seats; MC, V.* What a wonderful fair-weather experience it is to sit outside in the brick courtyard here under a sheltering umbrella. Among the profusely flowering gardens, diners peruse the menu while sipping icy cold margaritas and dipping freshly fried, crisp tortilla chips in tasty salsa. Excellent flautas consist of shredded beef rolled in a deep-fried tortilla and topped with guacamole. Tacos and enchiladas are also available. On weekends after 5 p.m. regional specialties join the menu. Red snapper Veracruz is available on Fridays, carne asada on Saturdays, and drunken chicken on Sundays. Limited amounts of these specialties are prepared, so diners must call to reserve their portion. Live music is scheduled on the outdoor stage each Saturday and Sunday from noon to 3:30.

San Juan Bakery *319 Third St, 408/623-4570; daily 7-6.* This old-fashioned bakery makes a wonderful sourdough French bread, a down-soft buttermilk bread, and an assortment of delicious breakfast pastries. The sugar cookies are particularly good and make a great car snack. Picnic supplies are also available.

– Salinas –

A LITTLE BACKGROUND

Salinas is one of the biggest cities in the Salinas Valley. Known as "the salad bowl of the nation," this valley is where author John Steinbeck spent his formative years. Many of his novels are set here. In fact, the first working title for *East of Eden* was "Salinas Valley."

VISITOR INFORMATION

Salinas Chamber of Commerce *P.O. Box 1170 (119 E. Alisal), Salinas 93902, 408/424-7611.*

GETTING THERE

Located approximately 20 miles south of San Juan Bautista via Highway 101. It is also possible to take Amtrak from Oakland or San Jose and return the same day. Call 800/872-7245 for more information.

ANNUAL EVENTS

California Rodeo *July; 408/757-2951.* First presented in 1911, this outdoor rodeo is ranked fourth largest in the world. It is especially noted for its trick riders, clowns, and thoroughbred racing. Prize money totals over $200,000, attracting the best of the cowboys to the competitions.

Steinbeck Festival *August; 408/758-7314.* Each year one of Steinbeck's many novels is emphasized in this intellectual festival honoring the town's native son. Bus and walking tours, films, lectures, and panel discussions are all part of the festivities.

WHERE TO EAT

The Steinbeck House *132 Central Ave., 408/424-2735; seatings at 11:45 & 1:15 M-F; $; 1 highchair, 1 booster seat; reservations suggested; MC, V.* In 1902, John Steinbeck was born in the front bedroom of this beautifully renovated 1897 Victorian house. In *East of Eden* he described it as ". . . an immaculate and friendly house, grand enough but not pretentious . . . inside its white fence surrounded by its clipped lawn and roses . . ." Now a volunteer group owns the house and operates it as a gourmet luncheon restaurant. Serving seasonal produce grown in the Salinas Valley, the restaurant's menu changes daily and includes items such as spinach sau-

Mary, John & Jill —
Salinas Aug 28.07

John Steinbeck and his sister Mary on Jill—the inspiration for The Red Pony.

sage en croute and green chili quiche. The fixed-price lunch *($10.78)* includes entree, dessert, beverage, and tax. Though the dining rooms are elegantly decorated, with Steinbeck memorabilia filling the walls, the atmosphere is casual. Comfortable travel attire is acceptable, and children are welcome and may share portions with their parents or siblings.

After lunch, a cellar gift shop invites browsing, and perhaps selecting a souvenir book by Steinbeck.

From here it's just a short walk down the Victorian home-bedecked street to the **Steinbeck Library.**

– Gonzales –

GETTING THERE

Located approximately 20 miles south of Salinas via Highway 101.

WHAT TO DO

The Monterey Vineyard *800 S. Alta St., 408/675-2316; tasting daily 10-5; tours daily 11-4.* This attractive modern winery displays a collection of Ansel Adams photographs that tell the *Story of a Winery*. Picnic tables, a pond populated with ducks and geese, and lush grassy areas offer a relaxing respite from traffic.

Pinnacles National Monument *in Soledad, approximately 20 miles southeast of town, 408/389-4578; $3/car.* Formed by ancient volcanic activity, this scenic area is home to craggy pinnacles and spires. It is particularly surprising to come across, because this area is otherwise so flat. Spring and fall are the best times to visit for hiking and camping, spring being particularly popular because of the stunning display of wildflowers. At other times the temperatures can be uncomfortable. A variety of raptors—prairie falcons, red-shouldered hawks, and golden eagles— nest in the rocks and can sometimes be observed.

The more developed east side of the park is reached by taking Highway 25 south, then Highway 146 west. There, a Visitor Center is open from 9 to 5 daily, and an easy 2-mile loop trail leads to the Bear Gulch Caves.

– San Miguel –

GETTING THERE

Located approximately 65 miles south of Soledad via Highway 101.

WHAT TO DO

Mission San Miguel Arcangel *801 Mission St., 805/467-3256; daily 9:30-4:30; by donation.* Founded in 1797, this is the sixth in the chain of California's 21 missions. The present mission building was constructed in 1816. Though the outside architecture is simple, the delicate neoclassical paintings inside, done by parish Indians, are especially noteworthy. Beehive ovens and olive presses are on view in the gardens, and shaded picnic tables are provided.

– Paso Robles –

VISITOR INFORMATION

Paso Robles Chamber of Commerce *548 Spring St., Paso Robles 93446, 805/238-0506.*

GETTING THERE

Located approximately 5 miles south of San Miguel via Highway 101.

WHERE TO EAT

A&W Rootbeer Drive-In *2110 Spring St., 805/238-0360; daily 10am-11pm; $; children's portions; no cards.* An oasis on this long and usually hot drive, this A&W stand is right out of the '50s. A waitress appears when a car's headlights are turned on, and food is served on a tray that attaches to a partially rolled-down window. Choices are simple: hamburgers, hot dogs, French fries, onion rings, and *cold* root beer.

WHAT TO DO

James Dean Memorial *on Highway 46, Cholame, 25 miles east of town, 805/238-1390.* Depending on a person's mood, this can be an interesting or bizarre side trip. This is where the legendary actor James Dean crashed his Porsche and died in 1955. An obelisk shrine, constructed and maintained by a Japanese national who comes to pay homage twice a year, is located in front of the town's post office.

Wine Tasting. For a free map to the area's wineries, contact the Chamber of Commerce.

– San Luis Obispo –

VISITOR INFORMATION

San Luis Obispo County Visitors & Conference Bureau *1039 Chorro St., San Luis Obispo 93401, 800/634-1414, 805/543-1323.*

GETTING THERE

Located approximately 30 miles south of Paso Robles via Highway 101. It is also possible to take Amtrak. Call 800/872-7245 for more information.

WHERE TO STAY

Embassy Suites Hotel *333 Madonna Rd., 800/EMBASSY, 805/549-0800; 185 rooms; $$-$$$; children under 12 free; cribs; all bathtubs; indoor heated pool, hot tub, exercise room; full breakfast, restaurant, room service.* This branch of the all-suites hotel chain is located adjacent to a large shopping mall with a series of fast-food outlets.

Hostels. Simer's Home Hostel *(805/543-0599)* has six beds and the **Alana Buckley Home Hostel** *(805/541-5510; Apr-Sept only)* has five beds. See also page 278.

Madonna Inn *100 Madonna Rd., 800/543-9666, 805/543-3000; 109 rooms; $$-$$$+; cribs; children under 18 free; cribs; some bathtubs, fireplaces; 2 restaurants.* Begun in 1958 with just 12 rooms, this big pink motel now has 109 guest rooms. All are uniquely (some might say weirdly) decorated—some more uniquely than others. Like the Cave Man Room, with its stone walls, ceilings, and floors, plus a cascading waterfall shower; and the Barrel of Fun Room, in which all the furniture is made from barrels. A photo file at the check-in desk is available to help guests decide which room to book.

For those who are not spending the night, a snack in the flamboyant coffee shop or dining room is a must, and don't miss the restrooms—especially the men's room.

Motel Inn *2223 Monterey St., 805/543-4000; 40 rooms; $; cribs; children free; heated pool; restaurant.* Opened on December 12, 1925, this is the world's very first motel. One-story stucco bungalow units are scattered about the well-maintained grounds. (This motel was recently closed for a major renovation. Call for current information.)

Quality Suites *1631 Monterey St., 800/221-2222, 805/541-5001; 138 rooms; $$-$$$; children under 18 free; cribs; all bathtubs; heated pool, hot tub; full breakfast.* This chain is known for its spacious rooms and made-to-order buffet breakfasts. A complimentary evening cocktail hour is also provided, giving guests a chance to relax and mingle.

Motel Row. A vast array of motels lines the north end of Monterey Street.

WHERE TO EAT

Farmers' Market *held downtown in the 600 & 700 blocks of Higuera St., 805/541-0286; Th 6:30-9pm.* Shoppers here can buy dinner fully prepared or pick up the fixings. This market is known for its delicious barbecued items, and live entertainment is provided free.

Hobee's *1443 Calle Joaquin, 805/549-9186; B, L, & D daily; $; highchairs, booster seats, children's portions; 100% non-smoking; AE, MC, V.* For description, see page 6.

Pepe Delgado's *1601 Monterey St., 805/544-6660; L & D Tu-Sun; $; highchairs, booster seats, children's portions; MC, V.* Comfortable booths and large, solid tables make this popular Mexican spot an especially good choice for families. The hacienda-style building features tile floors, velvet paintings, and papier-mâché parrots hanging from ceiling perches. Potent fruit margaritas and daiquiris come in small, medium, and large sizes and help diners get festive. A large variety of traditional Mexican items is on the menu, and many are available in small portions. Fajitas are particularly fun to order because they arrive sizzling on raised platters and are kept warm by candles.

Rhythm Cafe *1040 Broad St., 805/541-4048; B & L Tu-Sat, D Tu-Sun, SunBr; $-$$; highchairs, booster seats, children's portions; 100% non-smoking; reservations suggested;*

no cards. Featuring a small dining room and a teeny balcony perched above San Luis Creek, this pleasant cafe is best at lunch, when a variety of interesting sandwiches, salads, and pastas are on the menu. An informal afternoon tea is served from 2:30 to 5. The menu then features scones, muffins, and desserts as well as salads and soups.

WHAT TO DO

California Polytechnic State University (Cal Poly) *on Grand Ave., 805/756-2792; tours M, W, F at 10 & 2; free.* Tours of this attractive campus begin at the Information Desk in the University Union.

Gum Alley *next to 733 Higuera St.* For several decades gum chewers have been depositing their product on these brick walls. Some have even taken the time to make designs. A vulgar, tacky eyesore to many, it is a cheap thrill for gum aficionados and most children. So don't get stuck here without a stick. Stock up on different colors of gum before arriving, and note that Double Bubble is reputed to stick best.

Hot Springs. Located on the way to the coast, **Sycamore Mineral Springs** *(1215 Avila Beach Dr., 800/234-5831, 805/595-7302; 28 rooms; $$-$$$; some kitchens, bathtubs, fireplaces; heated pool, 23 hot tubs; restaurant)* has outdoor mineral spring hot tubs that can be rented by the hour and rooms with private hot tubs. At **Avila Hot Springs** *(250 Avila Beach Dr., 805/595-2359)*, inner tubes can be rented to use in a warm pool, and campsites are available.

Mission San Luis Obispo de Tolosa *782 Monterey St., 805/543-6850; daily 9-4; by donation.* Built in 1772, this mission complex includes a museum and a fragrant rose garden. Its charming chapel is still used for services. An adjacent plaza and park provide shady trees, large grassy areas, and paths hugging a stream. Inviting open-air cafes surround it.

The **County Historical Museum** *(696 Monterey St., 805/543-0638; W-Sun 10-4; free)*, which is appropriately filled with historical exhibits, is nearby.

San Luis Obispo Children's Museum *1010 Nipomo St., 805/544-KIDS; Thur & F 1-5, Sat & Sun 10-3; $2/person, under 1 free; strollers not permitted.* Located within a transformed transmission shop, this museum is especially for kids. It holds numerous hands-on exhibits that entice children to explore and interact. They can draw petroglyphs in a mock Chumash cave, fly a space shuttle, and anchor a newscast. Children under 16 must be accompanied by an adult.

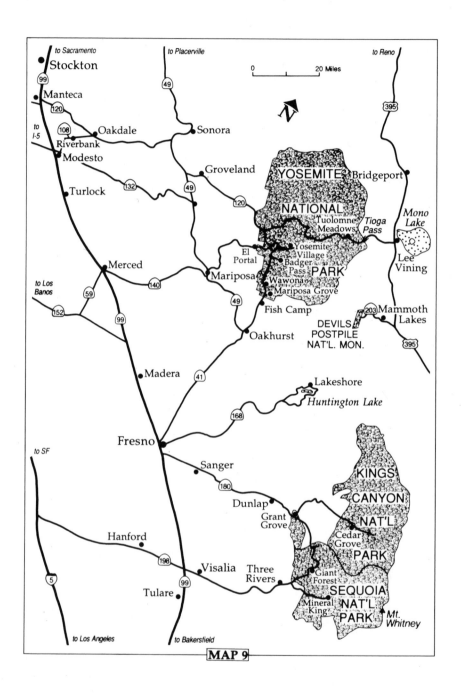

MAP 9

Yosemite National Park

A LITTLE BACKGROUND

Yosemite Park is a place of rest. A refuge . . . in which one gains the advantage of both solitude and society . . . none can escape its charms. Its natural beauty cleanses and warms like fire, and you will be willing to stay forever . . .

— John Muir

Yosemite is worth returning to in every season. Doing so permits enjoying the spectacular beauty of the park's dramatic seasonal changes. Most visitors see this grand national park in the summer, when it is at its busiest, with congested roads and accommodations filled to capacity. All this makes it hard to focus on what was the original draw—the scenic, natural beauty of the High Sierra. To catch a glimpse of the Yosemite described by Muir, it is essential to visit in the off-season: in fall when the colorful foilage change is spectacular; in winter when snow blankets the valley floor; in spring when the falls are at their fullest.

Yosemite's high country was designated a national park in 1890. The valley, which was under state supervision, was added to the national park in 1906. (It is

amazing to realize that the valley comprises just 1 percent of the park's terrain.) Among the park's scenic wonders are **El Capitan**—the largest piece of exposed granite in the world—and **Yosemite Falls**—the highest falls in North America.

Bear in mind that falls and rivers can be dangerous as well as beautiful. Be carefully, especially when hiking with children.

A $5 admission fee, which is good for 7 days, is collected at all park entrances. When they pay, visitors are given a copy of the *Yosemite Guide* (an activities newsletter) and a park map.

VISITOR INFORMATION

National Park Service *Yosemite National Park 95389, 209/372-0200.*

GETTING THERE

Located approximately 240 miles east of San Francisco. Take Highway 80 to Highway 580 to Highway 205 to Highway 120. To minimize the need for chains in winter, consider taking low elevation Highway 140 in from Merced.

ANNUAL EVENTS

Vintners Holidays *November & December.* Dinners at these special events are paired with complementary wines from esteemed winemakers. The sumptuous feasts and related wine seminars are held at The Ahwahnee hotel.

Bracebridge Dinner *December 22, 24, & 25.* Attending this memorable dinner at The Ahwahnee hotel is a pleasure not many get to enjoy. This expensive experience costs $125 per person *(children 8-12 $105, not appropriate for under 8)* and requires that participants apply for reservations a full year in advance. Still, applications are so numerous that guests must be chosen by lottery. Since 1927 the fare at the 3-hour mock-medieval feast has been seven courses of elegant Christmas dishes. Pageantry, carols, and jesters entertain diners between courses.

STOPS ALONG THE WAY

Oakwood Lake Resort *874 E. Woodward Rd., Manteca, 209/239-2500; May-Sept only, call for schedule; all day pass: over 4-feet-tall $15.95, under 4-feet free.* The main attraction here is the nine fiberglass waterslides. Most feature over 60 feet of enclosed tunnel and several 360-degree turns. A special slide for small children and timid adults is available at no charge. More daring is required for the Rapids Ride, which is maneuvered on an inner tube, and the Rampage Ride, in which riders sit on a plastic toboggan and drop 63 feet down a steep slide and then skim across the water. Resort facilities include a fishing lake, a playground, barbecue and picnic areas, and campsites. Several other rides, including Indy-style go-carts, are available at an additional fee. Special rates for half-day visits and picnic use are available.

Riverbank Cheese Company *6603 Second St., Riverbank, 209/869-4533; daily 9-5; call for tour schedule.* Specialty cheeses include teleme and assorted varieties of cheddars and Jacks. Picnic supplies are also stocked.

A riverside picnic may be enjoyed in town at **Jacob Myers Park,** located on First Street across the Burneyville Ferry Bridge.

Hershey Chocolate U.S.A. *120 S. Sierra Ave., Oakdale, 209/848-8126; tours M-F 8:30-3; free; strollers not permitted.* A good way to prepare for this visit is by reading the children's book, or seeing the movie, entitled *Charlie and the Chocolate Factory.* Tour participants sign-in at the Visitors Center and then ride a shuttle bus to the factory. Upon entering the factory the lucious chocolate smells become intense. It's easy to become quite stirred oneself when viewing the multiple 5-ton vats of liquid chocolate being stirred by heavy granite rollers. Workers in the noisy, warm, and fragrant factory look happy. *Real* happy. Maybe that's because they get to eat as much chocolate as they want for free. At the end of the tour, each participant receives a sweet treat.

Numerous cafes and produce stands are located along Highway 120. Fast-food heaven is in Oakdale.

Groveland. This rustic mountain town is home to the **Iron Door Saloon,** which was built in 1853 and claims to be the oldest saloon in the state. In summer, the inexpensive **Groveland Motel** *(209/962-7865)* gives pooped parents the option of renting a cabin for themselves and an adjacent carpeted tepee for the kids.

Knight's Ferry Covered Bridge *12 miles east of Oakdale; visitor center M-F 8-4, also Sat & Sun in summer; free.* Built in 1863 and measuring 330 feet long, this bridge is the longest and oldest covered bridge west of the Mississippi. It is closed to cars now, but pedestrian traffic is still permitted. A park with picnic tables, hiking trails, and a cold swimming hole is on the freeway side of the Stanislaus River. On the other side is a rustic Gold Rush-era town with a general store, several restaurants, and another park.

WHERE TO STAY

PARK LODGING

Reservations are essential. Call 209/252-4848 for information or to make reservations at any park hotel. It is especially difficult to obtain accommodations in the summer and on holiday weekends. Rates for two range from $27.50 to $208. Children under 2 stay free in their parents' room, and cribs are available. A bargain Midweek Ski Package is available in the winter.

In The Valley

The Ahwahnee *123 units; 45 non-smoking units; $$$+; cribs; some bathtubs, fireplaces; pool; restaurant, room service.* Built in 1927, this very sedate luxury hotel is also a National Historic Landmark. Some cottages are available.

Campgrounds *$; most Apr-Oct only, several year-round. For reservations call 800/365-2267.*

Curry Village *628 units; 20 non-smoking units; $-$$; cribs; some shared baths; pool; restaurant.* Accommodations and facilities are similar to Yosemite Lodge, but inexpensive tent-cabins, which are located along the Merced River and sleep up to six people, are also available.

Yosemite Lodge *495 units; 89 non-smoking units; $-$$; cribs; no TVs; some shared baths; pool; 2 restaurants.* Accommodations vary from old cabins without plumbing to comfortable modern hotel rooms.

Elsewhere

High Sierra Camps *56 units; $$; Sept-June only; unsuitable for children under 7; no TVs; communal bath house; dining tent.* Five camps provide dormitory-style tent accommodations that include linens and two meals. Reservations are assigned by lottery. Applications are accepted October 15 through November 30, and the drawing is held in mid-December.

Tuolumne Meadows Lodge *69 units; $; communal bath house; dining tent.* This all tent-cabin facility is located at the park's eastern entrance.

Wawona Hotel *on Highway 41, 30 miles from the valley, 209/375-6556; 104 rooms; 30 non-smoking rooms; $$; open Apr-Nov & Christmas vacation, weekends only Jan-Easter; cribs; no TVs; some bathtubs; some shared baths; unheated pool, 1 tennis court,* Built in 1879, this Victorian hotel is located 6 miles from the park's southern entrance near the Mariposa Grove of Big Trees. A National Historic Landmark, it is said to be the oldest resort hotel in the state. Most rooms accommodate only two people; a few in the annex, added in 1918, accommodate three. Facilities include a "swimming tank" built in 1917 and a 9-hole golf course.

A special Christmas program is scheduled each year. Details vary from year to year, but in 1991 it included a stagecoach ride across the covered bridge to the Pioneer History Center, where all the cabins were decorated for the holidays. Santa arrived in a horse-drawn wagon dating from the 1800s, and a special Christmas Eve and New Year's Eve dinner was served. Call for current details.

White Wolf Lodge *28 units; $; no TVs; shared bath house; dining tent.* Located at Tioga Pass, 31 miles from the valley, this complex consists of tent-cabins and a few cabins with private baths. Breakfast and dinner are available.

NON-PARK LODGING

Hostels. The **Midpines Home Hostel** *(on Highway 140, Midpines, 35 miles west of the park, 209/742-6318)* is a cabin with six beds. The **Yosemite Gateway Home Hostel** *(Merced, south of the park near Highway 99, 209/725-0407)* has four beds and is convenient to direct bus service into the park. See also page 278.

The Redwoods *Wawona, 6 miles inside the park's southern entrance, 209/375-6666; 82 units; 5 non-smoking units; $$-$$$; 2-night minimum, 3-night minimum in July & Aug; children under 4 free; cribs; all kitchens; some TVs, bathtubs, fireplaces; pets welcome in some units.* These rustic, modern homes and cottages are furnished with linens and kitchenware.

Yosemite Marriott Tenaya Lodge *1122 Highway 41, Fish Camp, 2 miles outside the park's southern entrance, 800/635-5807, 209/683-6555; 242 rooms; 150 non-smoking rooms; $$$-$$$+; children under 18 free; cribs; all bathtubs; 1 indoor heated pool & hot tub, 1 outdoor heated pool & hot tub, 2 saunas, 2 steam rooms, exercise room; 2 restaurants, room service.* Built in 1990, this plush new lodging facility is a cross between the park's Yosemite Lodge and The Ahwahnee hotel. A majestic public reception area features 3-story-tall beamed ceilings, and all of the comfortable rooms have forest views. Complimentary guided nature walks are scheduled most mornings, weather permitting, and crafts classes for all ages are scheduled regularly. In winter, ski and snowshoe rentals are available at the hotel, and guests may strike out on a scenic cross-country ski trail through adjacent **Yosemite National Forest**. In summer, campfire programs, wagon rides, and rentals of 21-speed mountain bikes are added to the agenda.

Camp Tenaya, a children's program, operates weekends and holidays fall through spring, daily in summer. It offers an afternoon program from 2 to 6 and an evening program from 6:30 to 10. A $15 to $20 fee is charged for each session.

Yosemite West Condominiums *16 miles from the valley, 209/454-2033; 48 units; $$-$$$; 2-night minimum; children under 3 free; cribs; all kitchens, bathtubs, fireplaces.* Tucked in the woods, this large complex offers fully-equipped condominiums.

WHERE TO EAT

PARK DINING

All of these valley facilities are open daily and equipped with highchairs and booster seats.

The Ahwahnee *209/372-1489; B, L, & D; $-$$$; children's portions; reservations essential for D.* The best time to dine in the rustic splendor of this elegant dining room is during daylight hours. Only then can the spectacular views of the valley offered by the 50-foot-tall, floor-to-cathedral ceiling leaded-glass windows be fully enjoyed. Dinner is expensive, and men are expected to wear a sport or suit jacket and women to dress accordingly. Guests of the hotel get first choice at reservations, so non-guests should be prepared for either an early or late seating. Children fit in best at breakfast or lunch. Ski buffets are presented on Thursdays, January through March.

Curry Village and **Yosemite Lodge Cafeterias** *B, L, & D; $.* Meals here are quick and informal.

Four Seasons Restaurant *Yosemite Lodge; B & D; $-$$; children's portions.* The dinner menu offers American fare—steak, fried chicken, fish, and hamburgers.

Mountain Room Broiler *Yosemite Lodge; D; $$-$$$; children's portions.* The walls in this stunning room are papered with striking black and white photo murals of mountain climbers, and floor-to-ceiling windows look out on Yosemite Falls. The menu features broiled fresh fish and aged beef as well as smoked trout, sauteed button mushrooms, and warm cheese bread.

Get rid of the kinks developed on the long ride in at the adjacent **Mountain Room Bar.**

Picnics. Box lunches can be reserved from hotel kitchens the evening before they are needed. Supplies can also be picked up at **Degnan's Deli** in the Village.

Wawona Hotel Dining Room *209/375-6556; B, L, & D daily, SunBr; children's portions; reservations suggested for D.* A visit for the inexpensive Sunday brunch is highly recommended. Served in the hotel's wonderful old dining room, where huge multi-paned windows provide views of the surrounding pines, it consists of simple, but satisfying, fare. Breakfast or lunch during the rest of the week is also pleasant.

NON-PARK DINING

Erna's Elderberry House *Oakhurst, 15 miles outside the park's southern entrance, 209/ 683-6800; L & D daily, SunBr; $$$; reservations essential.* Hillside dining "in the classic tradition of old Europe" is promised here. The staff prepares a different six-course, fixed-price ($45) meal every night. One meal enjoyed here in the elegantly appointed front room began with a flute of elderberry-flavored champagne. It continued with a scallop and sorrel timbale artistically positioned on a nest of pasta, followed by an unusual corn and cilantro soup, and then fresh pears poached in Riesling. The main course was alderwood-smoked chicken sausages, served with wild rice and a colorful array of vegetables. A simple, but elegant, salad followed. Dessert, which is optionally served outside on the candle-lit garden terrace, was a duo of Chocolate Decandence in fresh mint sauce and puff pastry filled with caramelized apples and creamed gourmand. Three wines are selected to complement each dinner and are offered by the glass.

Elegant, expensive lodging is available in the property's castle-like, newly constructed **Chateau du Sureau** *(209/683-6860, fax 209/683-0800).* (Sureau is the French word for elderberry.)

WHAT TO DO

PARK ACTIVITIES

The Ansel Adams Gallery *in the Village.* Exclusive special edition photographs by this well-known photographer may be purchased here.

Bicycle Rentals *Yosemite Lodge (209/372-1208; daily 9-5) & Curry Village (209/372-1200; daily 8-8), Apr-Oct only; $5/hour.* A map is provided with rentals, and helmets are available at no charge.

Bus Tours *209/372-1240; valley floor $13.75, grand tour $37.75.*

Glacier Point *1-hour drive from the valley.* From this spot gazers enjoy a 270-degree view of the high country and a bird's-eye view of the valley 3,214 feet below. Several trails lead down to the valley. Consider arriving in the morning (get a one-way ticket on the **Glacier Point Bus Tour**) and spending the rest of the day hiking back down.

Hiking. Participate in a ranger-guided walk or take any of the many self-guided trails. Maps may be purchased in the park stores.

Indian Cultural Museum *next to the **Village Visitor Center;** W-Sun 9-12 & 1-4.* Visitors learn about the Awaneechee Indians through artifacts, cultural demonstrations, and recorded chants. A reconstructed Indian village is located behind the museum. It features a self-guided trail that points out plants used by the Indians for food, clothing, and shelter.

Inner Tube Float Trip. Scenic and calm is the area on the Merced River between Pines Campground and Centinnel Bridge. Raft rentals are available in June and July.

Junior Ranger Program. This program is available for children in third grade and above. Consult the *Yosemite Guide* for details.

Mariposa Grove of Big Trees *on Highway 41, 35 miles from the valley; tours 8-7, May-Oct only; adults $5.25.* Five hundred giant sequoias are located in this 250-acre grove. Open-air trams take visitors on guided tours of a 6-mile scenic loop. In winter, this is a choice spot for cross-country skiing.

Movies. Scenic movies and slide shows are scheduled some evenings. Check the *Yosemite Guide* for times and locations.

Pioneer Yosemite History Center *on Highway 41, Wawona, 25 miles from the valley, 209/375-6321; daily dawn-dusk.* This village of restored historic pioneer buildings is reached by walking across an authentic **covered bridge.** Originally located in different areas around the park, the structures were moved here in the 1950s and '60s. In summer, history comes to life with demonstrations of soap making, yarn spinning, rail splitting, and other pioneer crafts. Horse-drawn carriage rides are sometimes available.

Rock Climbing Lessons *Curry Village (209/372-1244) & Tuolumne Meadows (209/372-1335; summer only).* Learn rock climbing at the **Yosemite Mountaineering School,** one of the finest in the world. Basic classes are held daily year-round. Beginners are taught safety essentials for dealing with the area's granite rock and can expect to climb as high as 80 feet in the first lesson. Oddly, snow and ice climbing are offered only in the summer. Children must be at least 14 to participate.

Valley Stables *guided 2-hour horse trips leave at 8, 10, & 1; $28/person; half-day mule trips/$36, all-day/$55; ponies $10/hour.* Said to have the largest public riding stock in the world, this concession can arrange for custom pack and fishing trips. Ponies may be rented for young children to ride; parents must walk and lead them.

Winter Activities. See page 267.

NON-PARK ACTIVITIES

The first three destinations are reached via the Tioga Pass.

Bodie State Historic Park *8 miles south of Bridgeport, 619/647-6445; daily dawn-dusk, May-Oct only; call for tour schedule; $3/car.* Located at the end of a 13-mile sideroad off of Highway 395, the last 3 miles of which are unpaved, this 486-acre park is the largest unrestored ghost town in the West. In 1879, when 10,000 people lived here, there were 2 churches and 65 saloons. It was said to be quite rowdy. A little girl who moved here in its heyday wrote in her diary, "Good, by God! We're going to Bodie." This passage has also been interpreted as "Good-bye God! We're going to Bodie." Due to fires in 1892 and 1932, only about 5 percent of the town remains. No food services or picnic facilities are available.

Devil's Postpile National Monument A shuttle bus is available from Mammoth Mountain. Visitors may take a pleasant 1-mile walk through the monument; another short hike leads to 101-foot-tall **Rainbow Falls.**

Mono Lake *off Highway 395, 619/647-6572. Nature Center: daily 9-8; guided nature walks daily in summer at 10 & 1, rest of year Sat & Sun at 1; call for directions.* John Muir described this desolate area as, "A country of wonderful contrasts, hot deserts bounded by snow-laden mountains, cinder and ashes scattered on glacier-

polished pavement, frost and fire working together in the making of beauty."
Mark Twain called it the Dead Sea of the West. An ancient Ice Age lake, estimated
to be at least 1 million years old, Mono Lake features an unusual terrain of pinnacles and spires formed by mineral deposits. It is filled with water that contains
more than 2-1/2 times the salt found in ocean water. Perhaps this is what attracts
the 50,000-plus seagulls that flock in here during April, stay into August, and then
head back to the coast. Situated at over 7,000 feet above sea level, it is one of the
largest lakes in the state. Campsites are available but are packed in summer, and
in winter the Tioga Pass is closed—making fall the best time for a visit.

For restaurant and lodging information call 619/647-6629.

Yosemite Mountain Sugar Pine Railroad *56001 Highway 41, Fish Camp, 4 miles
south of the park's southern entrance, a 1-hour drive from the valley, 209/683-7273; call
for schedule. Train: adults $8.50, 3-12 $4. Jennry railcars: adults $5.75, 3-12 $3.* A
reconstruction of the Madera Sugar Pine Co. railroad that made its last run in
1931, this narrow-gauge steam train takes passengers on a 45-minute, 4-mile scenic excursion through the **Sierra National Forest.** Passengers, sitting in open-air
touring cars upon logs that have been carved out to form long benches, are given
live narration on the area's history. They may stop over at the midway point to
picnic or hike. Moonlight rides, which include a steak-fry and campfire program,
are scheduled on Saturday nights in summer. Smaller Jenny railcars, powered by
Model A engines, take passengers on shorter 30-minute rides along the same
route when the train is not operating. A picnic area and snack shop are available.

Sequoia and Kings Canyon National Parks

A LITTLE BACKGROUND

Though located just south of Yosemite National Park, these two scenic national parks are often overlooked. It's a shame because they, too, offer spectacular scenery and are much less crowded.

Sequoia National Park was established in 1890. It was California's first national park, and it is the country's second oldest national park. (Yellowstone is the oldest.) Kings Canyon National Park was established in 1940. Combined they encompass 864,383 acres.

The main attraction at these parks is the enormous sequoia trees, with their vibrant cinnamon-colored bark. The trees may be viewed in both Sequoia Park's **Giant Forest** and Kings Canyon's **Grant Grove.** The largest is the **General Sherman Tree** in Sequoia National Park. It towers 275 feet high, measures 36-1/2 feet in diameter, and is between 2,300 and 2,700 years old. This makes it higher than Niagara Falls, as wide as a city street, and already middle-aged when Christ was born! It is said to be the largest living thing on the planet.

Mt. Whitney is also located in Sequoia Park and, at 14,494 feet, is the highest point in the United States outside of Alaska. From the east side of the Sierra, it is a 2- to 3-day hike to its peak; from the west side it is a 7- to 11-day hike.

Admission to the parks is $5 per car.

VISITOR INFORMATION

Sequoia and Kings Canyon National Parks *Three Rivers 93271, 209/565-3134.*

GETTING THERE

Located approximately 250 miles southeast of San Francisco. Take Highway 80 to Highway 580 to Highway 99 south, to either Highway 180 east or Highway 198 east.

ANNUAL EVENTS

Caravan to Nation's Christmas Tree *December; 209/875-4575.* Since 1926, the 267-foot-tall **General Grant Tree** in Kings Canyon National Park has been the site of a special Christmas service. In honor of its official status as the Nation's Christmas Tree, a wreath is placed at its base each year by members of the National Park Service. A car caravan leaves from the tiny town of Sanger, and seats are also available by reservation on a chartered bus.

General Grant Tree

WHERE TO STAY ·

Montecito-Sequoia Lodge. See pages 265 and 271.

Park Lodging *209/561-3314; 304 units; 40 non-smoking units; $-$$$; children under 12 free; cribs; no TVs; some bathtubs, fireplaces, wood-burning stoves; some shared baths; restaurant.* At Sequoia, lodging includes both spartan and deluxe cabins as well as motel rooms. Kings Canyon has similar facilities, but they are generally less luxurious and there are fewer of them.

Arrangements can be made to backpack 11 miles into the High Sierra tent-cabin camp at **Bearpaw**. Dinner and breakfast are included, and reservations are necessary.

Campsites are available on a first-come, first-served basis. In the summer reservations are accepted for Lodgepole Campground (see page 277).

For more information, request a park brochure that explains the various options in detail.

WHAT TO DO

Bicycle Rentals *in Cedar Grove.*

Caves.

Boyden Cavern *in Sequoia National Forest, just outside Kings Canyon, 209/736-2708; tours daily, May-Oct 11-4, June-Sept 10-5; closed Oct-Apr; adults $4, 6-12 $2; strollers not permitted.* This cave is located in spectacular 8,000-foot-deep Kings River Canyon—the deepest canyon in the United States. Guided tours take about 45 minutes.

Crystal Cave *in Sequoia; schedule varies, May-Sept only; adults $3, 6-11 $1.50.* This 50-degree marble cavern is reached via a steep 1/2-mile trail. The guided tour takes about an hour.

Fishing. The most popular spots are along Kings River and at the forks of the Kaweah River. A California fishing license is required. Ask about fishing regulations at park visitor centers.

Horse Rentals *in Cedar Grove, Wolverton, Grant Grove, & Mineral King.*

Trails. Over 900 miles of hiking trails are in these parks.

Unusual Trees. Many of these trees are encountered on the drive along the 46-mile **General's Highway** that connects the two national parks. Some require either a short walk to reach or a drive down a sideroad. From December through May, this highway is occasionally closed by snow.

Auto Log. Cars can be driven onto this fallen sequoia for a photograph.

Senate Group and **House Group of Sequoias**. These are among the most symmetrically formed and nearly perfect of the sequoias. They are reached via the Congress Trail, an easy walk beginning at the General Sherman Tree.

Tunnel Log. Cars may be driven through this tunnel carved through a tree that fell across the road in 1937.

Visitor Centers at *Lodgepole & Grant Grove; daily in summer 8-6, rest of year 9-5; free.* See exhibits on the area's wildlife as well as displays on Indians and sequoias. Inquire here about the schedule of nature walks and evening campfire programs.

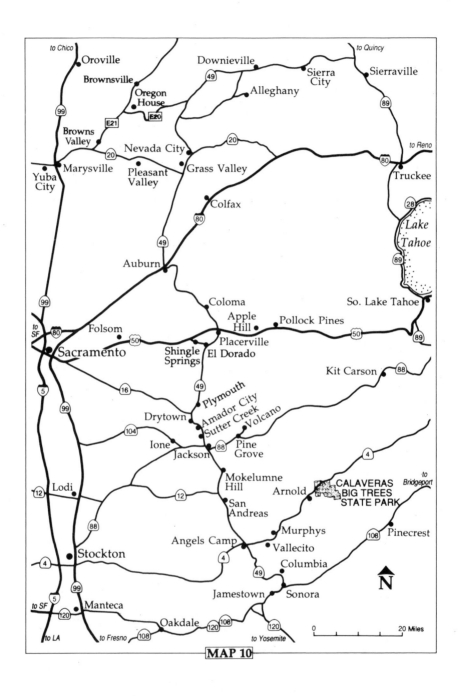

to Chico
Oroville
Brownsville
Oregon House
E21
E20
Browns Valley
99
Nevada City
20
Yuba City
Marysville
Pleasant Valley
Grass Valley
49
Downieville
Alleghany
Sierra City
Sierraville
to Quincy
89
20
to Reno
80
Colfax
80
Truckee
28
Lake Tahoe
89
49
Auburn
99
Coloma
Apple Hill
Pollock Pines
So. Lake Tahoe
to SF
80
Folsom
50
Sacramento
Shingle Springs
El Dorado
Placerville
50
89
5
99
16
49
Plymouth
Amador City
Sutter Creek
Volcano
Drytown
Kit Carson
88
104
Ione
Jackson
88
Pine Grove
12
Lodi
12
Mokelumne Hill
San Andreas
Arnold
CALAVERAS BIG TREES STATE PARK
to Bridgeport
4
88
Angels Camp
4
Murphys
Vallecito
Columbia
108
Pinecrest
Stockton
4
49
Jamestown
Sonora
N
99
5
Manteca
120
to SF
to LA
Oakdale
120
108
120
to Fresno
108
to Yosemite
0   20 Miles

MAP 10

Gold Rush Country

A LITTLE BACKGROUND

The Mother Lode, as this area is sometimes referred to, stretches along the entire route of Highway 49, south from Mariposa and north through Nevada City, ending in Downieville. (On the other hand the Mother Lode *vein*, which runs from Northern California to South America, surfaces in the area between Jamestown and Auburn.)

The main Gold Rush towns can all be visited by driving along Highway 49. But many scenic sideroads, leading to towns with intriguing names such as Fiddletown and Rescue, invite exploration.

This area provides history, adventure, and scenic beauty. Not yet heavily promoted and packaged, it also provides many low-key and inexpensive vacation joys for the hype-weary traveler. A thorough visit could take weeks, but a satisfying visit takes only a few days. For a weekend visit, don't attempt to drive the entire route. Visit one portion and then go back another time to see the rest.

Because the area is steeped in history, consider doing some reading for more background information. Two classic books about the area that are also good for reading out loud are *The Celebrated Jumping Frog of Calaveras County* by Samuel L. Clemens (Mark Twain) and *The Luck of Roaring Camp* by Bret Harte.

Currently there is said to be another gold rush on. Many nervous people are staking claims, so caution is advised when doing any unguided panning or prospecting. As far as the prospects for success, Mark Twain once said, "A gold mine is a hole in the ground with a liar at the entrance."

GETTING THERE

Located approximately 135 miles east of San Francisco. Take Highway 80 to Highway 580 to Highway 205 to Highway 120 to Highway 49.

– Jamestown –

WHERE TO STAY

♥**Jamestown Hotel** *Main St., 209/984-3902; 8 rooms; $$; unsuitable for children under 7; no TVs; all bathtubs; continental breakfast, restaurant.* Built in the 1850s, this hotel is furnished with Victorian antiques. Many spacious suites with sitting rooms are available.

Lunch and dinner are served daily in a nicely appointed dining room with an eclectic menu offering prime rib, seafood, chicken, veal, and pasta. Total consideration is given to children: highchairs, booster seats, children's portions, and even hamburgers are available. An attractive saloon adjacent to the dining room specializes in fancy drinks, California wines, and tasty appetizers.

♥**The National Hotel** *77 Main St., 800/894-3446, 209/984-3446; 11 rooms; $$; unsuitable for children under 10; some shared baths; full breakfast, restaurant, room service; pets welcome.* A sense of history awaits at this really *old* hotel. Built in 1859, it has been in continuous operation ever since. In fact, it is one of the ten oldest continuously operating hotels in the state and is now an official historical landmark. Until 1978 rooms were rented to men only and went for $4 a night. Indoor plumbing was added in 1981! Much of the antique furniture is original to the hotel, and that which has been added is right in tune with the era. Color TVs are not in the rooms but are available upon request.

The hotel's dining room is an especially inviting spot for dinner after the drive in. On warm evenings diners are seated outside on a pleasant patio. Strong points of the menu include fresh fish with interesting sauces, a wine list featuring the largest selection of Gold Country wines available anywhere, and exceptional desserts. Lunch and Sunday brunch are also served, and a children's menu is available. Located just off the parlor, an old-time saloon, featuring its original redwood long bar with brass rail and also an 1881 cash register, is the perfect spot for a nightcap.

Overall, everything is far more luxurious now than anything those gold-miners ever experienced.

WHERE TO EAT

Country Kitchen Cafe *18231 Main St., 209/984-3326; B & L daily; $; highchairs, boosters seats, children's portions; AE, MC, V.* Located in a circa 1865 structure that is one of the oldest wooden commercial buildings remaining in town, this cafe offers simple food in pleasant surroundings. Housemade soups, pastries, and pies are particularly good. Kids will probably be happy to find that both a hot dog and a peanut butter and jelly sandwich are on the menu. Ice cream treats are also available, and a candy counter dispenses a variety of sweets. A gift shop operating upstairs is worth a visit.

Smoke Cafe *18191 Main St., 209/984-3733; L Sat & Sun, D Tu-Sun; $-$$; highchairs, booster seats, children's portions; no reservations; MC, V.* This popular spot recently relocated into a modern Santa Fe-style building with soft stucco edges and lots of tile. Upscale Mexican menu items include specialties such as pollo de mole poblano and chile verde. A hamburger is also available.

WHAT TO DO

Gold Prospecting Expeditions *18170 Main St., 209/984-GOLD, fax 209/984-0711; tours daily 10-5; 1-hour tour $20/person, $35/family.* Operating out of the town's old livery stable, this business organizes prospecting trips appropriate for children as well as adults. It is claimed gold has been found on every trip, and the rule is "finders, keepers." Participants get down and dirty in a stream, where they are taught the basics. All equipment is supplied, and everyone finds something on trips of 2 hours or more. Full-day trips and trips by river raft or helicopter can also be arranged.

Children can pan for free in a gold-panning trough located in front of the shop. A pan may be rented for $1.

Railtown 1897 State Historic Park *Fifth Ave., 209/984-3953. Train: Sat & Sun at 10:30, 12, 1:30, & 3; closed Dec & Jan; adults $9, 3-12 $4.50. Roundhouse tours: daily 10-4; adults $2.50, 3-12 $1.50.* Be sure to allow time to watch the hubbub that surrounds preparing the train for departure. The depot is always full of excitement as the huge steam trains roll in and out, sounding their screaming whistles and belching a mix of fire, smoke, and steam. The **Mother Lode Cannonball,** an historic steam train, takes passengers on a 1-hour, 12-mile round trip to Chinese Station. Several special trips are also sometimes available. A 2-hour ride on the Keystone Special is offered in spring and fall. It includes snacks and a visit to a set for *Back to the Future III.* The Twilight Limited operates in summer. Riders get cocktails and snacks en route and a steak barbecue back at the station.

Tours of the old six-stall **roundhouse,** where the trains are still serviced, are also available.

If it all looks familiar, that might be because many TV shows and movies have been filmed here. The list includes *Bonanza, Little House on the Prairie, The Virginian, High Noon,* and *Pale Rider.*

– Sonora –

A LITTLE BACKGROUND

Once known as the "Queen of the Southern Mines," when it was the richest and wildest town in the southern Mother Lode, this town still bustles and is a popular stopover spot for skiers and other travelers on their way to vacation cabins and recreation. Because it is a crossroads, it has been built up more than most Gold Rush towns and is far from quiet. But off the main thoroughfares a taste of the old Sonora of Victorian homes and quiet streets is still to be found.

VISITOR INFORMATION

Tuolumne County Visitors Bureau *P.O. Box 4020 (55 W. Stockton), Sonora 95370, 800/446-1333, 209/533-4420, fax 209/533-0956.*

WHERE TO STAY

Gunn House Motel *286 S. Washington St., 209/532-3421; 25 rooms; $-$$; cribs; all bathtubs; heated pool (summer only); continental breakfast; pets welcome.* Built in 1850, this 2-story adobe house was once the residence of Dr. Lewis C. Gunn. Then it served for awhile as the offices for the *Sonora Herald*—the area's first newspaper. Rooms are restored and furnished with antiques. The cozy office is staffed with helpful personnel, and a poolside cocktail lounge is available to guests.

WHAT TO DO

Autumn Colors Drive. Take Highway 108 about 15 miles east for a dazzling display of fall leaf colors. Populated with Aspen, this entire area is usually vibrant with color. The road closes after the first snowfall, which is usually toward the end of October.

Mark Twain's Cabin *off Highway 49, midway between town & Angels Camp.* Built on **Jackass Hill,** this replica of Twain's cabin is built around the original chimney. Twain lived here in 1864 and '65, when he wrote *The Celebrated Jumping Frog of Calaveras County* and *Roughing It.* Picnic tables are available.

Tuolumne County Museum and History Center *158 W. Bradford Ave., 209/532-1317; M-Sat 10-4, in summer also Sun 10-3:30; free.* Located inside a jail built in 1866, this museum displays various relics from the Gold Rush era. Picnic tables are available.

– Columbia State Historic Park –

A LITTLE BACKGROUND

In her prime, with over 6,000 people calling her home, Columbia was one of the largest mining towns in the southern Mother Lode. Her nickname, "Gem of the Southern Mines," was reference to the $87 million-plus in gold mined here (a figure calculated when gold was $35 an ounce).

Since 1945 this reconstructed Gold Rush town has been a state historic park. It is open daily from 9 to 5, and admission is free. Streets are blocked off to all but foot traffic and an occasional stagecoach. A museum introduces visitors to the town's history, and more exhibits are scattered among the many restored historic buildings.

In fact, the whole town is basically a living museum. Private concessionaires operate modern versions of businesses that would have been found here in the 1800s. Cold mugs of beer and old-fashioned rootbeer-like sarsaparilla are poured in the town saloon. A blacksmith eeks out a living practicing his craft in a ramshackle shed, and a candy kitchen uses 100-year-old recipes and antique equipment to turn out such old-time favorites as horehound, rocky road, and almond bark. Customers in the photography studio don Gold Rush-era clothing for portraits taken with vintage camera equipment, but developed with modern quick-develop processes. Visitors can even tour a still-operating gold mine and learn to pan for gold in a salted sluice.

In case Columbia looks familiar, note that *High Noon* and episodes of *Little House on the Prairie* were filmed here.

VISITOR INFORMATION

Columbia State Historic Park *P.O. Box 151, Columbia 95310, 209/532-4301.*

ANNUAL EVENTS

Victorian Easter Parade and Egg Hunt *March or April (on Easter Sunday).*

Fireman's Muster *May.*

A Miners Christmas *first 2 weekends in December.*

WHERE TO STAY

City Hotel *Main St., 209/532-1479; 10 rooms; 100% non-smoking; $$; children under 2 free; cribs; no TVs; full breakfast, restaurant, limited room service.* This 1856 hotel provides overnight lodging in keeping with the town's flavor. The restored rooms are furnished with Victorian antiques from the collection of the California State Parks Department. Eager-to-please students from the Columbia College Hospitality Management program dress in period clothing and supplement the full-time staff by performing such esoteric duties as fluffing pillows and, in the beautifully appointed restaurant downstairs, de-crumbing tables. Guests are encouraged to congregate in the parlor in the evening for Sherry, conversation, and games. To make the trek down the hall to the bath more civilized, guests are loaned a wicker basket packed with shower cap, slippers, robe, soap, and shampoo.

The kitchen prepares elegant regional cuisine for weekend lunches and nightly dinners. Fixed-price, four-course dinners *($28.50-$29.50)* are available along with an a la carte menu. Reservations are suggested, and children are welcome. The cozy **What Cheer Saloon** adjoins.

Columbia Gem Motel *22131 Parrotts Ferry Rd., 1 mile from park, 209/532-4508; 12 units; $-$$; cribs; some bathtubs; pets welcome.* Typical motel-room decor greets guests inside tiny cottages scattered in an attractive pine tree setting.

Fallon Hotel *Washington St., 209/532-1470; 14 rooms; 100% non-smoking; $$; closed midweek Jan-Mar; no TVs; cribs; some shared bathrooms; continental breakfast.* This historic hotel, dating from 1857, has undergone a $4 million renovation and is now beautifully restored to its Victorian grandeur. Many of the furnishings are original to the hotel. The hotel is operated in similar style as the City Hotel and is under the same management, and an ice cream parlor operates on the premises. Packages that include lodging, dinner, and a theater performance are available.

WHAT TO DO

Fallon House Theatre *209/532-4644; summer only; reservations advised.* Located in the rear of the Fallon Hotel, this historic theater has been in operation since the 1880s. Call for current schedule.

– Murphys –

A LITTLE BACKGROUND

A map to the town's buildings and sights is available from merchants and at the check-in desk in Murphys Hotel.

ANNUAL EVENTS

Music from Bear Valley *July; Bear Valley, 209/753-2574.* Held high in the Sierra in a circus-style red-and-white-striped tent, this festival presents a musical smorgasbord.

WHERE TO STAY

♥**Dunbar House, 1880** *271 Jones St., 800/225-3764 ext.321, 209/728-2897; 4 rooms; 100% non-smoking; $$$; 2-night minimum on Sat; unsuitable for children under 10; all wood-burning stoves; full breakfast.* This restored Italianate-style home was the filming location for the TV series *Seven Brides for Seven Brothers.* Rooms are decorated with antiques, lace, and down comforters, and each is equipped with a VCR and access to a video library of classics. Guests are greeted each afternoon by an appetizer buffet, and a complimentary bottle of local wine awaits in each room's private refrigerator. Buggy rides through town can be arranged.

Murphys Hotel *457 Main St., 800/532-7684, 209/728-3444; 29 rooms; $$; 2-night minimum on weekends May-Sept; children under 12 free; cribs; some TVs; some shared baths; continental breakfast, restaurant.* This old hotel, built in 1856 and now a National Historical Monument, is said to have provided lodging for such Gold Rush-era luminaries as U.S. Grant, J.P. Morgan, Mark Twain, Horatio Alger, John Muir, and Black Bart—each of whom has a room he actually stayed in named after him. Modern motel rooms, with no legends attached, are available adjacent to the hotel. Though the hotel rooms are immeasurably more interesting, they have one big drawback: The noisy hotel bar, reputed to be the best in the Mother Lode, is kept jumping until the wee hours by townspeople and travelers alike. Those who want to sleep should opt for a less interesting, but quiet, motel room. Special skier rates are available in the winter.

A reasonably priced restaurant serves breakfast, lunch, and dinner daily. It is popular with locals, and the portions tend to be large. Menu choices consist of hearty, made-from-scratch American country fare such as fried chicken, hamburgers, and steaks. Complete facilities are available for children.

WHERE TO EAT

The Peppermint Stick *454 Main St., 209/728-3570; open daily; $; highchairs, booster seats, children's portions; 100% non-smoking; no reservations; no cards.* When it was built in 1893, this building served the town as an ice house. Now it is a cheerful ice cream parlor serving old-fashioned sodas and cleverly named sundaes. Sandwiches, soups, and candies are also available, and everything can be packed to go.

WHAT TO DO

Black Bart Players *209/728-8842; weekends in Apr & Nov only, 8pm; tickets $7.50; reservations suggested.* This little theater group performs musicals, melodramas, mysteries, comedies, and classics. Call for current schedule.

Calaveras Big Trees State Park *1170 E. Highway 4, Arnold, 15 miles east of town, 209/795-2334; daily dawn-dusk; $5/car.* This ancient forest houses the mammoth, and now rare, sequoia variety of redwood. The Big Trees Nature Trail is a choice trek for families with young children. Other trails are also available, as are campsites and picnic and barbecue facilities. In warm weather, the Beaver Creek Picnic Area has a good wading area for children. (Picnic provisions can be picked up in Arnold, where there are delis, markets, and restaurants.) A cross-country ski trail is available in winter.

Calaveras Big Trees State Park

Mercer Caverns *1665 Sheepranch Rd., off Highway 4, 1 mile north of town, 209/728-2101; daily 9-4:30 June-Sept, rest of year Sat & Sun 11-3:30; adults $5, 5-11 $2.50; strollers not permitted.* Discovered over 100 years ago in 1885, this well-lighted 55-degree limestone cavern takes about a half-hour to tour. It is said to be the longest continually operating commercial canvern in the state.

Moaning Cavern *on Parrotts Ferry Rd., west of town, Vallecito, 209/736-2708; daily 9-6 June-Aug, rest of year 10-5; adults $5.75, 6-12 $2.75; strollers not permitted.* The 45-minute tour ascends a 100-foot-high spiral staircase into the largest public cavern chamber in California. The cavern was originally discovered by Indians, many of whom are thought to have fallen to their death here. Later it was used as a burial site. In fact, the oldest human remains in the U.S. were found here. A more expensive 3-hour **rappel tour** allows a 180-foot rope descent into the cave; reservations are necessary. Camping is permitted at the cavern; call for further details.

Old Timers Museum *across the street from Murphys Hotel, 209/728-2607; Thur-Sun 11-4, in winter Sat & Sun only; free.* Dating from 1856, this is the oldest stone building in town. It is interesting to note that the stones were fitted together without mortar. The building now houses Gold Rush-era memorabilia.

WINERIES

Milliaire *276 Main St., 209/728-1658; tasting & tours daily 11-4:30.* Operating out of a converted carriage house, this tiny winery is known for its intense, full-bodied wines. It also produces three delicious dessert wines: a late harvest Zinfandel, a late harvest Sauvignon Blanc, and an orange Muscat.

Stevenot Winery *2690 San Domingo Rd., 1 mile past Mercer Caverns, 209/728-3436; tasting daily 10-5; tours by appt.* Located in a canyon on the site of the first swimming pool in Calaveras County, this relatively new winery (circa 1976) is housed in a series of old buildings. The cool, rustic tasting room has a sod roof and split-log walls. Picnic tables are sheltered under a grape arbor and feature a view of the vineyards.

Moaning Cavern rappel tour

– Angels Camp –

VISITOR INFORMATION

Calaveras Lodging and Visitors Association *P.O. Box 637 (1301 S. Main St.), Angels Camp 95222, 800/225-3764, 209/736-0049, fax 209/736-9124.*

ANNUAL EVENTS

Jumping Frog Jubilee *third weekend in May; 209/736-2561.* Visitors are invited to bring their own frog to enter in this historic contest, but rental frogs are available on site. In 1986 Rosie the Ribiter set the current world's record by landing, after three leaps, 21 feet 5-3/4 inches from the starting pad. She earned her jockey $1,500. The prize money is usually won by frog jockeys who are serious about the sport and bring 50 to 60 frogs. A rental frog has never won.

The **Calaveras County Fair** is part of the fun and features carnival rides, livestock exhibits, a rodeo, a destruction derby, headliner entertainers, and fireworks.

WHERE TO EAT

There are no recommended restaurants for this town. Could this have something to do with Mark Twain's description of some coffee ("day-before-yesterday dishwater") and soup ("hellfire") suffered long ago at the Hotel Angels?

PICNIC PICK-UPS

Informal picnic areas may be found by the river. Scenic **Utica Park** has picnic tables and a children's play area. **Angels Bakery** *(1277 S. Main, 209/736-4360)* makes great cheese-and-salt breadsticks, garlic bread, and fruit bars. The **Pickle Barrel Deli** *(1225 S. Main, 209/736-4704)* will pack picnic supplies to go and provides tables for those who decide to stay.

WHAT TO DO

Angels Camp Museum *753 S. Main St., 209/736-2963; daily 10-4 Apr-Nov, in winter M-F only; adults $1, 6-12 25¢.* Of special interest here are an extensive rock collection and a group of old wagons and buggies.

– San Andreas –

VISITOR INFORMATION

Calaveras County Chamber of Commerce *P.O. Box 115 (3 N. Main St.), San Andreas 95249, 209/754-4009.*

WHERE TO STAY

Black Bart Inn and Motel *55 Main St., 209/754-3808; 40 rooms; 8 non-smoking rooms; $; cribs; some bathtubs; some shared baths; unheated pool (unavailable during winter); restaurant.* This lodging facility is named after the infamous highwayman whose career ended in this town. Rooms are available in both the old hotel and a more modern motel located adjacent.

WHAT TO DO

Calaveras County Museum *30 N. Main St., 209/754-6579; daily 10-4; adults 50c, under 13 25¢.* Items on display upstairs in this restored 1867 courthouse include Miwok Indian and Gold Rush artifacts. Among the nicely organized exhibits is a full-size room display of a Gold Rush-era general store. The jail cell Black Bart once occupied is downstairs in a rustic courtyard planted with native California flora.

California Caverns at Cave City *off Mountain Ranch Rd., 10 miles east of town, 209/736-2708; daily 10-5 June-Oct, call for fall & spring schedule; closed in winter; adults $5.75, 6-12 $2.75; strollers not permitted.* This cavern was first opened to the public in 1850. The nearly level Trail of Lights tour, which takes 80 minutes, follows the footsteps of John Muir, Mark Twain, and Bret Harte.

Another more strenuous **spelunking tour** *($59)* through the unlighted portion of the cavern is available by reservation only. It "involves climbing rocks and a 60-foot ladder, squeezing through small passages, crossing 200-foot-deep lakes on rafts, and viewing breathtaking formations unequalled in any other cavern in the West." Reservations are necessary, and participants must be at least 12 years old, in good health, and not pregnant.

– Mokelumne Hill –

WHERE TO STAY

Hotel Leger *8304 Main St., 209/286-1401; 13 rooms; $$; 100% non-smoking; some bathtubs, fireplaces; some shared baths; unheated pool; restaurant.* Once considered among the most luxurious of Gold Rush hotels, this 1879 lodging still provides comfortable rooms. Many have sitting areas, and all are furnished with tasteful period pieces.

A restaurant and the old-time **Frontier Saloon** are located on the ground floor.

Sometimes plays are scheduled in the **Court House Theatre**. Call for current schedule.

(By the way, Leger is pronounced la-JAY. It was originally pronounced like it looks, with a soft G, but later new French owners changed tradition.)

– Jackson –

VISITOR INFORMATION

Amador County Chamber of Commerce *P.O. Box 596 (125 Peek St.), Jackson 95642, 800/649-4988, 209/223-0350.*

ANNUAL EVENTS

Italian Picnic *first weekend in June; in Plymouth, at the Italian Picnic Grounds at the Amador County Fair Grounds.* For over 100 years the public has been invited to this festive event. The fun includes kiddie rides for the children, dancing for the adults, and a parade (in Sutter Creek) and barbecue for everyone.

WHERE TO STAY

Broadway Hotel *225 Broadway, 209/223-3503; 14 rooms; 10 non-smoking rooms; $$; children under 4 free; some TVs, bathtubs; hot tub; continental breakfast; pets welcome.* Located just a few blocks from downtown, this former miner's hotel is furnished with antiques. Swings await young children.

Country Squire Motel *1105 N. Main St., 209/223-1657; 12 rooms; $; children under 1 free; cribs; continental breakfast; pets welcome.* Located out in the country adjacent to the old Kennedy Gold Mine site, this comfortable motel housed one of the last private gambling casinos in California. The casino was closed in 1952. Some of the units are restored and some are motel-modern. Gold panning may be practiced in the backyard "crick," and ducks, goats, and sheep roam freely on farm land across the way. Plenty of grass beckons children to romp.

National Hotel *2 Water St., 209/223-0500; 30 rooms; 2 non-smoking rooms; $-$$; Sat night reservations must include D & B reservations in restaurant.* This hotel claims to be the oldest in continuous operation (since 1862) in California. Room decor is modest, as are the prices. Prior guests have included every California governor since 1862, two Presidents (Garfield and Hoover), and John Wayne.

A cozy cellar dining room serves dinner Friday through Sunday and brunch on Sunday. Lunch is served Wednesday through Saturday in the bar.

WHERE TO STAY NEARBY

♥The Heirloom *214 Shakeley Lane, Ione, 12 miles from town, 209/274-4468; 6 rooms; 100% non-smoking; $$; 2-night minimum on Sat; no TVs; 1 bathtub, 1 fireplace, 2 wood-burning stoves; some shared baths; full breakfast.* Being located in a town that was once known as Bed Bug could be a bit of a disadvantage for some lodgings. This B&B is so charming, however, that this history is easily overlooked. Resembling a colonial mansion and featuring large, grassy grounds, this 1863 house is situated down a country lane right on Sutter Creek. Two rooms are in an adjacent sod-roof cottage. A full French country-style breakfast is served each morning.

Roaring Camp Mining Co. *Pine Grove, 209/296-4100; 20 cabins; $310/week/couple for a prospector cabin, $115/extra person, $75/child under 18; closed Oct-Apr; shared modern bath house; restaurant.* Guests leave their cars behind and make the 1-hour trip into the remote canyon here via truck. They stay in this former mining camp in rustic prospector cabins without electricity, and they must bring all their own gear and food. Recreation consists of swimming, fishing, and panning for gold in the Mokelumne River, as well as hiking and perhaps collecting rocks. Guests may keep up to 1 ounce of found gold; anything over 1 ounce per cabin must be split with Roaring Camp. A saloon, short order restaurant, and general store are available when guests get tired of roughing it. Weekly stays run Sunday to Sunday. For stays of less than a week, call the Monday before the anticipated date of arrival.

Shorter 4-hour day tours are also available. On Wednesday evenings a group of diners is trucked in for a riverside steak cookout; weekly guests are invited to join this event at no charge.

WHERE TO EAT

Right on Main *134 Main, 209/223-0611; L daily; $; 1 highchair, booster seats; no cards.* This old-fashioned ice cream parlor/candy store has been serving up sweet confections since the turn of the century. Nowadays soup and sandwiches are also available.

Wells Fargo Restaurant *2 Main St., 209/223-9956; B, L, D Tu-Sun; $; highchairs, booster seats; MC, V.* Daily dinner specials include such all-American fare as baked shortribs, roast lamb, roast pork, baked ham, and breaded veal. The restaurant is known for its steaks, chicken, and ribs, and well-prepared, generous portions keep the locals coming back. Hot and cold sandwiches and hamburgers are available at both lunch and dinner. An adjacent saloon dates back to the mid-1800s.

WHAT TO DO

Amador County Museum *225 Church St., 209/223-6386; W-Sun 10-4; by donation.* This museum is located inside an 1859 red brick house. A brightly painted wooden train engine, which was once used as a prop on TV's *Petticoat Junction,* is permanently parked in front. Scale models of the Kennedy Mine tailing wheels and head frame and the North Star Mine stamp mill are on display; they are operated hourly on weekends (fee).

Kennedy Mine Tailing Wheels *on Jackson Gate Rd; dawn to dusk; free.* Four huge 58-foot-diameter wheels, originally built in 1912 to carry waste gravel from the nearby mine, may be viewed by taking a short walk on well-marked trails on either side of the road. Two of the wheels have already collapsed. Better hurry to see this site before time takes its toll on the other two. The abandoned Kennedy Mine may be seen from the site. Picnic tables are available.

Wine Tasting. Many wineries are located in this area, with a heavy concentration occuring around the nearby town of Plymouth. Contact the Chamber of Commerce for a free map/brochure.

– Sutter Creek –

A LITTLE BACKGROUND

Seven gold mines were once located on this quiet Main Street. Now it is lined with modern gold mines—antique shops.

WHERE TO STAY

♥**Sutter Creek Inn** *75 Main St., 209/267-5606; 19 rooms; 9 non-smoking rooms; $$; 2-night minimum on Sat; unsuitable for children under 10; some fireplaces; full breakfast.* Opened as an inn in 1966, this 1859 Greek Revival structure was one of the first B&Bs west of the Mississippi. Rooms are available in the house as well as in an adjacent carriage house. As guests arrive each day, homemade lemonade and cookies are served in the garden. In the morning coffee is served by the fireplace, and then at 9 sharp a full sit-down breakfast is served family-style at long trestle tables in the dining room and kitchen. For those who have been longing to spend the night in a bed suspended from the ceiling by chains, this inn fulfills that and other yearnings. (The guests really *swing* here.) Some visitors may even see a friendly ghost, although it has been 26 years since the last sighting. Croquet and hammocks beckon from the gardens, and handwriting analysis and both foot and body massages are available at an additional fee by appointment.

WHERE TO EAT

Bellotti Inn *53 Main St., 209/267-5211; L & D W-M; $$; highchairs, booster seats, children's portions; reservations suggested; MC, V.* Located inside an historic building, this well-established saloon and restaurant serves bountiful Italian family-style dinners with veal, chicken, and steak entrees. A la carte items and a hamburger are also on the menu.

Inexpensive hotel rooms are also available.

– Volcano –

A LITTLE BACKGROUND

The scenic, rural drive here from Sutter Creek is ill-marked, poorly paved, and best maneuvered during daylight. And experience indicates that directions and information obtained around these parts are often vague or misleading, leaving plenty of room for error. A good map can be worth its weight in gold.

Because this tiny town is built in a depression on top of limestone caves, it is green year-round. Sleepy and quiet now, during the Gold Rush it was a boom town well-known for its boisterous dance halls and saloons. It also opened the state's first public library.

ANNUAL EVENTS

Daffodil Hill *from mid-Mar until bloom is over in Apr; 18310 Rams Horn Grade, off Shake Ridge Rd., 3 miles north of town, 209/296-7048.* Originally planted in the 1850s by a Dutch settler, then added to and maintained by Grandma McLaughlin, this 6-acre garden boasts more than 300 varieties of bulbs. There are many, many daffodils, with a few tulips and hyacinths mixed in, too. More bulbs are planted every year by McLaughlin's grandchildren and great grandchildren. Currently over 400,000 bloom together each spring, making for a spectacular display. Peacocks, chickens, and sheep wander the grounds, and there is a picnic area with tables. It is a pleasant surprise that this seasonal extravaganza of bloom is so non-commercial: Admission is by donation.

WHERE TO STAY

St. George Hotel *16104 Volcano-Pine Grove Rd., 209/296-4458; 20 rooms; $$, on Sat $$$ but includes D & B; special children's rates; closed Jan-Feb; 1 bathtub; some shared baths; full breakfast, restaurant.* This solidly constructed hotel offers a choice of rooms in either the main hotel, built in 1862, or in an annex built almost a hundred years later in 1961. For safety reasons families with children under 12 must stay in the newer and charmless annex located around the corner, their consolation being that they get a private bathroom. In the hotel there is a cozy memorabilia-crammed bar and a parlor area, with fireplace and games, to relax in.

Dinner is served in the dining room Wednesday through Saturday; reservations are necessary. A special chicken dinner is served on Sunday from 3 to 7, and breakfast is also available on weekends.

WHERE TO EAT

Jug and Rose Confectionery *Main St., 209/296-4696; B Sat & Sun, L W-Sun; closed Dec-Mar; $; 1 highchair, children's portions; reservations suggested; no cards.* Famous for all-you-can-eat sourdough pancake breakfasts, this charming spot has been in business since 1855. In the Gold Rush days it was located in a different spot and known as The Stone Jug Saloon. A prior owner had the ruins of the saloon moved to its present site stone by stone. Sourdough pancakes are served with a choice of warm spice syrup, strawberries and sour cream, or boysenberry topping. (The pancakes have been served only since 1958, when Sourdough Jack visited from Alaska with his crock of sourdough.) Lunch brings homemade soups and sandwiches to the menu. Teatime goodies and exotic sundaes lure afternoon customers. How about a Moss Rose Sundae (homemade rose petal syrup on vanilla ice cream topped, in season, with an antique-variety rose), or a Sierra Split (three flavors of ice cream, wild blackberry topping, and banana). A Plain Jane is available for scardy cats. All items are served with fresh flower garnishes. For kids there is a scaled-down version of the old-fashioned ice cream parlor-style tables and chairs and a basket full of toys.

WHAT TO DO

Indian Grinding Rock State Historic Park *14881 Pine Grove-Volcano Rd., Pine Grove, southwest of town, 209/296-7488; daily 11-3, in summer 10-5; $5/car.* The largest of the grinding rocks—a huge flat bedrock limestone measuring 175 feet by 82 feet—has over 1,500 mortar holes and approximately 130 **petroglyphs** (rock carvings). All were made by Miwok Indians who ground their acorns and other seeds here with pestles. A reconstructed **Miwok Village** contains a ceremonial roundhouse, a covered handgame area, several cedar bark houses, and an Indian game field. Additional facilities include a self-guided nature trail and a regional museum that orients visitors with a slide show and interpretive displays. Picnic facilities and campsites are also available.

A **"Big Time" Miwok Celebration** is scheduled each September.

"Old Abe" Volcano Blues Cannon. Located in the center of town in a protected shelter, this cannon—without firing a shot—helped win the Civil War. Cast of bronze and brass in Boston in 1837 and weighing 737 pounds, it somehow reached San Francisco and was smuggled to Volcano in 1863. It was used by the town to control renegades who were drawn here in search of quick wealth. For the complete story, ask around town.

Sing Kee's Store. Built in 1857 and formerly a general store, this building is now a gift shop.

Soldiers' Gulch. Rocky terrain, a gurgling stream, and scenic stone ruins, which include the facades of several ancient buildings, provide a picturesque backdrop against which to enjoy a picnic or just a few moments of quiet contemplation.

Volcano Pioneers Community Theatre Group *209/223-4663; F & Sat at 8pm, occasionally Thur & Sun; closed Nov-Mar; tickets $10; reservations necessary.* The first little theater group to form in California was the Volcano Thespian Society in 1854. Performances are held in the intimate 50-seat **Cobblestone Theater,** and children are welcome.

– Amador City –

A LITTLE BACKGROUND

With a population of 202, this is said to be the smallest incorporated city in the state.

WHERE TO STAY

Mine House Inn *14125 Highway 49, 209/267-5900; 7 rooms; $$; children under 2 free; continental breakfast; unheated pool (unavailable Oct-Apr).* Built in 1881 as the headquarters for the Keystone Mine, this attractive restored brick building now houses guest rooms furnished with Gold Rush-era antiques. Each room is named for its original function: the Mill Grinding Room, the Vault Room, the Retort Room. In the morning, guests just push a buzzer and breakfast is delivered to the door. One Easter, long ago, a family that was staying here arranged for an Easter basket to arrive in this same mysterious manner. The kid still hasn't figured out how the parents pulled that one off!

WHERE TO EAT

Buffalo Chips Emporium *14179 Highway 49, 209/267-0570; B & L W-Sun; $; 1 highchair, 1 booster seat; no cards.* Some folks just buy a simple cone here and then sit outside on one of the weathered benches to leisurely watch the busy world drive by. Others prefer to sit inside what was once the town's Wells Fargo Bank and indulge in a fancy fountain item.

– Drytown –

A LITTLE BACKGROUND

Once home to 27 saloons, Drytown is now known for its equally abundant antique shops.

WHAT TO DO

Piper Playhouse *on Highway 49, 209/245-4604; Sat at 8, some matinees; closed Oct-Apr; tickets $13.50-$15; reservations necessary.* The Claypipers have been performing raucous melodramas here for over 30 years. However, since a fire in 1988 burned to the ground the old Joaquin Murietta Dance Hall, which dated from the 1930s and used to occupy the site, the troupe now performs in a newer building. The less expensive tickets are in the balcony, and children who sit on a lap don't need a ticket. Call for current schedule.

– Shingle Springs –

WHERE TO EAT

Sam's Town *3333 Coach Lane, Cameron Park exit off Highway 50, 916/677-2273; B, L, & D daily; $-$$; highchairs, booster seats; AE, MC, V.* This is a funky combination restaurant/honky-tonk piano bar/general store/memorabilia museum/pinball arcade. The outside grounds are littered with covered wagons, and the inside floors are littered with peanut shells discarded by happy revelers. Food runs the gamut from a hamburger and soda to prime rib and champagne.

– El Dorado –

WHERE TO EAT

Poor Red's *4041 Main St., 916/622-2901; L M-F, D daily; $; highchairs, booster seats; no reservations; MC, V.* Judging just from the outside, which looks to be an unsavory bar, this spot could easily be passed by. But then weary travelers would miss the experience of dining on exquisite ham, ribs, chicken, and steak—all cooked over an open oakwood pit and served in generous portions. Because this restaurant is very popular and also very small, weekend dinner waits can run over an hour. Some patrons pass that time downing Gold Cadillacs at the old-time horseshoe bar. Some pass it studying the mural behind the bar that depicts the town as it appeared in the late 1800s. Others pass it feeding the jukebox. Yet others beat the wait by ordering take-out.

– Placerville –

A LITTLE BACKGROUND

Placerville was once known as Hangtown because hangings here were so common. This is where the Hangtown Fry (eggs, bacon, and oysters) originated. Railroad magnate Mark Hopkins, meat-packer Philip Armour, and automobile-maker John Studebaker all got their financial starts here as well.

VISITOR INFORMATION

El Dorado County Chamber of Commerce *542 Main St., Placerville 95667, 800/457-6279, 916/621-5885.*

ANNUAL EVENTS

Reenactment of Pony Express *June; in Pollock Pines, 916/644-3970.*

Apple Hill *September-December; 916/644-7692.* Located on a mountain ridge east of town, the route for the Apple Hill tour follows an historic path originally blazed out in 1857 by Pony Express riders. In the fall, 42 apple ranches along this route sell 22 varieties of tree-fresh apples at bargain prices. And they're *crunchy*, because they're fresh! An impressive selection of homemade apple goodies can also be purchased: fresh-pressed apple cider, hard cider, apple wine, spicy apple butter, caramel apples, apple jelly, dried apples, apple cake, apple sundaes, apple syrup, and, of course, apple pie. Many of the farms have picnic facilities, and some have snack bars. A few also have hiking trails, fishing ponds, pony rides, train rides, and live jazz. Two wineries are also located here. Several apple varieties are available into December, and five Christmas tree farms open on Thanksgiving weekend. Cherry season begins on Father's Day weekend. For a free map to the farms, send a legal-size stamped, self-addressed envelope with 75 cents postage to: The Apple Hill Growers, P.O. Box 494, Camino 95709.

WHERE TO EAT

The Sundae Times *3025 Sacramento St., 916/621-1921; daily 10-10; $; highchairs, booster seats, children's portions; MC, V.* It is often hot as blazes when travelers hit this lively boom town, so this cheerful, air-conditioned spot offers a welcome respite. Diners sit on ornate wire chairs, perched at cute little tables, while cooling their palates with generous portions of ice cream concoctions. The menu also offers soups, salads, and sandwiches, and a grilled peanut butter and jelly sandwich lurks among the special children's items.

WHAT TO DO

El Dorado County Historical Museum *100 Placerville Dr., 2 miles west of town at the El Dorado County Fairgrounds, 916/621-5865; W-Sat 10-4, Sun 1-4; free.* Historic exhibits in this "great hall" include a Wells Fargo stagecoach and a wheelbarrow made by John Studebaker in the days before he manufactured cars.

Gold Bug Mine *off Bedford Ave., 1 mile north of town, 916/642-5232; daily 10-4 in summer; Sept-Oct & Mar-Apr, Sat & Sun only; closed Nov-Feb; adults $1, 5-16 50¢, cassette tour $1.* Visitors here can take self-guided tours through a cool 1/4-mile-long lighted mine shaft, picnic at creek-side tables, and hike in rugged 61-acre **Bedford Park.**

WINERIES

Boeger Winery *1709 Carson Rd., (take Schnell School Road exit off Highway 50), 800/655-2634, 916/622-8094; tasting daily 10-5; tours by appt.* The stone cellar tasting room here is part of the original winery that operated from the 1860s through the 1920s. During Prohibition the winery became a pear farm. Then, in the early 1970s, it once again became a winery. Shaded stream-side picnic tables beckon, and a sandbox awaits children.

Sierra Vista Winery *4560 Cabernet Way, 916/622-7221; tasting M-F 10-4, Sat & Sun 11-5; tours by appt.* Enjoy a magnificent view of the entire Crystal Range of the Sierra Nevada while picnicking at this pleasant winery. Bring lawn toys for children.

– Coloma –

A LITTLE BACKGROUND

This is where James Marshall discovered gold in 1848. The entire town is now a National Historic Landmark.

WHERE TO STAY

Sierra Nevada House III *835 Lotus Rd., 916/621-1649; 8 rooms; $$; some bathtubs; restaurant.* Built near the ruins of two former hotels of the same name, which burned to the ground in 1907 and 1926, this is an authentic reconstruction. Some rooms are in the older hotel, and some are in a newer motel addition.

A cheery old-fashioned ice cream parlor offers seating at both round marble tables and at a long marble counter. A steak house serves prime rib and fried chicken in the dining room Tuesday through Sunday. Highchairs, booster seats, and children's portions are available.

Vineyard House *530 Cold Springs Rd., 916/622-2217; 7 rooms; 100% non-smoking; $$; children under 5 free; no TVs; some shared baths; full breakfast, restaurant, room service.* Rumored to be haunted by its 19th-century owners, who are buried across the street in **Pioneer Cemetery,** this comfortable 1878 Victorian inn's guest rooms are the house's original bedrooms. Each is uniquely decorated and characterized after well-known people from the late 1800s. The Emerald Room features walls covered with shirred deep-green chintz. The Red Room, which is dedicated to the memory of flamboyant Lola Montez, has walls covered with red flocked paper. Several rooms are also decorated in cheerier, lighter tones.

In the basement, the house's original wine cellar and a jail cell now serve as a bar with live music on Friday and Saturday nights. On the main floor, homemade dinners are served daily in a warren of dining rooms. Entrees include chicken and dumplings, beef stroganoff, fresh seafood, and prime rib. Dinners come with homemade soup, salad, fresh steamed carrots from the inn's garden, and homemade bread pudding. Children's portions are available, as are highchairs and booster seats.

The **Olde Coloma Theatre,** which is located adjacent, stages melodrama performances May through December. A dinner package is available through the Vineyard House.

WHAT TO DO

Gold Hill Vineyard *5660 Vineyard Lane, 916/626-6522; tasting Sat & Sun 10-5; tours by appt.* This modern tasting room is located on a quiet hill overlooking the vineyards. A picnic area is provided.

Marshall Gold Discovery State Historic Park *on Highway 49, 916/622-3470. Park: daily 8-sunset; $5/car. Museum: daily 10-5 in summer, shorter hours rest of year; free.*

This lovely 265-acre park encompasses 70 percent of the town. It contains a reconstruction of the original **Sutter's Mill** (where the Gold Rush began) as well as picnic facilities, nature trails, and Gold Rush-era buildings and artifacts. An exact replica of the piece of gold Marshall found is on display in the museum (the original is at the Smithsonian in Washington, D.C.). The mill is sometimes operated; call for schedule. Picnic facilities are available.

The **James W. Marshall Monument** is located on a hill overlooking the town. Marshall's grave is here, and a statue honoring him depicts him pointing to the spot where he discovered gold.

Whitewater Connection *800/336-7238, 916/622-6446, fax 916/622-7192; half- and full-day trips offered daily mid-Apr-Sept only; $59+/person.* The office and base camp for this whitewater rafting outfit is located adjacent to the state park. Participants on American River trips are permitted to camp out at the outfitter's riverside facility. Longer trips are also available. See also page 274.

– Auburn –

VISITOR INFORMATION

Placer County Visitors Information Center *13460 Lincoln Way, Auburn 95603, 800/ 427-6463, 916/885-5616.*

WHERE TO STAY

Motel Row. Many motels are located at the top of the hill on Lincoln Way, and across the freeway on Bowman Road.

WHERE TO EAT

Cafe Delicias *1591 Lincoln Way, 916/885-2050; L & D daily; $; highchairs, booster seats; AE, MC, V.* Located in one of the town's oldest buildings, this casual Mexican restaurant serves especially good flautas and homemade tamales. Mexican wedding cake makes a great dessert but is, unfortunately, often unavailable.

Ikeda's *13500 Lincoln Way, (1/4 mile east of Auburn Ravine-Foresthill exit off Highway 80), 916/885-4243; daily 9-7, to 9 in summer & on weekends.* Since the 1950s this casual snack bar has been serving travel-weary diners delicious fast-food fare. Among the goodies are hamburgers, corn dogs, burritos, deep-fried whole mushrooms, fruit pie, fresh fruit salad, frozen yogurt, ten flavors of hot chocolate, and absolutely wonderful, thick fresh fruit milkshakes. Not to be missed at the adjacent produce stand are the giant cashews and pistachios, which are grown in the area, and the baked and unbaked pies to go.

WHAT TO DO

Gold Country Museum *Museum: 1273 High St., in the Gold Country Fairgrounds, 916/889-4134. House: 291 Auburn-Folsom Rd., 916/889-4156. Both open Tu-Sun 10-4; by donation.* Located within a building constructed of logs and stones, this old-time museum emphasizes mining exhibits. Visitors may walk through a 48-foot mine shaft and view a working model of a stamp mill. Local Maidu Indian artifacts and an extensive doll collection are also on display.

Docent-led tours are available of the nearby Greek Revival-style **Bernhard House**, a restored Victorian farmhouse that was built in 1851 and is furnished with Victorian antiques.

– Grass Valley –

A LITTLE BACKGROUND

It was here, in what was once the richest gold mining region in the state, that gold mining became a well-organized industry. Many advanced mining techniques were developed and first used here.

VISITOR INFORMATION

Grass Valley/Nevada County Chamber of Commerce *248 Mill St., Grass Valley 95945, 800/272-5440, 916/273-4667.* Because of its location inside a replica of the historic home once occupied by scandalous Gold Rush personality Lola Montez, this office is worth visiting in person.

ANNUAL EVENTS

Bluegrass Festival *June; 209/464-5324.*

Cornish Christmas Street Faire *December.* Experience an old-time Christmas at this event celebrating the traditions of the Cornish miners who settled this Gold Rush town. Visitors can dance in the downtown streets, which are closed to traffic, and ride in a horse-drawn carriage.

WHERE TO STAY

Alta Sierra Resort Motel *135 Tammy Way, 800/992-5300, 916/273-9102; 14 rooms; $$-$$$; cribs; all bathtubs.* Finding this rustic modern motel is a little like going on a treasure hunt. Guests just keep following signs down a winding country road, and when they finally do find it, they usually agree it is somewhat of a treasure. Woodsy, spacious rooms overlook a small lake and picturesque, grassy grounds. Guests have complimentary access to a pool (summer only), 18-hole golf course, tennis courts, and inexpensive dining at a country club located across the street.

♥Holbrooke Hotel *212 W. Main St., 800/933-7077, 916/272-1989, fax 916/273-0434; 27 rooms; 12 non-smoking rooms; $$-$$$; some bathtubs, gas fireplaces; continental breakfast, restaurant.* Established in 1851, this grand hotel was meticulously restored in Victorian style and reopened in 1984. Past guests include four presidents (Grant, Garfield, Cleveland, and Harrison), stagecoach robber Black Bart, and author Mark Twain. Current guests can step back in time in the beautifully appointed rooms featuring brass beds and the original claw-foot tubs. Most rooms hold only two people, but in a few larger rooms a child can be accommodated with a rollaway bed. A century-old wrought-iron elevator cage lifts guests from floor to floor. This lodging facility, which consists of both the hotel and the 1874 **Purcell House** behind it, is conveniently located in the center of town.

Both the **Golden Gate Saloon**, which is said to be the oldest continuously operating saloon in the Gold Country and which features an ornate bar that was shipped around the Horn, and an elegant restaurant with full family amenities operate on the main floor.

Sivananda Ashram Vrindavan Yoga Farm *14651 Ballantree Lane, 916/272-9322; 8 rooms; 100% non-smoking; $$; children under 5 free; no TVs; all shared bathrooms; meals included.* The bell rings here at 5:30 each morning to awaken guests. Attendance at scheduled meditation and yoga classes is mandatory. In between guests dine on vegetarian meals and have plenty of free time to enjoy the natural surroundings of the 80-acre farm. Lodging consists of both dormitories and single and double rooms, and during the summer guests may bring their own tents.

WHERE TO EAT

Mrs. Dubblebee's Pasties *251 S. Auburn St., 916/272-7700; M-F 9-6, Sat & Sun 10-5:30; $; no cards.* Located inside a pristine white Victorian home, this unusual eatery specializes in pasties. (In fact, the original owner of this shop, William Brooks, invented the pasty-making machine now used throughout the world.) These meat and potato turnovers were once popular lunch fare among the area's Cornish miners, who carried them down into the mines in their pockets. At lunchtime, they reheated their pasties on a shovel held over candles secured in their hard hats. Fruit turnovers and drinks are also available. How about a hasty tasty pasty picnic? (Actually, pasty rhymes with nasty.)

More pasties are available at **Marshall's Pasties** *(203 Mill St., 916/272-2844)*, where they are made by hand, and at **King Richard's** *(217 Colfax Ave., 916/273-0286)*, where they are made using the Brooks machine—which can sometimes be observed in operation.

Tofanelli's *302 W. Main St., 916/273-9927; B & L daily, D M-Sat; $; highchairs, booster seats, children's portions; 100% non-smoking; MC, V.* Every kind of breakfast item imaginable is on this menu, including design-your-own-omelettes, whole wheat pancakes and waffles, and a large variety of teas. Salads, sandwiches, and several kinds of hamburgers—including a tofuburger and a veggieburger—join the menu at lunch. All this and an attractive brick and oak decor, too.

WHAT TO DO

Bridgeport Covered Bridge *Take Highway 20 west about 8 miles to Pleasant Valley, turn right (north) and follow the south fork of the Yuba River 5 miles.* Built over the south fork of the Yuba River in 1862 and in use until 1971, this is the longest (233 feet) single-span wood-covered bridge in the world. It is now a State Historical Landmark. Not currently maintained and in shaky condition, it should be walked across with caution. A scenic picnic area is situated on the riverbank, and there are several hiking trails.

Those who have witnessed it claim the wildflower display here in March is spectacular.

Empire Mine State Historic Park *10791 E. Empire St., 916/273-8522; daily 10-5; guided tours daily at 1; adults $2, 6-12 $1.* Once the largest and richest hard rock mine in the state, the Empire Mine was operated for over a century—from 1850 to 1956. Though it still holds millions of dollars worth of gold, the ore is too expensive to extract and the mine is now a 784-acre state park. Of special interest are the stone **Bourn Mansion** *(hours vary; guided tour on weekends)*, which was designed

and built by Willis Polk in 1897 in the style of an English country lodge, and the 13-acre formal gardens—featuring an antique rose garden and several reflecting pools—that surround it. The mining area illustrates many facets of the business and allows visitors to look down a lighted mine shaft. There are also approximately 22 miles of self-guided back country hiking trails. Picnicking is permitted only on the outskirts of the parking lot.

Grass Valley Museum *S. Church/Chapel Sts.; W, Sat, Sun 12-3; June-Sept only; by donation.* Built in 1863 as Mount Saint Mary's Convent and Orphanage, this was the state's first orphanage for non-Indian children. The building now displays Gold Rush memorabilia and furnishings, as well as a fully equipped doctor's office, classroom, parlor, and music room from that era.

Memorial Park *Colfax/Central Aves., 916/273-3171.* This is a good spot to picnic, get in a game of tennis, swim in the public pool, wade in the creek, or let the kids romp at the well-equipped playground.

North Star Mining Museum *Allison Ranch Rd./McCourtney Rd., 916/265-6044; daily 10-5; closed Nov-Apr; adults 50¢, under 18 free.* This rustic stone building, which was once the power house for the North Star Mine, houses a collection of old photographs, mining dioramas and models, and a 30-foot-diameter, 10-ton Pelton water wheel dating from 1896. It also displays the largest operational Cornish pump in the country. A grassy picnic area is located across adjacent Wolf Creek.

Oregon House. *Located 35 miles west of town. Take Highway 20 west to Browns Valley. Then take Highway E21 north to Oregon House, and follow E20 east.*

    Collins Lake Recreation Area *916/692-1600; $4/car, boat rentals $5-$10/hour.* Popular with fishermen, this 1,000-acre lake also has terraced campsites with a view of the lake.

    Renaissance Vineyard & Winery *12585 Rices Crossing Rd., Oregon House, 800/525-9463, 916/692-2222; tasting & tours by appt; tasting fee $5, applies to purchase or keep tasting glass.* The drive through the scenic Sierra Nevada foothills required to reach this isolated valley would be worthwhile even if this special winery weren't waiting at the end. Operated by the Fellowship of Friends, a non-denominational religious group, the winery is situated on a scenic hillside terraced with grapevines.

    This complex is also home to the **Museum of Classical Chinese Furniture** *(916/692-3142; M-Sat 11-3, Sun 3-6; by donation),* which is the only museum in the world dedicated to displaying Chinese hardwood furniture from the Ming (1368-1644) and early Qing (1644-1722) dynasties. Reached via a drive up a cypress-lined roadway, the museum is housed within a Louis XVI Versailles-style mansion surrounded by mandarin orange groves and a formal rose garden.

    The chef-owned **La Cucina Restaurant** *(916/692-2425; L & D W-Sun; $-$$; reservations required at dinner),* which is also on the property, serves a limited menu of well-prepared lunch items: a salad, a soup, a pasta, a hamburger. When the weather is nice, deck seating is available, and on warmer days, the air-conditioned interior of the dining room brings welcome relief.

– Nevada City –

A LITTLE BACKGROUND

Said to be the best privately preserved and restored small city in the state, this picturesque mining town is also said to contain residential and commercial buildings representative of all the major 19th century architectural styles. Scenically situated on seven hills, the town boasts a particularly fine assortment of lovely gingerbread-style Victorian homes. The entire downtown district is on the National Register of Historic Places.

VISITOR INFORMATION

Nevada City Chamber of Commerce *132 Main St., Nevada City 95959, 800/655-NJOY, 916/265-9019.*

ANNUAL EVENTS

International Teddy Bear Convention *April; 916/265-5804.* Bears from all over the world come out of hibernation for this warm, fuzzy event. Bearaphernalia and bear necessities and luxuries abound, and all kinds of bears are available for adoption. A tour of the charming bear-stuffed **Teddy Bear Castle** at 431 Broad Street is part of the fun.

4th of July Parade *July.* Held in Nevada City on even years and in Grass Valley on odd, this is a real old-fashioned celebration. It begins with a parade, followed by diversions—food stalls, competitions, entertainment—at the fairgrounds. As might be expected, it culminates in a fireworks extravaganza.

Constitution Day Parade *September.* The signing of the U.S. Constitution is honored with marching bands, drill teams, floats, fire engines, and horsemen. Pre-parade activities include a reenactment of the signing and a demonstration of colonial dancing.

Fall Colors *mid-October through mid-November.*

Victorian Christmas *December, on the three Wednesday evenings & usually all day on the Sunday before Christmas.*

WHERE TO STAY IN TOWN

♥Grandmere's Inn *449 Broad St., 916/265-4660; 7 rooms; $$$; 2-night minimum on weekends; unsuitable for children; some bathtubs; full breakfast.* Built in 1861, this 3-story Colonial Revival home is on the National Register of Historic Places. It is beautifully decorated in French country style, with antique pine furnishings and gorgeous floral fabrics, and is conveniently located at the **Top of Broad Street**—one of the town's earliest residential areas.

National Hotel *211 Broad St., 916/265-4551; 42 rooms; 4 non-smoking rooms; $-$$$; children under 12 free; some TVs, kitchens, bathtubs; some shared baths; unheated pool;*

restaurant, room service. Located on the town's main street, this claims to be the oldest continuously operating hotel west of the Rockies—maybe even west of the Mississippi. Among the luminaries who have been guests here are both Herbert Hoover, who stayed here when he was a mining engineer for the Empire Mine, and Mark Twain. Built in 1856, it is a State Historical Landmark and features high ceilings, cozy floral wallpapers, and old-time furniture. Families of four can be accommodated in two separate rooms with a bath between.

The plush, old-fashioned **Victorian Dining Room** serves a moderately-priced breakfast and lunch daily, as well as a Sunday brunch. Its steak and lobster dinner menu is more pricey. Highchairs and booster seats are available.

Northern Queen Inn *400 Railroad Ave., 916/265-5824, fax 916/265-3720; 93 units; 10 non-smoking units; $$; some kitchens, wood-burning stoves; heated pool, hot tub; restaurant.* Located on the outskirts of town beside Gold Run Creek, this pleasant lodging complex has modern motel rooms, cottages, and 2-story chalets.

Piety Hill Inn *523 Sacramento, 916/265-2245; 9 units; 100% non-smoking; $$; 2-night minimum on weekends; cribs; 1 bathtub; hot tub; full breakfast.* Cutesied up with floral wallpapers and antique furnishings, this 1930s auto court motel has one- and two-room cottages.

♥Red Castle Inn *109 Prospect, 916/265-5135; 7 rooms; 100% non-smoking; $$-$$$; 2-night minimum on Sat Apr-Dec; unsuitable for children under 10; no TVs; some wood-burning stoves; full breakfast.* Situated on a hilltop above town, this beautifully restored and plushly furnished Gothic Revival mansion was built in 1860. Said to be one of only two of this style left on the West Coast, it features gingerbread and icicle trim and has old-fashioned double brick walls.

WHERE TO STAY NEARBY

Herrington's Sierra Pines *on Highway 49, Sierra City, 60 miles north of town, 916/862-1151; 20 units; $-$$; closed Nov-Feb; cribs; 1 kitchen, 1 wood-burning stove; restaurant.* Located on the north fork of the Yuba River, this lodging facility features duplex units and one cabin.

The restaurant is known for its baked goods and rainbow trout, which are caught fresh each morning from the property's own trout pond. Breakfast and dinner are served daily, and highchairs and booster seats are available.

Kenton Mine Lodge *on Foots Crossing Rd., Alleghany, 40 miles north of town in a quiet canyon at the end of a 3-mile dirt road, 916/287-3212; $$-$$$; unsuitable for children under 10; no TVs; some kitchens, wood-burning stoves; some shared baths; sauna; includes meals.* One of the most favored areas of the current gold rush is the area surrounding the tiny Sierra town of Alleghany. City-slickers are advised to be careful around here, though, as many miners camp on top of their claims, and some have been known to get mean when confronted with trespassers. To assure safety and warmth while trying one's luck at panning for gold, consider spending time at this remote, semi-refurbished mining camp dating from the 1930s. Though vivid imaginations have been known to run wild here (several guests have commented that the winding forest road in from Nevada City is not unlike the one seen at the beginning of the horror movie *The Shining*), once the freaked-out city traveler relaxes and acclimates to the unaccustomed peace and tranquility, apprehensions dissolve. Guests sleep in either weathered cabins or B&B-style rooms and are fed home-cooked meals, served family-style at long tables in the Cookhouse. Gold-panning equipment may be borrowed for use in gurgling Kanaka Creek, which runs through the camp. An abandoned gold mine, dating from the late 1800s, and a stamp mill on the property provide for some interesting exploring. Campsites are also available.

Packer Lake Lodge *on Packer Lake Rd., Sierra City, 60 miles north of town, 916/862-1221; 14 units; $-$$; closed Nov-May; cribs; some kitchens, wood-burning stoves; some shared baths; restaurant.* Located at the end of a road in a remote corner of the Sierra Nevadas, this rustic resort has eight housekeeping cabins with sundecks overlooking Packer Lake. Cabins are rented by the week and include use of a rowboat. (No motorboats are permitted on the lake.) Six sleeping cabins are also available by the night.

Salmon Lake Lodge *10 miles from Sierra City, 415/771-0150 (reservations number is in San Francisco), 916/842-3108; 14 units; $$-$$$; 1-week minimum June-Aug; closed Nov-Apr; no TVs; all kitchens, wood-burning stoves; some shared baths.* Located in the glaciated high country of Sierra County, this remote resort has been in continuous operation for almost a century. Guests park their cars at the east end of Salmon Lake and are transported by a staff-operated barge across the lake. There they sleep in one of the rustic cabins or tent-cabins and are provided free access to an assortment of boats. One newer deluxe cabin comes fully equipped, but guests in the other cabins provide their own bedding, kitchen utensils, and supplies. The experience is a lot like camping, but with the added amenities of electricity and a kitchen. To ease cooking chores, guests are invited twice each week to a catered barbecue (additional fee) held on an island in the center of the lake.

Sierra Shangri-La *on Highway 49, Downieville, 45 miles north of town, 916/289-3455; 11 units; 3 non-smoking units; $$-$$$; 2-night minimum; cribs; some kitchens, wood-burning stoves.* There is little to do here except commune with nature. Guests can relax, do some fishing and hiking, and enjoy the sight and sound of the Yuba River rushing past their cabin door. Some units are perched right over the river, allowing guests to fish from their deck in the spring. Several B&B units are also available.

WHERE TO EAT

Apple Fare *307 Broad St., 916/265-5458; B & L daily; $; highchairs, booster seats, children's portions; 100% non-smoking; no reservations; AE, MC, V.* This pleasant, casual spot is popular with families and locals. Homemade soups and an assortment of sandwiches are on the lunch menu. Apple goodies include an apple-tizer (a creamy cheese and apple dip served with apple wedges and crackers) and cold apple cider. Don't miss a slab of fresh baked apple pie; the smooth French silk chocolate and lemon chess are also especially good.

Friar Tuck's *111 N. Pine St., 916/265-9093; L & D W-Sun; $$; highchairs, booster seats, children's portions; reservations suggested; AE, MC, V.* Operating in a building that dates back to 1857, this cozy restaurant offers a variety of casual fondue items. A chocolate dessert fondue is among them. The extensive menu also offers grilled fresh fish, chicken, and steak. The wine list runs the gamut from inexpensive local labels to expensive rare vintages; varietals are available by the glass. Non-drinkers and children can get high on a Princess Leia or Darth Vader—updated versions of the old-time Shirley Temple and Roy Rodgers. Relaxing live guitar music is piped throughout the many dining rooms furnished with large, comfortable wooden booths. An authentic 19th century pub bar from Liverpool, England adds to the atmosphere.

WHAT TO DO IN TOWN

Firehouse Museum #1 *214 Main St., 916/265-5468; daily 11-4; closed W Nov-Mar; by donation.* Located inside a charming 1861 Victorian firehouse, this museum is said to be haunted. Among the intriguing pioneer memorabilia on display are a Chinese altar, snowshoes made for a horse, and a noteworthy collection of Maidu Indian baskets.

Nevada City Winery *321 Spring St., 800/347-1497, 916/265-WINE; tasting daily 12-5; tours by appt (fee).* Housed now in an old foundry building where gold mining tools were once cast, this winery is located only 2 blocks from where it began a century ago. It is known for its Cabernets, Merlots, and Zinfandels.

Nevada Theatre *401 Broad St., 916/265-6161; most F & Sat evenings; tickets $10-$12, under 12 $6.* Opened in September of 1865 and lectured in by Mark Twain, this is said to be the oldest theater building in California. It has been refurbished to appear as it did when it first opened. The inside is very small and all seats are close to the stage, making it an excellent spot to expose children to a live performance. The audience is usually filled with locals, and they bring their children when the production is appropriate. Movies are often scheduled on Sunday evenings. Call for current program.

WHAT TO DO NEARBY

Consciousness Village/Campbell Hot Springs *1 Campbell Hot Springs Rd., Sierraville, off Highway 89, 80 miles north of town, 916/994-3737; baths open 24-hours daily; adults $6, under 12 free.* Swimsuits are optional in the indoor and outdoor hot tubs at this secluded spa, which has been open since the 1850s. A cool natural mineral water swimming pool rounds out the facilities. Rebirthing and conscious breathing seminars are sometimes scheduled, and a vegetarian restaurant serves breakfast and dinner.

Rooms in a lodge dating from 1909 are also available. The inexpensive rates include two vegetarian meals and unlimited use of the springs.

Independence Trail *off Highway 49, 6 miles north of town; free.* Basically level and easy for baby strollers and children to navigate, this 1-mile nature trail passes Transitional Zone vegetation. It features an outstanding display of wildflowers in April and May.

Malakoff Diggins State Historic Park *23579 N. Bloomfield Rd., off Highway 49, 17 miles northeast of town, 916/265-2740; $5/car. Museum: daily 10-4, May-Sept; rest of* *year, Sat & Sun only.* Inhabited by over 1,500 people in the 1800s, when it was the largest hydraulic gold mining operation in the world, **North Bloomfield** is now a ghost town. Several buildings have been restored, but there are no commercial stores. The park museum, a former dance hall, has an interpretive display on hydraulic mining, and visitors may hike on numerous trails and fish in a small lake. Picnic facilities are available.

Three primitive cabins, five walk-in campsites, and thirty regular campsites are available.

Note that the drive from town takes just under an hour, and a portion of the road is unpaved. Travelers with large motorhomes or trailers should enter the park via the Tyler-Foote route, located 11 miles north of Nevada City on Highway 49.

Oregon Creek Swimming Hole *on Highway 49, 18 miles north of town.* Located in the middle fork of the Yuba River, this popular spot has sandy beaches, both deep swimming and shallow wading spots, and picnic facilities. A **Tahoe National Forest** campground is also located here.

Sierra County Historical Park and Museum *on Highway 49, Sierra City, 60 miles north of town, 916/862-1310; W-Sun 10-5 June-Sept, Sat & Sun only in Oct; closed Nov-May; adults $4, 13-16 $2.* A 45-minute guided tour through the reconstructed 1850s **Kentucky Mine and Stamp Mill** located here permits viewing the original machinery, which is still intact and operable. The museum is set up inside a reconstructed woodframe hotel dating from the mid-19th century. Picnic tables and barbecue facilites are situated under a canopy of oak trees.

A **Kentucky Mine Concert Series** of eclectic material is held on Friday evenings in July and August in an amphitheater within the complex.

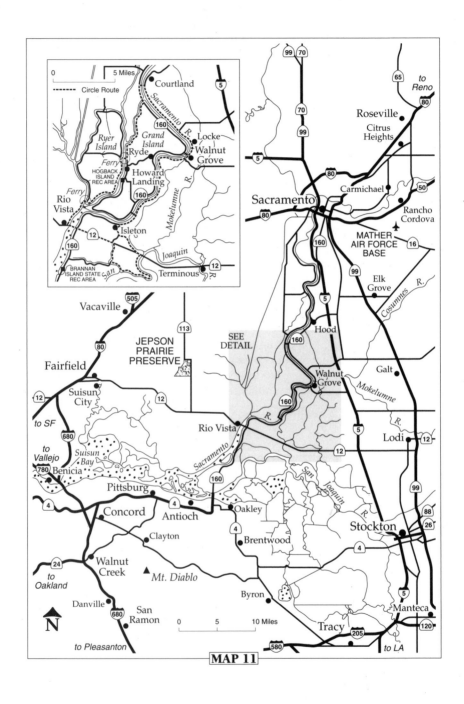

MAP 11

The Delta

A LITTLE BACKGROUND

Composed of flat land, criss-crossed by more than 700 miles of rivers and sloughs (pronounced *slews*), this area is filled with scenic roads running along raised levees. Bridges abound (there are at least 70), and many raise to accommodate large boats. Popular for a houseboat vacation (see page 272), this area is also pleasant for just a day trip. Do have a good detailed map, as the roads here are maze-like, and do try to avoid driving at night, when the levee roads can be dangerous.

Trendy hasn't yet hit this area and probably never will. Food is basic. Wine is sometimes mistreated. However, people in the area do enjoy a good time, and many eating establishments book live entertainment in the evening.

VISITOR INFORMATION

Isleton Chamber of Commerce *P.O. Box 758, Isleton 95641, 916/777-5880.*

Rio Vista Chamber of Commerce *60 Main St., Rio Vista 94571, 707/374-2700.*

Vallejo Convention & Visitors Bureau *Vallejo Ferry Terminal, 495 Mare Island Way #C, Vallejo 94590, 707/642-3653, fax 707/644-2206.* This bureau also offers information on Benicia.

Walnut Grove Area Chamber of Commerce *P.O. Box 100 (14133 Market St.), Walnut Grove, 95690, 916/776-2060.*

Also, *Hal Schell's Delta Map and Guide (P.O. Box 9140, Stockton 95208, 209/951-7821)* is an indispensable aid. It is available in many Delta stores for $2.25. To secure one in advance, send $3.25 to the above address.

GETTING THERE

Located approximately 60 miles east of San Francisco. Take Highway 80 north to Highway 4 east, and continue following Highway 4 as it turns into Highway 160 (River Road) and crosses the gigantic arch that is the John A. Nejedly Bridge. Highway 160 continues north into Sacramento.

ANNUAL EVENTS

Great Isleton Crawdad Festival *June; in Isleton, 510/782-7379, 916/777-5880.* Benefitting this small town's Children's Fund, this festival features live music and entertainment, plus plenty of crawdads. Activities include a Crawdad Race and a Crawdad Petting Zoo, and there are plenty of cooked crawdads for eating.

Pear Fair *July; in Courtland.* The Delta is the foremost pear growing area in the country. This annual celebration of the harvest is always held on the last Sunday in July and features a parade, kiddie rides, and, of course, plenty of pear foods. Contests include pear bobbing, pear pie-eating, and pear peeling—in which the longest continuous peel after 10 minutes wins. A competition to find the area's largest pear is also part of the fun.

WHERE TO STAY/WHERE TO EAT/WHAT TO DO

The following towns are listed in the order that they appear on the circle tour highlighted with broken lines on the map on page 210. It is possible to start the tour at any point. Following it takes drivers through the area's most scenic towns, across several different types of bridges, and on two car ferries.

Isleton

Located at the geographic center of the Delta, this town is one of the largest in the area.

Delta Daze Inn *20 Main St., 916/777-7777; 12 rooms; 9 non-smoking rooms; $$-$$$; full breakfast.* Located in the town's quiet Chinatown, this structure has served as a bordello, a gambling hall, a candy store, and an ice cream parlor. Now it is totally remodeled and expanded into a comfortable B&B. Afternoon snacks and breakfast are served in a cheery room dominated by an impressive arched window that is accented with stained glass. Rooms are uniquely decorated, and the Levee Suite, which has two queen beds and a balcony overlooking the town, is large enough for a family. Complimentary ice cream concoctions are served only to guests in the inn's own lobby soda fountain, and bikes are available for loan.

Croissanterie *7 Main St., 916/777-6170; B, L, & D daily; $-$$; MC, V.* The lunch menu offers a choice of hot and cold sandwiches on a variety of house-made breads, as well as pizzas and quiches. Box lunches for picnics can be packed to go. A house specialty at dinner is a crawdad scampi appetizer. Sunday brunch highlights include fresh orange juice, ham-asparagus crepes, seafood scramble, muffins, and house-made sorbet. An outdoor patio area is available for warm weather dining. (This appears to be the one exception to that comment at the beginning of this chapter about finding trendy food in the Delta.)

Hotel Del Rio *209 2nd St., 916/777-6033; B, L, & D daily; $-$$; children's portions; reservations suggested; MC, V.* The specialty of the house here is prime rib in three sizes: petite, regular, and double. Broasted chicken and deep-fried prawns round out the menu, and big plates of Cajun-style crawdads are sometimes available. All entrees include visits to the salad bar. Live music is scheduled in the bar on Saturday and Sunday nights.

Inexpensive rooms, furnished attractively with antiques, are available upstairs.

Moore's Riverboat *106 Brannan Island Rd., 916/777-6545; B, L, & D daily; $-$$; MC, V.* Now permanently moored on the Mokelumne River, this 156-foot river freighter, launched in 1931 as the *Fort Sutter*, has been refitted to serve as a restaurant. A jumbo crawdad platter is the house specialty, but seafood and steaks are also available. Live rock music is scheduled on weekends.

Walnut Grove

This town, which grew up on both sides of the river, is linked by the first cantilever bridge built west of the Mississippi. The decaying east side of town holds the remnants of a Chinatown, and the west side is a well-maintained residential area.

Giusti's *on Walnut Grove Rd., 4 miles west of town, 916/776-1808; L & D daily, SunBr; $$; no cards.* This rustic landmark building stands at the junction of the North Fork of the Mokelumne River and Snodgrass Slough. The restaurant has been dishing up family-style Italian meals here since 1896, and its dining room overlooks the river.

Locke

Said to be the only town in the country that was built entirely by and for Chinese immigrants, this tiny town dates back to 1915. Its narrow Main Street is lined with picturesque weathered wooden buildings, many of which are still inhabited. Aging Chinese residents are often seen sitting on benches on the wooden walkways, just watching. When leaving here, continue the circle tour as indicated or back track to Walnut Grove, cross the river, and continue south to Ryde.

Al's Place *on Main St., 916/776-1800; L & D daily; $; highchairs, booster seats; no cards.* Once a speakeasy, this restaurant's unsavory looks might cause many people to pass it by. But once through the bar, which can be rowdy even at lunchtime, diners enter a windowless back room and can seat themselves at plain formica picnic tables with benches. The only thing on the menu is a steak sandwich, served with a side of very good grilled garlic bread. Jars of peanut butter and jam adorn each table and are meant to be used with the steak. Parents can sometimes strike a deal with a waitress to bring extra bread so their kids can make peanut butter and jelly sandwiches. At dinner, when the place gets more crowded, the steak goes up a bit in price and is served with soup, salad, pasta, and sourdough bread.

When leaving, stop by the bar to find out how dollar bills get stuck to the 2-story-high ceiling. It only costs $1 to find out.

Dai Loy Museum *on Main St., 916/776-1684; W-Sun 11-5; free.* Located within what was the town gambling hall from 1916 to 1951, this museum fills visitors in on the town's history as a Chinese outpost. Visitors may view the Central Gaming Hall, with its original furniture and gaming tables, and the low-ceilinged dealers' bedrooms located upstairs. Interesting era photographs hang on the walls throughout.

Ryde

Grand Island Inn *14340 Highway 160, 3 miles south of Walnut Grove, 916/776-1318; L Sat, D F-Sun, SunBr; $$; reservations suggested; MC, V.* Built in 1926 and once owned by actor Lon Chaney, this colorful pink stucco, 4-story hotel operated a basement speakeasy during Prohibition. It is claimed that Herbert Hoover, who was a Prohibitionist, ironically announced his presidential candidacy in 1928 in this very hotel while standing above a large stash of bootleg booze. Now beautifully restored, this art deco hotel once again serves elegant dinners in its dining room. Live music accompanies Saturday night dinner, and an island barbecue is scheduled every Sunday evening. Guest rooms are also available.

Across the island, the **Grand Island Mansion** *(916/775-1705),* operated by the same owners, is open only on Sunday for an opulent brunch.

Car Ferrys. *Free.* Catch the old-time diesel-powered, cable-guided **Howard's Landing Ferry,** also known as the *J-Mack,* off Grand Island Road. It holds about

The Real McCoy

six cars, and waits are usually short. (Note that it closes down for lunch from 12 to 12:30.) Once on Ryer Island, take Ryer Road south to the **Ryer Island Ferry,** also known as *The Real McCoy*. After crossing, follow the road into Rio Vista.

Hogback Island Recreation Area *Grand Island Rd.; $3/car*. A grassy picnic area is bounded on one side by Steamboat Slough and on the other by a boat-launching lagoon. This isn't a good swimming area, but there are access spots that are good for getting feet wet.

Rio Vista

*This pleasant town has some beautiful Victorian homes on Second Street, which is also known as **Millionaires' Row.***

Foster's Big Horn *143 Main St., 707/374-2511; L & D W-M; $-$$; highchairs, booster seats*. Opened in 1931, this restaurant's walls are lined with more than 300 mounted big game heads—including a full-grown elephant and giraffe. Gathered by the late hunter William Foster, it is the world's largest collection of big game trophies. Diners walk through an attractive bar area in the front, into a open dining room with high ceilings and comfortable booths. Sandwiches and hamburgers are on the lunch menu, steak and seafood on the dinner menu.

The Point Restaurant *120 Marina Dr., in the Delta Marina, 707/374-5400; L & D Tu-Sat, SunBr; $$; highchairs, booster seats; AE, MC, V*. Overlooking the Sacramento River at its widest point, this comfortable, well-maintained restaurant has many roomy booths. The lunch menu features house-made soups and sandwiches. At dinner, entrees include prime rib, scampi, and chicken Dijon. Photos illustrating Humphrey the Whale's well-publicized visit to the area are displayed in the entryway.

Brannan Island State Recreation Area *17645 Highway 160, 3 miles south of town, 916/777-6671; $5/car*. Located on a high knoll, this 336-acre park offers slough-side picnic and swimming areas. Campsites are available.

Western Delta: Benicia

*Founded in 1847 by General Vallejo and named for his bride, this low-key town was the state capital for a short time in 1853. Situated on the Carquinez Strait, about 30 miles northeast of San Francisco, it was also a very busy port. Now it is known for its many **antique shops** (located along First Street) and **glass-blowing factories** (located on H Street).*

Union Hotel *401 First St., 707/746-0368, fax 707/746-6458; 12 rooms; $$-$$$; some bathtubs; continental breakfast, restaurant*. Located right on the main street, in the part of town reflecting the ambiance of a quieter era, this 1882 Victorian hotel offers individually decorated rooms. For example, the Victoriana Room is decorated with rich, dark floral wallpaper and furnished with an assortment of antiques, among them a substantial armoire. (All of the antiques for the hotel were purchased from **Red Rose Antiques,** located at 620 First Street.)

For dinner, guests just catch the elevator down to the attractive dining room. Diners dress in everything from a suit and tie to a tank top and jeans. One meal here began with an unusual and delicious papaya and avocado salad with hazelnut vinaigrette dressing. The main course was grilled ahi with a sweet and tangy pineapple-cilantro sauce, and dessert was a block of ice cream-like hazelnut parfait swimming in a dark chocolate sauce swirled with white chocolate sauce.

It's just a few steps over to the cozy lounge for a relaxing after-dinner drink. Featuring an impressive 110-year-old mahogany bar and faux tin walls, it is a showcase for live jazz.

Benicia Capitol State Historic Park *115 W. G St., 707/745-3385; daily 10-5; adults $1, 6-17 50¢.* Historic information and artifacts await visitors inside this 2-story, red brick capitol building.

Also in the park, the 1858 Victorian **Fischer-Hanlon House** holds an impressive collection of period furniture. It is sometimes open for tours on weekend afternoons; call for schedule.

Eastern Delta

Palace Showboat Dinner Theatre *10480 N. Highway 99, Stockton, 209/931-0274; F & Sat, dinner 6:30-7:30, show at 8:30; dinner & show $18-$23, show only $11.50, children under 12 discounted; reservations essential; MC, V.* The melodrama and vaudeville shows here seem to please everyone. On the *Palace Showboat*, which is a landbound replica of the old riverboats that once cruised the Sacramento River, all seats are excellent. True to the form, the melodramas offer plenty of opportunities for the audience to respond with hisses and cheers. The vaudeville part of the show allows the actors a chance to show their versatility with comedy sketches, singing, and dancing. Shows change twice each year.

The dinner menu is a choice of either the superb fried chicken for which they are justifiably famous, or prawns, steak, or a hamburger. Each is served with a tossed green salad, French fries, and a roll with butter and honey. Mixed drinks made with wine are served from a funky bar. Servers are also performers, and many of the helpers are family of the owner.

Sacramento

A LITTLE BACKGROUND

It is fiery summer always, and you can gather roses, and eat strawberries and ice-cream, and wear white linen clothes, and pant and perspire at eight or nine o'clock in the morning.
— Mark Twain

Sacramento has been the state capital since 1854. Most of its major historic attractions are concentrated in the downtown area.

VISITOR INFORMATION

Sacramento Convention & Visitors Bureau *1421 K St., Sacramento 95814, 916/264-7777.*

GETTING THERE

Located approximately 90 miles northeast of San Francisco. Take Highway 80 all the way.

By Cruise Ship. Special Expeditions *(800/762-0003)* operates 4-day, 3-night cruises through the Delta to Sacramento each November. Passengers sleep aboard a shallow-draft ship in outside accommodations, and all meals are included.

By Ferry. The Delta Travel Agency *(916/372-3690; fare $134, reduced rates for children)* offers a 2-day cruise from San Francisco through the Delta to Sacramento. The trip operates on Saturdays, May through October. It includes round-trip boat tickets, bus transfers, and hotel accommodations in Sacramento. One-day and one-way trips are also available.

By Train. Amtrak *(800/872-7245)* trains leave for Sacramento daily from San Jose, San Francisco (via bus connection to Oakland), and Oakland. Special family fares and an overnight hotel package are available. Call for fare and schedule information and to make reservations.

Scenic Route by Car. Take Highway 160 through the Delta (see page 212).

ANNUAL EVENTS

Camellia Festival *March; 916/442-8166.* Sacramento claims to be the camellia capital of the world. Floral exhibits, a parade, and a queen contest celebrate this gorgeous flower.

Sacramento Jazz Jubilee *May; 916/372-5277.* This, the world's largest traditional jazz festival, is always held on Memorial Day weekend.

California State Fair *August; 916/924-2000.* There's something for everyone at the oldest state fair in the West, which is also the largest agricultural fair in the U.S. Pleasures include monorail and carnival rides, thoroughbred racing, and educational exhibits. Special for children are a petting farm, pony rides, and a nursery where baby animals are born each day.

> **Waterworld USA Family Waterpark** *(1600 Exposition Blvd., 916/924-0555; daily 10:30-6, June-Aug only; over 4-feet tall $13.95, under 4-feet $9.95, under 3 free)* operates adjacent to the fair site. It features the largest wave pool in Northern California, the highest waterslides in the West, and an assortment of other attractions.

STOPS ALONG THE WAY

Western Railway Museum *5848 Highway 12, Suisun City, between Fairfield and Rio Vista (exit Highway 80 at Highway 12, then drive east), 707/374-2978; Sat & Sun 11-5, W-Sun in July & Aug; adults $4, 4-15 $2.* Located between two sheep pastures in the middle of a flat, arid no-man's land, this very special museum displays and

actually operates its collection of historic electric streetcars and steam train engines. Among the dozen or so operating electric cars are both an articulated car
(hinged so it can go around corners), which ran on the Bay Bridge from 1939 to
1958, and a bright red car from the Peninsular Railway. Several cars operate each
weekend and run along a 1.5-mile stretch of track with overhead electric trolley
wires. Cars are operated by the same volunteers who spent countless hours re-
storing them. Stationary cars, waiting for repairs, can be viewed in several large
barns. An oasis-like picnic and play area is available to visitors, and a bookstore
with a past (check out the plaque above the bench in front) offers a large collection of railroad books and paraphernalia. All fees collected are used to restore and
maintain the streetcars. (It costs between $25,000 and $50,000 to restore a car and,
because the labor is volunteer, it can take as long as 10 years!)

The museum also operates special trains over the Sacramento Northern Railway. They run from the museum to Jepson Prairie, usually on weekends in April
and May. **Ghost Trains** run at Halloween, **Santa Claus Specials** during December.

The Nut Tree *on Highway 80/Highway 505, Vacaville, 707/448-6411; B, L, & D daily;*
$$; highchairs, booster seats, children's portions; reservations suggested; AE, MC, V. An
outside snack bar serves a memorable frosted orange slush, a good hot dog, and
an assortment of other short-order items. The striking inside restaurant is more
expensive and features a large glass-enclosed area housing a variety of plants and
brightly-colored, exotic birds. And the food is as tasty as the architecture is dra-
matic. The breakfast menu offers fresh fruit items such as bananas with cashew
nuts and cream, pineapple slices with marshmallow sauce, and strawberries with
cream. Breakfast entrees include French toast made with orange nut bread, waffles
made with orange or date nut breads, and the more usual egg items. Lunch brings
on sandwiches, hot entrees, and a variety of salads and desserts. The dinner menu
includes entrees such as golden prawns with tropical fruit, a tamale stuffed with
turkey and green olives, and fresh fish. Less expensive sandwich items are also
available. Desserts are special: a banana praline sundae, a rocky road sundae (the
ice cream is put *on top* of almonds and both heated marshmallow and chocolate
sauces), and chess pie (walnuts and raisins in a butterscotch filling). Parents of

babies will be interested to know that even Gerber's baby food is on the menu!

There is plenty to do here besides eat. For a small fare a colorful miniature train transports passengers around the spacious grounds. Numerous shops are stocked with interesting merchandise, including a toy store with a good selection of children's travel games and books. Nearby there are free rocking horse rides, climbing structures for kids (and wooden benches for the old folks), and sometimes puppet shows.

Each October a month-long harvest festival culminates in a **Great Scarecrow Contest.** Held outdoors in an adjacent pumpkin patch, the contest is open to anyone who wants to enter. Visitors may view the creations, and pumpkins and pumpkin foods are for sale. Live music and other entertainment is also scheduled.

WHERE TO STAY

Modern motels abound. Call a favorite chain for reservations, or contact the Convention & Visitors Bureau for a list of lodgings.

Delta King *1000 Front St., Old Sacramento, 800/825-KING, 916/444-KING; 44 rooms; $$$; children free; cribs; some bathtubs; continental breakfast, restaurant.* Launched in 1927, this riverboat plied the waters between Sacramento and San Francisco in the late 1920s and '30s. After having spent 15 months partially submerged in the San Francisco Bay, she was treated to years of restoration work costing $9.5 million. Appropriately moored dockside in Old Sacramento, this flat-bottomed boat features rooms furnished with brass beds and wicker accent pieces. All have private bathrooms with an old-fashioned pedestal sink and pull-chain, tall-tank toilet. A few even have claw-foot tubs.

An elegant dinner with a river view can be enjoyed by guests and non-guests alike in the **Pilothouse Restaurant,** located on the Promenade Deck. Entrees include luxury items such as prawns, steak, and rack of lamb; a well-executed Caesar salad, which is dramatically prepared table-side, is not to be missed. An enticing dessert tray is also available.

Live performances are scheduled on weekends in an intimate theater down on the Cargo Deck. Intermissions are long, allowing plenty of time to visit the lobby bar. Dinner/theater and overnight packages are sometimes available.

In addition to these facilities, the Delta King has a cozy lounge-style bar adjoining the restaurant. Live music performed on a grand piano is provided most evenings. Wednesday through Saturday nights the **Paddlewheel Saloon,** a more lively bar that overlooks the boat's 17-ton paddlewheel, provides recorded 1950s and '60s rock & roll music and plenty of dancing space.

Gold Rush Home Hostel *1421 Tiverton Ave., 916/421-5954.* This four-bed hostel operates in a private home. See also page 278.

Radisson Hotel *500 Leisure Lane, 800/333-3333, 916/922-2020; $$-$$$+; children under 18 free; heated pool, hot tub, parcourse; restaurant.* Located on the outskirts of downtown, this low-rise hotel complex is run much like a vacation resort. Rooms are spacious and comfortable, and some overlook a natural spring-fed lake and koi pond. On weekends throughout the summer, jazz and orchestra performances (free to guests) are scheduled in the property's own amphitheater. Bicycle rentals are available for rides along the scenic Jedediah Smith bike trail, which runs along the American River Parkway adjacent to the hotel. (The 35-mile trail runs along the river from Old Sacramento to Folsom. The hotel is about 5 miles from the Old Sacramento end.) More amenities include a Health and Fitness Center (must be 21 or older), and a courtesy shuttle to the impressive indoor **Arden Fair Shopping Mall.**

WHERE TO EAT

Buffalo Bob's Ice Cream Saloon *110 K St., Old Sacramento, 916/442-1105; L & D daily; $; highchairs, booster seats; no cards.* A variety of sandwiches (including grilled cheese and peanut butter and jelly) and hot dogs are available here, as is old-time sarsaparilla to wash it all down with. Ice cream concoctions dominate the menu and include exotic sundaes such as Fool's Gold (butter brickle ice cream topped with butterscotch and marshmallow, whipped cream, almonds, and a cherry) and Sierra Nevada (peaks of vanilla ice cream capped with hot fudge, whipped cream, almonds, and a cherry).

Fanny Ann's Saloon *1023 2nd St., Old Sacramento, 916/441-0505; L & D daily; $; no reservations; no cards.* This narrow, 4-level restaurant has a raucous ambiance and funky decor that provide the makings for instant fun. Children and adults alike enjoy the casual atmosphere and American-style fare: good half-pound hamburgers, assorted styles of 9-inch hot dogs, curly French fries, and large bowls of homemade soup. A variety of sandwiches and salads are also available. After orders are placed with the cook at the window in back, diners can relax with a game of pinball or get a downright cheap drink at the old bar. When one mother inquired whether there were booster seats, the cheerful hostess replied, "I'll hold the kids on my lap."

Good Earth *2024 Arden Way, 916/920-5544.* For description, see page 6.

Los Padres *106 J St., Old Sacramento, 916/443-6376; L & D daily, B Sat & Sun; $$; highchairs, booster seats, children's portions; no reservations; AE, MC, V.* The lovely old brick walls of this nicely appointed restaurant are decorated with paintings of the California missions. The Early California/Mexican cuisine includes nachos (tortilla chips topped with refried beans and melted cheddar cheese), quesadillas (small corn tortillas topped with melted Jack cheese and guacamole), and a green enchilada (corn tortilla filled with king crab and guacamole and topped with green sauce and sour cream). Fresh tortillas and European pastries and breads, made in the restaurant's downstairs bakery, are available to go.

Suspects Mystery Dinner Theater *1023 Front St., Old Sacramento, 916/443-3600; F at 7:30, Sat at 5 & 8:30; tickets $28.50; reservations required; AE, MC, V.* In the show here professional actors mingle with diners, acting out a murder mystery during dinner. Then diners match wits with a detective/actor in an attempt to stop another murder. And the food's good, too!

WHAT TO DO

Money-Saving Note: A combination ticket is available that is good for the California State Railroad Museum, the Sacramento History Museum, the Crocker Art Museum, Sutter's

Fort State Historic Park, the California State Indian Museum, and the Governor's Mansion State Historic Park. It costs $11 for adults, $6 for children 6 through 17, and is good for 1 year. It may be purchased at any of the included locations.

American River Parkway *916/366-2066; $4/car.* This is basically 23 miles of water fun. Call for a free map and more information about facilities.

Bike Trail. The paved **Jedediah Smith National Recreation Trail** runs for 23 miles along the American River.

Fishing. The best month for salmon and steelhead is October. Favorite spots are the Nimbus Basin below the dam and Sailor Bar. A state license in required.

Nature Walks. The **Effie Yeaw Nature Center** *(in Ancil Hoffman Park, 3700 Tarshes Dr., Carmichael, 916/489-4918; daily 9-5)* has two self-guided nature trails.

Raft Trips. Trips begin in the **Upper Sunrise Recreation Area,** located north of the Sunrise Boulevard exit off Highway 50. In summer several companies rent rafts and provide shuttle bus return.

Blue Diamond Growers Visitor Center *1701 C St., 916/446-8409. Tours: by appt. M-F at 10 & 1; free. Gift Shop: M-F 10-5, Sat 10-4.* This tour of the world's largest almond processing plant includes almond tasting and a 25-minute film about the history of almonds. See how almonds are sorted, blanched, roasted, packaged, and canned. The Almond Plaza gift shop stocks an impressive selection of almond products and other specialty foods.

California State Capitol Building *10th/L Sts., 916/324-0333; tours daily 9-4; free.* In 1981 the Capitol was renovated to the tune of $68 million, in what is said to have been the largest restoration project in the history of the country. The main reason for the project was to make the building earthquake safe. Restored now to its turn-of-the-century decor, it is quite a showcase. Free tour tickets can be picked up in the basement a half-hour before each tour. A small museum with a 10-minute orientation film entertains visitors while they wait.

A short-order cafeteria operates in the basement for meals and snacks, and the full-service **Capitol Cafe** operates weekdays on the sixth floor.

Tours of the surrounding grounds, which is home to over 300 varieties of trees and flowers from all over the world and to one of the largest camellia groves in the world, are scheduled daily at 10:30 a.m. in the summer. The 22 shiny black granite panels of the **California Vietnam Veteran's Memorial** are located at the park's east end (15th St./Capitol Ave.).

Crocker Art Museum *216 O/3rd Sts., 916/264-5423; W-Sun 10-5, Thur to 9; adults $3, 7-17 $1.50.* Located within a Victorian building dating from 1874, this is the oldest public art museum west of the Mississippi. It features a permanent collection of American and European paintings and a gallery of special exhibitions. A hands-on Discovery Gallery is open to children of all ages on Saturdays from 1 to 3. Cultural events such as lectures, films, and Sunday afternoon concerts are often scheduled; call for current information. Picnic tables are available across the street in lovely **Crocker Park.**

Governor's Mansion State Historic Park *1526 H/16th Sts., 916/324-0539; tours on the hour daily 10-4; adults $2, 6-12 $1.* Built in 1877, this 30-room Victorian mansion was bought by the state in 1903 for $32,500. During the next 64 years it was home to 13 governors and their families. It remains just as it was when vacated by its last tenant—Governor Reagan. Now serving the public as an interesting museum, it displays 15 rooms of furnishings and personal items left behind by each family. Visitors see Governor George Pardee's 1902 Steinway piano, Earl Warren's hand-tied Persian carpets, and Hiram Johnson's plum velvet sofa and chairs. Among the interesting artifacts are marble fireplaces from Italy and gold-framed mirrors from France. The official State of California china, selected by the wife of Goodwin Knight in the late 1950s, is also on display.

Music Circus *1419 H St., adjacent to the Sacramento Convention Center, 916/557-1999; nightly in July & Aug; tickets $23-$27, children half-price at some performances.* Said to be the only tent theater west of the Mississippi, this 2,500-seat facility presents summer stock musicals suitable for the entire family. Call for current schedule.

Old Sacramento. Situated along the Sacramento River, Old Sacramento was the kickoff point for the gold fields during the Gold Rush. It was the western terminus for both the Pony Express and the country's first long distance telegraph, and the country's first transcontinental railroad started here. Said to be the largest historic preservation project in the West, Old Sacramento is a 28-acre living museum of the Old West. Vintage buildings, wooden sidewalks, and brick streets recall the period from 1850 to 1880. Restaurants, shops, and historic exhibits combine to make it both an entertaining and educational spot to visit.

Guided tours of the area begin at the California State Railroad Museum on selected Saturdays. For more information call 916/324-0040. Information on self-guided tours may be obtained at the **Visitor Information Center** *(1104 Front St., 916/442-7644; daily 9-5).* Several horse-drawn vehicles may be hired for rides from Old Sacramento to the Capitol.

California State Railroad Museum *111 I St., 916/448-4466; daily 10-5, in summer to 9; adults $5, 6-12 $2 (ticket also good on same day for admission to Central Pacific Passenger Depot at 930 Front St.).* This gigantic 3-story building holds the largest interpretive railroad museum in North America. Inside, 21 beautifully restored, full-size railroad locomotives and cars—representing the 1860s through the 1960s—are on display. Among them are an apartment-size, lushly furnished Georgia Northern private car, complete with stained glass windows, and a Canadian pullman that is rigged up so that it feels as if it is actually moving. A film, a 30-projector multi-image slide show, and assorted interpretive displays tell the history of American railroading. Docent-led tours are often available, and well-trained railroad-loving volunteers, wearing historically authentic railroad workers' garb, are always on hand to answer questions. Upstairs, great views of the trains below are available from an oversize catwalk. A large collection of toy trains—including a 1957 pastel pink Lionel train designed especially for little girls—is also displayed.

Nearby the **Central Pacific Passenger Depot** displays nine more locomotives and cars. Visiting this reconstructed train depot provides the opportunity to step back in time to 1876—an era when riding the train was the chic way to go. An audio tour wand that picks up recorded descriptions of displays is provided.

On scheduled weekends, the **Sacramento Southern Railroad excursion steam train** leaves from the depot and takes passengers for rides to **Miller Park**

(Sat & Sun 10-5 in summer, first weekend of month 12-3 rest of year; on the hour; adults $4, 6-17 $2).

Old Eagle Theatre *925 Front St., 916/446-6761; F & Sat at 8pm; tickets $7.* A reconstruction of California's first theater building that was built in 1849, the Eagle now presents Gold Rush-era plays and musicals. Children's programs are also sometimes scheduled. Call for current production information and for schedule of free tours.

Sacramento History Museum *101 I St., 916/264-7057; Tu-Sun 10-5; adults $3, 6-17 $1.50.* This 3-story brick building is a replica of Sacramento's first public building. The museum inside houses an extensive collection of gold specimens (worth $1 million), old photos, and historic farm equipment. The 113-foot freestanding fiberglass flagpole in front is said to be the tallest in the entire country.

Schoolhouse *Front/L Sts., 916/483-8818; M-F 9:30-4, Sat & Sun 12-4.* Now a museum, this one-room schoolhouse has a play yard with old-fashioned board swings kids can use.

Sacramento Science Center *3615 Auburn Blvd., 916/277-6180; W-F 12-5, Sat & Sun 10-5; adults $2.50, 3-15 $1.50. Planetarium: shows W-F at 3, Sat & Sun at 1; adults $2,*

6-15 $1. Of special interest to children, this museum features hands-on exhibits, a planetarium, and a self-guided Discovery Trail outside. A picnic area is also available.

Silver Wings Aviation Museum *on Mather Air Force Base, Rancho Cordova, east of town off Highway 50, 916/364-2177; M-F 10-4, Sat 12-4; free.* The history of the Air Force is documented here with an assortment of exhibits. The only surviving American 1934 Corben Superace with a Model A engine—painted a shiny blue and black and in mint condition—is on display. Small visitors can sit in a half-size scale model of a World War I German Junker CL1, and everyone can examine an LR-11 rocket engine of the type that was in Chuck Yeager's plane when he broke the sound barrier. A collection of over 200 wooden models hangs overhead, and visitors may view the aviation films of their choice from a collection of over 450.

Sutter's Fort State Historic Park *2701 L St., 916/445-4422; daily 10-5; adults $2, 6-12 $1.* A reconstruction of the settlement founded in 1839 by Captain John A. Sutter, this is the oldest restored fort in the West. Exhibits include carpenter, cooper, and blacksmith shops as well as prison and living quarters. Hand-held speakers are loaned free to visitors for self-guided tours.

The **California State Indian Museum** *(2618 K St, 916/324-0971; daily 10-5; adults $2, 6-12 $1)* is located adjacent. Established in 1940, its exhibits were recently renovated. The bark clothing samples are of special interest, as is the permanent basket collection featuring colorful Pomo feather baskets. Films are presented throughout the day. Picnicking is particularly pleasant beside a duck pond across from the museum.

Towe Ford Museum *2200 Front St., 916/442-6802; daily 10-6; adults $5, 5-14 $1.* Opened in 1987, this museum displays 180 antique cars. Every year and model of Ford from 1903 to 1953 is exhibited. It is the most complete antique Ford collection in the world. A shuttle bus from Old Sacramento operates on weekends.

Victorians. Elaborate Victorian homes can be found between 7th and 16th Streets, from E to I Streets. Also, don't miss the Heilbron house at 740 O Street and the Stanford house at 800 N Street.

William Land Park *on Freeport Blvd. between 13th Ave. & Sutterville Rd.* This 236-acre park has a supervised playground, children's wading pool, 9-hole golf course, and a fishing pond for children under 16. It also incorporates:

Fairytale Town *on Freeport Blvd., 916/264-5233; daily 10-4:30; adults $2.25-$2.50, 3-12 $1.75-$2.* Nursery rhymes and fairy tales come to life in this amusement park.

Funderland *1550 17th Ave., 916/456-0115; daily 11-6 May-Sept, Sat & Sun only rest of year; closed Dec & Jan.* Eight kiddie rides delight the little folk here. Pony rides are available adjacent.

Sacramento Zoo *3930 W. Land Park Dr., 916/264-5885; daily 10-4; adults $3.50-$4, 3-12 $2-$2.50.* This modest but spacious 15-acre zoo is home to over 150 species of exotic animals. It holds just enough exhibits to keep visitors busy for a pleasant few hours. A snack bar dispenses a limited, but appropriate and satisfying, menu: hot dogs, sodas, cookies, etc. Strollers may be rented in the gift shop.

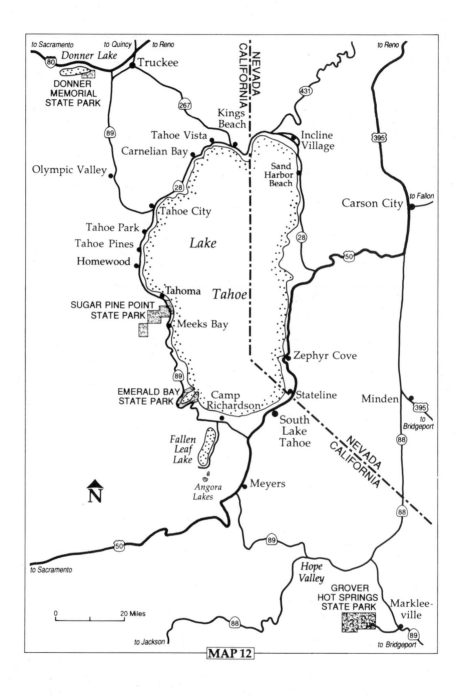

MAP 12

Lake Tahoe

– South Lake Tahoe –

A LITTLE BACKGROUND

. . . At last the Lake burst upon us—a noble sheet of blue water lifted six thousand three hundred feet above the level of the sea, and walled in by a rim of snowclad mountain peaks that towered aloft full three thousand feet higher still!

It was a vast oval. As it lay there with the shadows of the great mountains brilliantly photographed upon its surface, I thought it must surely be the fairest picture the whole earth affords . . .
— Mark Twain

Lake Tahoe lies two-thirds in California and one-third in Nevada. It is the largest (192 square miles surface) and deepest (1,645 feet) Alpine lake in North America and the second largest in the world. At 6,227 feet above sea level, its crystal clear, deep-blue summer waters provide a striking contrast with the extensive green forests and majestic mountains encircling it.

Once a remote area, Tahoe is now a popular and well-equipped vacation destination offering a wide range of recreational activities along with its spectacular scenery. Swimming, hiking, boating, tennis, golf, bicycling, horseback riding, river rafting, camping, fishing, water-skiing, and backpacking are among the summer outdoor activities to be enjoyed. In winter, the skiing is excellent.

On the Nevada side, gambling is another big attraction. Most lodgings provide transportation to the casinos and have discount casino coupons for their guests. In addition, the casinos offer on-demand pick-up shuttle service from most lodgings.

Children may go into a casino with adults but are not allowed to "loiter" (not even babies in backpacks!) or play the slot machines. Fortunately, childcare is relatively easy to find in this area. Many lodging facilities maintain a list of local sitters, and childcare centers that take drop-ins are listed in the Yellow Pages. Also, the Lake Tahoe Visitors Authority provides a free listing of day care providers. In addition to having more slot machines than any other casino at Lake Tahoe, Harrah's also has a supervised recreation center for children 6 to 14. It operates year-round from 9 a.m. to midnight. Admission is $6, and there is a 5-hour maximum. Children do need extra money for some of the facilities, which include a movie theater and both video and snack machines, and parents may rent a pager for $4. For older children, a gigantic video arcade is located just outside the center. Sure beats sitting on the curb reading comic books like some people did when they were kids. For further information call 800/648-3773 or 702/588-6611 (extension 447).

VISITOR INFORMATION

Lake Tahoe Visitors Authority *P.O. Box 16299, South Lake Tahoe 96151, 800/AT-TAHOE (lodging reservations referral service), 916/577-3550 (entertainment and special events information; road and weather conditions), 916/544-5050, fax 916/544-2386.*

GETTING THERE

Located approximately 200 miles north of San Francisco. Take Highway 80 to Highway 50 to the lake.

ANNUAL EVENTS

Autumn Colors *October.* The area around Kirkwood Ski Resort (see page 257) is home to groves of aspen. Hope Valley, north of Kirkwood on Highway 89, is particularly colorful.

STOPS ALONG THE WAY

Western Railway Museum. See page 218.

The Nut Tree. See page 219.

Sacramento. See page 217.

Folsom *off Highway 50, 25 miles east of Sacramento.*
This town makes a pleasant stop. Historic Sutter Street is lined with **antique shops,** and the **Folsom Zoo** *(Natoma/Stafford, 916/355-7200; Tu-Sun 10-4:15; adults $1.50, 5-12 50¢)* exhibits native animals, a few exotics, and the largest captive wolf pack in Northern California. A good breakfast can be enjoyed at the **Lake Forest Cafe** *(13409 Folsom Blvd., 916/985-6780; $; B & L W-Sun; highchairs, booster seats; AE, MC, V),* where omelettes, crepes, and homemade cinnamon rolls are on the menu.

Folsom Dam, built in 1955 by convicts from nearby Folsom Prison (the one Johnny Cash sings about), measures 340 feet high and 1,400 feet wide. Tours are available *(916/989-7274; Tu-Sat 10-1).* Overnight camping is permitted at 18,000-acre **Folsom Lake State Recreation Area** *(7806 Folsom-Auburn Rd., 916/988-0205).*

For more information about the town contact the **Folsom Chamber of Commerce** *(200 Wool St., 916/985-2698),* which is located inside the town's old train depot.

Sam's Town. See page 196.

Poor Red's. See page 196.

Placerville. See page 197.

WHERE TO STAY

LAKEFRONT

Inn By the Lake *3300 Lake Tahoe Blvd., 800/877-1466, 916/542-0330, fax 916/541-6596; 100 rooms; 34 non-smoking rooms; $$-$$$; children under 13 free; cribs; all bathtubs; some kitchens; heated pool, hot tub, sauna; continental breakfast.* Located in a grove of pine trees across the street from the lake, this attractive modern motel offers comfortable, quiet rooms and a free shuttle to the casinos and ski areas.

Royal Valhalla Motor Lodge *4104 Lakeshore Blvd., 800/999-4104, 916/544-2233, fax 916/544-1436; 80 units; $$$; cribs; all bathtubs; some kitchens; heated pool (unavailable Nov-Apr); continental breakfast.* Pick from one-, two-, or three-bedroom units, many of which have lake views. Guests have use of a private beach.

Tahoe Beach & Ski Club *3601 Lake Tahoe Blvd., 916/541-6220; 128 rooms; $$-$$$+; 2-night minimum on weekends Feb, Mar, & June-Sept; children under 6 free; cribs; all kitchens; some bathtubs; heated pool (unavailable Oct-Apr), hot tub, sauna; restaurant.* Located 1 mile from the casinos, this lakeside hotel provides a convenient shuttle. Added ammenities include 400 feet of private beach and a **Marie Callenders** restaurant.

Timber Cove Lodge *3411 Lake Tahoe Blvd., 800/528-1234, 916/541-6722, fax 916/541-7959; 262 rooms; 130 non-smoking rooms; $$; 2-night minimum on Sat July-Sept; children under 12 free; cribs; some bathtubs; heated pool, hot tub; restaurant, room service.* This motel has a private beach, marina, and pier, and many of the rooms have lake views.

CONDOS AND HOMES

Accommodation Station *800/344-9364, 916/542-5850; $$-$$$+; 2-night minimum, 5-night minimum during holidays; all kitchens, fireplaces.* Privately-owned condominiums, cabins, and homes may be rented through this agency. Rate is determined by the number of bedrooms and type of accommodation.

    Lake Tahoe Accommodations *(800/544-3234, 800/228-6921, 916/544-3234; 2-night minimum)* is a similar service.

Lakeland Village *3535 Highway 50, 800/822-5969, 916/544-1685, fax 916/544-0198; 210 rooms; $$-$$$; 2-night minimum on weekends; cribs; all kitchens, bathtubs, fireplaces; 2 heated pools, children's wading pool (unavailable in winter), hot tub, 2 saunas, 2 tennis courts (fee).* Though located on a bustling highway, this condominium complex manages to retain a secluded, restive feeling. Many of the units are lakefront; all are within a short walk. Amenities include a lakefront playground. During the Christmas holidays, sleigh rides are available through the resort's 19 wooded acres.

OTHER

Casinos. The major casinos offer large numbers of luxury hotel rooms. Call for details: **Caesars** 800/648-3353, **Harrah's** 800/648-3773, **Harvey's** 800/648-3361, **Horizon** 800/648-3322.

The Christiana Inn *3819 Saddle Rd., 916/544-7337, fax 916/544-5342; 6 rooms; 100% non-smoking; $$-$$$; children under 12 free; all bathtubs; some fireplaces; continental breakfast, restaurant.* Built in 1965 as a Scandinavian ski dormitory, this charming inn has been converted into a cluster of suites. A decanter of warming brandy awaits guests in each room.

    An elegant and expensive restaurant, known for its extensive wine cellar, is also open to non-guests.

Embassy Suites Resort *4130 Lake Tahoe Blvd., 800/EMBASSY, 916/544-5400; 400 units; 200 non-smoking units; $$$-$$$+; children under 12 free; cribs; all bathtubs; indoor heated pool, hot tub, sauna; full breakfast, restaurant, room service.* The first new hotel to be built in the Tahoe Basin since restrictions were imposed, this link in the popular Embassy Suites chain features a nightclub, a fitness center, and a garden atrium with waterfalls. Winter amenities include on-site ski rental, repair, and storage, plus next-day lift ticket sales and a complimentary shuttle to the Heavenly Valley ski area. And, as an ad for the hotel declares, ". . . you don't have to gamble to get a free breakfast and free drinks." Breakfast and evening cocktails are complimentary to guests. But for those who do want to gamble, Harrah's is right next door.

Tahoe Seasons Resort *3901 Saddle Rd., 800/551-2044, 916/541-6700, fax 916/541-0653; 180 units; $$-$$$; cribs; all kitchens, bathtubs; some fireplaces; heated pool, hot tub; 2 tennis courts; restaurant, room service (special children's items).* Each unit here is a spacious suite equipped with a mini-kitchen and an oversize whirlpool spa bathtub big enough to hold two people. And since it is located just across the street from the Heavenly Valley ski area, skiers who stay here can just walk there in the morning. No chains. No parking hassles. And if someone in the party doesn't want to ski, it's possible to get a room with a view of the slopes where they can stay cozy in front of a fireplace. The resort also provides on-site ski rentals and both chain installation and removal services.

Motel Row. Highway 50 into town is littered with more motels than is to be believed. However, this may be changing. South Lake Tahoe's redevelopment plan, which focuses on upgrading rather than expanding, dictates that for every new hotel room built, 1.31 old rooms must be removed.

FURTHER AWAY

Sorensen's Resort. See page 257.

Zephyr Cove Resort *760 Highway 50, Zephyr Cove, Nevada, 4 miles north of Stateline, 702/588-6644, fax 702/588-5021; 36 units; $-$$$; cribs; all bathtubs; some kitchens, fireplaces; restaurant; dogs welcome.* Located in a lovely forested area by the lake, these rustic cabins and lodge rooms are run by the Forest Service and provide a convenient yet out-of-the-way spot to stay. Facilities include a beach, marina with boat rentals, stables, and arcade. Campsites are also available. Do reserve early; cabins are usually booked-up a year in advance!

WHERE TO EAT

Cantina Los Tres Hombres *765 Emerald Bay Rd., 1/4 mile north of the Y, 916/544-1233; L & D daily; $-$$; highchairs, booster seats, children's portions; no reservations; AE, MC, V.* There is almost always a wait to be seated in this popular spot, but that's no reason to stay away. Waiting time can be passed sitting in the bar. A pitcher of margaritas (tasty niña coladas for kids), and some nachos (tortilla chips mixed with green chiles, melted cheese, and chorizo and topped with sour cream and guacamole) make it easy to settle into the festive surroundings. Wonderful menu selections include: crab enchiladas, carnitas (roast pork), a large variety of giant burritos, and fresh fish on Fridays. The menu has changed a lot over the years, but it just keeps getting better. If there's room left, try fried ice cream for dessert.

Casinos. For some of the best and least expensive food in this area, try the casino restaurants and buffets. Favorites include:

Caesars Cafe Roma *800/648-3353, 702/588-3515; B, L, & D daily; $; highchairs, booster seats, children's portions; no reservations; AE, MC, V.* This coffee shop is open round-the-clock.

Harrah's Forest Buffet *800/648-3773, 702/588-6611; B & L M-Sat, D daily, SunBr; $-$$; highchairs, booster seats, children's portions; no reservations; AE, MC, V.* Located on the 18th floor, this classy restaurant provides spectacular lake and mountain views plus outstanding food at a reasonable price.

Harvey's Carriage House *800/553-1022, 800/648-3361, 702/588-2411; B, L, & D daily; $-$$; highchairs, booster seats, children's portions; no reservations; AE, MC, V.* Open round-the-clock, this restaurant is known for its delicious fried chicken dinners. This casino also holds **Classic Burgers,** a '50s-style malt shop, and the largest video arcade at the lake.

When the lines at the casino restaurants are too long, consider opting for fast food at the **McDonald's** located inside **Bill's Casino.** It can be a sanity saver. The first McDonald's ever built in a casino, it features a separate entrance for families. In Bill's, be sure to take a free pull on **Billy Jean**—the world's largest free-pull slot machine.

In addition to bargain dining, the casinos also offer fine dining. The elegant **Summit** *(800/648-3773; D daily; $$$; reservations suggested; AE, MC, V)* restaurant, located on the 16th and 17th floors of Harrah's, offers heady views and refined cuisine. Located in what was originally the Star Suite, where the rich and famous headliners were put up, it offers a new menu every day. One meal enjoyed here began with crispy-crusted mini baguettes and sweet butter shaped like roses. An appetizer of chilled gulf shrimp was arranged in a red seafood sauce swirled with horseradish hearts, and a salad of baby lettuces was arranged in a scooped-out tomato so that it resembled a bouquet. The entree was a perfect rack of lamb with an anise crust and a side of mashed potatoes sprinkled with truffles. Dessert was a Frangelico souffle with a hazelnut-praline crème frâiche. The entire meal was beautifully presented, and service was impeccable. It was truly an experience befitting the rich and famous.

The Fresh Ketch Lakeside Restaurant *2433 Venice Dr. E., 916/541-5683; L & D daily; $$; highchairs, booster seats; reservations suggested; AE, MC, V.* Located at the Tahoe Keys Marina, the lake's only protected inland marina, this restaurant has water views and fresh seafood. In addition to a daily special, the menu also has scampi, calamari steak topped with anchovy butter, cioppino, king crab legs, and live Maine lobster. Plenty of non-fish items are also offered, including steaks and hamburgers. Among the interesting desserts are both Key lime and hula pies.

Heidi's Restaurant *3485 Lake Tahoe Blvd., 916/544-8113; B, L, & D daily; $; highchairs, booster seats, children's menu; 100% non-smoking; no reservations; MC, V.* Breakfast is served all day long in this cozy, casual restaurant. There is a large selection of pancakes, French toast, crepes, Belgian waffles, and omelettes, as well as just about any other breakfast item imaginable. Orange juice is fresh-squeezed. At lunch, a variety of sandwiches, hamburgers, and salads are added to the menu, and at dinner more substantial entrees join the choices.

Monument Peak Restaurant *top of Ski Run Blvd., Wildwood/Saddle Dr., 702/586-7000; L M-Sat, D daily, SunBr; call for winter D schedule; closed Oct, Nov, & May; $$; highchairs, booster seats, children's portions; 100% non-smoking; reservations suggested; AE, MC, V. Tram: adults $10.50, under 12 free.* A bright red aerial tram lifts diners 2,000 feet above Lake Tahoe to enjoy magnificent views while dining. Call for the current menu.

WHAT TO DO

Amusement Centers. These spots are open daily in summer and as the weather permits in winter.

    Magic Carpet Golf *2455 Lake Tahoe Blvd., 916/541-3787.* This is the kind of colorful miniature course that has giant plaster dinosaurs and a new theme at each hole. Choose from either 19- or 28-hole rounds.

    Tahoe Amusement Park *2401 Lake Tahoe Blvd., 916/541-1300.* Facilities include a variety of kiddie rides and a giant slide.

Angora Lakes Trail *on Spring Creek Rd., off Highway 89.* Take the road to Fallen Leaf Lake, which passes a falls, and then turn left at the sign to Angora Lakes. It is an easy 1/2-mile hike from the end of the road to the lakes, where quiet picnic and swimming spots can be found.

Beaches/Biking. The **Pope-Baldwin Recreation Area** *(on Highway 89, between the Y and Emerald Bay, 916/573-2600; daily 8-6; closed in winter; $2/car)* is lined with good beaches. This same stretch of highway has a number of bike rental facilities and a nice bike trail.

Boating.

    Tahoe Queen *at foot of Ski Run Blvd., 800/23-TAHOE, 916/541-3364; call for schedule; adults $14, under 12 $5; reservations required.* This big paddlewheeler offers 2-hour cruises to Emerald Bay. The boat has a large window area in its floor for underwater viewing. Call for information on the sunset dinner/dance cruise and the winter ski shuttle to the North Shore.

    M.S. Dixie *760 Highway 50, Zephyr Cove, Nevada, 4 miles north of Stateline, 702/588-3508; call for schedule; closed Oct-Mar; adults $12, 3-11 $4; reservations suggested.* Actually used on the Mississippi River as a cotton barge in the 1920s, this paddlewheel steamer cruises to Emerald Bay. She boasts a glass-bottom viewing window. Dinner cruises, with live music for dancing, and breakfast/brunch cruises are also available at an additional charge.

    Woodwind *760 Highway 50, Zephyr Cove, Nevada, 702/588-3000; call for schedule; closed Nov-Mar; adults $14, 2-12 $7; reservations advised.* Only 30 passengers fit on this 4l-foot trimaran with glass-bottom viewing window. A sunset champagne cruise is also available at additional charge.

M.S. Dixie

Rentals of various kinds of boats are available at **Ski Run Marina** *(916/544-0200)*, **Tahoe Keys Marina** *(916/541-2155)*, and **Timber Cove Marina** *(916/544-2942)*. Water-skiing and wind-surfing lessons and rentals also are available at Ski Run Marina.

Camp Richardson Corral and Pack Station *on Highway 89 North, Camp Richardson, 916/541-3113; daily, June-Oct only; guided rides $16/hour; reservations necessary; riders must be 6 or older.* Breakfast rides *($28.50)* leave at 8 a.m. Dinner rides *($29.50)* and wagon rides *($10, under 4 free)* are also available. Fishing trips, overnight pack trips, and spot pack trips may be arranged, and sleigh rides are available December through March when there is enough snow.

Casino Shows. Big name entertainment is always booked into these showrooms. Call ahead for reservations to the early or late cocktail shows. Seats are assigned. Children 6 and older are usually admitted, but it depends on the show's content.
    Caesars Circus Maximus *800/648-3353, 702/588-3515.*
    Harrah's South Shore Room *800/648-3773.*
    Harvey's Emerald Theater *800/648-3361, 702/588-2411.* Holding just 288 seats, this is said to be the only mini-showroom in the world. There are no bad seats, and it is 100 percent non-smoking.
    Horizon's Grande Lake Theatre *800/322-7723, 702/588-6211.*

Drive Around the Lake. A leisurely drive around the 72-mile perimeter of Lake Tahoe takes about 3 hours. Allow all day, though, as there are many tempting places to stop for picnicking, swimming, and exploring.

Grover Hot Springs State Park *in Markleeville, 35 miles southeast of town, 916/694-2248; daily 9-9 in summer, call for winter hours; adults $4, under 18 $2.* Beautifully situated in a valley meadow ringed by pine-covered slopes, this state park was operated as a resort from 1878 to 1959. It features a 3-feet deep, 104-degree mineral pool filled by six nonsulfurous springs and a 70- to 80-degree fresh-water pool. The pools are well-maintained, and lifeguards are on duty. The number of bathers permitted is limited, so sometimes there is a wait, and swimsuits are required. Short trails, picnic facilities, and campsites are also available. In winter this is a popular après-ski destination.

Lake Tahoe Historical Society Museum *3058 Highway 50, 916/541-5458; daily 11-4 in summer, Sat & Sun 12-4 rest of year; adults $1, 5-12 50¢.* The history of Lake Tahoe's south shore is chronicled here.

Lake Tahoe Visitor Center *on Highway 89, north of Camp Richardson, 916/573-2674; daily 8-6; closed Nov-May; free.* Campfire programs and guided nature tours are scheduled regularly, and there are several self-guided trails.

Mountain stream life may be viewed from an underwater perspective in the **Taylor Creek Stream Profile Chamber** *(open 10-4).* Visit in October to see the annual run of the Kokanee salmon and to take part in the annual **Kokanee Salmon Festival.**

The Outdoorsman *2358 Lake Tahoe Blvd., 916/541-1660; open daily, call for hours.* This is the place to go for recreational equipment and clothing. In winter the store has an especially impressive selection of brands and styles of ski clothing and après-ski boots.

Tahoe Trout Farm *1023 Blue Lake Ave., off Highway 50, 916/541-1491; daily 10-7, June-Aug only; charged by size of fish caught.* Though there is, of course, no challenge to catching trout here, there are some compelling reasons to give it a try. No license in required, bait and tackle are furnished free, and there is no limit. Anglers are virtually guaranteed to go home with tasty dinner fare. Young children, who frustrate easily, will also probably succeed in catching a fish. So do bear in mind that some children are appalled at just the idea of catching a fish—let alone actually *eating* it.

Tallac Historic Site *off Highway 89, 3 miles north of Highway 50, 916/573-2600; museum: daily 10-4 in summer; free.* Three 19th century mansions and 23 cottages are situated on this 74-acre site. Special cultural and historical programs are sometimes scheduled.

A **Great Gatsby Festival** is held each August. Celebrating this area's partying past, this festival brings history to life. There are era arts and crafts demonstrations, plus some old-fashioned fun and games.

Vikingsholm Castle *on Highway 89, Tahoma, 916/525-7277; tours daily 10-4, June-Aug only; adults $2, 6-17 $1; strollers not permitted on tour.* Butterflies, waterfalls,

Tallac Historic Site

and wildflowers are enjoyed on the steep, dry 1-mile trail that descends to this magnificent 39-room, sod-roof Swedish home. Built completely by hand using native materials, it was completed in one summer. It is part of **Emerald Bay State Park.** Picnic tables are available, and swimming is permitted in an area with a sandy beach.

Winter Activities. See page 257.

– North Lake Tahoe –

VISITOR INFORMATION

North Lake Tahoe Chamber of Commerce *P.O. Box 884 (245 North Lake Blvd.), Tahoe City 96145, 916/581-6900.*

Tahoe North Visitors & Convention Bureau *P.O. Box 5578 (950 N. Lake Blvd.), Tahoe City 95730, 800/TAHOE-4-U (reservations service), 916/583-3494.*

GETTING THERE

Located approximately 210 miles north of San Francisco. Take Highway 80 to Truckee, then Highway 267 south to the lake.

The Chicago-bound Amtrak train leaves Oakland daily at 10:40 p.m. and arrives in Truckee at 4:13 p.m. For fare and schedule information and to make reservations call 800/872-7245

ANNUAL EVENTS

Music at Sand Harbor *July; held in Lake Tahoe State Park in Nevada; 916/583-9048.* Imagine sitting in a natural sandbowl amphitheater overlooking beautiful Lake Tahoe while enjoying great, live contemporary music. Then try adding a sprinkling of stars, both celestial and earthly. That's "Tunes in the Dunes"—the nickname given by locals to this event.

Shakespeare at Sand Harbor *August, 916/583-9048.* "Bard on the Beach," another nickname bestowed by fond locals, is the biggest event of the summer at the lake.

STOPS ALONG THE WAY

Western Railway Museum. See page 218.

The Nut Tree. See page 219.

Sacramento. See page 217.

Auburn. See page 200.

Grass Valley. See page 200.

Nevada City. See page 205.

WHERE TO STAY

CONDOS ON THE LAKE

Rates in condos vary tremendously depending on how many people are in the party, how many nights the stay is for, and what time of year it is. Call for current details.

Brockway Springs *101 Chipmunk Ave., Kings Beach, 916/546-4201, fax 916/546-4202; 78 units; hot springs pool, children's wading pool, sauna, 2 tennis courts.* Most units here have stone fireplaces and balconies overlooking the lake.

Chinquapin *3600 North Lake Blvd., Tahoe City, 800/732-6721, 916/583-6991, fax 916/583-0937; 172 units; cribs; all TVs, kitchens, fireplaces, bathtubs; heated pool (June-Sept only), sauna, 7 tennis courts, 3 private beaches, boating facilities, fishing pier, 1-mile paved beachfront path.* Some of these units also have private saunas, and all of them have washers and dryers.

Coeur du Lac *136 Juanita Dr., Incline Village, Nevada, 800/869-8308, 702/831-3318, fax 702/831-8668; recreation center, heated pool (June-Aug only), indoor hot tub, sauna.* This attractive complex is located 1 block from the lake.

Tahoe Escape *245 North Lake Blvd., Tahoe City, 800/488-2177, 916/583-0223; 170 units; $$-$$$+; cribs; pets welcome in some units.* This service handles private condominium properties located on the north and west shores.

CONDOS FURTHER OUT

Carnelian Woods *5005 North Lake Blvd., Carnelian Bay, 800/486-6705, 916/546-5924, fax 916/583-8540; 1/4 mile from lake; 30 rental units; recreation center with heated pool (June-Sept only), 2 hot tubs, 2 saunas, 3 tennis courts; sports facilities, bicycle rentals, 1-mile parcourse, 2-mile cross-country ski course, snow play area.*

Granlibakken *end of Granlibakken Rd., Tahoe City, 800/543-3221, 916/583-4242; 1 mile from lake; 125 rooms; children under 2 free; cribs; all bathtubs; some kitchens, fireplaces; heated pool & children's wading pool (May-Sept only), hot tub, sauna, parcourse, jogging trail, 6 tennis courts; full breakfast; ski and snow play area.* See also page 260.

Kingswood Village *1001 Commonwealth Dr., off Highway 267, Kings Beach, 916/546-2501 (call collect for reservations); 3/4 mile from lake; 60 rental units; heated pool (June-Aug only), hot tub, sauna, 3 tennis courts, access to private lakefront beach club.*

Northstar-at-Tahoe *2499 North Star Dr., off Highway 267, Truckee, 800/533-6787, 916/526-1010; 6 miles from the lake; 230 units; 16 non-smoking units; 3-night minimum in winter; cribs; all bathtubs; some kitchens, fireplaces, wood-burning stoves; heated pool (June-Aug only), 2 hot tubs, 2 saunas, exercise room, parcourse, 10 tennis courts; children's playground, gameroom, 3 restaurants.* Northstar has been described by the Sierra Club as a "model development." Hotel rooms and homes are also available for rental. A complimentary shuttle bus makes it unecessary to use a car within the complex. Additional facilities, available at an additional fee, include a supervised summer children's recreation program for ages 2 through 10, an 18-hole golf course, and horseback riding. Mountain bike trails are also available. See also page 260.

Squaw Valley Lodge *201 Squaw Peak Rd., Olympic Valley, 800/922-9970, 916/583-5500; 154 rooms; heated pool (June-Aug only), 3 indoor hot tubs, 1 outdoor hot tub, sauna, steam room, health club, 2 tennis courts.* Claiming to be "just 84 steps from the Squaw Valley tram," this resort is convenient for both skiers and non-skiers. Staying here allows skiers to avoid a congested early morning commute to Squaw's parking lot. When ready to ski, it is possible to just walk, or even ski, over to the lifts. For non-skiers, a room facing the slopes allows complete warmth and comfort while watching the rest of the group whizz by. All condos are equipped with a kitchen (microwaves only; no stoves), cable TV, and all-goose down comforters. It is interesting to note that the pool here is treated with gentle-on-the-eyes bromine instead of chlorine.

LAKEFRONT MOTELS

Dunes Resort *6780 North Lake Blvd., Tahoe Vista 916/546-2196; 9 units; $-$$$; cribs; some kitchens, fireplaces.* Both motel rooms and cottages are available here, and weekly rates are discounted. Facilities include a private beach.

Lakeside Chalets *5240 North Lake Blvd., Carnelian Bay, 916/546-5857; 5 units; $$-$$$; 2 night minimum on weekends; children under 2 free; all bathtubs, fireplaces; pets welcome.* Facilities include a pier and sundeck. A wind-surfing school operates on the premises in the summer, and equipment rentals are available.

Mourelatos' Lakeshore Resort *6834 North Lake Blvd., Tahoe Vista, 800/2RELAX-U, 916/583-5334; 33 units; $$-$$$; children under 1 free; cribs; some kitchens.* These woodsy cottages and motel rooms are situated in a pine forest that opens onto a private beach on the lake. A children's playground is provided.

Villa Vista Resort *6750 North Lake Blvd., Tahoe Vista, 916/546-3333, fax 916/546-4100; $$; 2-night minimum in cottages; children under 1 free; cribs; some kitchens, fireplaces, bathtubs; heated pool (June-Aug only).* Both motel rooms and cottages are available. Facilities include a sandy beach and a deck overlooking the lake.

OTHER

The Captain's Alpenhaus *6941 West Lake Blvd., Tahoma, 2 miles from Homewood, 916/525-5000; 13 units; 100% non-smoking; $$-$$$; 2-night minimum in summer & winter; cribs; some TVs, kitchens, bathtubs, fireplaces; heated pool (unavailable Nov-May), hot tub; full breakfast (for guests in lodge rooms only), restaurant; pets welcome.* This rustic 1930s-era lodge, built with plenty of knotty pine paneling in the Old Tahoe architectural style, has several snug rooms and two-bedroom suites. Larger cottages are scattered in the adjacent woods. In summer, activities include playing horseshoes or Ping Pong under the pines, relaxing in a hammock, and crossing the road for swimming in the lake. A bike path circling the west and north shore begins right in front of the inn.

The restaurant serves European and American country cuisine (beef stew, schnitzels, pastas) for lunch and dinner. Most Wednesdays are Basque Nights, when the fixed-price menu features country French and Spanish-style foods from the Pyrenees. These dinners include two entrees, soup, salad, dessert, and coffee. Entertainment is provided by an accordian player conducting sing-alongs. Reservations are necessary for the 5:30 and 8 p.m. seatings; the price is $13.95 for adults, $6.95 for kids under 13.

In the winter, discount lift tickets are available for Homewood. Nordic skiing can be enjoyed at nearby Sugar Pine Point State Park, and a groomed sledding area and a snowmobile concession are easily accessible. In front of the fireplace in the lodge's lounge is a comfortable spot to warm up with an après-ski drink from the adjacent **Alpine Bar.**

Hyatt Regency Lake Tahoe Casino *on Lakeshore/Country Club Dr., Incline Village, Nevada, 800/228-9000, 702/831-1111, fax 702/831-7508; 458 rooms; $$$-$$$+; children under 18 free; cribs; some bathtubs, fireplaces; heated pool, indoor hot tub, exercise room, 2 tennis courts; 3 restaurants, room service (special children's items).* Guests here have a choice between a room in an 11-story highrise, in a 3-story annex, or in a lakeside cottage, and Lady Luck can be tested 24 hours a day in the 13,000-square-foot casino. Of special note is the resort's magnificent private beach, complete with beach boys who set up lounge chairs and umbrellas wherever desired. In summer, guests may relax with the water lapping at the shore just beneath their toes. When thirsty, a server can be beckoned by raising a little red flag on the lounge chair—causing one to ponder, "Can it get better than this?" Jet skis and paddle boats may be rented at an adjacent marina. During ski season, free shuttle service is provided to nearby ski resorts, and both ski rentals and discounted lift tickets are available on the premises. Packages come and go. When making reservations, be sure to ask about current specials.

A wonderful **Camp Hyatt** program for children ages 3 to 15 operates on weekends year-round, daily during summer and holidays. There is a fee to participate during the day, but a special evening program is always free. And the inexpensive room service menu for kids is unbelievable: applesauce, corn-on-the-cob, gooey chocolate cake, hot chocolate with marshmallows!

Motel Row. Last-minute lodging can often be found among the numerous motels and cabins lining the lake in Kings Beach and Tahoe Vista. Chances are best, of course, on weekdays and in the off-season.

WHERE TO EAT

Alexander's Bar & Grill *Olympic Valley, 916/583-2555; L & D daily; booster seats; reservations suggested. Tram: 916/583-6985; daily 10-4; adults $10, 4-13 $5.* This restaurant is located on the slopes of the Squaw Valley ski area and is reached via a scenic tram ride. Call the restaurant for dining details.

A lovely but difficult hike to Shirley Lake begins at the tram building. Hikers pass waterfalls and huge boulders as they follow Squaw Creek about 2-1/2 miles to the lake.

Cantina Los Tres Hombres *8791 North Lake Blvd., Kings Beach, 916/546-4052.* For description, see page 231. Though the menu and atmosphere of these two restaurants remain similar, they are now under separate ownership.

Hacienda del Lago *760 North Lake Blvd., in Boatworks Shopping Center, Tahoe City, 916/583-0358; D daily, L daily in summer; $; highchairs, booster seats, children's portions; no reservations; MC, V.* It is definitely worth a wait to be seated here in the front room featuring panoramic views of the lake. People tend to pass the wait drinking fruit margaritas in the bar. (Smoothies are popular with children.) Anesthetized by these potent, tangy drinks, it is quite easy to over-indulge on the large portions of tasty Mexican food. The menu includes a variety of burritos, chimechangas (deep-fried burritos), and enchiladas. A huge taco salad consists of a crispy-fried flour tortilla bowl filled to the brim with salad goodies, and make-your-own tacos are available with pork, turkey, or beef stuffings. For those who know when to stop, there are a la carte portions. For those who don't, there is a dessert flan topped with whipped cream.

Lakehouse Pizza *120 Grove St., Tahoe City, 916/583-2222; L & D daily; $; highchairs, booster seats; no reservations; MC, V.* This casual spot offers a view of the lake and a choice of sitting either inside or outside on a deck. Menu choices include pizza, sandwiches, salads, hamburgers, and exceptionally good homemade potato chips.

Sunnyside Restaurant *1850 West Lake Blvd., Tahoe City, 800/822-2-SKI, 916/583-7200; D daily, B & L daily July-Sept; $-$$; highchairs, booster seats, children's portions; reservations suggested; MC, V.* In the past it has been hard to beat a summer meal enjoyed here outside on the huge deck—watching the sailboats on the lake or listening to live jazz on Sunday afternoons. This restaurant has a history of regularly changing its menu format and phone numbers, so call before visiting. Overnight lodging is also available.

Water Wheel *1115 West Lake Blvd., Tahoe City, 916/583-4404; D daily; closed M Mar-May & Sept-Nov; $$; booster seats; reservations suggested; AE, MC, V.* Diners here are treated to a river view and some of the tastiest Chinese Szechwan cuisine in Northern California. Hailing from Taipei, Taiwan, chef Nelson has a way with a wok and whips up old family recipes to delight his loyal customers. The portion of the menu devoted to spicy Szechwan dishes appears flawless. Highly recommended are the beef Szechwan (beef in a marvelous crunchy sauce of minced woodear, water chestnuts, and green onions), twice-cooked pork (a colorful arrangement of brilliant chartreuse cabbage, bright orange carrot rounds, and pork in a spicy hot sauce redolent of sesame oil and garlic), and Szechwan spicy pork (shredded pork with minced water chestnuts, mushrooms, garlic, and peppers in a flavorful sauce—served with little pancakes). Indeed, the entire menu holds promise. Several window tables overlooking the Truckee River are tucked behind the bar, where Lily mixes drinks that are almost as tasty as the food.

♥**Wolfdale's** *640 North Lake Blvd., Tahoe City, 916/583-5700; D W-M; $$-$$$; reservations suggested; AE, MC, V.* The attractive circa 1880 house this restaurant is located in was floated over on a barge from the Nevada side of the lake at the turn of the century. It was converted into a restaurant in the 1960s. During the two seatings scheduled each evening, talented owner/chef Douglas Dale combines French and Japanese cooking techniques to produce exceptional fresh fish and meat entrees—all artistically arranged and served with house-baked herb bread. Appetizers and desserts are also generally very good. Adding to the aesthetics of this dining experience, everything is served on handmade pottery designed to enhance the food.

WHAT TO DO

Best Beaches.

Commons Beach *Tahoe City; stairway is across from 510 North Lake Blvd.; parking lot is behind Tahoe City Fire Station.* This family beach boasts a large grassy area and a lakefront playground.

Sand Harbor Beach *in Nevada, 4 miles south of Incline Village; $4/car.* This is a perfect beach. The sand is clean and fine, lifeguards are usually on duty, and there are plenty of parking spaces and picnic tables.

William Kent Beach *south of Tahoe City; $2/car.* Parking is difficult, but this small, rocky beach is worth the hassle.

Bike Trails begin in Tahoe City and follow the shoreline. Rentals are available in Tahoe City and at other spots along the lake.

Donner Memorial State Park *12593 Donner Pass Rd., off Highway 40, 2 miles west of Truckee, 916/587-3841; open daily; closed Nov-Apr; $5/car. Museum: daily 10-4, in summer to 5; closed Nov-Apr; adults $2, 6-12 $1.* Located on Donner Lake, this park is a monument to the tragic Donner Party that was stranded here by blizzards in 1846. Picnic facilities, lake swimming, hiking trails, nature programs, and campsites are available.

The **Emigrant Trail Museum** features exhibits on the area's history.

Fanny Bridge/Truckee River Bridge *at junction of Highways 89 & 28 (the Y), Tahoe City.* The only outlet from the lake, the dam below this bridge has gates that control the flow of water into the river. Spectators gather here to view and feed the giant rainbow trout that congregate beneath the bridge. (They like to eat bread and crackers.) The nickname comes from the sight that develops as people bend over the bridge.

Fishing Charters. Get the names of captains and a fishing license at one of the local sporting goods shops. The captains usually supply bait and tackle.

Gatekeeper's Museum *130 West Lake Blvd., in **William B. Layton Park**, Tahoe City, 916/583-1762; daily 11-5 June-Aug, W-Sun in Sept; closed Oct-May; free.* The structure this museum is located within—a replica of a 1910 lodgepole pine log cabin—was originally inhabited by a succession of keepers whose job it was to raise and lower the gates of the dam. Displays include Indian artifacts and Lake Tahoe memorabilia. The surrounding 3-1/2-acre lakeside park is equipped with picnic tables and barbecue facilities.

Ponderosa Ranch *100 Ponderosa Ranch Rd., Incline Village, Nevada, 702/831-0691; daily 9:30-5; closed Nov-Apr; adults $7.50, 5-11 $5.50; breakfast hayride $2/person.* Created especially for filming scenes for the TV show *Bonanza*, this ranch is now open to the public for tours. Visitors get a bumpy ride from the parking lot up the hill to the ranch, and then a guided tour. After the tour, there is time to explore and visit both a petting farm and what is said to be the world's largest collection of antique farm equipment. Fast-grub is available, and the tin cups in which beer and soft drinks are served make great souvenirs.

A breakfast haywagon ride is offered between 8 and 9:30 a.m.

Squaw Valley Stables *1525 Squaw Valley Rd., Olympic Valley, 916/583-RIDE; daily*

9-5, June-Oct only; 1-hour guided rides $15; riders must be 7 or older; ponies $6. The proprietor here says, "We have all kinds of horses . . . gentle horses for gentle people, spirited horses for spirited people, and for those who don't like to ride we have horses that don't like to be ridden." Pony rides are available for children ages 2 through 7. Parents must lead the pony in a large arena area.

Sugar Pine Point State Park *on the west shore, Tahoma, 9 miles south of Tahoe City, 916/525-7982, 916/525-7232 (winter); daily 8-dusk; $5/car. Mansion: tours on the hour 11-4, July-Sept only.* In this gorgeous, peaceful setting, the 3-story 1902 Queen Anne **Ehrman Mansion** has 16 rooms open for public viewing. The **General Phipps Cabin**, built in 1870 of hand-split logs, is also on the property. A magnificent beach invites swimming and sunning. Picnic tables, hiking trails, and a 1930s tennis court are also available, and campsites are open year-round. In winter, cross-country skiing and ranger-led snowshoe walks join the agenda.

Truckee *located 40 miles from the lake via Highway 267.* Much of the original architecture in this old mining town is preserved. It can be viewed by walking down the main street and stopping in at the many shops and restaurants operating within historic buildings.

Breakfast at the long, narrow **Squeeze In** *(10060 Donner Pass Rd., 916/587-9814; B&L daily; $; highchairs, booster seats; 100% non-smoking; no reservations; no cards)* gives diners a choice of 57 kinds of omelettes. A variety of other breakfast dishes and sandwiches are also on the menu.

For more information on this area, contact **Truckee-Donner Visitor Information** *(P.O. Box 2757 (10065 Commercial Row), Truckee 96160, 800/548-8388, 916/587-2757).*

Truckin' on the Truckee/River Rafting *begins at the Y in Tahoe City; daily 9-3:30, June-Oct only; adults $15, 4-12 $10; no children under 4.* What better way to spend a sunny summer Alpine day than floating down the peaceful Truckee River a la Huckleberry Finn? All that's needed is a swimsuit, water-friendly shoes, and some suntan lotion. Packing along a picnic and some cold drinks is also a good idea, and a daypack keeps hands free for paddling. White-water enthusiasts stay away. This trip is so civilized that there are even portable toilets strategically placed along the riverbank. The 4-mile, 3-hour trip ends at **River Ranch** *(800/535-9900, 916/583-4264)*, a restaurant and lodging facility featuring an outdoor barbecue luncheon that is perfect for an after-rafting snack. Tahoe City concessionaires offer a package that includes raft, life jacket, paddles, and return ride. It is first-come, first-served, so get here before 11 a.m. to avoid crowds and to get an early-bird discount.

Note that a 3-1/2-mile off-road bicycle trail runs along the river from the River Ranch into Tahoe City. Note, also, that the drought of the early 1990s dried up the river and stopped the fun here. Check with the Visitors Bureau for the current status of the river. Rates reflect those in effect before the drought.

Watson Cabin Museum *560 North Lake Blvd., Tahoe City, 916/583-8717; daily 12-4, June-Aug only; free.* Built in 1908 and 1909, this log cabin is the oldest building at the north end of the lake still on its original site.

Winter Activities. See page 259.

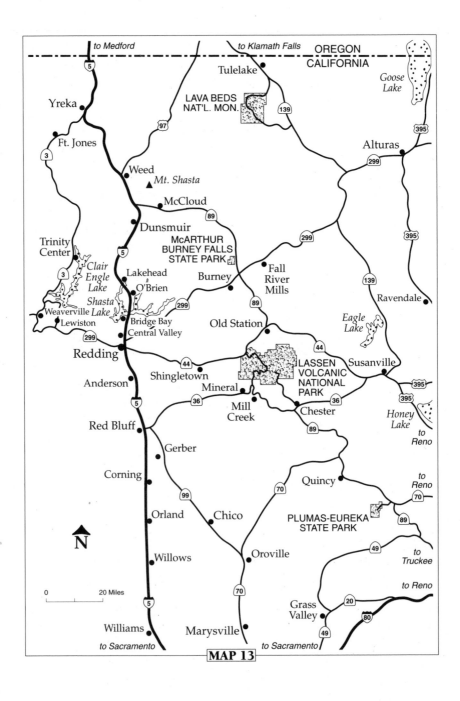

MAP 13

Mt. Shasta and Vicinity

A LITTLE BACKGROUND

Poet Joaquin Miller, who considered Mount Shasta the most beautiful mountain in the West, described it as "lonely as God and white as a winter moon." New Agers rank it up there with Stonehenge and the Egyptian pyramids, apparently because of its unusual energy fields. Peculiar stories, involving UFOs and even Big Foot, abound in this area.

VISITOR INFORMATION

Shasta-Cascade Wonderland Association *1250 Parkview Ave., Redding 96001, 800/ 326-6944, 916/243-2643.*

GETTING THERE

Located approximately 235 miles north of San Francisco. Take Highway 80 north to Highway 5 north.

ANNUAL EVENTS

South Shasta Model Railroad *Sun in April & May; in Gerber, 12 miles south of Red Bluff, 916/385-1389.* This miniature 1/4-inch O-gauge reproduction of the Southern Pacific line from Gerber to Dunsmuir operates in a farmhouse basement. It includes 16 steam locomotives, 100 cars, and over 900 feet of track. Visitors may ride on a 2-foot gauge steam train and visit a museum of antique farm equipment.

– Lake Shasta Area –

WHERE TO STAY

Hostel. Sitting in the shadow of Mount Shasta, the Bavarian-style **Alpenrose Cottage** *(204 E. Hinckley St., Mt. Shasta, 916/926-6724)* has 12 beds. See also page 278.

Houseboats. See page 272.

Railroad Park Resort *100 Railroad Park Ave., Dunsmuir, 800/974-RAIL, 916/235-4440; 28 units; 4 non-smoking units; $$; all bathtubs; unheated pool, hot tub; restaurant.* Guests here can sleep in an authentic antique caboose or a deluxe box car unit furnished with antiques and a claw-foot tub. Special family units have bunk beds. Three cabins and some campsites are also available. The nearby Cascade Mountains and their granite Castle Crags Spires can be observed while frolicking in the pool, and a prime rib or seafood dinner may be enjoyed in an authentic McCloud River Railroad car.

Motel Row. Inexpensive motels are located at Bridge Bay and in the Lakehead area. Some inexpensive hotels are in McCloud.

WHAT TO DO

Lake Shasta Caverns *in O'Brien, 15 miles north of Redding, 916/238-2341; tours daily, call for schedule; adults $12, 4-12 $6.* Discovered in 1878, these caverns weren't opened for tours until 1964. The 2-1/2-hour tour begins with a 15-minute catamaran cruise across the McCloud arm of Lake Shasta. Then visitors board a bus for a scenic, winding ride up the steep mountainside to where the caverns are located. In this case, getting there really is half the fun. Gold-panning, nature trails, picnic facilites, and a snack bar are also available.

McCloud. Set in the shadow of Mt. Shasta, this scenic lumbermill town was owned by the McCloud Lumber Company from 1897 to 1965. Try the **McCloud Cookhouse** *(424 Main)* for a lumberjack breakfast and Mexican-style dinners, or **Bellissimo Restaurant** *(204 Lake St.)* for homemade waffles and blintzes. The **McCloud Guest House** *(606 W. Colombero, 916/964-3160)* has five rooms and a good restaurant.

Shasta State Historic Park *on Highway 299 west of town, Old Shasta, 916/243-8194; daily 10-5; adults $2, 6-13 $1.* This was a prosperous town during the Gold Rush. Now it is an interesting museum of restored buildings and relics. Picnic facilities are provided. The fee includes same-day admission to the Joss House State Historic Park in Weaverville (see page 253).

– Lassen Volcanic National Park –

A LITTLE BACKGROUND

Now a dormant volcano, imposing 10,457-foot Lassen Peak last erupted in 1915 and is thought to be the largest plug dome volcano in the world. Visitors can take several self-guided nature walks. Guided hikes and campfire talks are scheduled in the summer. Wooden catwalks supplement the trail through popular **Bumpass Hell,** an area featuring geological oddities such as boiling springs and mud pots, pyrite pools, and noisy fumaroles. The trail covers 3 miles and takes about 3 hours round-trip. The park also offers over 150 miles of back country trails, including a 17-mile section of the **Pacific Crest Trail.**

A free park program and map orients visitors and lists daily activities. It is best to visit July through September, when the 35-mile road through the park is least likely to be closed by snow. Eight campgrounds are available on a first-come, first-served basis. For skiing information, see page 257.

Park admission is $5 per car.

VISITOR INFORMATION

Park Headquarters *P.O. Box 100 (38350 Highway 36E), Mineral 96063, 916/595-4444.*

GETTING THERE

Take Highway 36 east from Red Bluff or Highway 44 east from Redding.

WHERE TO STAY IN THE AREA

Drakesbad Guest Ranch *end of Warner Valley Rd., 18 miles from Chester, 916/529-1512; 19 units; $$$+, special children's rates, children under 3 free; closed Oct-May; 2-night minimum; cribs; no TVs; some bathtubs; some shared baths; natural hot springs pool, hot tub; includes 3 meals/day; restaurant.* Located in a secluded, scenic mountain valley in Lassen Volcanic National Park, this rustic resort was a hot springs spa in the mid-1800s. It has been a guest ranch since the turn of the century and is now the only dude ranch located within a national park. Most of the rustic cabins, bungalows, and lodge rooms have no electricity, so kerosene lanterns are used for light. The ranch is close to some of Lassen's thermal sights: 1 mile from the steaming fumaroles at **Boiling Springs Lake** and 2 miles from the bubbling sulfurous mud pots at the **Devil's Kitchen.** Guests may rent horses from the ranch stables and take guided rides into these areas. Pack trips may also be arranged. All this and a good trout-fishing stream, too! Day visitors should call ahead for stable or dining reservations. Overnight guests should book one year in advance.

Hat Creek Resort *on Highway 89 just north of Highway 44, Old Station, 11 miles from northern entrance to Lassen Park, 916/335-7121; 17 units; $; 2-night minimum in cabins; some kitchens.* These bargain motel units and old-time housekeeping cabins—the kind with linoleum floors and homemade curtains—are located beside rushing Hat Creek. The cabins are available May through October only. Guests can fish in the creek, roast marsmallows over an open fire, and check out the stars at night.

WHERE TO STAY FURTHER AWAY

Spanish Springs Ranch *Ravendale, east of Lassen on Highway 395, 40 miles north of Susanville, 80 miles north of Reno, 800/272-8282, RAVENDALE-30; $100/day, children 3-12 $50, under 3 free; all meals included.* Located in the remote northeast corner of the state, this 70,000-acre working cattle ranch offers a variety of vacation options.

Guests can opt for the main lodge, where the luxurious amenities congregate and where kids can bunk in separate boys and girls dormitories. Or they can sign up for week-long cattle drives in the spring or fall. Weekly rates and special packages—including wilderness pack trips, fishing trips, and camp-outs in an Indian tepee village—are also available.

Wild Horse and Burro Sanctuary *on Wilson Hill Rd., Shingletown, 5 miles south of Highway 44, 21 miles from Lassen, 916/474-5770; 5 units; 2 nights/$235, 3 nights/$335; May-Sept only; unsuitable for children under 14; no TVs; shared bath house; all meals included.* This protected preserve for wild mustangs and burros is the only wild horse sanctuary in the nation. Guests ride out of a base camp to observe the 300-

plus population in their natural habitat. Meals are served by an open campfire, and overnight accommodations are in new, but rustic, cabins overlooking Vernal Lake.

Little other lodging is available in this area, but many forest campsites are available on a first-come, first-served basis. Visitors should bear in mind that this area is remote and does not offer big-city facilities such as supermarkets.

WHERE TO EAT

Uncle Runt's Place *on Highway 44, Old Station, 916/335-7177; L & D Tu-Sun Apr-Jan, Thur-Sun rest of year; $; highchairs, booster seats, children's portions; reservations suggested; no cards.* This cozy restaurant caters to locals and has a short-order menu of sandwiches, hamburgers, and dinner specials.

WHAT TO DO

McArthur-Burney Falls Memorial State Park *on Highway 44, Burney, 30 miles north of Old Station, 916/335-2777; $5/car.* A lovely 1-mile nature trail winds past the soothing rush of the 129-foot falls, allowing for closer inspection of the volcanic terrain for which this area is known.

Paddle boats may be rented at man-made **Lake Britton.** Facilities include picnic tables, a sandy beach, and a wading area for children. Swimming is allowed only in designated areas, as the lake has a steep drop-off. Campsites are also available.

Twelve miles away, the town of Burney offers modern motels and supermarkets.

Spattercone Crest Trail *1/2 mile west of Old Station, across the street from Hat Creek Campground; free.* This 2-mile, self-interpretive trail winds past a number of volcanic spattercones, lava tubes, domes, and blowholes. It take about 2 hours to walk and is most comfortably hiked in early morning or late afternoon.

Subway Cave *1 mile north of Old Station, near junction of Highways 44 & 89; free.* Lava tubes were formed here about 2,000 years ago, when the surface of a lava flow cooled and hardened while the liquid lava beneath the hard crust flowed away. This cave, actually a lava tube, winds for 1,300 feet (about 1/4 mile). Always a cool 46 degrees, it makes a good place to visit on a hot afternoon. However, it is completely unlighted inside, so visitors are advised to bring along a powerful lantern. Even "chickens" can enjoy the cave—by making a furtive entry and then picnicking in the lovely surrounding woods.

Lava Beds
– National Monument –

A LITTLE BACKGROUND

It doesn't hurt to be warned ahead of time that this national monument is located in the middle of nowhere. Perhaps you've heard of the expression "out in the tules." This could be where it originated.

The monument has a campground, but the nearest motels and restaurants are far away in Tulelake. It's a good idea to pack-in picnic supplies as there is nowhere to buy food within many miles of the monument.

The area also buzzes with insects, is a haven for rattlesnakes, and sometimes has plague warnings posted. Still, it is an unusual place that is well worth a visit.

The Visitors Center at the southern entrance offers a good orientation. Historically this area is known as the site of the 1872 Modoc War—the only major Indian war to be fought in California. Geologically the area is of interest because of its concentration of caves—approximately 300.

Park admission is $3 per car.

VISITOR INFORMATION

Monument Headquarters *P.O. Box 867, Tulelake 96134, 916/667-2282.*

GETTING THERE

Continue north from Lassen Park to Highway 299. Then head north on Highway 139 through sparsely populated forest and farmland.

STOPS ALONG THE WAY

Fort Crook Museum *on Highway 299, Fall River Mills, 916/336-5110; daily 12-4,*

May-Oct only; free. Composed of a 3-story main building and five outer buildings, this large museum complex displays six rooms of antique furniture, the old Fall River jail, and a collection of early farm implements and Indian artifacts.

WHAT TO DO

Caves. Mushpot Cave, located in the Visitors Center parking lot, is the only lighted cave. It also has interpretive displays.

A loop road provides access to most of the other 19 caves that are open without passes. They have such descriptive names as Blue Grotto, Sunshine, and Natural Bridge. Catacombs must be crawled through.

To explore some of the other caves, it is required that visitors register at the Visitors Center . . . just in case. Also, lanterns are available to borrow. The Visitors Center is open from 9 to 5:30 in summer, 8 to 4:30 in winter.

Klamath Basin National Wildlife Refuge *4 miles south of the Oregon state line, 916/ 667-2231. Visitor Center: daily 8-4; free.* The gravel road north out of the monument passes through the Tule Lake portion of this scenic area. The refuge is home to a variety of interesting birds that can easily be viewed from a car. In winter it has the densest concentration of bald eagles in the U.S. south of Alaska.

– Trinity Alps –

A LITTLE BACKGROUND

Densely forested, this is wonderful camping country. There really isn't much to do here except relax and perhaps fish, boat, or hike.

WHERE TO STAY

Cedar Stock Resort and Marina *on Highway 3, Lewiston, 15 miles north of Weaverville, 800/982-2279, 916/286-2225; 12 units; $-$$; 1 week minimum in summer; closed Dec-Feb; no TVs; all kitchens, bathtubs; restaurant; dogs welcome.* This quiet spot offers lodging in a cabin in the woods or on a houseboat on **Clair Engle Lake.** Guests provide their own bedding and linens. The marina also rents boats and slips, and the bar and restaurant offer a terrific view of the lake.

Coffee Creek Guest Ranch *off Highway 3, Trinity Center, 40 miles north of Weaverville, 800/624-4480, 916/266-3343; 15 units; $100-$119/person/day; special rates for children; 2-night minimum in spring & fall, 1-week minimum June-Aug; cribs; no TVs; some bathtubs, fireplaces, wood-burning stoves; heated pool (unavailable Nov-Mar), children's wading pool, hot tub, exercise room; all meals included; restaurant.* The private one- and two-bedroom cabins here are located in the woods. Activities include hayrides, movies, steak-frys, outdoor games, square dancing, archery, gun practice on a rifle range, panning for gold, and supervised activities for children 3 to 12. Horseback riding is available at additional charge. Cross-country skiing and ice skating are available in winter.

Trinity Alps Resort *on Highway 3, Lewiston, 12 miles north of Weaverville, 916/286-2205; 43 units; $400-$700/cabin/week; 1-week minimum June-Aug; spring & fall prices by the day, 3-night minimum; closed Oct-May; all kitchens; 1 tennis court, restaurant.* Arranged especially to please families, this 90-acre resort offers rustic 1920s brown-shingle cabins with sleeping verandas—all scattered along rushing Stuart Fork River. Guests provide their own linens or pay additional to rent them. Simple pleasures include crossing the river via a suspension bridge, hanging out at the General Store, and gathering for theme meals in the dining room or riverside patio. Scheduled activities include square dancing and evening movies. Horseback riding is available at additional cost, and kids can ride their bikes endlessly.

WHAT TO DO

J.J. (Jake) Jackson Memorial Museum and **Trinity County Historical Park** *508 Main St., 916/623-5211; daily 10-5, May-Oct only; by donation.* Trinity County's history is traced here through mining equipment, old bottles, and photographs. A reconstructed blacksmith shop and miner's cabin are also on display. Outside a creekside picnic area beckons.

A full-size stamp mill, located on the block just below the museum, is operated on holidays.

Joss House State Historic Park *412 Main St., Weaverville, 916/623-5284; tours on half-hour, daily 10-4 in July & Aug, Thur-M rest of year; adults $2, 6-13 $1.* Located in a shaded area beside a creek, this Chinese Taoist temple is still in use and pro-

vides a cool respite on a hot summer day. Built in 1874, it is the oldest continuously used Chinese temple in the state.

The fee includes same-day admission to the Shasta State Historic Park (see page 247) and **Courthouse Museum** located outside of Redding.

– Yreka –

A LITTLE BACKGROUND

This town is filled with beautifully maintained **historic homes** *(on the four blocks of Third Street located between Lennox & Miner).* The Chamber of Commerce provides a brochure pointing out the many homes built before 1900, a few of which are open to the public.

VISITOR INFORMATION

Yreka Chamber of Commerce Tourist Information Center *117 W. Miner St., Yreka 96097, 800-ON-YREKA (recorded message about sights and special events), 916/842-1649.*

WHAT TO DO

Siskiyou County Museum *910 S. Main St., 916/842-3836; daily 9-5 in summer, Tu-Sat rest of year; free.* Local artifacts and history are emphasized. Of special interest is the exhibit on the pioneer Terwilliger family.

The **Outdoor Museum** is located adjacent. Among its original and reconstructed historic buildings are a schoolhouse, a Catholic church, a blacksmith shop, a miner's cabin, and an operating general store.

Yreka Western Railroad *300 E. Miner St., 916/842-4146; W-Sun at 10am, June-Sept only; adults $9, under 13 $4.50.* The ride on the Blue Goose excursion train, pulled by a restored 1915 Baldwin steam locomotive that had a role in the movie *Stand by Me*, treats passengers to spectacular views of Mount Shasta. There is an hour layover in Montague, where passengers can tour the historic town and enjoy a treat in an old-fashioned ice cream parlor.

A 1,000-square-foot **model railroad** is displayed in an adjacent freight warehouse.

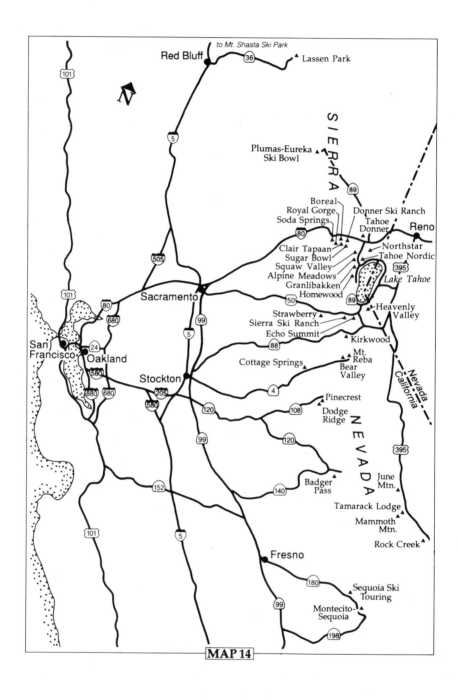

to Mt. Shasta Ski Park

Red Bluff

Lassen Park

36

101

5

N

SIERRA

Plumas-Eureka
Ski Bowl

89

Boreal
Royal Gorge
Soda Springs

Donner Ski Ranch
Tahoe
Donner

Reno

80

Clair Tapaan
Sugar Bowl
Squaw Valley
Alpine Meadows
Granlibakken
Homewood

Northstar
Tahoe Nordic

395

Lake Tahoe

505

Sacramento

50

89

Heavenly
Valley

80

99

Strawberry
Sierra Ski Ranch
Echo Summit

5

680

Kirkwood

San
Francisco

24

Oakland

Mt.
Reba
Bear
Valley

Nevada
California

88

Cottage Springs

101

580

Stockton

4

880 680

205

Pinecrest

580

120

Dodge
Ridge

108

395

99

120

NEVADA

152

140

Badger
Pass

June
Mtn.

101

Tamarack Lodge

Mammoth
Mtn.

5

Rock Creek

Fresno

180

Sequoia Ski
Touring

99

Montecito-
Sequoia

198

MAP 14

Winter Snow Fun

– Downhill Skiing –

Downhill ski areas are plentiful in Northern California. The season runs from the first snow, usually in late November, through the spring thaw in April. Several resorts are known for staying open longer.

Lifts usually operate daily from 9 to 4. To avoid parking problems and long lines for lift tickets and rentals, arrive early. On-site equipment rentals are usually available and convenient.

The least crowded times at the resorts are the 3 weeks after Thanksgiving, the first 2 weeks in January, and late in the season. The 2 weeks around Christmas are ridiculous.

Those who know say it is worthwhile to buy ski equipment if someone skis more than 15 days per season. Otherwise, it is financially beneficial to rent. Avoid buying children plastic skis; they break very easily.

– Cross-country Skiing –

Cross-country skiing is becoming more popular each year. One reason for this surging popularity is the advantages it has over downhill skiing. There are no lift tickets to purchase, and the equipment is less expensive. Also, the sport is considered safer, can be enjoyed in groups, and allows escape from crowds. But it also requires more stamina and is less exhilarating.

Specialized cross-country centers offer equipment rentals, lessons (average cost is $6 to $10 and reservations are usually required), maintained trails, and warming huts. Trail maps are usually available at the center headquarters. Some centers also offer lodging, guided tours, and the option of downhill facilities.

Children age 4 and older are usually taught in classes with their parents, but some centers have special children's classes. Parents who have the strength can carry younger children in a backpack or pull them along in a "pulk."

It is a good idea for beginners to rent equipment and take a few lessons to learn safety guidelines and basic skiing techniques. Once the basics are learned, this sport can be practiced just about anywhere there is 1 foot of snow.

The state **Sno-Park** program makes it easier to park at popular trailheads. Parking areas are kept cleared of snow, and overnight RV camping is permitted at some locations. The permit is $20 and is good from November 1 through May 30. One-day permits are $3. For more information call 916/322-8993.

– Snow Play –

Toboggans, saucers, inner tubes, and sleds are the equipment people use for snow play. For safety's sake, take note that sleds are lots of fun to use but extremely dangerous. Truck inner tubes are also extremely dangerous, because the rider is high off the ground with nothing to hold on to and no way to steer.

When people do not pay attention to safety rules, snow play can become dangerous. (I once had the wind knocked out of me by an antsy bear of a man who didn't wait for me and my young child to come to a stop before he pushed down the same hill in his saucer. After the collision he said, "Sorry. But you shouldn't have been there." I'm sure worse stories are waiting to be told.)

Some commercial snow play areas allow people to use their own equipment, but others require that people rent the concession's equipment.

Dress for cold, wet weather. Wear wool when possible, and pack a change of clothes. Protect feet with boots. When boots aren't available, a cheap improvisation is to wrap feet in newspapers, then in plastic bags, and then put shoes on. Also, a large plastic garbage bag can be used as a raincoat. Always wear gloves to protect hands from sharp, packed snow. (For information on dressing kids for the snow, see page 292.)

The high-speed fun of **snowmobiling** is an exciting adventure. Many snowmobile concessions provide protective clothing and equipment. Though not inexpensive, especially for a family, it is an exhilarating, memorable experience.

Note: In the following listings, difficulty of terrain is specified in percentages: %B (beginner), %I (intermediate), %A (advanced). Adult lift ticket prices are given first/followed by children's prices (discounts are often available on weekdays).

– Way Up North –

Coffee Creek. See page 251.

Lassen Park Ski Area 2150 N. *Main #7, Red Bluff, 916/595-3376, snow phone 916/595-4464; 49 miles east of Red Bluff; open Thur-Sun only. Downhill: 1 triple, 2 surface; 40%B, 40%I, 20%A; lifts $22/$13 (8-12), under 8 free; children's ski school (4-8). Cross-country: 916/595-3376; (80 km), all ungroomed. Lodging nearby; packages available; snow play area.* California's "undiscovered National Park" is an excellent area for families and beginners. The scenery includes hot steam vents and mud pots—allowing for unusual and interesting cross-country ski touring. Snowshoe walks are sometimes scheduled. See also page 247.

Mt. Shasta Ski Park 104 *Siskiyou Ave., Mt. Shasta, 916/926-8610, snow phone 916/926-8686; 10 miles east of Mt. Shasta City; downhill & cross-country; 2 triples, 1 surface; 20%B, 60%I, 20%A; lifts $25/$3 (1-7); children's ski school (4-7); lodging nearby 916/243-2643.* Snowboard rentals and lessons and night skiing are available at this low-key, family-oriented ski area.

Plumas-Eureka Ski Bowl in *Plumas-Eureka State Park, 916/836-2317; 25 miles east of Quincy; downhill only; W, Sat, & Sun only; 2 poma lifts, 1 rope tow; 45%B, 50%I, 5%A; lifts $12/$9 (1-12).*

– South Lake Tahoe –

Heavenly Valley *South Lake Tahoe, 916/541-1330, snow phone 916/541-SKII; downhill only; 1 aerial tram, 7 triples, 9 doubles, 6 surface; 25%B, 50%I, 25%A; lifts $38/$15; childcare (2-4), children's ski school (4-12); lodging nearby 800/2-HEAVEN, adjacent townhouses 800/822-5967, packages available.* This is one of the largest and most scenic ski areas in the country. Situated in two states, the runs on the California side offer breathtaking views of Lake Tahoe. Heavenly has been rated as having the best intermediate skiing in California. It also has exhilarating expert slopes and offers both night and helicopter skiing.

Hope Valley Cross-Country Ski Center at Sorensen's *Hope Valley, 916/694-2203; on Highway 88, 16 miles south of Lake Tahoe; cross-country only; 100 km trails, 18 km groomed; by donation; lodging on premises 800/423-9949.* Small and informal, this is a great place for families. Lodging is available in 30 housekeeping cabins. Some are newish log cabins equipped with fully equipped kitchenettes and wood-burning fireplaces. Others are older and smaller. A sauna and cafe are among the resort's facilities. Open year-round, this modestly priced spot is 100% non-smoking. In the summer it offers both a family-oriented fly fishing school and history tours of the Emigrant Road and Pony Express Trail.

Kirkwood Ski Resort *Kirkwood, 209/258-6000, snow phone 209/258-3000; on Highway 88, 30 miles south of South Lake Tahoe; downhill only; 4 triples, 6 doubles, 1 surface;*

15%B, 50%I, 35%A; lifts $35/$17 (1-12); childcare center (3-6), children's ski school (4-12); lodging on premises in condominiums 209/258-7247. This is a very large, uncrowded family area that is reputed to have the best natural snow, and food, in the Sierra. It is said to usually be snowing here when it is raining at other Tahoe ski areas. Snowboard rentals and lessons are available, as are horse-drawn sleigh rides.

The adjacent **Kirkwood Cross Country** *(209/258-7240; 21 trails (80 km), all groomed; 20%B, 60%I, 20%A; trail fee $12/$7; childcare center (3-6))* offers inexpensive Family Days as well as guided overnight trips that include lodging and meals.

Sierra Ski Ranch *Twin Bridges, 916/659-7535, snow phone 916/659-7475, 415/427-6011; on Highway 50, 12 miles west of South Lake Tahoe; downhill only; 2 quads, 2 triples, 4 doubles; 20%B, 60%I, 20%A; lifts $29/$15 (1-12); children's ski school (3-6); lodging nearby 800/AT-TAHOE.* This family-run ski area is reputed to be particularly popular with college students and families with teenagers.

SNOW PLAY

Borges' Sleigh Rides *on Highway 50 next to Caesar's Tahoe casino, Stateline, 916/541-2953, 916/957-6066; daily 12-dusk, as snow conditions permit; couple $15, under 12 $5, reduced family rates.* Take a ride around a meadow in an old-fashioned "one-horse open sleigh."

Hansen's Resort *1360 Ski Run Blvd./Needle Peak Rd., 3 blocks from Heavenly Valley, South Lake Tahoe, 916/544-3361; daily 9-12 & 1-4; 3-hour session $9/person.* Facilities include a saucer hill and a packed toboggan run with banked turns. All equipment is furnished, and lodging is available.

Husky Express *in Hope Valley, 15 miles south of Lake Tahoe, 702/782-3047; by appt.; $95/sled; reservations required.* On these enjoyable excursions, as the sled swooshes over the scenic trails through the trees, the frisky, well-tempered huskies seem to be having as much fun as the passengers. So does the "musher," who never utters the word "mush" but instead hollers "Hike!" or "Let's Go!" Two sleds are available, and each can carry two adults or a combination of kids and adults that doesn't exceed 375 pounds. Three-hour picnic tours ($175) are also available.

Snow Hikes. *Sierra State Parks, P.O. Drawer D, Tahoma 96142, 916/525-7232.* Request a schedule of free ranger-led snowshoe and cross-country hikes in Lake Tahoe area state parks by sending a stamped, self-addressed legal size envelope to the above address. Hikes are scheduled October through April, depending on the snow level.

Winter Wonderland *3672 Verdon/Needle Peak Rd., South Lake Tahoe 916/544-7903; daily; free.* This snow play area is an open field located behind the Winter Wonderland ski rental shop—the oldest ski shop at Tahoe. Saucers may be rented from the shop for $3 per day.

– North Lake Tahoe –

Alpine Meadows *800/441-4423, 916/583-4232, snow phone 916/583-6914; off Highway 89, 4 miles north of Tahoe City; downhill only; 1 quad, 2 triples, 8 doubles, 1 surface; 25%B, 40%I, 35%A; lifts $38/$13 (7-12), under 7 $5; childcare snow school (3-6), children's ski school (6-12); lodging nearby 800/TAHOE-4-U, packages available.* Alpine is usually open through Memorial Day and some years is open into July—giving it the longest ski season at Lake Tahoe. A 5-day learn-to-ski program begins each

Monday. Free 1-hour guided tours show participants the main runs and how to avoid crowds. They are offered on Saturdays and Sundays at 9:30 a.m., and reservations are required. Alpine also hosts a free ski clinic for amputees and is known for having excellent ski instruction for the physically and mentally handicapped. Snowboarding is banned.

A **Family Ski Challenge** is scheduled each March.

Granlibakken *800/543-3221, 916/583-9896; 1 mile south of Tahoe City; 2 surface; 50%B, 50%I; lifts $12/$6 (1-12), free to lodging guests; snow play area.* This small ski area is protected from the wind and caters to beginners and families with small children. It is said to be the oldest ski resort at Tahoe and to have the least expensive lift ticket. See also page 238.

Homewood *916/525-7256; on Highway 89, 6 miles south of Tahoe City; downhill only; 1 quad, 2 triples, 2 doubles, 5 surface; 20%B, 50%I, 30%A; lifts $27/$9 (1-12); childcare center, children's ski school (4-6); lodging nearby 800/822-5959.* The slopes here are ideal for intermediates and provide great views of Lake Tahoe.

Northstar-at-Tahoe *snow phone 916/562-1330; off Highway 267, 6 miles south of Truckee. Downhill: 916/562-1010; 1 gondola, 2 quads, 3 triples, 3 doubles, 2 surface; 25%B, 50%I, 25%A; lifts $38/$15 (5-12), under 5 free; childcare center (2-6), children's ski school (5-12). Cross-country: 916/587-0273; 34 trails (65km), all groomed; 30%B, 40%I, 30%A; trail fee $13/$6 (5-12), under 5 free. Lodging in modern condos on premises 800/533-6787, packages available.* This attractive ski area is said to be the least windy at Tahoe. Catering to families, it is good for beginners and excellent for intermediates. Lift ticket sales are limited to assure that the slopes don't get overcrowded, so arrive early. Organized activities are scheduled throughout the week, and free 2-hour introductory tours, in which participants are shown the best runs and given a history of the area, are given on Fridays and Sundays at 11 a.m. Sleigh rides are available, as are snowboard rentals and lessons. See also page 238.

Squaw Valley U.S.A. *Olympic Valley, 800/545-4350, snow phone 916/583-6955; off Highway 89, 5 miles north of Tahoe City; downhill only; 1 aerial tram, 1 6-passenger gondola, 13 quads, 17 triples, 16 doubles, 4 surface; 25%B, 45%I, 30%A; lifts $38/$5 (1-12); childcare (6 mo.-2), childcare snow school (3-5), children's ski school (6-12); lodging on premises 800/327-3353; packages available.* Squaw Valley made its name in 1960 when it was home to the VIII Winter Olympic Games. Today it is a world-class ski area known internationally for its open slopes and predictably generous snowfall—which usually allows Squaw to stay open into May. Expert skiers consider it to be the best ski resort in the state because it has the steepest, most challenging slopes. Indeed, there are good slopes for every ability level. Squaw Valley's Papoose Ski School, a special area for children under 6, is equipped with two rope tows. Ice skating is available at the **Olympic Ice Pavilion** at High Camp, and night skiing is available on weekends. A free 1-hour introductory tour is offered each day at 1 p.m.

Tahoe Nordic Ski Center *925 Country Club Dr., Tahoe City, 916/583-9858, 916/583-0484; off Highway 28, 2 miles east of Tahoe City; weekends only; cross-country only; 12 trails (65 km), all groomed; 30%B, 40%I, 30%A; trail fee $12/$4, under 7 free; children's lessons (4-10); lodging nearby 800/824-6348.* Moonlight tours are available.

SNOW PLAY

Carnelian Woods Condominiums. See page 238.

North Lake Tahoe Regional Park Ski Area *off Highway 28 at the end of National Ave., Tahoe Vista, 916/546-7248*. This 108-acre park has a snow play area for toboggans and saucers. Snowmobiles may be rented on weekends for use on a 1/4-mile oval racing track and 2-1/2 miles of trails. Cross-country trails *(3 trails (6.6 mi); trail fee $3/$2 (1-12))* and picnic tables round out the facilities.

Sugar Pine Point State Park. See page 243.

Snowfest *916/583-7625*. Held for a week each year in March, this is the largest winter carnival in the West. In the past activities have included a fireworks display over the slopes at Squaw Valley, followed by the awe-inspiring sight of scores of torch-bearing skiers making a twisting descent down Exhibition Run. Other popular events include The Great Ski Race (a 30-kilometer nordic ski competition) and the Localman Triathlon (a competition in winter survival skills in which participants must stack firewood, shovel snow, and put on tire chains).

– Donner Summit –

Boreal *916/426-3666, snow phone 916/426-3663; Castle Peak exit off Highway 80, 10 miles west of Truckee; downhill only; 1 quad, 2 triples, 7 doubles; 30%B, 55%I, 15%A; lifts $29/$14 (1-12); childcare center (2-12), children's ski school (4-12); lodging on premises 916/426-3668; packages available*. This area is known for being relatively inexpensive and convenient to the Bay Area. Facilities are especially good for beginners and low-intermediates, and the Sierra's most extensive night skiing facilities are available. Snowboard lessons and rentals are also available.

Clair Tapaan Lodge *Norden, 916/426-3632; on Highway 40, 3 miles east of Norden/ Soda Springs exit off I-80; cross-country only; 6 trails (7 km), all groomed; 30%B, 60%I, 10%A; trail fee: $5 donation*. This area is said to be the snowiest in the continental U.S. Both the massive timbered lodge, which was built by volunteers in 1934, and track system are owned and operated by the Sierra Club. A special package *($36/ $22.50 (12 and under)/$31 members)* includes bunk bed lodging, three hearty meals served family style, and use of the trails. As in hostels, everyone is expected to do a chore. Overnight trips to wilderness areas can be arranged.

Donner Ski Ranch *Norden, 916/426-3635; on Highway 40, 3 miles from the Norden/ Soda Springs exit off Highway 80; downhill only; 1 triple, 4 doubles; 25%B, 50%I, 25%A; lifts $20/$10; lodging on premises; packages available*. This area offers no frills and is best for beginners and intermediates. Snowboard rentals and lessons are available.

Royal Gorge Cross Country Ski Resort *Soda Springs, 916/426-3871, snow phone 916/426-3873; at Soda Springs/Norden exit off Highway 80, near Donner Pass; cross-country only; 77 trails (317 km), all groomed; 39%B, 41%I, 20%A; trail fee $16/$8.50;*

children's ski school (4-9); lodging on premises; packages available. Modeled after Scandinavian ski resorts, this was the first cross-country ski resort in California. The overnight **Wilderness Lodge** here is not easily accessible. Guests are brought in by snowcat-drawn sleigh (sorry, no reindeer or horses yet) and leave by skiing the 2 miles back out. Accommodations are rustic. In the old 1920s hunting lodge, everyone shares the same toilet area. Bathing facilities—showers, a sauna, and an outdoor hot tub—are reached by a short trek through the snow. Sleeping facilities are rustic roomettes, each with a bunk bed and cloth-covered doorway. Several three-bed rooms are available for families. The food, however, is remarkably civilized. A chef works full-time in the kitchen preparing attractive, tasty, and bountiful French repasts. Oh, yes. The skiing. Guests may cross-country ski whenever they wish, and the capable staff gives lessons each morning and afternoon. Guided moonlight ski tours are scheduled after dinner. A two-night weekend *($265/ person, $215/kids 5-14)* includes everything except equipment, which may be rented on the premises. Lower rates are available midweek.

Royal Gorge also operates a more accessible B&B, **Rainbow Lodge** *(916/426-3661),* nearby.

The cross-country ski center is open to non-guests and features the largest cross-country track system in the U.S. A new Interconnect Trail allows skiers to enjoy 8 miles of scenic downhill cross-country skiing; shuttle buses return skiers to the trailhead. A special program is available for skiers with disabilities.

Soda Springs Ski Area *Soda Springs, 916/426-3666, at Soda Springs exit off Highway 80, 4 miles west of Donner Summit; F-Sun only; downhill only; 1 triple, 1 double; 30%B, 50%I, 20%A; lifts $21/$11 (1-12); children's ski school (4-12), children's lessons; lodging nearby.* Built on the former site of one of the first Sierra ski resorts, this relatively new ski area is very close to the Bay Area. It is possible to rent all or part of the resort on weekdays, and snowboard rentals and lessons are available.

Sugar Bowl Ski Resort *Norden, 916/426-3651, snow phone 916/426-3847; on Highway 40, 3 miles from the Soda Springs exit off Highway 80; downhill only; 1 gondola, 1 quad, 6 doubles; 20%B, 30%I, 50%A; lifts $33/$14 (6-12); childcare (3-5), children's ski school (6-12); lodging on premises 800/435-4004; packages available.* Exuding a 1930s Tyrolean charm, this ski resort is one of the Sierra's oldest and is said to have had the first chairlift in the state. It is further known for having short lift lines, good runs at all ability levels, and a lack of hotdoggers. Skiers park their cars carefully (to avoid tickets), and then ride a gondola or chairlift up to the resort. Night skiing is available.

Tahoe Donner *Truckee, snow phone 916/587-9494; on Highway 40, 1/2 mile from the Truckee/Donner Lake exit off Highway 80. Downhill: 916/587-9444; 2 doubles, 1 surface; 50%B, 50%I; lifts $20/$10; children's ski school (3-6). Cross-country: 916/587-9484; 32 trails (65 km), all groomed; 30%B, 40%I, 30%A; trail fee $13/$11 (13-17), $8 (under 13); children's ski school (4-6 & 7-10). Lodging in modern condos and homes on premises 916/ 587-6586, 916/587-5411.* This small resort is good for families. The number of lift tickets is limited, assuring that it never gets too crowded. The cross-country ski center offers lighted night skiing and schedules special tours: Ski With Santa, Morning Nature Tour, Sauna Tour, Donner Trail Tour. Sleigh rides are also available.

SNOW PLAY

Sierra Sweepstakes Sled Dog Races *annually in January; held at the Truckee Tahoe Airport off Highway 267, 4 miles south of Truckee, 916/587-2757.* The largest such races in the West, this two-day event features three-, six-, and eight-dog teams of huskies, samoyeds, setters, and bloodhounds.

Western Ski Sport Museum *at Boreal Ridge exit off I-80, 916/426-3313; Tu-Sun 11-5 during ski season, W-Sun rest of year; free.* Here is an opportunity to see how cumbersome old-time ski equipment was. Vintage ski films are shown upon request.

– East –

Bear Valley Cross-Country *Bear Valley, 209/753-2834; on Highway 4, 49 miles east of Angels Camp; cross-country only; trail fee $12.50/$8, under 8 free; 34 trails (120 km), all groomed; 35%B, 50%I, 15%A; children's ski program (3-7); childcare (1-5) and lodging nearby.* This resort ranks second in Northern California in length of groomed trails. Overnight tours, complete with lodging and food, are available, as are snowbound cabins reachable only by snowcat.

An **ice skating rink** *($4, skate rental $3)* on a natural pond is also available here. A trail pass permits free entry.

Bear Valley Ski Company *Bear Valley, 209/753-2301, snow phone 209/753-2308; on Highway 4, 55 miles east of Angels Camp; downhill only; 2 triples, 7 doubles, 2 surface; 30%B, 40%I, 30%A; lifts $32/$13 (7-12), under 7 $10; childcare center (1-5), children's ski school (3-7); lodging in condos, homes, and lodge on premises 209/753-BEAR.* Intermediate or better ability skiers staying in this secluded resort village can ski the 3-mile Home Run trail back to the resort area at the end of the day. A bus takes skiers to and from the village area lodgings and the slopes. Bear is one of the biggest ski areas in the state and generally has short lift lines. However, that Ski Bare campaign must have caught people's attention: Now there are lines where once there were none. It is popular with families and especially good for beginners and intermediates. Snowboard rentals and lessons are available.

Inexpensive modern rooms, with bathrooms down the hall, are available at nearby **Red Dog Lodge** *(209/753-2344).*

Cottage Springs *209/795-1401; on Highway 4, 8 miles east of Arnold; downhill only; 1 double, 2 surface; 75%B, 25%I; lifts $18/$10; lodging nearby; snow play area (rental fee).* This is a good area to learn to ski. Night skiing is available on Fridays and Saturdays.

Dodge Ridge *Pinecrest, 209/965-3474, snow phone 209/965-4444; 32 miles east of Sonora off Highway 108; downhill only; 2 triples, 5 doubles, 4 surface; 20%B, 60%I, 20%A; lifts $30/$15 (9-12), under 9 free; childcare center (2-8), children's ski school (3-10); lodging nearby 800/446-1333.* This low-key, family-oriented ski area is known for short lift lines. Snowboard rentals and lessons are available.

SNOW PLAY

Bear River Lake Resort *on Bear River Reservoir, 209/295-4868; 42 miles east of Jackson, 3 miles off Highway 88; daily 8am-8pm; free, parking $5/car.* Visitors may use their own equipment in this groomed snow play area. Snowcats, cross-country equipment, snowshoes, saucers, and tubes are available for rental, and back country cross-country trips may be arranged.

Long Barn Lodge Ice Rink *Long Barn, 209/586-3533; 23 miles east of Sonora off Highway 108; call for schedule; adults $4.50, under 13 $3.50, skate rental 50¢.* Located behind a bar and restaurant built in 1925, this rink is covered but has two sides open to the outdoors.

– South –

Badger Pass *Yosemite National Park (see page 165); off Highway 41 on Glacier Point Rd., 23 miles from the valley. Downhill: 209/372-1330, snow phone 209/372-1000; 1 triple, 3 doubles, 2 surface; 35%B, 50%I, 15%A; lifts $25/$11.75 (4-12); childcare center (3-9), children's pre-ski school (4-6). Cross-country: 209/372-1244; 3%B, 14%I, 83%A; 13 trails (550km), 32km groomed; trail use free with park admission. Lodging nearby;*

The old days

packages available. Badger Pass opened in 1935, making it California's first, and oldest, organized ski area. It is a prime spot for beginners and intermediates and is especially popular with families. Its natural bowl has gentle slopes and provides shelter from wind. A free shuttle bus delivers valley guests to the slopes. Tickets must be picked up the day before at any lodging reservations desk.

A snow play area is located several miles from the slopes; it is not always accessible, and there are no equipment rentals. Cross-country skiing is arranged through **Yosemite Cross-Country Ski School**—the oldest cross-country ski school on the West Coast. Survival courses, snow camping, and overnight tours that include lodging and meals are also available. Ask about the bargain Midweek Ski Package.

June Mountain *June Lake, 619/648-7733; 4 miles south of Highway 395, 58 miles north of Bishop; downhill only; 1 aerial tram, 2 quads, 5 doubles; 35%B, 45%I, 20%A; lifts $35/ $17 (7-12), under 7 free; childcare center (4-5), children's ski school (3-12); lodging nearby.* This compact, uncrowded area is excellent for beginners and popular with families. Snowboard rentals and lessons are available.

For lodging try **June Lodge** *(714/648-7713).* A former hunting lodge, it was once a popular retreat for movie stars such as Clark Gable and Humphrey Bogart.

Mammoth Mountain *Mammoth Lakes, 619/934-2571, snow phone 619/934-6166; 50 miles north of Bishop; downhill only; 2 gondolas, 1 express, 4 quads, 7 triples, 14 doubles, 2 surface; 30%B, 40%I, 30%A; lifts $35/$17 (7-12), under 7 free; infant care, childcare center (2-8), children's ski school (4-12); lodging on premises 800/367-6572, 619/934-2581.* One of the three largest ski areas in the country, Mammoth is located on a dormant volcano and has the highest elevation of any California ski area. It also is said to have some of the longest lift lines and one of the longest seasons—usually staying open through June and sometimes into July. Snowboard rentals and lessons are available. A 7-hour drive from the Bay Area, it is understandably more popular with Southern Californians.

The 22-bed **Hilton Creek Youth Hostel** *(619/935-4989; family rooms available)* is located about 20 miles away. The focus here is on cross-country skiing, and special packages are available. See also page 278.

Montecito-Sequoia Cross Country Ski Center *(see page 271); 800/227-9900, snow phone 209/565-3324; on Highway 180 between Kings Canyon and Sequoia National Parks; cross-country only; 30%B, 35%I, 35%A; 16 trails (84km), 35km groomed; trail fee $10/$5; childcare (6mo.-6), children's lessons (7-11); lodging on premises; packages available.* Skiers here enjoy breathtaking ski tours and snowshoe walks through groves of giant sequoias. Arrangements can be made for videotaping lessons, and parents may rent "pulkas" to pull their children along in. Because of its high altitude location at 7,500 feet, this resort usually retains its snow and stays open for skiing through spring.

Lodge guests have plenty to do besides skiing. In the lodge they feast on "California fresh" cuisine. There are board games, Ping Pong, and plenty of movies for the VCR. Outside activities include snow sculpture, igloo building, and ski football. A session on the natural lake **ice skating rink** is also a possibility. But there is also the option of just resting in front of the massive stone fireplaces.

Rock Creek Cross-Country *Mammoth Lakes, half-way between Mammoth Lakes and Bishop, 619/935-4452; cross-country only; 30%A, 45%I, 25%B; 14 trails (75km), 25km groomed; trail fee $6/$3; lodging on premises.* The ski package ($160) here includes snowcat transportation to the remote off-road lodge, two nights in either the lodge or a cabin heated by a wood-burning stove, breakfasts and dinners in the lodge, and a 2-hour ski lesson. Children ages 5 to 9 are charged half-price; under 5 are free. Midweek rates are even lower.

Sequoia Ski Touring Center *Sequoia National Park; Giant Forest, 209/565-3435; Grant Grove, 209/335-2314; cross-country only; 25%B, 25%I, 50%A; 8 trails (40km), none groomed; trail use free with park admission; children's lessons; lodging nearby (see page 177).* The big attraction here is the scenic national park ski trails leading through groves of cinnamon-colored giant sequoias. Free hot drinks are provided, and moonlight tours and overnight tours are available. Snow play areas are located at Azalea campground and Big Stump picnic areas. See also page 175.

Tamarack Cross-Country Ski Center *Mammoth Lakes, 800/237-6879, 619/934-2442; on Twin Lakes, 2-1/2 miles from Mammoth Lakes Village; cross-country only; 48%B, 37%I, 15%A; 22 trails (55km), all groomed; trail fee $13/$8 (12-18), under 12 free; lodging on premises.* For the hearty, expedition tours are scheduled in which participants spend the night in a snow cave or tent. Lodging is a choice of either rooms in a rustic 1923 alpine lodge or housekeeping cabins with wood-burning stoves.

SNOW PLAY

Yosemite *(see page 165)*. Ice skate in the shadow of Glacier Point, with a spectacular view of Half Dome, at the scenic outdoor rink in Curry Village. Skating pointers are free *(209/372-1441; call for schedule; adults $4.50, under 13 $3.75, skate rentals $1.75)*.

Open-air snowcat rides leave from Badger Pass *(209/372-1330; daily 10-3; reservations suggested; adults $5, under 13 $3.50)*.

Free ranger-led snowshoe walks are also available at Badger Pass *(209/372-4461; $1 snowshoe maintenance fee)*. A good place to snowshoe without a guide is the Sequoia Forest Trail in Mariposa Grove.

Miscellaneous Adventures

– Family Camps –

Most adults remember the good old days when they were a kid and got to go away to summer camp. Most adults think those days are gone for good. Well, they're not. A vacation at a family camp brings it all back!

Family camps provide a reasonably-priced, organized vacation experience. They are sponsored by city recreation departments, university alumni organizations, and private enterprise. The city and private camps are open to anyone, but some university camps require a campus affiliation.

And its isn't necessary to have children to attend. One year at one camp a couple was actually *honeymooning!* Elderly couples whose children have grown occasionally attend alone, and family reunions are sometimes held at a camp. Whole clubs and groups of friends have been known to book in at the same time.

Housing varies from primitive platform tents and cabins without electricity, plumbing, or bedding to comfortable campus dormitory apartments with daily maid service. Locations vary from the mountains to the sea. Predictably, costs also vary with the type of accommodations and facilities. Some camps allow stays of less than a week, but most require a week-long committment. Children are usually charged at a lower rate according to their age.

Most family camps operate during the summer months only. Fees usually include meal preparation and clean-up, special programs for children, and recreation programs for everyone. Activities can include river or pool swimming, hikes, fishing, volleyball, table tennis, badminton, hayrides, tournaments, campfires, crafts programs, songfests, tennis, and horseback riding.

Each camp has its own special appeal, but all offer an informal atmosphere where guests can really unwind. Often over half the guests return the following year. Repeat guests and their camp friends tend to choose the same week each year.

For detailed rate information, itemization of facilities, session dates, and route directions, contact the camp reservation offices directly and request a free brochure. Reserve early to avoid disappointment.

City/Group Camps

Berkeley Tuolumne Family Camp *City of Berkeley Camps Office, Berkeley, 510/644-6520; daily rates; located on the south fork of the Tuolumne River near Yosemite National Park; platform tents without electricity, provide own bedding, community bathrooms; family-style meals; programs for toddlers-6, 6-12, & teens; swimming instruction in river, cookout and breakfast hikes.*

Camp Concord *Concord Department of Leisure Services, Concord, 510/671-3273; daily rates; located near Camp Richardson at South Lake Tahoe; cabins with electricity, provide own bedding, community bathrooms; cafeteria-style meals; special program for ages 3-6 & 7-16; horseback riding and river rafting available at extra charge.*

Camp Mather *San Francisco Recreation and Park Department, San Francisco, 415/666-7073; daily rates; located on the rim of the Tuolumne River gorge near Yosemite National Park; cabins with electricity; provide own bedding, community bathrooms; cafeteria-style meals; playground area, program for age 6 and older; pool; extra fee for horseback riding.*

Camp Sacramento *Department of Parks and Recreation, Sacramento, 916/264-5195; daily rates; located in the El Dorado National Forest 17 miles south of Lake Tahoe; cabins with electricity, provide own bedding, community bathrooms; cafeteria-style meals; program for ages 2-16, babysitting available at extra charge.*

Camp Sierra *Associated Cooperatives Inc., Berkeley, 510/538-0454; weekly rates; located in a pine forest between Huntington and Shaver Lakes about 65 miles east of Fresno; some cabins with electricity, lodge rooms, or bring own tent; provide own bedding, community bathrooms; family-style meals; special activities for teens, playground and crafts program for younger children; discussion groups.*

Cazadero Music & Arts Family Camp *CAMPS Inc., Berkeley, 510/549-2396; weekly rates; located in the Russian River area; platform tents without electricity or provide own tent; provide own bedding, community bathrooms; family-style meals; daycare for ages 1-5, program for ages 6 and older; heated pool.* The music classes are open to everyone regardless of ability or experience. Campers may learn anything from beginning musical theory to advanced steel drums. Private lessons are available on all instruments. Dance, drama, and art classes are also scheduled.

Echo Lake Family Camp *CAMPS Inc., Berkeley, 510/549-2396; weekly rates; located on the western rim of the Lake Tahoe basin near the Desolation Wilderness Area; tent-cabins without electricity, provide own bedding, community bathrooms; family-style meals; daycare program for ages 1-5, supervised program for ages 6-12; heated pool.* Just one 1-week session is scheduled each year, and it always includes July 4th. Hiking is the focus.

Feather River Camp *Office of Parks and Recreation, Oakland, 510/238-2267; daily rates; located in the Plumas National Forest north of Lake Tahoe near Quincy; cabins and platform tents without electricity, provide own bedding, community bathrooms; family-style meals; play area and activities for ages 2-6, program for age 6 and older; theme weeks.*

Gualala Family Camp *Berkeley-Albany YMCA, Berkeley, 510/848-9622; 2-3 night weekend in July; located 7 miles inland from the coast near Gualala; shared cabins with electricity & lodge rooms, community bathrooms; meals provided; childcare for 1-6, programs for older children; fitness classes, canoeing, swimming, arts & crafts, hiking, campfire programs.*

San Jose Family Camp *San Jose Parks and Recreation Department, San Jose, 408/277-4666; daily rates; located in the Stanislaus National Forest 30 miles from Yosemite National Park; platform tents without electricity (5 with electricity at additional fee), provide own bedding, community bathrooms; buffet (B & L) and family-style (D) meals; play area, program for age 3 and older; dammed-off river pool.*

Silver Lake Family Resort *Department of Parks and Recreation, Stockton, 209/944-8206; daily rates; located 40 miles south of Lake Tahoe; platform tents and cabins with electric lights; provide own bedding, community bathrooms; cafeteria-style meals; program for toddlers and older children; swimming in lake, horseback riding nearby.*

Private Enterprise Camps

Coffee Creek Guest Ranch. See page 251.

Emandal Farm. See page 137.

Greenhorn Creek Guest Ranch *800/334-6939, 916/283-0930; weekly rates; open Mar-Dec; located 70 miles north of Lake Tahoe in Feather River country; rustic cabins and lodge rooms with maid service, private bathrooms; family-style meals; childcare for children 3-5 during horseback rides, babysitting available at additional charge; heated pool, horseback riding, hayrides, fishing pond, hiking; golf and tennis nearby.* Most people seem to come here for the heavy schedule of horse-related activities. A Thanksgiving Weekend is scheduled each year, and special daily and weekend rates may be secured on a space-available basis by calling 2 weeks in advance. This is where to go to rough it in comfort.

Kennolyn's Family Camp *408/475-1430; no children under 3; 1-week session at end of Aug; located 4 miles from Soquel in the Santa Cruz mountains; cabins with electricity, provide own bedding, some private bathrooms; family-style meals; programs for all ages; 3 tennis courts, 2 solar-heated pools, darkroom access for photographers; instruction in horseback riding, riflery, archery, gymnastics, crafts, sailing, windsurfing, skin diving, and soccer.*

Montecito-Sequoia High Sierra Vacation Camp *800/227-9900, 415/967-8612; weekly rates; located in Sequoia National Forest between Kings Canyon and Sequoia National Parks; lodge, bedding provided, private baths; also open cabins, provide own bedding, community bathrooms; buffet meals; nursery for babies 6mo.-2, programs for age 3 and older; 2 tennis courts, lake swimming, pool, sailing, canoeing, boating, archery, fishing, riflery; extra fee for water-skiing and horseback riding.* See also page 265.

University Camps

Lair of the Golden Bear *sponsored by the California Alumni Association at the University of California, Berkeley, 510/642-0221; weekly rates; located in the Stanislaus National Forest near Pinecrest; tent cabins with electricity, provide own bedding, community bathrooms; family-style meals; supervised play for ages 2-6, program for 6-17; heated pool, 3 tennis courts, swimming and tennis lessons, complete athletic facilities.* This is actually two separate camps—**Camp Blue** and **Camp Gold**—that operate side by side. Each has its own staff and facilities.

– Houseboats –

Living in a houseboat for a few days is an unusual way to get away from it all. It is possible to dive off the boat for a refreshing swim, fish for dinner while sunbathing, and dock in a sheltered, quiet cove for the night.

Houseboats are equipped with kitchens and flush toilets. Most rental agencies require that renters provide their own bedding, linens, and groceries. Almost everything else is on the floating hotel—including life jackets.

Rates vary quite dramatically depending on the time of year and how many people are in the party. Summer rentals are highest, and a group of six to ten people gets the best rates. In-season weekly rates for six range from $785 to $1,900 —

depending on the size and quality of the boat. Fuel is additional. Some rental facilities have enough boats to offer midweek specials and 3-day weekends; some offer a Thanksgiving special that includes the turkey and pumpkin pie. During the off-season, rates drop by approximately one-third, and some facilities will rent their boats for just a day. Contact rental facilities directly for current stock and rates.

Clair Engle Lake

Cedar Stock Resort and Marina. See page 251.

Lake Oroville

Bidwell Marina *800/637-1767, 916/589-3152.*

Lime Saddle Marina *800/834-7517, 916/877-2414.*

For more information on this area contact:
Oroville Chamber of Commerce *1789 Montgomery, Oroville 95965, 800/655-GOLD, 916/533-2542.*

Lake Shasta

Bridge Bay Resort & Marina and **Digger Bay Resort & Marina** *800/752-9669, 916/275-3021.*

Holiday Flotels *at Packers Bay Marina, 916/245-1002.*

Holiday Harbor *800/776-2628, 916/238-2383.*

For more information on houseboating on Lake Shasta contact:
Shasta-Cascade Wonderland Association (see page 245).

The Delta

Herman & Helen's Marina *209/951-4634.*

Paradise Point Marina *800/752-9669.*

For more information on houseboating on the Delta contact:
Delta Houseboat Rental Association *6333 Pacific Ave. #152, Stockton 95207, 209/477-1840.*

Rio Vista Chamber of Commerce *60 Main St., Rio Vista 94571, 707/374-2700.*

Stockton Chamber of Commerce *445 W. Weber Ave. #220, Stockton 95203, 209/466-7066.*

Stockton Convention & Visitors Bureau *46 W. Fremont St., Stockton 95202, 209/943-1987.*

See also page 211.

– Rafting Trips –

The adventure of rafting down a changing and unpredictable river offers a real escape for the harried, city-weary participant. But don't expect it to be relaxing. Participants are expected to help with setting up and breaking camp, and they are sometimes mercilessly exposed to the elements. While usually not dangerous when done with experienced guides, an element of risk is involved. Still, most participants walk away ecstatic and addicted to the experience.

The outfitter will provide shelter, food, and equipment for the trip. Participants need only bring sleeping gear and personal items. Costs range from $170 to $450 per person for an overnight run. Some day trips are available. Seasons and rivers vary with each company.

Most outfitters offer special trips for families with young children. The minimum age requirement for children ranges from 4 to 8. For details, contact the tour operators directly.

The American River Touring Association *Groveland, 800/323-ARTA, 209/962-7873.*

ECHO: The Wilderness Company *Oakland, 800/652-ECHO, 510/652-1600.*

Mariah Wilderness Expeditions *Point Richmond, 800/4-MARIAH, 510/233-2303.* This is California's only woman-owned and operated whitewater raft and wilderness company. Special mother/child trips are scheduled, as well as father/child trips (with both female and male guides). A professional storyteller accompanies all family trips.

O.A.R.S. *Angels Camp, 800/446-7238, 209/736-4677.*

Turtle River Rafting Company *Mt. Shasta, 800/726-3223, 916/926-3223.* Special trips include personal growth workshops.

Whitewater Connection. See page 199.

Whitewater Voyages *El Sobrante, 800/488-RAFT, 510/222-5994.* Several bargain half-price Clean-Up Trips are scheduled each year. Participants get the same amenities as on any other trip, but they are expected to pick up any debris they encounter.

For information on more California river outfitters contact:
California Outdoors *800/552-3625.*

– Pack Trips –

Packing equipment onto horses or mules allows for a much easier and luxurious trek into the wilderness than does backpacking.

Campers need simply to choose the type of pack trip desired. On a spot pack trip the packers will load the animals with gear, take them to a prearranged campsite, unload the gear, and return to the pack station with the pack animals. They will return to repack the gear on the day the campers are scheduled to leave. Campers may either hike or ride on horses to the campsite. If riding, campers usually have a choice of keeping the horses at their campsite or of having the packers take them back out. If keeping them, campers need to arrange in advance for a corral and feed, and they should be experienced with horses. Children who haven't had at least basic riding instruction should not be included on such a trip.

A more rugged trip (where the campsite is moved each day) or an easier trip (with all expenses and a guide included) can also usually be arranged with the packer.

This is not an inexpensive vacation. Prices will vary according to which of the above options are selected. Often there are special rates for children, who must be at least 5 years old. Trips are usually available only in the summer.

For general information and a list of packers contact **Eastern High Sierra Packers Association** *(690 N. Main St., Bishop 93514, 619/873-8405).*

One of the bigger, more organized packers is **Red's Meadow Pack Stations** *(Mammoth Lakes, 800/292-7758, 619/934-2345, in winter 619/873-3928),* which schedules a large number of pack trips each summer. Horses, saddles, and meals are included. Discounts are available for children under 15. Day rides are also available, and occasional cattle and horse drives are scheduled.

Guided pack trips can also be taken with llamas. They're familiar with this chore, having been used for it for over 2,000 years in the Andes. And they are so gentle even a 4-year-old can lead one. For details, contact either **Shasta Llamas** *(P.O. Box 1137, Mt. Shasta 96067, 916/926-3959),* which offers a special family trip, or **Sierra Llama Adventures** *(P.O. Box 478, Diamond Springs 95619, 916/626-6777),* which schedules trips in the Sierra and at Point Reyes National Seashore.

– Camping –

Because there are excellent resources available that provide information on campgrounds, this book mentions only briefly those that fit into the text. For convenience, they are also included in the Index under "campsites." For more complete information, consult the following references:

The California-Nevada Camp Book and its companion maps list camping facilities and fees. They are available free to California State Automobile Association members.

The *California State Parks Guide* is an informative brochure with a map that pinpoints all state parks, reserves, recreation areas, historic parks, and campgrounds. It is available free by calling 800/444-7275.

CAMPSITE RESERVATIONS

Reservations are advisable at most state park campgrounds. For a small service fee, they can be made by phone as early as 8 weeks in advance. For general information on state park campgrounds and to make reservations call 800/444-7275 or 619/452-5956.

– Miscellany –

American Hiking Society *Washington, D.C., 703/385-3252.* This group organizes volunteer vacations using teams of volunteers for work trips in remote back-country areas.

Their annual directory, *Helping Out in the Outdoors,* tells how to get a job as a state park or forest volunteer—hosting a campground, helping improve trails, collecting data on wildlife, or explaining an area's history to visitors. Very few of these jobs reimburse travel and food costs or provide accommodations. Opportunities are available in all 50 states; most are not appropriate for children. For a copy of the directory send $5 to: American Hiking Society, P.O. Box 20160, Washington, D.C. 20041-2160.

American Youth Hostels *San Francisco, 415/863-1444, fax 415/863-3865.* The idea behind hosteling is to save money, so accommodations are simple. Women bunk in one dormitory-style room and men in another. Some hostels have separate rooms for couples and families. Guests provide their own bedding and linens (sleepsets can be rented), and bathrooms and kitchens are shared. All guests are expected to do a chore. Hostels are closed during the day, usually from 9:30 to 4:30, and lights go out at 11 p.m. Fees are low, ranging from $8 to $14 per person per night, and children under 18 with a parent are charged half-price. Hostel members receive a discount at most hostels, as well as a newsletter and handbook of U.S. hostels. Package tours are available. Call for further information and for a free brochure detailing the hostels in Northern California.

Backroads *Berkeley, 800/GO-ACTIVE, 510/527-1555, fax 510/527-1444.* Weekend bicycle trips include the Wine Country, Russian River, and Point Reyes Seashore. Many more trips are scheduled in Southern California, as well as in other states and countries. The emphasis is not on endurance but on getting some exercise. Two or three tour guides accompany bikers, and a support vehicle transports equipment and tired cyclists. Allowing for different ability levels, several routes are available on each trip. Accommodations are in either interesting hotels or comfortable campgrounds, and meals are included. Special family trips are available. Children are welcome on most other trips as well, and they qualify for discounted rates. Walking and cross-country ski trips are also available.

Bed & Breakfast International *San Francisco, 800/872-4500, 415/696-1690, fax 415/696-1699.* This B&B reservations service books travelers into private homes, inns, and vacation homes throughout Northern California. Many of the 300 host homes located in 42 cities are appropriate for children. Though most cannot accommodate more than two people in a room, a discount is given for children staying in a second room. Amenities, of course, vary with the property, and there is a 2-night minimum.

Bike Trek *Davis, 800/827-2453, 916/758-8778.* Sponsored by the American Lung Association of California, these bicycle trips are fully supported and are led by an experienced staff. Vans carry gear, and mechanics are available for repairs. Camping accommodations and both breakfast and dinner are provided. Though prices are reasonable, it is possible for participants to raise pledges for the organization and go along for even less.

Cal Adventures *Department of Recreational Sports, University of California, Berkeley, 510/642-4000.* Adventure trips include rock climbing, backpacking, snow camping, cross-country skiing, river rafting, kayaking, sailing, and wind surfing. Day classes and a special program for children in grades 3 through 12 are also available.

California Academy of Sciences *San Francisco, 415/750-7098.* These nature study trips are led by members of the academy staff. On some trips participants camp out and cook their own meals. On other less strenuous trips, motel lodging and restaurant meals are included. Destinations include Lava Beds National Monument and Santa Cruz Island. The Junior Academy offers similar 1-day and weekend trips for children ages 6 through 16.

Coastwalk *Sebastopol, 707/829-6689.* Since 1983, Coastwalk has organized summer hikes in California's coastal counties. Hikers can sign up for walks ranging from 4 to 6 days, with camping gear shuttled by vehicle. Participants bring and prepare their own food. It is also possible to join a walk for just a day, or for a shorter portion of the trip. The goals of this non-profit organization are to nurture an awareness of the coastal environment and to promote development of a continuous California Coastal Trail.

Green Tortoise *San Francisco, 800/227-4766, 415/821-0803.* Travel on this laid-back alternative bus line is enjoyed at bargain rates. The clientele tends to be the under-30s crowd, but all ages are welcome. Trips are available to almost anywhere on this continent. There are cross-country trips with stops at national parks, and there are river rafting trips to Baja. Usually the scenic route, which is not necessarily the most direct route, is followed. Overnight accommodations are often arranged in hostels, but sometimes riders must bring their own bedding. The jack-of-all-trades bus drivers often organize cookouts, and they get out and fix breakdowns themselves. Passengers have also been known to get out and push when necessary. All in all, a trip on this bus line is really a trip.

Near Escapes *San Francisco, 415/386-8687.* Guided tours of unusual, closer-in destinations are the specialty of this tour company. Past escapes have included Shop Till You Drop (a shopping spree of clothing outlets) and Graveyard Shift: The Colma Cemeteries (a visit to the graves of Wyatt Earp, Levi Strauss, and Benny Bufano, plus a visit to a pet cemetery). Transportation, guide, and snack were included on both these trips. Children are welcome on most trips.

Owner Builder Center *Berkeley, 510/848-6860, fax 510/848-2512.* One-, two-, and three-week camp programs that give participants experience in house-building are held each summer in the Sierra foothills near Grass Valley. Students receive comprehensive classroom instruction one day, then spend the next day putting theory into action. Step-by-step they learn everything from foundations to finishing. But because it's also vacation time, there are rafting trips, barbecues, and softball games, too.

Owner Builder Center Summer Camp

Point Reyes Field Seminars *Point Reyes National Seashore, 415/663-1200.* These interpretive programs are co-sponsored by the National Park Service and the Point Reyes National Seashore Association. Instructors are experts in their fields, and courses include both day trips and overnight trips. Some trips are designed especially for families. Subjects include natural arts and crafts, photography, natural history, bird watching, and Indian culture.

San Damiano Retreat *Danville, 510/837-9141.* A person goes on a retreat to experience solitude and meditate. Retreat weekends here are scheduled for groups of men, women, young adults, engaged couples, married couples, etc.

Sierra Club *San Francisco, 415/923-5630.* Service trips take participants to remote wilderness areas to maintain trails and clean up trash. Nature appreciation trips and special family trips are also scheduled. All trips are 1 to 2 weeks long and are described in the January/February issue of *Sierra Magazine,* which is sent free to all club members. Shorter day and overnight trips are scheduled through the local chapter *(510/653-6127).*

Slide Ranch *Muir Beach, 415/381-6155.* Perched dramatically on the ocean side of Highway 1 near Muir Beach, this coastal farm offers the city-slicker a chance to get back to the land . . . a chance to learn about a self-sustaining rural lifestyle through exposure to frontier arts . . . a chance to slow the pace. During Family Days programs, children and adults learn together about things like cheese-making, composting, and papermaking. Though the program varies according to the season and the ages of participants, a typical day begins with smiling staff members greeting visitors in a fragrant grove of eucalyptus. A visit to the sheep pen usually follows—giving children the chance to "pet a four-legged sweater." Then, turning the tables, children who really just want to be kids can don a sheep-skin and wander disguised among the goats—who tend to stare quizzically and then run. A picnic lunch, nature walk, and visit inside the chicken pen round out this family experience. In addition to these day-long programs, the ranch offers Family Overnights in which participants spend the night in tents overlooking the ocean.

University Extension and Research Programs. Many state colleges and universities have travel/study programs.

    San Jose State University offers a program of family vacations through their Extension Division *(408/924-2625).*

    The **University of California** sponsors a program of research expeditions *(510/642-6586).* These trips are not appropriate for children under 16.

Wellspring Renewal Center *Philo, 707/895-3893.* Founded in 1979 as an interfaith center, this facility offers programs focused on deepening spirituality and engendering creativity. Regularly scheduled programs include planting and harvesting weekends, meditation and healing retreats, an arts and crafts week, and storytelling workshops. A variety of lodging is available—lodge rooms, both rustic and improved cabins, and a campground at which guests may either pitch their own tent or rent a tepee or tent cabin. Prices vary, and children ages 2 through 15 are half-price. Meals, which feature mostly vegetarian entrees, are available at an additional charge. Individuals, families, and groups are welcome.

Appendixes

APPENDIX I

– Traveling With Children –

Just because you have kids doesn't mean you have to stop having fun. Or traveling. But if you want to travel with your kids and have fun too, you are going to have to do some pre-planning. It is crucial for a successful trip.

One of the most important things to find out in advance is whether the lodging facility you plan to say at welcomes children. Though it is actually illegal in California to prohibit children, I think we parents all know we will have a better time if the management likes them.

It is also a good idea to plan a daily itinerary. But don't pack it too tightly. Leave time for simple pleasures such as napping and slurping ice cream cones. On longer trips allow for some "separation" time: adults going their separate ways, each with one child; adults taking turns staying with the kids while one gets free time; etc.

You might also consider doing what the military daddy did in the movie *The Great Santini*. He moved his family out for a car trip in the middle of the night. It could work. Traffic is lighter then, and the kids just might sleep. However, the Great Santini didn't have to deal with carseat laws and the accompanying physical restrictions.

Planning Trips

• Write or call the Chamber of Commerce or Visitors Bureau in the area you plan to visit. Ask for specific recommendations for families, and request pertinent literature.

• Have your children help pick a destination and plan the trip. Look at maps together. (You may want to consider joining the California State Automobile Association, which offers excellent maps and services to members.) Create a flexible travel schedule. Allow sufficient travel time between destinations so that you can make spontaneous exploration stops along the way.

• Establish guidelines on spending money, snacks, bedtime, TV use, etc.

• Plan to start the trip early in the morning and to arrive at your destination early in the day, so you will have time to relax.

283

- When you arrive, read again the appropriate sections in this book to familiarize yourself with local facilities. Check the Yellow Pages in the telephone book for further information on things to do:

babysitting service	public swimming pools/plunges
bicycle rentals	restaurants
horseback riding/stable	skating rinks

Also check the local newspapers and tourist magazines for current special events and activities.

- Hang a detailed map of California on a wall in your home. Use colored push-pins or flags to mark places you have visited. Children especially enjoy doing this.

LODGING RESERVATIONS

- To avoid disappointment and a frantic, last-minute search for anything—and the possiblity of finding nothing—make advance reservations at motels and campgrounds. Inquire about special rates, discounts for automobile club members, and packages. Reservations sometimes also save you money, because inexpensive rooms often are reserved first, leaving the expensive (albeit usually more luxurious) rooms for last-minute arrivals. Always ask for a written confirmation. Take it along as proof of your reservation. If you must cancel, do so as soon as possible. A complete refund is usually available with at least 48 hours notice.

C.T.M.'s Rule of the Road: *The tendency for some family member to get sick increases in direct proportion to the approach of a trip. This is even more likely if you've paid a non-refundable deposit on accommodations.*

- If you require a crib, reserve one at the time you make your room reservation. Otherwise, you may find none available when you arrive. Better yet, purchase a portable crib to use when traveling. Or make one yourself. A pattern for making a particularly nice fabric and wood crib appears in *Sunset* magazine (May 1983; page 182).

- If your child still wets, take along a plastic sheet to protect the bed.

- Children are sometimes allowed to sleep on the floor of their parents' room at no charge. If you want to do this, you'll need to take along sleeping bags for them. Inquire in advance about the lodging's policy.

- On longer trips, an occasional splurge on two rooms, or a suite, can be a treat for everyone—especially if you have two or more older children. Also consider all-suite hotels and condominiums.

PACKING

- Make a checklist of all the items you need to gather or buy for your trip. For instance, if you are going to a beach or river area in the summer, you will want to consider taking along the following items:

swimsuit	sand toys
towels	inner tubes
suntan lotion	sandals/tennis shoes
beach blanket	air mattress
back rest	beach ball
sun umbrella	

If you do forget something, most of the destinations mentioned in this book are near a store where you can buy emergency replacements.

• Pack one outfit per day per child in separate plastic zip-lock bags. It is helpful if each child can have their own suitcase.

• If you have a toddler, pack electrical outlet covers and a safety gate. You might also want to pack a night light.

• Take along travelers' checks or adequate cash. Surprisingly, some lodging and dining facilities in vacation areas do not accept either out-of-town checks or credit cards.

Helpful Hints In The Car

Traveling anywhere in a car with children can be a trying experience for everyone concerned. Even short trips can be exhausting and leave everyone in real *need* of a vacation. (Does anyone know where I can purchase the kind of taxi that has bulletproof, soundproof glass separating the parents from the kids—I mean the driver from the passengers?)

Here are some suggestions on how to make a family car trip a more pleasurable experience.

SAFETY AND COMFORT

• California residents are required by law to use a car seat for children who are under age 4 or who weigh less than 40 pounds. It is mandatory that the driver and *all* passengers wear seat belts. (For detailed information on the importance of car seats and brand recommendations, refer to *Consumer Reports* at your library.) A fabric liner makes a car seat easier to clean and protects a child from the danger of hot plastic.

• Use a luggage rack to handle trunk overflow. For comfort, leave as much space as possible in the passenger section.

• Take along blankets and pillows for napping. Pillows are also wonderful as a lap tray, an arm rest, and as a divider between siblings. Be sure to pack one pillow per child.

• Buy some new towels for your bathroom, and put the old ones in the trunk of your car. They make good covers for hot car seats and can be used in countless other ways: rolled up as a pillow, for mopping up spills, etc.

• Removable screens for the car's windows keep the sun off baby and out of eyes.

- Keep a first-aid kit in your trunk. Stock it with:

bandages	children's aspirin and aspirin substitute
antiseptic	thermometer
safety pins	scissors
tweezers	adhesive tape
a roller bandage	gauze pads
cotton swabs	soap
washcloth	flashlight
sunscreen	a compact sewing kit
a few dimes for emergency phone calls	

These items will fit inside a large, empty coffee can or in an old lunchbox.

- Keep a package of medium-size self-locking plastic bags in your car's trunk. These are handy for holding many things: messy items such as bibs, diapers, and wet bathing suits; items children collect; etc.

FOOD

- A quick, inexpensive breakfast stop at a donut shop can help you get on the road fast.

- Pack a supply of non-messy snacks for the road. Some ideas:

fruit rolls	dried apple rings
raisins	granola bars
cheese	apples
animal crackers	bananas
fig newtons	small boxes of dry cereal
small cans or boxes of juice	

- You might want to pack these snacks in a separate lunch box or shoe box for each child. Let them eat as they are hungry.

- Provide the kids with a bag of Cheerios or Froot Loops and some dental floss for stringing edible necklaces. They will love you, and their dentist will, too.

- For clean-ups, pack moist towelettes. Or make your own by putting either damp paper towels or a damp washcloth in a plastic bag or covered container.

- Consider packing only water for drinks. When spilled, it isn't sticky. A fun idea for older children is to recycle those commercial plastic containers that resemble lemons and limes. Empty the citrus juice, remove the insert (an ice pick helps), rinse, and fill with water. Children can then squirt drinks into their mouths with a minimum of mess and bother. Another idea is to give each child their own small thermos of water. Or give each a collapsible cup to use for drinks from the family thermos. Many years ago I bought a stainless steel thermos for our family car trips. It has turned out to be a wise investment.

- For long trips, stock an ice chest with milk and fruit and other nutritious, but perishable, foods.

- Avoid eating meals in the car. Though it saves time, eating in offers no chance to stretch, and it's very messy.

- Picnic when possible. After the cramped experience of a car ride, a restaurant can sometimes feel too confining. Gas station attendants can be helpful in providing directions to a local park with a playground.

- Bring a molded plastic bib for babies. Such a bib is especially wonderful for catching ice cream drips. To clean it, all you have to do is wipe or rinse.

- Make disposable bibs by using an old "sweater guard" to hold a table napkin around baby's neck.

- A bottle warmer that plugs into the car's cigarette lighter can be useful when traveling with a baby.

- For a baby no longer on formula but still on a bottle, try putting 1/3 cup (2-2/3 ounces) of powdered milk in a baby bottle. When milk is needed, add water to make 8 ounces and shake. (This eliminates the need for refrigeration and is handy any time you are away from home.)

ENTERTAINMENT

- Turn your children into navigators. Give each their own map and let them figure out how far it is to the next town. Give them a wide felt-tip highlighter pen to trace the route as you go.

- To help younger children deal with distances, string a number of Cheerios or Froot Loops onto a string. At specific intervals (5 miles, 10 miles, 50 miles) let them take one off and eat it. Arrange it so that when they eat the last one, you're there.

- Provide each child with a notepad to use as a trip diary. Encourage them to make entries each day. Older children can do this alone. For younger children, you can write down what they dictate. Have crayons available for illustrations. If you have an instant print camera, let each child take a few pictures each day to illustrate their diary.

- Provide each child with a portable tape player. My family enjoys listening together to story tapes. But when one of our children turns on the music in our car, they also put on their earphones. If you have the kind of player that also records, it is fun to record a travel diary as you go.

- Colorforms plastic cutouts are fun for younger children. They adhere easily to the passenger's side window and leave no marks.

- Have a few wrapped presents on hand to use for distracting children during restless times. Select items that make good additions to the goodie bag (see page 289). If they're learning to tell time and have their own watch, consider writing specific instructions such as, "Open at 10:42."

- Store games and miscellaneous items in a shoebag hung on the back of the front seat or on the car door.

- Keep a travel game book in the glove compartment. (One especially good one is *Miles of Smiles: 101 Great Car Games & Activities*. I should know—it was written by me! For ordering information, see page 321.) Use it only when necessary. When everyone is happy, leave well enough alone.

REST STOPS

• Make a rest stop every few hours or as the situation dictates. This is a good time to eat, to enjoy a sightseeing side trip, or to let children run off some pent-up energy in a park.

• Organize a scavenger hunt during a park stop or after a picnic. Give each child a list of items (pine cone, twig shaped like a letter, something from an animal, two different leaves, etc.) and see who can find the most in a given amount of time. Have a prize for all participants.

• Keep an inflatable beach ball in your trunk. When you stop, blow it up and use it to encourage active movement. Other good items to have along for rest stops:

bubbles	chalk (for hopscotch)
jump rope	jacks
frisbee	

• Buy gas in small quantities. Never fill the tank unless you are driving in desolate areas. This will require you to stop more frequently, giving passengers time to stretch, get drinks, and visit the restroom.

WHEN THINGS DEGENERATE

As Erma Bombeck once said, "Families that play together get on each others nerves," so . . .

• Try the "mad bag/glad bag" trick. Give each child a bag filled with nickels or dimes at the beginning of the trip. (It seems pennies are no longer exciting.) Mom and dad begin the trip with an empty bag. When a child has been deemed naughty, they must give up a coin to the parents' bag. If you are a liberated parent, you can let it work the other way, too. Any coins left in the children's bag at the end of the trip are theirs to keep. This works even better with dollars.

• Adults take turns driving. The non-driving adult sits in the back seat with one (two, three . . .) child while the other child sits in the front seat with the driver. This helps keep squabbles to a minimum and also gives the back-seat parent and child a chance to spend some time together. And, even though many adults will not jump at the chance to sit in the back seat, most children will jump at the chance to sit in the front seat.

• I've heard tell of one desperate parent who keeps a fly swatter with her in the front seat. It allows her to easily reach a troublemaker in the back seat.

• When all else fails, travel in a motorcycle with a sidebucket. Daddy and one kid sit on the cycle; mommy and another sit in the bucket. This may be a very unsafe and inconvenient form of travel, but you won't hear a word.

If you ever find yourself wondering why you brought the kids along, keep in mind that they are very useful in figuring out how to turn strange TVs on and off.

And above all remember, as someone once observed, "Happiness is a journey, not a destination."

Hints For When You're There

MOTEL GAMES

What *will* you do when you finally arrive at the motel and the kids aren't ready to go to sleep? If there is a pool, a swim can be refreshing, and a TV can keep them occupied for awhile. But what will you do when you're all in the room and the kids are *bored?*

Try these special games that everyone in the family can enjoy together:

• **Card Games.** Keep a deck of cards in your car's glove compartment. They come in very handy to build card houses. They are also great for tossing into a trash basket. And, of course, you can always play the more standard card games with them.

• **Hide the Ashtray.** It's good for a few minutes of diversion. To prolong the activity, hide several ashtrays.

• **Wastebasket-ball**. Using a trash can for a hoop, players take turns tossing socks (rolled into balls). The trash basket can be left on the floor, or higher up on a desk or dresser. Use a belt to make a line behind which players must stand when tossing.

• **Bathtub Cups.** Give each child two plastic or paper cups from the room's medicine cabinet. Let them pour water back and forth, back and forth, back and forth.

• **Bubble Bath.** Pack along a bottle of bubbles. Bring it out at bathtime and let them blow, let them blow, let them blow.

POST CARD SOUVENIRS

Post cards make an inexpensive souvenir. Let your children select a few at each destination. Encourage your children to:

• Use them to illustrate their trip diaries.

• Keep them as a collection, held together with a rubber band or ribbon.

• Write diary entries on the back and keep a post card diary.

• Keep a post card diary. Then have them send each post card to themselves as you travel so that they will have mail when they get home.

• Write a post card to a friend. For an instant post card puzzle, cut it up and send it in an envelope.

Or assign each of the kids a number of relatives to send post cards to. When the natives get restless in the condo, notice that it's time for them to write post cards.

Here's a trick I used at Disneyland. Buy a post card depicting your child's favorite Disney character. Compose a message from the character and sign their name. Mail it to your home before you leave. My daughter had stardust in her eyes as she told people how her friend Minnie had sent her a card from Disneyland. You may be able to think of creative adaptations.

AT THE BEACH
• To help get all your gear from the car to the beach, consider using a molded plastic sled (borrowed from your winter gear). Pack everything in the sled and drag it along the sand to your chosen spot. Filled with a little water, it also makes a great place for a baby to splash and play safely.

• Remove the floor from an old playpen and use it to corral a toddler at the beach. Or turn your regular one upside down to provide shade.

• When you're ready to leave, have the kids fill their buckets with water and carry them back to the car for rinsing sandy feet.

The Goodie Bag

A good way to keep children occupied and happy on a car trip is to provide each with his own goodie bag. For the bag itself you might use an old purse, a recycled lunch box, a backpack (especially good for plane trips), a small basket, a shopping bag, a small suitcase, a plastic bucket, or a covered metal cake pan. Whichever container you choose, be sure to have a separate one for each child, and try to fill them with the same items (or equivalent items if their interests differ). Labeling the contents with each child's name will avoid some conflict. A flat, hard container makes a good foundation for writing and coloring. Things you might put inside include:

pads of paper	play dough
scotch tape	small scraps of colored paper
colored pencils	gummed paper shapes
washable felt pens	stickers
midget cars	magic slate
finger puppets	eraser
little people toys	magnetic games
car games	shoestring sewing cards
workbook	magnifying glass
pencil box	photo viewer toy
blunt scissors	small chalkboard and chalk
card games	felt board and shapes
non-melting crayons	glue stick
coloring books	etch-a-sketch toy
pipe cleaners	plastic sponge puzzle
snap-lock beads	plastic bags to hold collectibles
paper dolls	spiral notebook
origami paper	story books

The items you choose to put in the goodie bag will depend on your child's age. Be sure to keep the bag stocked and ready to go, and keep your eyes open for new items to unveil on future trips. For younger children, don't forget to bring along their lovies—teddy bear, blanket, etc.

Have older children shop with you for new goodie bag items a few days before the trip. The anticipation of playing with the newly selected items will work in your favor.

I think you will find the goodie bag so useful that you will begin using it in other ways—on a rainy day, when your children are sick, when you leave them with a babysitter, when you dine out in a restaurant.

PICNIC GOODIE BAG

I like to stop at a delicatessen for picnic fare. To help make our picnics more comfortable, I always keep in the trunk of our car: a picnic blanket, a day pack (for those picnic spots that require a hike to reach), and a plastic pull-string bag stocked with paper plates, cups, napkins, plastic eating utensils, straws, a can opener, and a corkscrew.

MUSICAL GOODIE BAG

The following items provide family fun by the campfire or fireplace and can be purchased inexpensively in most music shops:

slide whistle	plastic flute
kazoo	whistle
small tambourine	wooden rhythm blocks
jew's-harp	ratchet
gongs	rasps
bells	harmonica
cymbals	

BEACH PLAY GOODIE BAG

Many of these items can be gathered from your kitchen. Remember to avoid glass. I like to store them all in one big plastic bucket, which I save especially for trips to the water.

spray bottle	bucket
spatula	funnel
scoop	cookie cutters
pastry brush	strainer
plastic cups	pancake turner
measuring spoons	

APPENDIX II

– Traveling With Teens –

Since my oldest child has become a teenager, I've often lamented the trials of traveling with one. Of course, I had trials even before he was a teen. Now I just have different ones. (Did you know that "teen" is a Scottish word for grief?)

I've found that the very best solution to the problem is to let him stay home. This really does work best for everyone concerned. I like him to stay with a friend or relative when he doesn't accompany us, and I only allow this option for weekend trips. (Whatever you do, don't leave them home alone. If you do consider leaving them in your home alone, be sure to see the movie *Risky Business.* That should stop you in your tracks!) For longer family vacations, I still insist he come with us. I believe that traveling together strengthens family bonds, and that it is important that we have these experiences together. (Be careful about letting teens stay with someone else for long periods while you vacation without them. A side effect can be that a letting-up on your rules by the temporary caretaker can make it difficult to re-establish order when you return.)

Since I have another younger child who is still fairly enthused about going places and doing things with her parents, I don't feel a void when the teen is not with us. I find, instead, that we have a much more enjoyable time, and the physical void that occurs can be filled with extra trip paraphernalia. And on those now rarer occasions when he does accompany us, we all consider it a special treat.

If you are able to get your teen to accompany you on a trip, don't expect them to wax enthusiastic as well. You've heard the old saying, "You can lead a horse to water, but you can't make him drink." Teenagers are a lot like horses.

Other suggestions include:

• Let them invite a friend along.

• Plan a trip somewhere they desperately want to go.

• Plan a one-parent, one-child trip—perhaps a river rafting trip or a backpacking expedition.

• Put them in charge of something they enjoy: taking photographs, planning several outings, preparing a music tape for the trip, etc. (As our children reach adolescence, it is important that we parents have carrots of hope dangled before us. So I want you to know that my own son once introduced the family to Paul Simon's *Graceland* album as we drove to Los Angeles. We all loved it, and his choosing it reflected his consideration of the family's mutual tastes.)

• My teen enjoys staying behind in our room while we adults go out to dinner. He especially enjoys this when he can watch a movie on cable TV and/or order from room service. Sometimes we hire him to babysit for his younger sister, which is a real win-win situation: He earns extra trip money, and we adults get a break.

• Use the ultimate bribe: Let them drive.

– Dressing Kids For Snow –

The following is a comfortable, warm way to dress children for the snow. Most of the ideas work for adults as well. You probably have many of the items on hand. Those items that need to be purchased make excellent presents for Christmas or Hanukkah—both of which are celebrated at the beginning of the winter season.

Dress children in thermal underwear, which afterwards can be used for pajamas. Then put on a cotton turtleneck to keep out drafts. On top of that put a wool or wool-blend pullover sweater and either insulated bib-front water-repellant pants or regular overalls treated with a water-repellant spray. Top it off with their regular winter jacket. For insulation use two layers of socks: a thin cotton liner and a thicker wool pair—unribbed to avoid blisters. Leg-warmers, worn over or under pants, add an extra layer of warmth.

On their heads, put a wool hat that can be pulled down over the ears (20 to 30 percent of body heat is lost through uncovered heads). A hat that converts to a face mask is particularly nice on windy days. For neck warmth use a square bandana; wool is best but cotton is better than nothing. (Avoid long neck scarves as they have been known to become entangled in lift equipment. Remember what happened to Isadora Duncan.) Sunglasses with a safety strap or goggles are necessary to cut the glare.

Before letting them loose, zip into their pockets: sun-block lotion, chapstick, loose change for a snack, tissues, an identification slip (with name and address or location of parents), and perhaps a box of raisins or a candy bar for a snack.

The best places to find good winter clothing for children include Sears, REI Co-op *(call 800/426-4840 for a free catalogue)*, and Patagonia *(call 800/638-6464 for a free catalogue)*.

Helpful Hints

• Borrow clothing from friends or relatives until it is determined what is needed.

• To avoid loss of children's gloves or mittens, thread a length of elastic or thick yarn through their jacket sleeves and pin mittens to the ends.

• A warm pair of water-proof boots for after-skiing is useful. Avoid rubber as it gets very cold. Good-looking, popular, and warm "moon boots" can be purchased inexpensively.

Never let children ski alone. Lifts can be very dangerous without proper supervision. If time is desired to ski without children, consider signing them up for lessons in the morning and then spending the afternoon skiing together. Another alternative is the all-day childcare and ski schools available at many resorts.

APPENDIX IV

– Condominium Rentals –

Condominiums are a good choice for family lodging, especially when the stay is for longer than a weekend. Prices are usually competitive with motels, and you get additional space in the form of extra bedrooms, a living room, and a kitchen.

Vacation money can be stretched by making use of the kitchen to prepare breakfast and to put together a picnic lunch. Barbecues, which are sometimes provided, can make cooking the evening meal more fun. Occasional meals out then become more affordable.

Many condo complexes offer shared recreational facilities such as a pool, a hot tub, and tennis courts. They also usually have appreciated amenities such as laundry facilities and fireplaces. In the winter, packages with nearby ski resorts are often available.

Sharing a condo with another family can cut expenses even further. Pooling monies might allow a choicer property. Cooking and shopping chores can be shared, and each couple can get a night out by taking turns babysitting. Be sure, though, to get it clear what happens if one family cancels out after the deposit is paid.

The reservation numbers listed in this book are usually for an owners' rental service. Because maid service and office expenses have to be covered, the units usually cost more than when rented directly from the owner. Though money can often be saved when renting directly from the owner, it usually is required that the unit be cleaned by the renter before leaving.

APPENDIX V

– Superlative Quiz –

Superlatives are words that refer to something that is superior to, or excels over, all others. How many of these superlative Northern California sights can you name?

1. Which winery music series is the **oldest** in the U.S., as well as the **largest** in the world? (see page 5.)
2. Where can you see the **largest collection** of Japanese bamboo in the western world. (See page 7.)
3. Which is California's **oldest** state park? (see page 10.)
4. Where is the **tallest** covered bridge in the U.S.? (See page 10.)
5. Where is the **only** elephant seal rookery on the U.S. mainland? (See page 16.)

6. Where can you see the **largest** antique plane fly-in and air show held on the West Coast? (See page 18.)
7. Which amusement park is the **oldest** in California and is also home to the **largest** classic carousel in Northern California? (See page 20.)
8. Which town was the the state's **first** seaside resort and is, as well, the **only** town in the U.S. to host an annual Begonia Festival? (See page 24.)
9. Which was the **first** condominium complex in California? (See page 24.)
10. Who was California's **first** artichoke queen? (See page 27.)
11. Which city annual hosts the **oldest** continuously presented jazz festival in the country? (See page 27.)
12. Where is the world's **tallest** aquarium exhibit tank? (see page 32.)
13. Where is the **oldest** continuously operating lighthouse on the Pacific Coast? (See page 38.)
14. Which park has been described as "the **greatest** meeting of land and water in the world?" (See page 45.)
15. Where can you play chess on **one of the two largest** chess boards in the U.S.? (See page 59.)
16. In what state park is the world's **third largest** bird sanctuary? (See page 59.)
17. Which shop has the **largest** selection of sea shells on the West Coast? (See page 59.)
18. What forest did naturalist John Muir deem "the **best** tree lover's monument in . . . all the world"? (See page 62.)
19. Where have winds been recorded blowing at the **highest rate** in the continental U.S.? (See page 66.)
20. Where is the world's **largest** salmon barbecue held each year? (See page 79.)
21. Where is the **largest** town square in the state? (See page 89.)
22. Which winery is California's **oldest**? (See page 91.)
23. Which California winery has been owned continuously by the same family for the **longest** of any in the U.S.? (See page 92.)
24. Where can you see the world's largest collection of carved oak wine casks? (See page 92.)
25. Which resort has the **largest** tennis complex in Northern California? (See page 95.)
26. Which winery produced the country's **first** designated Meritage wine? (See page 96.)
27. Which California winery has the **most extensive** system of wine-aging caves in the U.S.? (See page 99.)
28. Which winery deli claims to have the **largest** selection of international cheeses on the West Coast? (See page 106.)
29. Which lake is California's **largest**? (See page 112.)
30. Which county has the **cleanest** air in the state? (See page 113.)
31. Which lake is reputed to be the **best** bass fishing spot in the West? (See page 115.)
32. Where is the **first** winery tasting room north of San Francisco? (See page 119.)
33. Which winery is the **only one** in the country making Ehrenfelser wine, which is the **only** wine in the country produced in a blue bottle? (See page 119.)

34. Where is the **oldest** and **largest** gathering of the clans, ouside of Scotland, held each year? (See page 120.)
35. Where can you find the **largest** selection of *Peanuts* cartoon strip merchandise in the world? (See page 123.)
36. Which is the **only** family-owned and -operated winery/restaurant in the state? (See page 128.)
37. Which winery is the nation's **oldest** producer of methode champenoise champagne? (See page 129.)
38. Which winery is the **only one** in the country that produces the Cinsault varietal? (See page 135.)
39. Which brewpub was the **first** to open in California after Prohibition? (See page 135.)
40. Which resort has the **only** naturally carbonated mineral baths in North America? (See page 136.)
41. Which mansion is said to be the **most** photographed house in the U.S.? (See page 141.)
42. Which California boat has the **smallest** licensed bar in the state and is the **oldest** operating passenger vessel in the U.S.? (See page 142.)
43. What is the **most** westerly point on the continental U.S.? (See page 143.)
44. What is the world's **largest** grove of virgin redwoods? (See page 145.)
45. Which national park contains the world's **tallest** tree, as well as the world's **second, third, and fifth tallest** trees? (See page 146.)
46. Which city is California's **oldest**? (See page 149.)
47. Which is the **largest** children's museum in the West? (See page 150.)
48. Where is the world's **largest** indoor movie screen? (See page 151.)
49. What establishment was the **first** place west of Detroit to serve ice cream and sodas? (See page 152.)
50. Which is the **oldest** winemaking family in the country? (See page 152.)
51. Where are the **fastest** waterslides this side of the Rockies? (See page 153.)
52. Which museum has the **largest** exhibit of Egyptian, Babylonian, and Assyrian artifacts on the West Coast? (See page 153.)
53. Which flea market is the world's **largest**? (See page 153.)
54. Which was the world's **first** motel? (See page 161.)
55. What is the **largest** piece of exposed granite in the world? (See page 166.)
56. Which falls is the **highest** in North America? (See page 166.)
57. What is the **longest** and **oldest** covered bridge west of the Mississippi? (See page 167.)
58. Which is the state's **oldest** resort hotel? (See page 169.)
59. Which stable has the **largest** public riding stock in the world? (See page 172.)
60. What is the **largest** unrestored ghost town in the West? (See page 173.)
61. Which national park was California's **first**, and is also the country's **second oldest**? (See page 175.)
62. What is the **largest** living thing in the world? (See page 175.)
63. Which is the **tallest** mountain in the U.S., not counting Alaska? (See page 175.)
64. Which is the **deepest** canyon in the U.S.? (See page 177.)
65. Which hotel dining room has the **largest** selection of Gold Country wines available anywhere? (See page 180.)

66. Which is the **longest** continually operating commercial cavern in the state? (See page 186.)
67. Which cavern has the **largest** public chamber in California? (See page 186.)
68. Where were the **oldest** human remains in the U.S. found? (See page 186.)
69. Which hotel claims to be the **oldest** in continuous operation in California? (See page 190.)
70. Which town opened the state's **first** library? (See page 193.)
71. Which was the **first** little theater group to form in California? (See page 195.)
72. What is the **smallest** incorporated city in the state? (See page 195.)
73. Which bar is said to be the **oldest** continuously operating saloon in the Gold Country? (See page 202.)
74. Which is the **longest** single-span wood-covered bridge in the world? (See page 203.)
75. Which was once the **largest** and **richest** hard rock mine in the state? (See page 203.)
76. Which was the state's **first** orphanage for non-Indian children? (See page 204.)
77. Where is the **largest** operational Cornish pump in the country on display? (See page 204.)
78. Which is the **only** museum in the world dedicated to displaying Chinese hardwood furniture from the Ming and early Qing dynasties? (See page 204.)
79. Which is the **best** preserved and restored small city in the state? (See page 205.)
80. Which is the **oldest** continuously operating hotel west of the Rockies? (See page 205.)
81. Which is the **oldest** theater building in California? (See page 208.)
82. In the 1800s, where was the **largest** hydraulic gold mining operation? (See page 209.)
83. Where is the **foremost** pear growing area in the country? (See page 212.)
84. Where is the **first** cantilever bridge built west of the Mississipppi? (See page 213.)
85. Which town is the **only** one in the country that was built entirely by and for Chinese immigrants? (See page 213.)
86. Which bar/restaurant has its walls lined with the world's **largest** collection of big game trophies? (See page 215.)
87. What is the world's **largest** traditional jazz festival? (See page 218.)
88. What is the **oldest** state fair in the West and the **largest** agricultural fair in the U.S.? (See page 218.)
89. Where is the **largest** wave pool in Northern California and the **highest** waterslides in the West? (See page 218.)
90. Where can you tour the world's **largest** almond processing plant? (See page 222.)
91. What was the **largest** restoration project in the history of the country? (See page 222.)
92. What is the **oldest** public art museum west of the Mississippi? (See page 222.)
93. What is the **only** tent theater west of the Mississippi? (See page 223.)
94. Where did the country's **first** transcontinental railroad start? (See page 223.)
95. What is the **largest** historic preservation project in the West? (See page 223.)

96. What is the **largest** interpretive railroad museum in North America? (See page 223.)
97. Where is the **tallest** free-standing fiberglass flagpole in the country? (See page 224.)
98. Where is the **only** surviving American 1934 Corben Superace with a Model A engine on display? (See page 225.)
99. Which is the **oldest** restored fort in the West? (See page 225.)
100. Where is the **most complete** antique Ford collection in the world displayed? (See page 225.)
101. What is the **largest** and **deepest** Alpine lake in North America? (See page 227.)
102. Where is the **largest** captive wolf pack in Northern California? (See page 229.)
103. Which casino holds the **first** McDonald's ever built in a casino? (See page 232.)
104. Which is the world's **largest** free-pull slot machine? (See page 232.)
105. Which casino showroom is the **only** mini-showroom in the world? (See page 234.)
106. Where is the world's **largest** collection of antique farm equipment? (See page 242.)
107. Which mountain is the **largest** plug dome volcano in the world? (See page 247.)
108. Which is the **only** dude ranch located within a national park? (See page 247.)
109. Where was the **only** major Indian war fought in California? (See page 250.)
110. Where is the **densest** concentration of bald eagles in the U.S., south of Alaska? (See page 251.)
111. Which is the **oldest** continuously used Chinese temple in the state? (See page 252.)
112. What is the **largest** winter carnival in the West? (See page 261.)
113. Which was the **first** cross-country track system in the U.S.? (See page 262.)
114. Which ski resort had the **first** chairlift in the state? (See page 262.)
115. What is the **largest** sled dog races in the West? (See page 263.)
116. Which is California's **first**, and **oldest**, organized ski area? (See page 264.)
117. What is the **oldest** cross-country ski school on the West Coast? (See page 265.)

Annual Events

JANUARY
AT&T Pebble Beach National Pro-Am, Pebble Beach

MARCH
Camellia Festival, Sacramento
Daffodil Hill, Volcano
Easter Egg Hunt, Roaring Camp & Big Trees Narrow-Gauge Railroad, Felton
Family Ski Challenge, Tahoe City
Russian River Wine Road Barrel Tasting
Snowfest, North Lake Tahoe
Slug Fest, Guerneville
Victorian Easter Parade and Egg Hunt, Columbia

APRIL
Adobe House Tour, Monterey
Apple Blossom Festival, Sebastopol
Butter & Egg Days, Petaluma
Fisherman's Festival, Bodega Bay
International Teddy Bear Convention, Nevada City
South Shasta Model Railroad, Gerber
Steam Donkey Days, Fort Humboldt State Historic Park, Eureka
Victorian Home Tour, Pacific Grove
Wildflower Show, Pacific Grove

MAY
Chamarita, Half Moon Bay
Fireman's Muster, Columbia
Jumping Frog Jubilee, Angels Camp
Living History Day, Adobe State Historic Park, Petaluma
Sacramento Jazz Jubilee
Sheep Shearing/Kids Day, Abode State Historic Park, Petaluma
West Coast Antique Fly-In and Air Show, Watsonville
World Championship Great Arcata to Ferndale Cross Country
    Kinetic Sculpture Race

JUNE
Bluegrass Festival, Grass Valley
Great Isleton Crawdad Festival, Isleton
Open House, Dry Creek Vineyard, Healdsburg
Napa Valley Wine Auction, Rutherford
Paul Masson Summer Series, Saratoga
Reenactment of Pony Express, Pollock Pines

Summer Concert Series, Lakeport and Clearlake
Ugly Dog Contest, Petaluma

JULY
American Pops Concert and Fireworks Display, Mirassou Winery, San Jose
Bohemian Grove, Russian River area
Cabrillo Music Festival, Santa Cruz
California Rodeo, Salinas
California Wine Tasting Championships, Philo
Carmel Bach Festival
Early Days at San Juan Bautista
4th of July Parade, Nevada City
Italian Picnic, Plymouth
Kentucky Mine Concert Series, Sierra City
Mendocino Music Festival
Monterey Scottish Festival and Highland Games
Music from Bear Valley
Music at Sand Harbor, Lake Tahoe
Old Adobe Day Fiesta, Adobe State Historic Park, Petaluma
Pear Fair, Courtland
Robert Mondavi Summer Festival, Oakville
World Pillow Fighting Championship, Kenwood
World's Largest Salmon Barbecue, Fort Bragg

AUGUST
Blackberry Festival, Clearlake
California State Fair, Sacramento
Concours d'Elegance, Pebble Beach
Gravenstein Apple Fair, Sebastopol
Great Gatsby Festival, Tallic Historic Site, South Lake Tahoe
Historic Automobile Races, Monterey-Salinas
International Calamari Festival, India Joze Restaurant, Santa Cruz
Petaluma River Festival
Petaluma Summer Music Festival
Shakespeare at Sand Harbor, North Lake Tahoe
Steinbeck Festival, Salinas

SEPTEMBER
Antique Apple Tasting, Healdsburg
Apple Hill, Placerville
Begonia Festival, Capitola
"Big Time" Miwok Celebration, Pine Grove
Castroville Artichoke Festival, Castroville
Constitution Day Parade, Nevada City
Fiesta, Carmel Mission
Great Sand Castle Contest, Carmel

OCTOBER
Art and Pumpkin Festival, Half Moon Bay
autumn colors, Hope Valley
Brussels Sprout Festival, Santa Cruz
Butterfly Parade, Pacific Grove
fall colors, Nevada City
Fall Colors Festival, Geyserville
Ghost Trains, Western Railroad Museum, Suisun City
Grand Prix, Monterey-Salinas
Great Scarecrow Contest, The Nut Tree, Vacaville
Harvest Festival, Konocti Winery, Kelseyville
Halloween Tours, Winchester Mystery House, San Jose
Kokanee Salmon Festival, Lake Tahoe Visitor Center
Pumpkin Festival, Westside Farms, Healdsburg
Wrist Wrestling Contest, Petaluma

NOVEMBER
Monterey Jazz Festival
Russian River Jazz Festival, Guerneville
Scottish Gathering and Games, Santa Rosa
Valley of the Moon Vintage Festival, Sonoma
Vintners Holidays, Yosemite National Park

DECEMBER
A Miner's Christmas, Columbia
Bracebridge Dinner, Yosemite National Park
Caravan to Nation's Christmas Tree, Kings Canyon National Park
Christmas at the Castle, San Simeon
Christmas in the Adobes and La Posada, Monterey
Christmas Show, Redwood Empire Ice Area, Santa Rosa
Cornish Christmas Street Faire, Grass Valley
La Posada and La Virgin del Tepeyac, San Juan Bautista
Santa Claus Specials, Western Railway Museum, Suisun City
Victorian Christmas, Nevada City

Categorical Index

303

Quality Inn, Petaluma
The Redwoods, Yosemite
    National Park
The Sea Ranch homes,
    The Sea Ranch
Sears House Inn, Mendocino
Serenisea, Gualala
Stanford Inn by the Sea, Mendocino
Tahoe Escape, Tahoe City
Vagabond House Inn, Carmel
Vintage Inn, Yountville
Zephyr Cove Resort, Zephyr
    Cove, Nevada

**LODGINGS WITH
TENNIS COURTS**
Brockway Springs, Kings Beach
Carmel Valley Inn
Carnelian Woods, Carnelian Bay
Chinquapin, Tahoe City
Flamingo Resort Hotel & Fitness
    Center, Santa Rosa
Granlibakken, Tahoe City
Hyatt Lake Tahoe Casino, Incline
    Village, Nevada
Hyatt Regency Monterey
John Gardiner's Tennis Ranch,
    Carmel Valley
Kingswood Village, Kings Beach
Konocti Harbor Resort & Spa,
    Kelseyville
Lakeland Village, South Lake Tahoe
Little River Inn, Little River
The Lodge at Pebble Beach
Northstar-at-Tahoe, Truckee
Pajaro Dunes, Watsonville
Pine Beach Inn, Fort Bragg
Quail Lodge Resort & Golf Club,
    Carmel Valley
Silverado Country Club and
    Resort, Napa
Sonoma Mission Inn, Sonoma
Squaw Valley Lodge,
    Olympic Valley
Tahoe Seasons Resort, South
    Lake Tahoe
Timberhill Ranch, Timber
    Cove-Cazadero
Trinity Alps Resort, Lewiston
Vintage Inn, Yountville
Wawona Hotel, Yosemite National
    Park

**LODGINGS WITH
INDOOR POOLS**
Cambria Pines Lodge, Cambria
Dr. Wilkinson's Hot Springs,
    Calistoga
Embassy Suites Hotels & Resorts, San
    Luis Obispo & South Lake Tahoe
Inn at Napa Valley, Napa
Konocti Harbor Resort & Spa,
    Kelseyville
Stanford Inn by the Sea, Mendocino
Tenaya Lodge, Fish Camp
West Wind Lodge, Monterey
Yosemite Marriott Tenaya
    Lodge, Fish Camp

CHEAP SLEEPS
*Some rooms are available for
under $50 for two people.*
Ben Lomond Hylton, Ben
    Lomond, $44
Black Bart Inn and Motel, San
    Andreas, $47
Butterfly Grove Inn, Pacific Grove, $45
Calistoga Inn, Calistoga, $45
Cedar Stock Resort and Marina,
    Lewiston, $45
Columbia Gem Motel, Columbia, $35
Country Squire Motel, Jackson, $35
Creekside Inn & Resort,
    Guerneville, $35
Curry Village, Yosemite National
    Park, $31.50
Dr. Wilkinson's Hot Springs,
    Calistoga, $49
Dry Creek Inn,
    Healdsburg, $45
Dunes Resort, Tahoe Vista, $48
Fern River Resort, Felton, $49
Gunn House Motel, Sonora, $40
Hartsook Inn, Piercy, $39
Johnson's Beach & Resort,
    Guerneville, $25
Jules Resort, Clearlake, $28
Miranda Gardens Resort,
    Miranda, $45
National Hotel, Nevada City, $42
Ocean Echo Motel & Cottages,
    Santa Cruz, $45
Ocean View Lodging, Fort Bragg, $45
Orr Hot Springs, Ukiah, $40
Packer Lake Lodge, Sierra City, $48
Ripplewood Resort, Big Sur, $45
Riverlane Resort, Guerneville, $45
Salt Point Lodge, Jenner, $45
Seabreeze Motel, Pacifica, $45
Sea Gull Inn, Mendocino, $35
Sequoia and Kings Canyon
    National Parks Lodging, $40
Skylark Motel, Lakeport, $40
Steep Ravine Cabins, Stinson
    Beach, $30
Tuolumne Meadows Lodge, Yosemite
    National Park, $36.75
Village Inn, Monte Rio, $25
White Wolf Lodge, Yosemite
    National Park, $31.75
Yosemite Lodge, Yosemite
    National Park, $28.50
Zephyr Cove Resort, Zephyr
    Cove, Nevada, $45

CHILD-FRIENDLY WINERIES
Buena Vista Winery, Sonoma
    (Gewurztraminer juice)
Chateau Julian Winery, Carmel
    Valley (juice and crackers)
Chateau Montelena Winery,
    Calistoga (crayons and paper)
Geyser Peak Winery, Geyserville
    (grape juice and balloons)
Hallcrest Vineyards, Felton
    (premium varietal grape juice)
The Hess Collection Winery,
    Napa (Valser mineral water)
Mark West Winery, Forestville
    (organic grape juice)
Navarro Vineyards, Philo
    (varietal grape juices)

Rodney Strong Vineyards,
    Healdsburg (grape juice and soda)
Topolos at Russian River Vineyards,
    Forestville (sparkling apple cider)
Viansa, Sonoma (balloons)

HAUNTED PLACES
Firehouse Museum #1,
    Nevada City
Mission San Francisco Solano,
    Sonoma
Shadowbrook Restaurant, Capitola
Stevenson House, Monterey State
    Historic Park, Monterey
Sutter Creek Inn, Sutter Creek
Vineyard House, Coloma

MINERAL HOT SPRINGS
Avila Hot Springs, San Luis Obispo
Calistoga Spa Hot Springs,
    Calistoga
Consciousness Village/Campbell
    Hot Springs, Sierraville
Drakesbad Guest Ranch, Chester
Dr. Wilkinson's Hot Springs,
    Calistoga
Grover Hot Springs State Park,
    Markleeville
Indian Springs Spa & Resort,
    Calistoga
Morton's Warm Springs, Kenwood
Orr Hot Springs, Ukiah
Sycamore Mineral Springs, San
    Luis Obispo
Tassajara Zen Mountain Center,
    Carmel Valley
Vichy Springs Resort, Ukiah
Wilbur Hot Springs Health
    Sanctuary, Williams

**RESORTS WHERE CLOTHING IS
OPTIONAL AROUND THE POOL**
Consciousness Village/Campbell Hot
    Springs, Sierraville
Esalen Institute, Big Sur
Orr Hot Springs, Ukiah
Tassajara Zen Mountain Center,
    Carmel Valey
Ventana-Big Sur Country Inn
    Resort, Big Sur
Wilbur Hot Springs Health
    Sanctuary, Williams

**VEGETARIAN RETREATS AND
RESTAURANTS**
Consciousness Village/Campbell Hot
    Springs, Sierraville
Good Earth, Los Gatos (see Index for
    other locations)
Hobee's, Saratoga (see Index for
    other locations)
The Restaurant, Fort Bragg
Sivananda Ashram Vrindavan Yoga
    Farm, Grass Valley
Tassajara Zen Mountain Center,
    Carmel Valley
Wellspring Renewal Center, Philo

Alphabetical Index

Credits

Typesetting, layout, and cover design: Betsy Joyce
Maps: John Parsons and Mark Williams, Eureka Cartography
Printing: Malloy Lithographing, Inc.
Computer Wizardry: Gene Meyers

Photos:
cover: reading top to bottom, left to right, credits are same as below for pages 53, 256, 97, 147, 274, 151, 236
page 11: Roaring Camp & Big Trees Narrow-Gauge Railroad
pages 17, 21: Santa Cruz Beach & Boardwalk
page 25: Shadowbrook
pages 30, 45, 46, 50, 53, 61, 90, 139, 142, 144, 183, 201, 203, 217, 224, 267: California Department of Parks and Recreation
page 32: Jerry Lebeck, Monterey Peninsula Visitors & Convention Bureau
page 33: Monterey Bay Aquarium
page 35: Pete Amos, California Department of Parks and Recreation
page 56: Theodore Osmundson California Department of Parks and Recreation
page 57: John Kaestner, California Department of Parks and Recreation
pages 63, 78, 82, 111, 112, 277: Redwood Empire Association
page 68: Sharon Taussig, Sonoma County Convention & Visitors Bureau
page 72, 147: Ansel Adams, Redwood Empire Association
page 87: *Sonoma Index-Tribune* & Sonoma Valley Visitors Bureau
page 93: Smothers Brothers Wine Store
page 97: Balloon Aviation of Napa Valley, Redwood Empire Association
page 101: Meadowood Napa Valley
page 107: Penn, Dr. Wilkinson's Hot Springs
page 118: Scott Hess, Petaluma Area Chamber of Commerce
pages 132, 162: Carole Terwilliger Meyers
page 136: Vichy Springs Resort
page 140: Eureka Inn
page 151: Great America
page 154: Winchester Mystery House
page 158: Valley Guild, courtesy of the Steinbeck Library
page 159: John Michael Flint, Oakwood Lake
pages 165, 168, 171, 264, 266: Yosemite Park and Curry Company
pages 173, 268: John M. Giosso, San Francisco Recreation and Park Department
page 176: Sanger District Chamber of Commerce
page 181: Gold Prospecting Expeditions
pages 186, 194, 199: Larry Paynter, California Department of Parks and Recreation
page 187: Moaning Cavern
page 188: 39th District Agricultural Association
pages 211, 215: Hal Schell
page 219: Harre W. Demoro
page 228: Greater Reno Chamber of Commerce
page 234: Travel Systems Ltd.
page 236: Lake Tahoe Visitors Authority
page 238: Northstar-at-Tahoe
pages 245, 249, 252: John F. Reginato, Shasta-Cascade Wonderland Association
page 248: Lela Joslin, Spanish Springs Ranch
page 256: Royal Gorge Nordic Ski Resort
page 259: Bob Everson, Alpine Meadows
page 272: Shasta-Cascade Wonderland Association
page 274: Dick Linford, ECHO
page 275: Wilderness Adventures
page 276: Shasta Llamas
page 280: Owner Builder Center
page 319: Mike Maloney, San Francisco Chronicle

Acknowledgments: Special thanks to Keith Walklet at Yosemite National Park, Malinee Crapsey at Sequoia and Kings Canyon National Parks, and Laurie Armstrong at the Lake Tahoe Visitors Authority for their extensive help in updating the information in the chapters pertaining to their areas.

About the Author

Carole Terwilliger Meyers, a native San Franciscan, holds a B.A. degree in anthropology from San Francisco State University and an elementary teaching credential from Fresno State University. Her articles have appeared in *Family Circle, Parenting, Family Fun, New Choices,* and *San Francisco Focus* magazines, as well as in numerous other magazines and newspapers, and she has been a columnist for *California* magazine, the *San Francisco Examiner,* the *San Jose Mercury News,* and *Parents' Press.* She is a contributor to *The Berlitz Travellers Guide to San Francisco & Northern California.* Ms. Meyers resides in Berkeley, California with her husband and two children.

More Travel Publications from Carousel Press

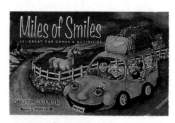

Miles of Smiles: 101 Great Car Games & Activities

128 pages; 8-1/2 x 5-1/2; 26 line drawings; charts, map. $8.95. Anyone who has ever been trapped in a hot car with bored kids is well aware that the world needs a sure-fire way of easing the resulting tensions. This clever book fills that need. In fact, according to one enthusiatic user it just "may be the ultimate solution for back seat squabbling." The book is filled with games and activities that have travel-related themes. Ninety-seven require just your minds and mouths to play, and the other four need only simple props: a penny, pencil, and some crayons. A helpful index categorizes each game and activity according to age-appropriateness, and humorous illustrations that kids can color add to everyone's enjoyment.

San Francisco Family Fun

296pp; 6x9; b&w photos and illus, maps. $12.95. With the help of this book, parents can easily plan a daytrip or a week-long vacation. In fact, there is enough information included to keep a family busy throughout an entire childhood! Information about the family-friendliness of lodgings and restaurants is detailed, and all the best attractions are described. In addition to San Francisco, the book covers the East, South, and North Bay areas. Helpful indexes guide you to the best spots for brunch, for the big splurge—even where to go with *teens!*

Best Bets for Great Getaways Newsletter.

Sample issue $4. Published six times a year by Marge Best, this newsletter features different areas of Northern California in each issue. Sample includes subscription information.

Travel Papers are short, information-packed articles about a particular destination. Most supplement general guidebooks by including useful, detailed information of value to families. Articles range in length from one to seven pages. They are single-spaced and printed on one side of letter-size paper. Travel Papers are available only through Carousel Press.

The Family Travel Guides Catalogue

includes over 200 family-oriented travel books and children's travel activities. A free copy is included with every order from Carousel Press. If you are not ordering anything now but would like a copy of the catalogue, fill out the Order Form and include $1 for postage and handling.

Order Form

These books and Travel Papers are written by *Weekend Adventures* author Carole Terwilliger Meyers and can be purchased by mail:

QTY.	TITLE	PRICE
	BOOKS	
____	Weekend Adventures for City-Weary People: Overnight Trips in Northern California	$13.95
____	San Francisco Family Fun	$12.95
____	Miles of Smiles: 101 Great Car Games & Activities	$8.95
	TRAVEL PAPERS	
____	Ashland Shakespeare Festival in Oregon	$4.00
____	Beverly Hills 90210—with Kids	$4.00
____	The California Missions	$4.00
____	Camping Favorites in Oregon	$3.00
____	Creative Ways to Use Post Cards	$1.00
____	Death Valley Daze	$4.00
____	Disneyland	$4.00
____	The English Side of Victoria, BC	$3.00
____	Family-Friendly London	$4.00
____	Fun in New York City—with the Kids!	$4.00
____	Germany's Fairy Tale Road	$4.00
____	Going Hollywood: In Search of the Stars	$4.00
____	Highway Attractions on Highways 101 and 5 in Oregon	$4.00
____	Home Exchanging	$2.00
____	Hot Spots on the Beach: Southern California Resorts that Welcome Kids	$4.00
____	Knott's Berry Farm, plus A Trip Back in Time	$3.00
____	On the Road to Hana in Maui, HI	$4.00
____	Pooped Parents Visit Poipou Beach in Kauai, HI	$4.00
____	Portland, OR	$4.00
____	Reno, NV	$4.00
____	San Diego, CA	$4.00
____	Santa Barbara, CA	$4.00
____	Seattle, WA	$3.00
____	Solvang, CA	$3.00
____	A Southern California Family Cruise . . . With a Teen!	$3.00
____	Staying on Top of a Volcano in Hawaii	$3.00
____	Vacationing with Grandchildren	$3.00
____	Waikiki Wiki Wiki (Fast) with the Keikis (Kids)	$4.00
____	Washington, D.C.	$4.00
____	*Best Bets for Great Getaways* newsletter	$4.00

Tax: California residents add 8¼% sales tax.

Shipping: If your order totals less than $5, add $2; from $5.01 to $10, add $3; from $10.01 to $25, add $4; over $25, add $5. For optional UPS 2nd Day Air, add $5 more. **Foreign orders** must use MasterCard or VISA and specify surface or air. Charge will be exact shipping cost plus a $2 processing fee.

Make check payable to CAROUSEL PRESS , or charge to: [ ] Visa   [ ] MC

Acct # _____   Exp. date _____   Signature _____

Ship to: Name _____

Address _____

City, State, Zip _____

☐ Send me just *The Family Travel Guides Catalogue*. I'm enclosing $1 for postage and handling. (The catalogue is included *free* if you order a book or Travel Paper.)

Mail to: 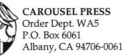 **CAROUSEL PRESS**
Order Dept. WA5
P.O. Box 6061
Albany, CA 94706-0061

Reader Feedback

I get annoyed when I find out that a place doesn't actually have a feature I've been led to expect. Please let me know if this happens to you at any of the listings in this book. I'll look into it and complain on your behalf, and I'll fix the misinformation in the next edition of WEEKEND ADVENTURES FOR CITY-WEARY PEOPLE. Please, also, let me know about your discoveries.

Sincerely,
Carole Terwilliger Meyers
c/o Carousel Press
P.O. Box 6061
Albany, CA 94706-0061

Your Name _____

Address _____

City, State, Zip _____

Telephone _____

Listing Name _____

Address _____

City, State, Zip _____

Telephone _____

Describe your annoyance or discovery: